Russian Symbolism and
Literary Tradition

Russian Symbolism and Literary Tradition

Goethe, Novalis, and the Poetics of Vyacheslav Ivanov

Michael Wachtel

THE UNIVERSITY OF WISCONSIN PRESS

The University of Wisconsin Press
114 North Murray Street
Madison, Wisconsin 53715

3 Henrietta Street
London WC2E 8LU, England

Copyright © 1994
The Board of Regents of the University of Wisconsin System
All rights reserved

5 4 3 2 1

Printed in the United States of America

Library of Congress Cataloging-in-Publication Data

Wachtel, Michael
　　Russian symbolism and literary tradition: Goethe, Novalis, and the poetics of Vyacheslav Ivanov / Michael Wachtel.
　　260 p.　　cm.
　Includes bibliographical references and index.
　ISBN 0-299-14450-X
　　1. Ivanov, V. I. (Viacheslav Ivanovich), 1866–1949—Criticism and interpretation. 2. Symbolism (Literary movement)—Russia. 3. Goethe, Johann Wolfgang von, 1749–1832—Influence. 4. Novalis, 1772–1801—Influence. I. Title.
　PG3467.I8Z96　　1995
　891.71'3—dc20　　　94-25682

For Anna

Contents

Note	ix
Acknowledgments	xi
Introduction	3

Part I: Ivanov and Goethe

1	The Years of Apprenticeship: Vyacheslav Ivanov's *Lehrjahre*	21
2	Ivanov's Bride of Corinth: Introduction to a Syncretic Poetics	43
3	*Faust* and Ivanov's Conception of the Symbol	62
4	Faustian Allusions in *Pilot Stars*, *Transparence*, and *Tender Mystery*	78
5	Goethe's Poetry in the Mythology of *Cor Ardens*	97

Part II: Ivanov and Novalis

	Preliminary Remarks	111
6	Novalis in Russia	113
7	Ivanov's Translations from Novalis: Stylistic and Semantic Preconceptions	128
8	Zhiznetvorchestvo: The Conflation of Art and Life	143
9	Beyond Translation: Novalis as a Source for Ivanov's Poetry	157
10	Metrical Semantics and the "Hymns to the Night"	181

Conclusion	210
Works Consulted	231
Index	243

Note

In this book, I use an abbreviated footnote form, giving the author's last name and page number. When more than one work of an author has been consulted, I include the date of the relevant work and occasionally the place of publication in the footnote to avoid confusion. Full bibliographical information can be found, alphabetically by author, in the "Works Consulted." Vyacheslav Ivanov's *Complete Works* (*Sobranie sochinenii*) are referred to as *SS*, followed by the volume and page number.

In the case of anonymous publications, reference works (i.e., dictionaries, etc.) and archival sources, I give all relevant information in the footnotes. German archives are named in full, while the Ivanov family archive in Rome is referred to as "Rome archive." Russian archives are designated by the following abbreviations:

RGB   Russian State Library, Moscow
GPB   Saltykov-Shchedrin Library, St. Petersburg
TsGALI   Central State Archive of Literature and Art, Moscow

To assist specialists who may wish to consult the archival materials, dates of letters are cited precisely as they appear on a given document. In other words, some dates are given in old style and some in new; in cases where the original writer gave old and new styles, I also include both.

Since some readers may not know Russian, let me explain that I have used a simplified system of transliteration in the text and notes (that found in Victor Terras, *A Handbook of Russian Literature*, New Haven, 1985, p. xix) and the more precise, but less readable British system in the "Works Consulted." The differences concern only endings; anyone familiar with Russian should have no trouble recognizing, for example, that "Bely" and "Belyi" are the same person. Those who do not will not be affected in any case.

Occasionally Russian authors published their work in Germany and used the German system of transliteration (e.g., Voloshina became Woloschin, Metner became Medtner). Confusion is almost unavoidable in such cases. I attempt to simplify things by using the Russian version of the name in the text and expository section of the notes, but including in parentheses within the note the German rendering, since it appears this way in the "Works Consulted."

In both the main text and the notes, longer Russian citations appear in Cyrillic, shorter ones in transliteration. Unless otherwise indicated, all translations (from German and Russian) are my own. In a few instances, I do not translate because the passages are cited to demonstrate nonsemantic features that cannot be retained in English. In translations of verse, I aim only for semantic accuracy; the line breaks (indicated in the footnotes by a /) are maintained when this can be done without detriment to English syntax. Verse translations are included in the main text whenever a poem is cited in its entirety or when, in my judgment, it can be done without unduly distracting the reader from the discussion.

Acknowledgments

First and foremost, I wish to thank friends and mentors whose advice and suggestions have left their mark on this book. Konstantin Azadovsky, Mikhail Gasparov, John Malmstad and Igor Smirnov patiently guided me through the initial stages of this project, greatly adding to my understanding of Symbolism and poetics. Vladimir Alexandrov, Caryl Emerson and Andrew Wachtel gave detailed and much needed help in revising the manuscript. Ol'ga Kuznetsova, Gena Obatnin and Andrei Shishkin generously shared unpublished archival materials with me. Charles E. Townsend and Ellen Chances sacrificed many hours to assist with proofreading and editing. I owe a special debt of gratitude to Dimitri Ivanov, whose kindness, patience, and good will have continually inspired me.

This book could not have been completed without the financial support of three organizations: IREX, Fulbright, and the Princeton Committee for Research in the Humanities and Social Sciences. I truly appreciate their commitment to my work.

I would also like to thank publicly the people connected with the University of Wisconsin Press who assisted in the publication of this book: David Bethea, Allen Fitchen, Raphael Kadushin, Lydia Howarth, and the two outside readers, Steven Cassedy and André von Gronicka.

Last but certainly not least, I wish to acknowledge with gratitude the contributions of two Princeton students. Adam Logan's computer expertise is reflected on every page of the text, while Nicole Monnier proofread the entire book and compiled the index.

Russian Symbolism and
Literary Tradition

Introduction

> . . . denn ich war längst überzeugt, es gebe nichts Neues unter der Sonne, und man könne gar wohl in den Überlieferungen schon angedeutet finden, was wir selbst gewahr werden und denken, oder wohl gar hervor bringen. Wir sind nur Originale weil wir nichts wissen.[1]
> —Goethe, *Naturwissenschaftliche Schriften*

Whether labeled "influence," "reception," or "intertextuality," the question of a writer's relationship to tradition has long been of central importance to literary study. All art both belongs and contributes to a system, yet artists themselves rarely acknowledge the extent and significance of their own connectedness. Some altogether deny or reject their heritage, others assiduously avoid mentioning those who have left an imprint on their work. Still others expend boundless energy questing for precursors, discovering (or claiming to discover) myriad organic links to the literature of previous generations.

The work of Harold Bloom, perhaps the best known student of poetic influence in Anglo-American criticism, provides a convenient, if extreme, point of departure. Arguing for a literary history that focuses on a poet's relationship to his predecessors, Bloom maintains that no poet can understand himself—or be understood by others—outside the tension-ridden context of the larger literary tradition. In a characteristically provocative pronouncement, he insists that "the caveman who traced the outline of an animal upon the rock always retraced a precursor's outline."[2]

---

1. ". . . for I had long ago become convinced that there is nothing new under the sun, and that we can already find in the works of our predecessors hints of what we ourselves notice and think, or even of that which we create. We are only original insofar as we know nothing." Goethe, *Writings on the Natural Sciences*, in Trunz, vol. 13, pp. 111–12.

2. Bloom, p. 4.

Of course, Bloom by no means celebrates such repetition. In his view, tradition is the primary problem that confronts the would-be poet: "Any poet (meaning even Homer, if we could know enough about his precursors) is in the position of being 'after the Event,' in terms of literary language. His art is necessarily an *aftering,* and so at best he strives for a selection, through repression, out of the traces of the language of poetry; that is, he represses some of the traces, and remembers others."[3] In short, each great poet struggles with the legacy of his predecessors or, in Bloomian terms, his belatedness. According to this highly competitive—even combative—view of creativity, the tradition, by virtue of its very excellence, becomes more of an obstacle than a source of inspiration. Bloom offers only one solution to this problem: a poet cannot ignore the tradition, but he can *repress* it. Poetic creation thus becomes a matter of willful forgetting. It should be recalled that Bloom develops his theory of poetry in order to explain a specific set of English (and American) texts. His model of literary creation may indeed describe English Romanticism, but—despite his assurances—it does not necessarily apply to other national traditions.

It is the thesis of this book that the Russian Symbolists' creativity was based on a type of reception diametrically opposed to that posited by Bloom. Symbolism, the most prominent movement of the 1890s and the first decade of the twentieth century, ushered in the period of artistic achievement that has come to be known as Russia's "Silver Age." The Symbolists, an erudite group of poets and thinkers, shared a reverence for past accomplishment. If the English Romantics strove to escape the burden of the past, the Russian Symbolists sought with equal fervor to integrate themselves with it. Rather than exemplifying Bloom's notorious "anxiety of influence," the works of the Symbolists evince what might be termed an "anxious desire to be influenced." Rarely has a creative movement so eagerly and energetically looked backwards.

In a retrospective conclusion to the essay "The Emblematics of Meaning" (1909), Andrei Bely emphasized the way that Russian Symbolism affirmed, broadened, and even justified previous movements: "The Symbolist school shifted the borders of our conceptions of artistic creation; it showed that the canon of beauty is not merely an academic canon, that this canon cannot be the canon of only Romanticism, only Classicism, or only Realism. Rather, the Symbolist school justified all three trends as different expressions of a single creativity."[4] In the continuation of this same passage, Bely made explicit the

---

3. Ibid.
4. Bely (1910), p. 113.

organic connection of Symbolism to tradition: "The novelty of contemporary art lies only in the enormous quantity of the entire past that has suddenly surfaced before us; today we are experiencing in art all centuries and all nations . . . "

For the Symbolists, the past "surfaced" in numerous ways. With few exceptions, the major Symbolists translated extensively, thereby enriching Russia with a wide variety of linguistic and cultural traditions. They devoted critical and philosophical essays to foreign writers, artists, and philosophers. Delving into their own poetic heritage, they published the first complete editions of major nineteenth-century Russian poets. Through journals, regular meetings, and public lectures, they educated each other as well as the larger intellectual community. Polymaths and polyglots, they spent lengthy periods abroad, honing their language skills and acquainting themselves with other countries' cultural history. Reception, in short, was not simply an aspect of Russian Symbolism; it was one of its guiding principles and lifelong pursuits.

Valery Bryusov's comments on originality exemplify the Symbolist approach to literary creation. Beginning with the assumption that no writer has ever had the power "to free himself from the influences of the past, of his predecessors," Bryusov proceeds to delineate various types of "originality," the first of which has particular relevance to the present study: "A writer is original if he brings into his native literature that which has been created by writers of another nation."[5]

In contrast to the Bloomian model of willed forgetfulness, then, the Russian Symbolists operated with the fundamental concept of tenacious remembrance. In particular, the work of Vyacheslav Ivanov (1866–1949), is based on a virtual cult of memory. For Ivanov, memory is more than a link to past achievement. Repeatedly emphasizing that Mnemosyne is mother of the muses, he recognizes in memory the very source of artistic creativity.[6] Finally, as anamnesis, memory connects past, present, and future, offering the promise of immortality: "He in whom eternal memory lives, / Eternally triumphs over death."[7]

Vyacheslav Ivanov's reception (and canonization) of Goethe and Novalis serves as the focal point of the present study. Ivanov's interest in these poets can be understood as part of his nation's ongoing fasci-

---

5. Bryusov (1975), vol. 6, p. 390.
6. *SS*, vol. 2, p. 99; vol. 3, p. 392.
7. From the poem "Vechnaya Pamyat'" ("Eternal Memory"), *SS*, vol. 1, p. 568. For a discussion of the religious implications in Ivanov's usage of this term, see Stepun (1964), pp. 259–60.

nation with a country which, already decades before his birth, had beckoned to Russians. While France influenced all spheres of Russian nineteenth-century society (from popular reading to salon culture to dueling conventions), Germany's attractiveness lay almost exclusively in the realm of the intellect. It was a land of universities, of "thinkers and poets" ("Dichter und Denker," according to the time-honored cliché). In the 1820s and 1830s, Russian students immersed themselves in Hegel and Schelling with as much—and perhaps more—enthusiasm than their German counterparts. Through numerous, often excellent translations, Russians made a number of German poets their own (most notably Goethe, Schiller, and Heine). So great was Germany's allure that several leading nineteenth-century writers (e.g., Tyutchev, Zhukovsky, Turgenev) spent significant portions of their lives there.

Yet Ivanov's relationship to German culture provides more than an additional chapter in the history of Russo-German relations. Because of the crucial role that reception played in the Symbolist literary process, a study of Ivanov's reception of Goethe and Novalis leads beyond the Germans to issues that lie at the very heart of Russian Symbolism: the theory of the symbol, poetry as theurgy, the relationship between literary creation and "real life," poetics and mythopoesis, the theory and practice of translation.

While no Symbolist can be considered typical, Ivanov embodied to a very high degree the characteristics that made Symbolism unique. A poet-scholar, he was equally at home reciting his own verse, discussing that of his contemporaries, or lecturing on the history and theory of poetics. Combining linguistic brilliance with critical, philosophical, religious and mystical depth, he succeeded—as many Russian polymaths (e.g., Leo Tolstoy) could not—in integrating these disparate realms. Perhaps most importantly, his worldview was formed through direct contact with both Russian and foreign models. As Ivanov wrote: "I am half a son of the Russian earth, from where I was nonetheless driven out, and half a foreigner, from the apprentices of Sais, where race and tribe are forgotten."[8] Although of purely Russian lineage, Ivanov considered himself European by cultural heritage. He agreed with Dostoevsky, "that a true Russian was before all else a 'universal man' ['vsechelovek'] and that for this reason he is in Europe more European than a Frenchman or an Englishman or a German, each of whom considers himself precisely a Frenchman or an

---

8. *SS*, vol. 3, p. 412. Ivanov gave a similar account of his origins when discussing his mother: "And while she was pregnant, she constantly looked now at a portrait of Pushkin, now at a portrait of a certain very wise and industrious German that was hanging on her wall. And I inherited something from Pushkin and even more, perhaps, from that German." Al'tman, p. 309.

Englishman or a German and only conditionally and abstractly—a European."[9]

In the estimation of his peers, Ivanov occupied a preeminent position among the luminaries of Russian pre-revolutionary culture. Nikolai Berdyaev described him as "the central figure of that time" and "one of the most remarkable people in an epoch rich with talents."[10] In the words of Fedor Stepun, he was "the most multi-faceted and at the same time most organic figure of the Russian Symbolist school."[11] In short, from a literary-historical point of view, it is appropriate to place Ivanov at the center of the Symbolist movement. Ironically, the very qualities that make him complex and difficult to grasp for modern readers made him exemplary for his contemporaries.

Ivanov's breadth of interests can be traced in part to his biography, unusually peripatetic even by Symbolist standards. He came from relatively humble origins, the son of a land surveyor (who died in 1871, when his son was five years old). His mother, a devout, well-read, and artistically inclined woman, seems to have been the most significant influence on him during his youth.[12] He grew up in Moscow, finishing gymnasium with a gold medal and receiving a prize in classical languages at Moscow University. Encouraged by his professors, he left the University after two years (1884–86) in order to continue studies in Germany. Together with his wife Dar'ya Mikhailovna Dmitrievskaya, Ivanov spent the next five years at the University of Berlin, where he concentrated on ancient history and classical philology. In these years, he continued a secondary interest that he had begun in Russia: writing verse. Early in 1892, Ivanov, accompanied by his wife and daughter, left Berlin for Paris and Rome. The purpose of this trip was to complete the dissertation (on Roman tax law), which, in the custom of that time, Ivanov was writing in Latin. While in Rome, he met the strong-willed and impetuous Lidiya Dimitrievna Zinov'eva-Annibal. A passionate affair developed between them in 1895, and Ivanov divorced his wife and remarried. This decision also inspired him to break with the conventional world of academic scholarship and focus his energies on poetry. While Ivanov ultimately completed his dissertation, he never sat for the final oral examination and thus failed to receive a degree.

---

9. Letter to A. G. Godyaev of 7 October 1935 (Rome archive).
10. Berdyaev, p. 154.
11. Stepun (1989), p. 123.
12. "She was an original woman, with a penetrating mind and a lively imagination, gifted with a sense of elegance especially in music and word, and with a deep mystical feeling." From Ivanov's autobiography of 1904, first published in Kuznetsova (1993), p. 82.

Numerous legal complications (Lidiya was also engaged in divorce proceedings) ensured that Ivanov and Lidiya would spend their first years together outside Russia. Their daughter, also named Lidiya, was born in 1896. The next years were spent in France, Switzerland, England, and Greece, with Ivanov writing poetry and gathering material for a study of Dionysus and Dionysian cults. In 1903, Ivanov gave a series of lectures on the religion of Dionysus in Paris; among his listeners was Bryusov, who encouraged Ivanov to join forces with the Russian Symbolists. In that same year, Ivanov's first book of poetry appeared in Russia. This work, together with numerous theoretical essays that followed (many as contributions to Bryusov's journal "Libra") quickly earned Ivanov the reputation of a major Symbolist.

Ivanov and Lidiya returned to St. Petersburg in 1905. Their apartment, known as "The Tower," became the focal point of Petersburg culture. On Wednesdays (beginning late in the evening and lasting almost until morning), the apartment turned into a creative laboratory: the foremost poets read from their recent work, the most illustrious thinkers lectured and debated. With his encyclopedic knowledge and wide-ranging interests, Ivanov officiated at these legendary symposia, serving as critic, teacher, and interlocutor for an entire generation of Russian intellectuals.

In 1907 Lidiya died suddenly outside Petersburg, after tending to peasant children who were suffering from scarlet fever. Ivanov was devastated. While he continued to write and lecture (his major statements on Symbolism date from this time), the next few years mark an unusually dark period in the poet's life. Ivanov emerged from his depression by heeding Lidiya's advice proffered from beyond the grave. In accordance with her wishes (which he learned of through visions and automatic writing), Ivanov "rediscovered" Lidiya in the form of his stepdaughter Vera Shvarsalon (Lidiya's daughter from her first marriage). When, in 1912, it became evident that Vera was pregnant, the couple departed for Western Europe.

A year later, Ivanov returned to Russia with his young wife and son, taking up residence in Moscow. In this new new location, he picked up precisely where he had left off in Petersburg, spending the war years as an active participant in Moscow's cultural life. Like many intellectuals, Ivanov had little sympathy for the tsarist regime. However, he immediately recognized that the October Revolution was an unacceptable solution for Russia's ills. By 1918, Ivanov had published poems and essays in which he unambiguously criticized the senseless cruelty and godlessness of the revolutionaries.[13] Personal tragedy was soon to follow: Vera died from the privations of civil war in the summer of 1920. Shortly thereafter, together with his daughter Lidiya and his and Vera's son Dimitri, Ivanov left for Baku, where he managed to secure a professorship in classical philology. In 1924, through the personal intercession of the Soviet Commissar for Education A. V. Lunacharsky (a former friend and participant in the Wednesdays at the "Tower"), Ivanov was given permission to travel abroad. He departed for Italy, where he spent the last twenty-five years of his life. He died on 16 July 1949.

It will be helpful to focus on those elements of this brief biographical survey that illuminate Ivanov's German orientation and inclinations. His nine semesters at the University of Berlin play an especially significant role in this regard, for they were in many respects his formative years. In the most extensive published source on this period (the retrospective "Autobiographical Letter" of 1917),[14] Ivanov mentions that the first semester (fall, 1886) was spent "mastering the German language"[15] and that his views of German culture formed quickly: "As concerns things German, my interests were determined immediately and forever.... I reveled in the multi-volume edition of Goethe, I lovingly immersed myself in Schopenhauer, I knew nothing in the world more sweet and spiritually satisfying than German classical music."[16]

Archival holdings amplify this laconic account. Notebooks from the Berlin period indicate that, in addition to his rigorous academic program, Ivanov was constantly writing poetry. Several titles should be noted, for they reflect his awakened interest in German culture: "Na Reine" ("On the Rhine"),[17] "V gorod Minnesang" ("Into the City of Minnesang"),[18] "Kel'nskii sobor" ("The Cologne Cathedral"),[19] "Germanskomu professoru istorii" ("To a German Professor of

---

13. See the cycle of poems entitled "Pesni smutnogo vremeni" ("Songs of the Time of Troubles") in *SS*, vol. 4, pp. 72–75, and the essays from the newspaper *Luch Pravdy (The Ray of Truth)*, reprinted in Obatnin and Sobolev.

14. Despite its name, it is not a "letter" in the strict sense. It was written in 1917 at the request of S. A. Vengerov for the series *Russian Literature of the Twentieth Century*.

15. *SS*, vol. 2, p. 16.

16. Ibid., p. 18.

17. RGB, f. 109, k. 1, ed. khr. 26.

18. RGB, f. 109, k. 1, ed. khr. 31.

19. RGB, f. 109, k. 1, ed. khr. 26. Ivanov later added another stanza and renamed the poem "V goticheskom sobore" ("In a Gothic Cathedral"), cf. RGB, f. 109, k. 1, ed. khr. 23. An earlier version also exists under the title of "Goticheskii khram" ("The Gothic Church"), RGB, f. 109, k. 1, ed. khr. 33.

10   Introduction

History"),[20] "Gete" ("Goethe"),[21] and even "Faust. Russkie varianty obshchechelovecheskoi legendy" ("Faust. Russian Variants of a Universal Legend").[22] While Ivanov ultimately decided against publishing these poems, he thought highly enough of some to include them in the group he sent for evaluation to Vladimir Solovyov in 1895.[23] In *Kormchie Zvezdy (Pilot Stars)*, his first collection of poetry, Ivanov included one German-oriented poem written during the years in Berlin: "Missa Solemnis, Betkhovena" ("The Missa Solemnis of Beethoven").[24]

By his third semester (fall, 1887), Ivanov had begun to write German poetry. In contrast to the generally contemplative tone of his Russian poems, Ivanov's German verse is often marked by irreverence and levity. However, as the following verses demonstrate, Ivanov was also experimenting with formal aspects of German poetics:

Fräulein [H?]

Vieles gab dir der liebende Gott; die übrige Gabe,
    Ein vollkommenes Glück, schenke der liebende Mensch.[25]

Miss [H?]

The loving God gave you many things; the remaining gift,
    Complete happiness, may the loving man give you.

This brief poem, addressed to an anonymous woman, deserves attention less for its theme than for its versification. It is an example of the elegiac distich, a classical meter popularized in the modern German tradition by Goethe and Schiller. In Russian poetry, it was occasionally used by Pushkin, and ultimately became a favorite form of Ivanov

    20. RGB, f. 109, k. 1, ed. khr. 26.
    21. Ibid.
    22. This is the title of the second scene of Ivanov's "Russian Faust," which I discuss at length in chap. 1.
    23. Solovyov mentioned "To a German Professor of History," "In a Gothic Cathedral," and "Into the City of Minnesang," including the latter two among the five poems that he considered "especially interesting." Ivanov learned of Solovyov's reactions to these poems in a letter from his first wife of 2 July 1895. RGB, f. 109, k. 25, ed. khr. 30.
    24. RGB, f. 109, k. 1, ed. khr. 26.
    25. RGB, f. 109, k. 1, ed. khr. 33. Below these verses Ivanov wrote "Zur Erinnerung an einen alten Herrn" ("In Remembrance of an Old Man") and dated it "30. XII. 87."

himself.[26] It should be emphasized that Ivanov's realization of this ancient form (i.e., his numerous trochaic substitutions for dactylic feet) reflects German rather than Russian usage. For Ivanov, then, German was not merely the language of the seminar room; his poems reflect a creative interest in and sensitivity to the German language as such.

It was surely as a result of his intensive academic studies that Ivanov also mastered ornate, literary German.[27] His stylistic command is apparent in his correspondence with his adviser, Professor Otto Hirschfeld, during the years 1892 to 1894. The content of these letters is rather formulaic; they begin with a florid exordium (concerning either the addressee's health or the writer's poor letter-writing performance) and proceed to enumerate various unforeseen and unavoidable obstacles that impede progress on the dissertation. The opening sentences of Ivanov's first letter to Hirschfeld (from December 30, 1892) set the tone for the entire correspondence:

Hochverehrter Herr Professor,

Es werden im nächsten Frühjahr zwei volle Jahre verflossen sein, seit ich von Ihnen für eine, wie ich damals hoffte, viel kürzere Frist Abschied genommen habe. Wollen Sie mir das Fehlen meiner Briefe während dieser langen Zeit gütigst verzeihen! Ich bin mir der Schuld des Schweigens völlig bewußt, sowohl angesichts der Güte, mit welcher Sie mich zum Schreiben aufgefordert hatten, als in Anbetracht dessen, daß ich Sie dadurch in eine Ungewißheit in Bezug auf das Schicksal Ihres von mir unter Ihrer Leitung bearbeiteten Themas vielleicht versetzt habe. Aber abgehalten hat mich vom Schreiben gerade der Wunsch, Ihnen etwas Bestimmteres über den Gang eben dieser Arbeit mitzuteilen, die ich nicht aufhörte weiter zu fördern.[28]

---

26. An entire section of *Pilot Stars* is entitled "Distichs." It includes poems from as early as 1892 ("Laeta").

27. According to a course schedule Ivanov himself drew up (Humboldt University in Berlin: Rektor und Senat, Abgangszeugnisse vom 16.11.95 bis 4.3.96), Ivanov enrolled in as many as eight courses a semester. It is worth noting that almost all of his academic work was in the general area of history and philology. Only five of the forty-seven courses were devoted to literature (these focused exclusively on Latin and Greek texts). While Ivanov would go through life described as a "student of Mommsen," archival evidence shows that he worked more closely with Otto Hirschfeld (twelve courses) than with Mommsen (five courses), although this is likely explained by the fact that the septuagenerian Mommsen rarely taught in these years.

28. The letter is in the Hirschfeld archive (Deutsche Staatsbibliothek Berlin, Handschriftenabteilung, Literaturarchiv). "Most Honored Herr Professor, This coming spring two years will have passed since the time I took leave from you for a (as I then hoped) much shorter time. Please kindly forgive the absence of my letters

The tortuous history of Ivanov's doctoral dissertation has little relevance to the concerns of this study; what does deserve emphasis is the fact that by 1892—more than a decade before he was to play a leading role in the Russian Symbolist movement—Ivanov had acquired an extraordinary stylistic command of literary German.

When Ivanov burst upon the Russian cultural scene in 1903, he possessed a formidable knowledge not only of the German language but also of the literary and philosophical tradition. Numerous references to German thinkers in his first published essays make clear that he had already internalized their works. As contemporary documents indicate, Ivanov's authority in matters of German language and culture soon became widely known and respected. Already in 1903, Bryusov asked Ivanov to translate *The Birth of Tragedy* for a Russian edition of Nietzsche's works.[29] Somewhat later, the influential publisher Z. I. Grzhebin turned to Ivanov when he needed an evaluation of Russian translations of Wedekind.[30] In 1908, Johannes von Guenther (a translator from the Russian and unofficial emissary of German culture) prompted Ivanov to write a cycle of German poems under the title "Gastgeschenke."[31] Friedrich Fiedler, another native speaker and translator, testified to Ivanov's fluency in his diary in 1910: "Today Vyacheslav Ivanov was here. How beautifully the man speaks German and even writes German, and even in verses. He wrote some to me in my album 'At My House,' even if I did help out a bit with the

---

during this long period! I am fully aware of the guilt of silence, both in view of the kindness with which you had urged me to write and also in consideration of the fact that I perhaps put you in a position of uncertainty regarding the fate of the subject that I was working on under your supervision. Yet it was precisely the desire to inform you more specifically about the course of this very work—which I never ceased to expedite—that kept me from writing."

29. *Literaturnoe nasledstvo*, vol. 85 (Moscow, 1976), p. 441. A few years later, Ivanov happily agreed to translate *Thus Spoke Zarathustra* for the same edition (Ibid., p. 507). However, neither plan was realized.

30. RGB, f. 109, k. 26, ed. khr. 42. The letter is undated, but the fact that Grzhebin sends regards to Ivanov's wife, Lidiya Dimitrievna, makes clear that it was written before October, 1907.

31. Ivanov subsequently published them in *Cor Ardens*. For the history of their composition, see *SS*, vol. 2, p. 737. The title of the cycle is probably a (jocular or immodest!) reference to Goethe's play *Torquato Tasso*, act 1, lines 77–79: "Und es ist vorteilhaft, den Genius bewirten: gibst du ihm ein Gastgeschenk, So läßt er dir ein schöneres zurück." ("And it is advantageous to treat the genius generously: if you give him a gift, he leaves a nicer one behind.") Ivanov had first met Guenther a few years earlier: cf. his letter (of 17 March [1906]) to M. M. Zamyatina: "The young man v[on] Günther just visited me and read me a series of translations into German from my lyric poetry. A handsome and talented young man." RGB, f. 109, k. 9, ed. khr. 33.

rhymes."[32] In 1913, Ivanov was asked to supervise and write a foreward for a Russian translation of Rilke's "Book of Hours."[33]

As a translator, Ivanov actively encouraged Russian assimilation of German literature. His major accomplishment consists of the first, and, to this day, most complete Russian rendering of Novalis's lyric poetry. Other lengthy translations include "Die Doppeltgänger" ("The Doubles"),[34] one of E. T. A. Hoffmann's tales, and Goethe's verse drama "Prometheus."[35] For illustrative purposes in his critical essays, Ivanov carefully rendered into Russian select passages from Goethe and Schiller.

During his four-year tenure at the University of Baku, Ivanov taught three courses in German literature and thought—on German Romanticism, Nietzsche, and Goethe.[36] It is significant that, in 1923, when hoping to leave the Soviet Union, he considered Germany his only possible haven.[37] When, a year later, he succeeded in leaving Russia for Italy, Ivanov's command of German proved valuable and practical. It allowed him to contribute to mainstream European cultural life and thereby escape the intellectual isolation that was to become the fate of so many émigrés. Ivanov wrote a number of philosophical and literary essays in German that appeared in two well-known journals *(Hochland* and, with regularity, *Corona)*. In that language, he corresponded with luminaries of European culture, including Martin Buber, Ernst Robert Curtius, and Karl Muth.[38] He translated some of his own essays and select Russian lyric poetry (Tyutchev, Baratynsky, Pushkin) into German. In the 1930s, he worked on German versions of his own works: selected lyric poetry,

---

32. Azadovsky (1993), pp. 46–47, cites this passage as well as the poem itself.

33. The translator, Yulian Pavlovich Anisimov, was at the time affiliated with the Russian Futurists of the "Lirika" group. His translations appeared in 1913, without Ivanov's foreward.

34. According to the original plan (of 1919), Ivanov was to translate three Hoffmann tales, which were to be illustrated by Golovin, Benois, and Dobuzhinsky. Only one volume appeared (in 1922, with illustrations by Golovin). Cf. Kupreyanov, p. 122.

35. This work, along with translations of fifteen lyric poems, was commissioned in 1929 for the 1932 centenary edition of Goethe. Only "Prometheus" appeared in print. The original contract as well as Ivanov's versions of two of the shorter poems ("Rastlose Liebe" and "Paria") can be found in the Rome archive.

36. Kotrelev (1968), pp. 326–27.

37. See letter to Bryusov of 12 July 1923, in *Literaturnoe nasledstvo,* vol. 85 (Moscow, 1976), p. 543.

38. Their letters are in the Rome archive.

the long poem "Man," as well as the *magnum opus* of the emigration years, the unfinished "Tale of Prince Svetomir."[39]

In their retrospective quest to impose order on an unusually amorphous movement, literary historians traditionally divide the Russian Symbolists into an "older" and "younger" generation. The first group includes "aesthetes" and decadents (Bryusov, Bal'mont, Gippius, and others), who are contrasted with a more philosophical and mystico-religious triumvirate (Blok, Bely, Ivanov). Such a model, while oversimplified, is essentially accurate.[40] Attempts to develop it, however, have led to misleading assertions. Scholars have distinguished between the older and younger generations in terms of a shift in orientation from France to Germany.[41] While Blok, Bely, and Ivanov were indeed interested in German culture (as were, albeit to a lesser extent, Bryusov and Bal'mont), it would be inaccurate to suggest that a German orientation *unified* such diverse thinkers. Each Symbolist discovered aspects of German culture that spoke to his own spiritual and poetic needs, and each created in accordance with his own idiosyncratic "German tradition."

Bely's fascination with Neo-Kantian thought, for example, was not shared by Ivanov. This fact comes out clearly in a letter Ivanov wrote to Mintslova:

> My aspirations and those of Andrei Bely are not only close, but essentially coincide. As A[ndrei] Bely is well aware, I am skeptical of his attempt to make Rickert the basis for the realization of those aspirations in the sphere of thought—i.e., I do not think that this tactic will succeed; but this does not hinder me from wishing [him] such success in the name of [our] common aspirations. It would be sad if A[ndrei] Bely needed Rickert for himself, for his own intellectual and spiritual needs.[42]

By 1910, Neo-Kantianism had come to occupy a central place in Russian thought.[43] Of all the Neo-Kantians, Rickert was the most fundamental to Bely's conception of Symbolism.[44] Yet Ivanov viewed Bely's interest in Rickert as unnecessary and, ultimately, unproduc-

---

39. The German version of "Man" was first published in Doubrovkine, pp. 319–25. The German "Svetomir" (as yet unpublished) can be found in the Rome archive.
40. "Older" and "younger" should not be understood in strict chronological terms. The two generations coexisted (and often cooperated).
41. Cf. Donchin, p. 26; Bristol, p. 71.
42. RGB, f. 109, k. 10, ed. khr. 20. The letter is dated 15 January 1910.
43. See Bezrodnyi.
44. See Cassedy (1987), pp. 297–300, 308–10, 315–16.

tive.⁴⁵ The two poets' spiritual affinity rested on general principles which, according to Ivanov, had no connection to Neo-Kantian philosophy. In a similar way, when Bely began to embrace Anthroposophy, German culture again served not to link Ivanov and Bely, but to separate them.⁴⁶

Such disagreement was not limited to philosophical issues; it also concerned the reception of the Germanic poetic tradition. Heine, traditionally a favorite of Russian writers and readers, received a varied reception in the Symbolist period. Blok's immersion in the work of this German poet is well-known.⁴⁷ He translated Heine (numerous poems as well as a fragment of the prose) and devoted several essays to him. Yet Heine was inimical to everything Ivanov held dear in the German tradition. Ivanov blamed him for the loss of faith in the religious ideals of German Romanticism. "In the person of Heine the guilt is still heavier: it is the guilt of a deep inner rejection of the religious idea and of a blasphemous mocking of the ancient testaments of the school."⁴⁸ Ivanov mentions Heine approvingly only in his book on Dostoevsky, where he quotes "Nächtliche Fahrt" ("Night Journey"), one of Heine's most mystical and enigmatic poems, emphasizing its eerie closeness to the plot of *The Idiot.*⁴⁹ Curiously, this Heine poem, the single one that finds Ivanov's approval, is completely alien to Blok. Blok discusses the poem in a 1902 letter, but with a different evaluation: "There is a very obscure 'romanzero' of Heine called 'Night Journey.' I have not delved into it, nor do I wish to do so."⁵⁰

Ivanov's command of the German language and intimate familiarity with German culture set him apart from his fellow Symbolists of the "younger generation." (Both Blok and Bely, at least in the early years of the twentieth century, had only a rudimentary command of the language and must have relied to a considerable extent on translations.)⁵¹ It is thus not surprising that Ivanov's own writings

---

45. "Rickert's philosophy is alien to me," he noted in another letter. RGB, f. 109, k. 10, ed. khr. 20. This letter, also to Mintslova, is dated [11?] January 1910.

46. Once again Ivanov continued to respect Bely, without sharing his specific interests; cf. Wachtel, 1990, p. 133.

47. Cf. Bailey; Knipovich; Landa; Lavrov and Toporov; Tynyanov (1921).

48. *SS*, vol. 4, p. 255.

49. *SS*, vol. 4, pp. 550–51.

50. In *Literaturnoe nasledstvo*, vol. 89. Aleksandr Blok, Pis'ma k zhene (Moscow, 1978), p. 97.

51. Testimony to Blok's poor command of the language is the amusing, but grammatically incoherent German missive he wrote to his mother in September, 1905, after receiving a flattering letter from Johannes von Guenther. Beketova, p. 149. It seems probable that Bely learned German reasonably well in his years with Steiner. However, in the early Symbolist period, he appears to have relied on

touch on myriad aspects of German culture: music (particularly Beethoven and Wagner), philosophy (Kant, Hegel, and especially Schopenhauer and Nietzsche), as well as literature (Goethe, Schiller, Novalis, E. T. A. Hoffmann, Platen, George, and others). While he alludes to innumerable German cultural figures, the frequency and significance of the references vary considerably. Nietzsche and Wagner, for example, were central to Ivanov's theory of theater. However, his interest in them decreased greatly after about 1905. Ivanov admired Platen for his poetic mastery and was interested in his application of classical metrics to modern poetry.[52] Yet Platen's direct influence appears to have been limited to questions of form.

It is noteworthy that Ivanov showed little serious interest in contemporary German artistic trends. In the "Autobiographical Letter," he speaks of the "pretentious tastelessness and the depersonalized force of the most recent German culture."[53] Ivanov remained distant even from the leading German poets of his day. While he clearly respected Rilke, he mentioned him extremely infrequently.[54] Contemporaries familiar with the German cultural milieu repeatedly compared Ivanov with Stefan George, since both occupied the central position in their respective traditions.[55] Ivanov spoke highly of

---

translations. Berdyaev claims that before he came under Steiner's spell, Bely hardly knew German. Cf. Berdyaev, p. 192.

52. Ivanov became familiar with Platen's poetry in 1896. In a letter of 1 January 1897, he wrote to Lidiya Dimitrievna: "I also bought Platen's poems, which I have long wanted to get to know better as a result of the virtuosity of their form. Their soul is their luxurious rhythms, the most rare and refined. Platen has drawn my attention to certain classical ['antichnye'] rhythms that I would like to make use of." RGB, f. 109, k. 9, ed. khr. 41. Ivanov quotes Platen approvingly in his "Sporady," *SS*, vol. 3, p. 122.

53. *SS*, vol. 2, p. 218. It should be emphasized that Ivanov wrote this fierce condemnation of modern Germany in 1917. After the outbreak of the First World War, Ivanov, like many Russians, harshly criticized German culture. Cf. Stepun (1964, p. 239) and Stammler (p. 260).

54. A draft of a letter from Ivanov to Anisimov (of 14 October 1913) contains, to my knowledge, Ivanov's only evaluation of Rilke as a poet. According to Ivanov, Rilke demands "an almost meditative attention. Clear and simple in and of himself, he is nevertheless unexpected in his images and too profound, at times even intricate (yet all the while extremely laconic) to be easily understood." RGB, f. 109, k. 9, ed. khr. 2. Ivanov's essay "Vom Igorlied" ("On the Lay of Prince Igor"), which appeared in *Corona* (1936, No. 6), was originally conceived of as an introduction to Rilke's posthumously published translation of the Russian medieval epic. Cf. Ivanov's letter to Herbert Steiner of 24 February 1930 (Deutsches Literaturarchiv, Marbach), where he says that he would be "proud" to take on the task.

55. Guenther (p. 120) emphasizes the similarities in their belief in the hieratic nature of poetry. According to Henry von Heiseler (p. 72), "Ivanov's position corresponds approximately to that of Stefan George. Yet he is more comprehensive

George, yet their similarities were surely a matter of coincidence rather than influence.[56]

Throughout his life, Ivanov's love for Germany was firmly anchored in the classics of the late eighteenth and early nineteenth centuries. Among the celebrated writers and thinkers of this epoch, Goethe and Novalis stand out in Ivanov's estimation. Historically speaking, this pairing is somewhat curious: Weimar classicism (Goethe and Schiller) and Jena Romanticism (Novalis, Tieck, the Schlegels) were, after all, opposing contemporary movements. Their complicated relationship was marked at times by respect but more frequently by polemic and scorn. In terms of German literary history, it would therefore have been logical for Ivanov to ally himself with one or the other of these factions. Instead, Ivanov selects the leading exponent of each and reconciles them. According to this unabashedly ahistoric approach, characteristic of Ivanov's historical and philosophical views, Goethe and Novalis become *complementary*. In numerous theoretical essays, Ivanov describes the basic impulse of Russian Symbolism in terms of these two writers. This is particularly telling in "The Testaments of Symbolism," where Ivanov's avowed purpose is to demonstrate Russian Symbolism's national roots. In enumerating the movement's purely Russian lineage, he twice refers to Goethe and once to Novalis.[57] For his second collection of essays (published in 1916), Ivanov planned a section entitled "Towards the History of Symbolism," which was to consist of only two essays—one on Goethe and one on Novalis.[58] Finally, in important and complicated ways,

---

and a leader not only in lyric poetry." It is noteworthy that Heiseler, as translator of Ivanov's drama "Tantalus," sought to introduce Ivanov and his works to the George circle. In a letter to Ivanov from 2 November 1912, Heiseler wrote: "Incidentally, through a number of private readings, I have attempted to make 'Tantalus' known at least to a few valuable people, among them Dr. Karl Wolfskehl of the 'Blätter für die Kunst,' who was greatly impressed by it. You must definitely meet Wolfskehl; he is one of the most vital and richly endowed people who now exist. I cannot say today whether the 'Blätter' will publish 'Tantalus.' It seems to me that the initiative must come not from me, but from the 'Blätter,' because it would be for me too great a pity were 'Tantalus' to be rejected." (RGB, f. 109, k. 15, ed. khr. 59).

56. Two 1910 references indicate Ivanov's attitude towards George. In a diary entry from 30 March 1910, Fiedler records the following: "[Ivanov] holds Stefan George in extremely high esteem, not so much as a poet, but more as a 'master' (of the word)." In Azadovsky (1993), p. 46. In *Apollon* (1910, No. 7), Ivanov lauds "the great master of the most recent German poetry, Stefan George" (reprinted in *SS*, vol. 4, p. 182). Nonetheless, there is no reason to conclude that Ivanov was intimately acquainted with George's work.

57. *SS*, vol. 2, pp. 596–99.

58. *SS*, vol. 4, p. 738. The section was not included due to the paper shortages during the war.

Ivanov expressed his homage to these two "proto-Symbolists" by incorporating them into his own poetry.

Ivanov, unlike Harold Bloom's "strong poets," did not conceal his interest in and debt to his precursors. To compile a lengthy list of his explicit references to Goethe and Novalis would thus be a simple but meaningless task. I have chosen, therefore, to concentrate on those instances of Ivanov's reception that most clearly reflect his general aesthetic principles and poetics. Detailed analysis of exemplary passages will allow me to demonstrate that Ivanov's poetry and cultural philosophy represent a uniquely Symbolist approach to literary tradition and creativity. Bloom has characterized his own approach to literary influence as "antithetical criticism." I would suggest that the Russian Symbolist's use of reception can best be understood through a "synthetic criticism," which understands literary genealogy as smooth, albeit idiosyncratic, succession rather than a constant struggle between fathers and sons.

PART I

IVANOV AND GOETHE

Chapter 1

The Years of Apprenticeship: Vyacheslav Ivanov's *Lehrjahre*

> Lehrjahre im vorzüglichen Sinn sind die Lehrjahre der Kunst zu leben. Durch planmäßig geordnete Versuche lernt man ihre Grundsätze kennen und erhält die Fertigkeit nach ihnen beliebig zu verfahren.[1]
> —Novalis, *Vermischte Bemerkungen*

Many years after the fact, Vyacheslav Ivanov recalled a curious incident that reflected his state of mind before he set off to begin studies in Germany. The twenty-year-old selected a passage from Goethe's *Faust* (ll. 1198–1201) and carved it into the wooden wall of the room where he was living:

> Vernunft fängt wieder an zu sprechen,
> Und Hoffnung wieder an zu blühn;
> Man sehnt sich nach des Lebens Bächen,
> Ach! nach des Lebens Quelle hin.[2]

This image of a Russian youth zealously engraving Faust's verses into his bedroom wall serves as an eloquent, if also somewhat comical, testimony to Goethe's immense stature in Russia. Such behavior reveals more an uncritical adulation of a cultural icon rather than a thoughtful interpretation of his works. Yet it demonstrates in crude form a basic impulse that can be considered paradigmatic for Ivanov's entire reception of Goethe. Stated simply: Goethe's words are turned into credos. In far more subtle but essentially similar ways, the mature

---

1. "Years of apprenticeship in the true sense are the years of apprenticeship in the art of living. Through carefully planned experiments one becomes acquainted with art's fundamental rules and gains the ability to act freely in accordance with them." Novalis, *Miscellaneous Remarks*. In Novalis (1981), p. 424.
2. *SS*, vol. 2, p. 15. "Reason begins to speak again, / And hope begins to bloom again; / One yearns for the streams of life, / Oh! for the source of life."

Ivanov would repeatedly find in Goethe an expression or confirmation of his own sentiments. In poetry, theoretical essays, even personal letters, Ivanov cites Goethe as a source of irreproachable authority.

It is not surprising that Ivanov, on the eve of his departure for Germany, should have found his hopes embodied in Faust. In nineteenth-century Russia, Goethe was considered one of the towering figures of European letters; Russian writers continually studied, discussed, and translated his works.[3] Many even made the pilgrimage to his house in Weimar.[4] For Ivanov, as for any educated Russian of his time, Goethe's name was synonymous with German culture.

According to tradition, Ivanov's literary biography begins in 1903, with the appearance his first book of poetry, *Pilot Stars (Kormchie Zvezdy)*. The poet appears, as it were, from nowhere, fully matured. In Bryusov's words: "the debutante steps out as a genuine master."[5] By refraining from publishing his early poetic efforts, Ivanov consciously created this impression. However, it should be emphasized that the "debutante" was already thirty-six years old. As Bryusov himself recognized, Ivanov was not a poet without development: "One senses long work, an intimate closeness to his chosen models, the completion of searchings of many years. Behind *Pilot Stars* must be hiding preparatory études, the exercises of an apprentice . . . "[6]

Ivanov's unpublished writings from the Berlin period contain a wealth of material for evaluating this unknown phase of his literary biography. Such "juvenilia" should not be evaluated on the same terms as later published work, yet they serve as an invaluable indicator of the poet's early poetic and spiritual affinities. A particularly striking aspect of this work is its orientation on Goethe. The following passage, from an otherwise unexceptional prose sketch of 1887 entitled "Prizraki" ("Phantoms"), serves as a simple example:

> Меня преследуют призраки; они стоят вокруг меня темною толпою колоссальных образов. Уйдите, уйдите! Я устал слушать ваши однообразные вздохи, ваши темные песни.
>
> Я знаю: вы всегда обвевали меня. Вы вставали в чаще ветвей, глядели с неба несчетными глазами, прятались в стрельчатых сводах готического храма, смотрели робко из-за блестящих мраморных колонн языческих капищ. Вы учили меня угадывать смысл природы лучше других учителей, ибо вы были та же

---

3. According to Zhirmunsky (1937), p. 5, the history of Russian Goethe reception "illuminates to various degrees the entire history of Russian literature."
4. For a detailed account, see Durylin.
5. Bryusov (1975), vol. 6, p. 295.
6. Ibid.

природа. Вы были мне всех ближе, ибо вы были мой собственный дух, разлитый по небу, земле и морю. Вы говорили мне подобно тому бесу, спутнику Фауста: "смотри более глубоким взором в обычные явления: в них есть чудо". И я глядел и касался рукой — и из мертвого дерева брызгали потоки животворного вина.

> Phantoms pursue me; they stand around me in a dark crowd of enormous shapes. Be gone, be gone! I am tired of listening to your monotonous sighs, your dark songs.
> I know that you always surrounded me. You stood up in the thicket of branches, you stared from the sky with innumerable eyes, you hid in the arched vaults of the Gothic church, looked timidly from behind the gleaming marble columns of pagan temples. You taught me to guess nature's meaning better than other teachers, because you were that very nature. You were nearer to me than all others, because you were my own spirit, poured across the sky, the earth and the sea. You spoke to me like that demon, Faust's traveling companion: "look with a deeper glance into everyday phenomena: there is a miracle in them." And I looked and touched with my hand—and from the dead tree gushed forth streams of life-giving wine.

Ivanov here refers to the scene in Auerbach's Cellar *(Faust I)*, where Mephistopheles magically draws wine from a wooden table. It is significant that Ivanov painstakingly emphasizes his debt to Goethe. The narrator explicitly casts his own relationship to the "phantoms" in terms of Faust and Mephistopheles. Moreover, in case the reader has been nodding, Ivanov supplies a footnote to this passage in which he refers the reader to the relevant *Faust* verses: "Ein tiefer Blick in die Natur: Hier ist ein Wunder,—siehe nur! Göthe [sic], Faust, Auerbach's Keller."[7]

At approximately the same time, Ivanov commenced a much more ambitious project that involved Goethe: a "Russian Faust." This work deserves our close attention. It was not a translation, but a Russian variation on the German theme. Ivanov, of course, was not the first Russian poet to conceive of such an idea; Pushkin, Aleksei Konstantinovich Tolstoy, and Konstantin Sluchevsky had all written poems that refashioned elements of Goethe's most celebrated work. The idea for a new version of *Faust* might also have been inspired by a recent event in Germany: in 1887, Erich Schmidt, a professor at the University of Berlin, published the newly discovered *Urfaust,* thereby

---

7. "A deep glance into nature: Here is a miracle,—just look!" (*Faust I*, ll. 2288-89). In accordance with a time-honored Russian tradition, Ivanov slightly misquotes the passage. The final words are actually "Glaubet nur!" ("Just believe!").

acquainting readers with the earliest version of Goethe's masterpiece. Even if Ivanov never encountered Schmidt through coursework, it is unlikely that a scholarly sensation of this magnitude would have escaped his notice.

Ivanov's own text, written in the final days of December, 1887, consists of two complete scenes (182 lines in free iambs).[8] The first, a dialogue between God and Mephistopheles, clearly recalls the "Prologue in Heaven" from Goethe's *Faust* (the scene is not part of the *Urfaust*).

> Бог: Ты здесь опять? Зачем ты, искуситель?
> Решился наш давнишний спор:
> Я победил: спасен мой верный чтитель
> Мой Фауст — и правдив святой мой приговор.[9]
>
> God: You're here again? Why, you tempter?
> Our ancient quarrel has been decided.
> I have triumphed: my faithful admirer is saved,
> My Faust—and my sacred sentence is just.

Already in these opening lines, one finds an oblique reference to the German model. Goethe's most radical departure from the traditional Faust legend occurs in the famous final scene of the second part, when Faust ascends to heaven. By mentioning that Faust has been saved, Ivanov suggests that he is continuing Goethe's story. His own version begins, as it were, where Goethe's concluded.

Ivanov's portrayals of God and Mephisto owe an obvious debt to Goethe. God solemnly pronounces lofty *sententiae*, which Mephisto, the crafty and sometimes comic sophist, denies or contradicts. In a lengthy and rambling rebuttal to God's verses, Mephisto explains that he has come "with a humble proposal"—he offers his services to God.

> Мефист.
> Не мыслю вновь вступить на состязанье
> О силе нашего влиянья
> По человеческим сердцам...
>
> Но дело нужно мне для сердца и ума —
> Я к людям попривык, скучна мне стала тьма...

---

8. The first scene is undated, but the second was written from 27 to 30 December 1887.

9. The complete text can be found in Wachtel (1991, Paris).

Mephisto:
>   I do not think of competing again
>   About the power of our influence
>   On the hearts of men . . .
>
>   But the matter is important for my heart and mind—
>   I have grown accustomed to man, darkness now bores me . . .

God responds to this suggestion with scorn, exclaiming that evil cannot serve him. Mephisto parries this with his personal credo:

> Девиз мой доблестный я повторял не раз:
>   Я благодетельная сила,
> Что, вечно к злу стремясь, всегда добро творила.
>
> I have repeated my valiant slogan many a time:
> I am that virtuous force
> Which, eternally striving for evil, always did good.

This "slogan" comes directly from the mouth of Goethe's Mephisto, who at one oft-quoted point (ll. 1336–37) describes himself as "ein Teil von jener Kraft, die stets das Böse will und stets das Gute schafft" ("a part of that force, that always wants evil and always does good"). Building on the same opposition of good and evil but giving it a new twist, Mephisto returns to the Faust theme:

>   . . . вы — любите приличье
> И праведен для вас, кто, благо возлюбя,
> Всю жизнь лишь зло творит для ближних и себя,
>   Как Фауст, доктор преподобный,
> Но как бы ни было, я вам слуга удобный.
>   Мне хочется на шар земной слететь
>   Апостолом горячим идеала,
> Поборником добра . . .
>
> . . . You love propriety
> And for you a just person is he who, loving good,
> His entire life does nothing except evil for himself and his
>   neighbors,
> Like Faust, the venerable doctor.
> But however that may be, I am a convenient servant for you.
> I want to fly down to the earthly sphere
> As the ardent apostle of the ideal,
> As the champion of good . . .

The specifics of Mephisto's new plan become clear only at the scene's conclusion:

> Бог: Чего ты требуешь? Как речь твоя длинна!
>
> Меф: Прошу я презабавной штуки:
> Есть презабавная на севере страна,
> Край благочестия и сна,
> Недоумения и скуки.

> God: What do you demand? How lengthy your speech is!
>
> Mephisto:
> I ask for a most amusing thing.
> There is a most amusing country in the north,
> A land of piety and sleep,
> Bewilderment and boredom.

This "most amusing country in the north" is, of course, Russia. Mephisto intends to pay a visit to the "Russian Faust."

Above the second scene Ivanov wrote the title: "Faust. Russian Variants on a Universal Legend." The basic idea for this scene, which consists solely of a lyric monologue by a character designated as *N*, is derived from the famous opening soliloquy of Goethe's *Faust* (also the very first scene of the *Urfaust*). Like his German counterpart, Ivanov's hero expresses his profound dissatisfaction with life. However, as if to underline the differences, Ivanov takes care to create an appropriately Russian setting. Rather than pontificating in a scholar's study, Ivanov's hero stands alone on the terrace of an estate surrounded by birch trees.

> Какая скука! скука! скука!..
> Пришла, подкралася опять
> Ее холодная мне ведомая мука...

> What boredom! boredom! boredom!
> Its cold torture, long-known to me
> Has arrived, crept up again...

The emphatic repetition of the word "boredom" in the opening line recalls not only the despondency of Goethe's protagonist, but also Pushkin's "Scene from Faust," which begins with Faust's laconic statement to Mephistopheles: "Mne skuchno, bes." ("I am bored, demon.")

In his lengthy monologue, the protagonist relates various unsuccessful attempts to escape from his tenacious ennui. He has retreated from society to lead an introspective life ("I waited, joyous in advance, to find in solitude an invaluable treasure within my soul... And I listened greedily to my soul's voice, but it was silent, joyless... "). He has tried to become learned. ("With a naive and youthful ardor, I thirsted for learning and wisdom, but soon I understood the limit of narrow science.") He has developed a social conscience, liberating his serfs in the best tradition of the Russian gentry:

> В мои поместия к крестьянам удивленным
>   С доверчивой любовью я пришел;
> Народ хотел я знать освобожденным,
>   Забытым прежний произвол.
> Я отпускал рабов, давал рукою щедрой —
> И успокоился, лишь тяжко разорен.
> И что ж народ? в его таинственные недра
> Проникнуть я не мог: остался тот же он,
> Все так же пьян и нищ, выносливый, голодный,
>   Покорный, недоверчивый, холодный...

> Into my lands, to the astonished peasants
> I went with trustful love;
> I wanted to see the people set free,
> [To see] the former tyranny forgotten.
> I freed the serfs, gave to them generously
> And then calmed down, only severely ruined.
> And what of the people? Into their mysterious depths
> I was unable to penetrate: they remained the same,
> Still drunk and destitute, enduring, hungry,
> Submissive, disbelieving, cold...

The most direct source for this passage is again Pushkin, in this case the seventh scene of *Boris Godunov*, where the eponymous hero laments the ingratitude of his subjects.[10] However, Ivanov carries this paradigm from the "time of troubles" to the nineteenth century, replacing the cruel autocrat with the well-meaning gentry. By 1887, of course, the image of an "enlightened" landowner with an awakened conscience was a cliché of Russian literature. Ivanov's protagonist thus claims lineage to a distinctly Russian tradition of "superfluous men."

In Goethe's work, Faust's soliloquy comes to a sudden end when Wagner enters. The two then go outside to see the local people cele-

---

10. "Я думал свой народ / В довольствии, во славе успокоить / Щедротами любовь его снискать — / Но отложил пустое попеченье: / Живая власть для черни ненавистна". ("I thought / To make my people satisfied and glorious, / To win their love through generosity—/ But I have laid aside that plan / The rabble hates living power.")

brating Easter. In Ivanov's version, there is no second character, but the protagonist hears the local people singing songs in honor of the Russian folk holiday "Ivan Kupala." Recalling the rituals that accompany this day ("Ancient pagan charms!"), the protagonist momentarily forgets his morbid thoughts. Yet the scene closes on a dark note. Comparing the people's search with his own, he concludes that all are waiting for a miracle that will never come.

> Так не изменится в холодной глубине
> Состав сырой земли от перемен наружных,
> Хотя б морской потоп разлился сверху вновь,
> И почву залила избитых полчищ кровь.

> Thus in the cold depths, the composition of damp earth
> Will not alter from external changes,
> Even if a flood from the sea poured down on it again,
> And the blood of slaughtered hordes inundated the soil.

With this somewhat turgid imagery, the scene—and, as it turned out, the entire work—concludes.

With these two scenes, Ivanov set the stage for a meeting between Mephisto and *N*, but then he seems to have lost interest (or inspiration) in his "Russian Faust." There is little purpose in speculating on the direction this work might ultimately have taken. Nor would it be appropriate to judge these two scenes by the same standards one uses in evaluating a published text; in terms of theme and style, they have little in common with the poetry of *Pilot Stars*. Nonetheless, the text offers a valuable glimpse into the early phase of Ivanov's poetic development. For the twenty-year-old Russian poet, Goethe was not simply a giant of literary history, but a model to be followed. Rather than turning to contemporary literature (German or Russian) for ideas, Ivanov decided to rework the most celebrated masterpiece of the German literary tradition.

The problem with orienting one's own work on a model as well-known and respected as Goethe's *Faust* lies in the inevitable comparison. Ivanov's major thematic change, substituting Russia for Germany, does not alter the basic configuration of characters or the order and construction of the scenes. Even his choice of meter (free iamb) recalls Goethe's "Prologue in Heaven."

It is curious that Ivanov focuses so intently on the opening scenes of *Faust I*. Already in *Pilot Stars* (and throughout his long creative life), he displays a marked preference for the mystical, lyrical, less plot-oriented second part of Goethe's *Faust*. The opening scenes of *Faust,* which draw on a canon of realistic theater that in time became too constricting for Goethe himself, had limited relevance for the mature Ivanov. Yet the young Ivanov seems to lavish attention on matters of plot construction and the depiction of individual characters.

If nothing else, then, this work demonstrates a fervent desire to build on Goethe's legacy. Like most poets' juvenilia, the "Russian Faust" relies too closely on its source, repeating rather than responding to it. In his mature work, Ivanov treats his sources much more freely, not hesitating to alter and supplement them. In this regard, one further aspect of Ivanov's early Goethe reception should be noted, for it only intensifies in later years. As early as the "Russian Faust," Ivanov is already combining subtexts. While the work is fundamentally (almost slavishly) modeled on Goethe, Ivanov nevertheless includes ample allusions to the Russian literary tradition. The mixing of sources, so characteristic of Ivanov's mature poetics, can already be detected in embryonic form in the "Russian Faust."

In 1889, Ivanov wrote another poem that expresses his attitude toward Goethe. Entitled "Goethe" and written in trochaic tetrameter, it is a hymn to a genius:

> В мир твой входит посетитель,
> Но тебя не видит в нем:
> Ты сокрыл свою обитель,
> Как Творец сокрыл Свой дом.
>
> Ты как Он, разлит незримый,
> Многоличен и един;
> Ты, как Он, непостижимый,
> Мира часть и господин.
>
> Хладный бытия свидетель
> И участник бытия,
> Ты порок и добродетель,
> Подсудимый и судья.
>
> Нет ни цели произвольной,
> Ни иных тебе дорог,
> Всеблаженный, вседовольный
> Микрокозма смертный бог.[11]
>
> A visitor enters your world,
> But he does not see you in it,
> You have concealed your abode,
> Just as the Creator concealed His house.

---

11. RGB, f. 109, k. 1, ed. khr. 26. I quote from Ol'ga Kuznetsova's as yet unpublished manuscript.

> You, like Him, are everywhere invisible,
> Many-faced and unified;
> You, like Him, are unknowable,
> Both a part of the world and its master.
>
> A cold witness of existence
> And a participant in existence,
> You are vice and virtue,
> The defendant and the judge.
>
> There is for you no arbitrary goal,
> [For you] no other paths,
> All-blessed, all-satisfied
> Mortal god of the microcosm.

With these verses, Ivanov continues a Russian tradition (begun by Baratynsky and Tyutchev) of poems that celebrate Goethe as the highest exponent of mankind.[12] Ivanov's poem, structured as an extended apostrophe to Goethe, develops through a series of direct comparisons. Ivanov portrays the German poet as a second God, who is invisible, yet omnipresent. His superhuman accomplishments give him a status that can be expressed only through a series of paradoxes; many-faced and unified (stanza 2), an observer and a participant (stanza 3). This "*mortal* god of the microcosm" stands above all men, but still somewhat beneath God.

While interesting as an illustration of the early phase of Ivanov's adulation of Goethe, this poem has limited artistic value. Its lexicon, style, and imagery are extremely distant from Ivanov's mature verse. Moreover, except for its title, the poem contains nothing specifically Goethean. One can hardly be surprised that Ivanov never included it in his published collections.

Another, "extra-literary" side of Ivanov's early Goethe reception deserves attention. Numerous passages in his personal correspondence indicate that, for the young Ivanov, Goethe was more than a literary model; he was also a model for life.

The year 1895 marked a crucial turning point in Ivanov's personal development. Since 1892, he had been living in Rome with Dar'ya Mikhailovna, his wife of eight years, and their daughter Aleksandra. Little is known about Ivanov's activities of this time; he appears to have been working mainly on his dissertation, although his slow progress suggests that he also found time to enjoy life in the "eternal

---

12. In 1932, to commemorate the centennial of Goethe's death, Ivanov translated these poems into German and wrote a short essay on them. *SS*, vol. 3, pp. 158–62.

city."[13] What seems to have been a rather idyllic routine ended suddenly when Ivanov met Lidiya Dmitrievna Zinov'eva-Annibal, the woman who eventually became his second wife. Ivanov viewed their meeting as "a powerful dionysian spring thunderstorm, after which everything in me was rejuvenated, bloomed and became verdant."[14]

Ivanov's love affair with Lidiya began in the first months of 1895. At first their love was mixed with profound feelings of guilt, doubt, and regret. Given the extremely intimate nature of their correspondence, it is remarkable to note the frequency with which Ivanov, in both isolated phrases and entire paragraphs, alludes to Goethe. Ivanov's letter of 28/16 January 1895, could be called his first genuine love letter to Lidiya. In it, he refers to a "Demon" (probably a reference to Goethe's poem of that name in "Urworte. Orphisch")[15] that controls their actions and desires. " ... But why speak about our desire? As long as the Demon wants, we will involuntarily love each other; and passion, whether forged by our rational will or set free, will all the same be present in our love and penetrate it with its inner flame,—for as long as the Demon wants. And in the meantime, Lidiya, we will both strive constantly 'zum höchsten Dasein.'[16] That is the dawn, these are the raptures that I predicted."[17] Ivanov would later cite the phrase "zum höchsten Dasein" repeatedly, in the poetry as well as the theoretical works.

On February 16, Ivanov writes,

> ... In my tortuous spiritual condition of the last days I was *consoled* by the following lines of Goethe:
>
> *Ja, in der Ferne fühlt sich die Macht,*
> *Wenn zwei sich redlich lieben;*
> Drum bin ich in des Kerkers Nacht
> Auch noch lebendig geblieben

---

13. In the "Autobiographical Letter," Ivanov states that he was hindered in his work by malaria. His own letters of 1894 (to Krumbacher and Hirschfeld) make clear that he did indeed suffer from malaria for the last four months of 1893. However, this does not entirely explain the slow progress that characterized his other two and a half years in Rome.

14. *SS*, vol. 2, p. 20.

15. Goethe understood a "demon" as something unchangeable within the individual. The line that would apply here is: "So mußt du sein, dir kannst du nicht entfliehen ... " ("Thus you must be, you cannot escape yourself ... "). In later years, Ivanov often referred to Goethe's notion of the "demonic." See *SS*, vol. 2, p. 597; *SS*, vol. 3, p. 191; or in Al'tman, p. 315.

16. These words ("to the highest [form of] existence") come from Faust's monologue at the beginning of *Faust II*.

17. All quotes from the correspondence with Lidiya are from RGB, f. 109, k. 9, ed. khr. 37, 38.

> Und wenn mir fast das Herze bricht,
> So ruf' ich nur: *Vergiß mein nicht!*
> Da komme ich wieder ins Leben...[18]
>
> It was as if your letter confirmed the consolation of these words...

Ivanov quotes here the final stanza of Goethe's ballad "Das Blümlein Wunderschön" ("The Wonderful Flower"). Subtitled "Song of the Captive Count," the poem describes a nobleman whose imprisonment is made bearable only by his knowledge of his faithful beloved.

On 21 February, Ivanov returns to "The Wonderful Flower": "... In a word, it is enough to come to an agreement, to conclude pacts and treaties, to contrast 'Sehnsucht' ['yearning'] and 'Leidenschaft' ['passion'] (they are not opposite, and about myself I can only say with Goethe: 'ich trage nach dir Verlangen')[19]—and dry the flowers that are already blooming."

On 23 February, Ivanov alludes to the main characters of Goethe's novel *Die Wahlverwandtschaften (Elective Affinities)*: "Are you not sorry for me? You see, I am not dreaming about anything, I only want your closeness.... Let's remember Eduard and Ottilie in the final epoch, in the epoch after the catastrophe that destroyed all hopes: they also made do with closeness alone... "

On 2 March, he writes:

> "Die Leidenschaft bringt Leiden,"[20] Goethe says, and this is why it brings me suffering to read your lines and to write to you.... Why do I write this? In order to reawaken in you your smoldering flame?.. What have we done, my beloved, what have we done?
>
> Die Lebensfackel wollten wir entzünden:
> Ein Feuermeer umgiebt uns—welch' ein Feuer.[21]

On 17 March, a new Goethean theme appears—Gretchen.

---

18. "*Yes, power can be sensed from far away, when two people truly love each other.* This is why I still remain alive even in the the prison's night. And when my heart almost breaks, I just call out: *Forget me not!*—Then I am again rejuvenated." (These are Ivanov's italics.)

19. From the opening lines of "Das Blümlein Wunderschön": "Ich kenn ein Blümlein Wunderschön / Und trage darnach Verlangen" ("I know a beautiful little flower / And bear a desire for it.") The phrase in question has an extremely archaic ring.

20. "Passion brings suffering." The phrase is from the "Trilogie der Leidenschaft" ("Trilogy of Passion").

21. "We wanted to light the torch of life / A sea of fire surrounds us—what a fire." From Faust's monologue at the beginning of *Faust II*.

> You are now playing the role of the repentant Magdalene under the ferule of your tyrannical confessor. What a disgraceful scene; you ask her if they believed in your honesty, she answers "I don't know"—and this "doubt" fills your soul with "cold horror," and you, sobbing, beg for death.... What a humiliation of you, of me, of our love! The repentant Gretchen repented only before God, and profaned her feeling, condemning it before people.

The Gretchen theme reappears four days later, on 21 March: "When you write about your moral tortures, I experience a feeling like that of Faust entering Gretchen's jail. Then I ask myself with horror: 'What have you done with her?'"

Ivanov develops the *Wahlverwandtschaften* theme delicately in a letter of 27 March: "My Lidiya, our 'Wahlverwandtschaft' brings about an entire series of analogical phenomena in our spiritual and physical life and this thought encourages me in regard to your present state, forcing [me] to assume that you are the victim of the same—for us, sensitive natures, (pardon, my dear, I'm joking), sweet—illusion, in whose power I myself have been more than once..." In this same letter, he again mentions the Faust motif: "Never have I felt within myself such strength for life and such a Faustian thirst to experience, to know all of life in full."

The *Wahlverwandtschaften* theme returns at length in an apologetic letter of 18 June that Ivanov sent from Berlin.[22]

> I received your second letter and your sad parcel. This letter is already different. Here are different sounds. They penetrate directly to the heart and force me to suffer.... Yes, of course, my feeling is not what you want. I am not Eduard. I am not an "illusion" that you created. But I also don't want to be anything but myself. This is not cynicism (although, from a certain point of view, any self-affirmation can seem like cynicism). I do not praise myself and am not proud of myself; but I cannot and do not want to become different and I am worried only about being as just as possible and not hypocritical. Remember with what sincerity I pointed out to you the specific quality of my feeling every time I felt it. Remember with what care I always characterized our love. Imbued with a sense of its elemental quality, I compared it to a "Wahlverwandschaft," but only with the provision that I was uncertain about the full correspondence of this comparison and that it would be more probable to assume only certain sides of our beings were somehow exclusively predestined for mutual conjunction and completion...

---

22. I quote from a draft of the letter, as the final version appears not to have survived.

In sum, Ivanov charts his relationship to Lidiya in terms of recurring motifs from Goethe's works. There is the motif of optimism, exemplified by Faust's desire to experience life in all of its fullness. Longing is expressed through the words of the captive Count from the ballad "The Wonderful Flower." Guilt is associated with Faust's treatment of Gretchen. The theme of elemental love comes out in the references to Eduard and Ottilie from *Elective Affinities*. This last example warrants particular attention. In letters of 23 February and 27 March, Ivanov uses Goethe's pair of lovers to explain the miraculous, almost supernatural attraction that brought him and Lidiya together. (Years later, Ivanov described this novel as "the ultimate revelation about the mystery of love, about its cosmic roots.")[23] However, the final reference (in the letter of 18 June) suggests that Ivanov, having carried the suggestive analogy too far, is forced to shy away from his own comparison. As he explains: "I was uncertain about the *full* correspondence of this comparison"[24] (my emphasis).

It is noteworthy that Ivanov uses Goethe to characterize not only the vicissitudes of his new, passionate extramarital relationship with Lidiya, but also to clarify his cooled relationship with his wife, Dar'ya Mikhailovna. In a letter of 31/19 June 1895, Ivanov wrote to her from the Bibliothèque Nationale of Paris:

> There is no return: this is recognized by me to the same degree as by you, and the double certainty of the impossibility of resurrecting the old,—a certainty springing up in me from an awareness of my situation and the conditions of my inner life, in you from the awareness of your situation and the demands of your character,—[this double certainty] lies like a heavy tombstone on the grave of our former happiness, on which I have cried bitterly. Contemplating our relationship, this is the conclusion to which I, and you as well, come, and with inexpressible pain I bury "mein früh verlornes höchstes Gut,"[25]—as Faust says of his first love.[26]

---

23. *SS*, vol. 4, p. 147. Ivanov describes the book's "message" as follows: "True love is a chemical affinity of human monads; they are elementally attracted to one another by the invincible necessity of a law of nature. In the spiritual and physical make-up of those predestined by nature to be joined, a series of inherent correspondences is found."

24. Ivanov originally wrote, "I was uncertain about the *correctness* of this comparison," but, in the same draft, replaced "correctness" with "full correspondence."

25. "My highest good, which was lost early." Ivanov makes a curious (Freudian?) slip. The actual line (cf. *Faust II*, l. 10059) reads "jugenderstes längstentbehrtes höchstes Gut" ("highest good, first of my youth, which I have done without for a long time").

26. RGB, f. 109, k. 10, ed. khr. 8.

How should one interpret the remarkably "literary" quality of these deeply intimate letters? Some of these Goethe passages and situations (e.g., the Gretchen theme, the slogan "zum höchsten Dasein") play a central role in Ivanov's later poetic and philosophical works. Others never reappear in his writings (e.g., "The Wonderful Flower"). In short, Ivanov's allusions do not "add up" to a unified, carefully formulated, canonic image of Goethe. Indeed, their function is not so much aesthetic as practical; taken together, they represent a voice of authority and spiritual anchor. Goethe's words "sanction" Ivanov's own views and behavior.

The larger issue transcends Goethe, however. Whether composing poetry or writing about his own feelings, Ivanov thought in terms of literary analogies. His letters, at once highly literary and intensely personal, reveal a belief in a fluid boundary between literature and life. As a result, the words and actions of fictional characters are accorded the same ontological status as the thoughts and deeds of living people. In fact, Goethe's texts seem more truthful than Ivanov's own sentiments. Ivanov views Goethe as an infallible source of wisdom: these are statements whose veracity cannot be disputed. And since Goethe was so articulate on such a diversity of topics, a knowledgeable reader could find advice—or confirmation—for almost any decision.

It should be emphasized that, with the exception of the Goethe allusions, Ivanov's letters of this period contain relatively few quotations. While references to other writers appear, they occur infrequently. A Schiller reference provides an interesting contrast: on 10 February 1895, Ivanov wrote to Lidiya: "The ideal of knight Toggenburg has never been so foreign, even hateful, to me, as it is now, when my predominant will has sentenced me to the role of Toggenburg." Ivanov here alludes to Schiller's ballad "Ritter Toggenburg," where the protagonist agrees to separate from his beloved. Schiller's hero thus provides Ivanov with a *negative* model; he is a character who should not be emulated. The case of Nietzsche also deserves mention, since Ivanov at one point (5 July 1895) approvingly quotes his "Das trunkene Lied" ("The Intoxicated Song"), stating that it contains "a total rejection of pessimism." Nonetheless, it is the only time in these letters that Ivanov gives Nietzsche such exemplary status.[27] One must con-

---

27. In the "Autobiographical Letter," (*SS*, vol. 2, pp. 19-20) Ivanov does indeed grant such status to Nietzsche. "Nietzsche became more fully and more powerfully the sovereign of my thoughts. This Nietzscheanism helped me—cruelly and with full accountability, but correctly, according to my conscience—to decide the choice that confronted me in 1895 between the deep and tender closeness that my feeling of love for my wife had become and the love that consumed me entirely, which from that time was destined to grow and spiritually deepen through my whole life, but which in those first days seemed only a criminal, dark, and demonic passion to me myself and to her

clude that at this critical juncture in Ivanov's personal life (1895), Goethe possessed unprecedented authority and influence.[28]

Ivanov's densely allusive technique implies a certain artistic and even philosophical outlook according to which reality is inextricably linked to fiction. Such a view has good precedent in nineteenth-century literature and thought. On the one hand, it prevailed in the work of the Russian radical critics, who frequently treated fictional characters as real-life people. These critics generally sought in Russian literature "types" who embodied the spirit of the epoch.[29] In a different way, the Romantics also sought to combine literature and

---

whom I loved." This claim is supported, in oblique fashion, by a letter to Ivanov of 2 June 1895 from D. M. Ivanova (his first wife), in which she describes her meeting with Vladimir Solovyov: "I told him that you had an artistic nature and that you are now a Nietzschean and I asked him to write a critique of Nietzsche. He said, 'That is not his final conclusion—he will not stop there [i.e., with Nietzsche] . . . '" (in Kotrelev, 1989). The question of Nietzsche's role in Ivanov's early development remains unclear. However, in Ivanov's letters to Lidiya of 1895 (surely the most important personal documents of these years), Nietzsche's role is decidedly minor, particularly in comparison to that of Goethe.

28. It is tempting, and to a remarkable extent justifiable, to compare Ivanov's experiences of Italy with Goethe's celebrated Italian journey of 1786–87 and all the discoveries associated with it (eros, poetry, antiquity). Archival documents suggest that Ivanov's reactions to this trip reflected those of his chosen precursor. When, in his first letter to Hirschfeld (Deutsche Staatsbibliothek Berlin, Handschriften-abteilung, Literaturarchiv), Ivanov writes of his joy at being for the first time "auf dem klassischen Boden ("on classical ground"), he echoes Goethe's famous formulation in the fifth "Roman Elegy": "Froh empfind ich mich nun auf klassischem Boden begeistert" ("I now find myself happily inspired on classical ground"). In a diary of travels dating from August, 1892 (RGB, f. 109, k. 1, ed. khr. 9), Ivanov, writing of the sunset in Taormina, makes this orientation more explicit: "I waited impatiently for the appearance of the sun, and I recalled ["mne vspominalis'"—the passive nuance of the Russian verb is significant here, but cannot be rendered adequately in English] Goethe's words: 'Look up! The enormous peaks of mountains already announce the beginning of the most festive hour. They are allowed to enjoy earlier the eternal light, which only later descends to us. But now the new brightness and clarity are announced to the green meadows; and this occurs gradually . . . And, lo, the sun itself comes forward!' The sun quickly rose, like a sphere of liquified gold, from behind the foggy-violet Calabrian peaks. Brightly and happily the sea turned blue, and its waves began to play beneath the sun in the form of golden arabesques. In a few minutes everything shone in the peaceful and fresh morning sunshine." The Goethe passage (from the famous opening monologue in *Faust II*, ll. 4695–98) had enormous signficance for Ivanov's own poetics (see chap. 3). In the context of the diary, however, it is noteworthy how Ivanov instinctively turned to a Goethean model when formulating his own observations.

29. Belinsky is the founder of this tradition, but Dobrolyubov's interpretation of Oblomov is perhaps the best-known single example. Cf. Ginzburg, p. 17.

life.³⁰ However, they generally stressed the unity of *their own* life and literature, rather than their own life and another poet's literature. Ivanov's early Goethe references make clear that his favorite German poet served as both an artistic ideal and a guide for personal behavior. This underlying belief in the interconnectedness of one's own literature and life with that of past writers would eventually evolve into a belief in "zhiznetvorchestvo," a fundamental aspect of Russian Symbolist theory and practice.³¹

These letters, together with the poetry of the Berlin years, establish beyond a doubt that Goethe's works made an enormous impact on the young Ivanov. A more important question, however, concerns Goethe's continuing influence on him. A recently discovered preface that Ivanov wrote for *Pilot Stars* provides invaluable assistance in tracing Ivanov's attitude toward the "sage of Weimar." Ol'ga Kuznetsova, who has researched and prepared the text for publication, convincingly argues that it was written in about 1900. I quote it in full:

> The following "Book of Lyric Poetry," the fruit of long and drawn-out years of study and wandering ("Lehr- und Wanderjahre"), is of necessity a collected and complicated whole, contradictory in mood and uneven in style. The removal of the purely juvenile, which I had set as my rule, could not be carried out to the end, given the lack of exact borders, and two undoubtedly immature works ("Worlds of the Possible" and "Ars Magna"), which are joined with the whole by a certain organic tie, are included in the collection in spite of the rule. "Spät erklingt, was früh erklang"—one can say with Goethe about the majority of the book, of which only six poems appeared earlier in print (in "Kosmopolis" and "The European Herald" in 1898 and 1899); this does not satisfy the poet . . .
>
> > Doch schäme dich nicht der Gebrechen,
> > Vollende rasch das kleine Buch;
> > Die Welt ist voller Widerspruch,
> > Und sollte sich's nicht wiedersprechen?
>
> [Thus] Goethe gives his approval. The unity of contemplation of the lofty guiding principles (from whatever angle these Pilot Stars might appear in various conditions of the fleeting moment) is the true unity, and it gave the entire collection its general title, which was approved by him, before whose eyes the book grew

---

30. Ginzburg (pp. 20–21) sees the need to merge literature and life as a fundamentally Romantic impulse.
31. See chap. 8 for a detailed discussion.

> and ripened, with the thought about whom so many of these poems were written, and to whom in all fairness this book would have been dedicated, were it not that a more holy light made it an 'ex-voto' to the poet's deceased mother . . . —tu duca, Vladimir Sergeevich, alas! That which he desired reached its fulfillment too early. He was a mystagogue, a good laborer of God's work in the fleeting and eternal of his activity, in his enthusiasm and his clairvoyance, both in the logos and the symbol of his philosophical speculation and in the penetration of his inspirations of Russian poetry's precious treasures.[32]

This admittedly verbose preface might strike the uninitiated as presumptuous. An unknown Russian poet begins his first book of poetry with three explicit allusions to Goethe (in German), one slightly veiled reference to Dante (in Italian), and a lengthy paean to Vladimir Solovyov. Yet, as the poetry of *Pilot Stars* attests, these names are chosen carefully. In bringing together this triumvirate, Ivanov introduces his main spiritual guides and poetic forebears.

The specific quotations from Goethe require explanation. At the outset, Ivanov describes his book as the fruit of "Lehr- und Wanderjahre" ("years of apprenticeship and wandering"), thereby recalling, to any reader with even rudimentary knowledge about the German literary tradition, the titles of Goethe's two Wilhelm Meister novels. In the context of Ivanov's biography, this reference is easily clarified: Ivanov spent years studying in Berlin, took a lengthy dissertation-writing sojourn in Italy, and traveled extensively throughout and even beyond Europe.

The second two references, much less familiar, are far more revealing. Both date from 1814 and were written specifically for the *Complete Works* edition of 1815. A few words are in order about this edition; Goethe spent much effort devising its format and he was to maintain it, with minor adjustments, throughout all subsequent editions. His most important editorial decision was to reject chronology as an ordering principle. Instead of offering the reader a "lyric diary," he placed the poems into sections based on roughly defined genres (songs, ballads, elegies, etc.) or general themes (e.g., "God and World," "Art"). With few exceptions, he prefaced each section with a "motto," a brief (often merely two lines) poetic "fragment" composed specifically for this purpose.

In Goethe's *Complete Works*, adjacent poems within a single section were often penned at various periods of the poet's life. The two Goethe quotations chosen by Ivanov both refer to this fact. "Spät

---

32. Ol'ga Kuznetsova, "Gete v poeticheskom samoopredelenii Vyach. Ivanova," as yet unpublished manuscript.

erklingt, was früh erklang" ("That which rang out early, rings out late"), served as the motto to "Lieder" ("Songs"), the book's opening section. These lines were therefore among the first that a reader of Goethe's collected poetry would encounter. Ivanov selected his second quotation from "Vorklage," (best rendered in English as "a complaint in advance"), the very first poem in the "Lieder" section. The passage is best understood in the context of the entire poem.

> Vorklage
>
> Wie nimmt ein leidenschaftlich Stammeln
> Geschrieben sich so seltsam aus!
> Nun soll ich gar von Haus zu Haus
> Die losen Blätter alle sammeln.
>
> Was eine lange, weite Strecke
> Im Leben voneinander stand,
> Das kommt nun unter *einer* Decke
> Dem guten Leser in die Hand.
>
> Doch schäme dich nicht der Gebrechen,
> Vollende schnell das kleine Buch;
> Die Welt ist voller Widerspruch,
> Und sollte sich's nicht widersprechen?[33]

The poem consists of two sections that contrast in theme and intonation. In the first two quatrains the author laments the chronological (and spatial) inconsistencies among the poems that follow. In the final stanza (the only one quoted by Ivanov), the poet urges himself to finish the book despite these shortcomings. Given the poem's message, it is not surprising that Goethe wrote it expressly for the 1815 edition and that he gave it a position of maximum importance—as the first poem of the first section.

Why did Ivanov choose these two poetic quotations? While *Pilot Stars* includes a number of direct quotations from Goethe's poetry, these particular passages never reappear. The reason for their inclusion in the preface, I believe, has little to do with inherent aesthetic value or profound theoretical implications. Rather, their presence must be explained in terms of Goethe's exemplary status. When

---

33. "How a passionate stutter looks so strange when written down! Now I have to gather all the stray pages from house to house. What in life stood long and wide apart now comes to the good reader under a single cover. But don't be ashamed of the defect, finish the little book quickly; the world is full of contradiction, and should it [i.e., the book] not contradict itself?"

preparing his first collection of poetry for publication, Ivanov looked to Goethe as a model. He therefore decided to begin his book the same way Goethe began his—with a lament about the variegated nature of what follows. The finest expression of this sentiment could of course be found in Goethe's own work. In short, the larger context of these passages gives them a meaning that transcends their immediate "message." They function as markers that announce the beginning of a book of poetry. It should be noted that in larger, structural terms, *Pilot Stars* does in fact follow Goethe's model. Like Goethe, Ivanov ignores chronology, choosing to divide his book into sections grouped by broad themes ("Impulse and Borders," "Oreads") or, in a smaller number of cases, by genre (e.g., "Sonnets," "Distichs").[34] Moreover, in both Goethe and Ivanov, the vast majority of sections begins with a motto. In terms of sources, one recognizes a fundamental difference; Goethe usually wrote his own mottos, whereas most of Ivanov's are quotations from other poets. Yet the fact that Ivanov's first motto comes from *Faust* suggests that Goethe supplied the very idea of mottos.

To summarize, the Goethe quotations in the preface serve a practical rather than philosophical function. They confirm Ivanov's general editorial practice and justify, as it were, the diversity of poems included in the collection. With Goethe's "approval," Ivanov offers the reader his book.

If the first part of the preface rests on Goethe's authority, the second moves back to Russia, focusing on the person of Vladimir Solovyov. Since there are no intertextual references to Solovyov (except for a paraphrase of his dying words: "difficult is the work of the Lord"), the passage requires little elucidation. Ivanov begins his tribute with a warm personal remembrance. (He notes that Solovyov had praised his poems and sanctioned the book's title[35]—thus, for the second time in the preface, the crucial notion of "approval" resounds.) As the tone becomes increasingly animated, Ivanov apostrophizes Solovyov with the Italian phrase "tu duca" ("you, my leader"). These words, spoken by Dante to Virgil in the "Inferno," (II, 140) add an

---

34. In Goethe's collection, the majority of sections are grouped by genre. In this regard, it is curious to remark that, sometime after 1913, Ivanov drew up a plan for a new edition of his works in which the sections were designated solely by genre—odes and hymns, dithyrambs, dithyrambic mysteries, ancient ballads, songs, elegies, lyric [moments?], odes, songs and elegies from [the book?] "Eros," sonnets, sonnets and canzones from the book "Love and Death," ghasels, spiritual verses, long poems. GPL, f. 304, ed. khr. 47. This collection never materialized, but the plan strongly suggests that the Goethean model still was influential in Ivanov's thinking.

35. For details, see Kotrelev (1989) and Kuznetsova (unpublished manuscript).

additional intertextual level to the preface's already complicated fabric. Ivanov refers to a scene where one poet addresses his predecessor. In this new context, Ivanov's predecessor ("leader") becomes not only Solovyov, but also Dante himself. Having established these connections, Ivanov closes the preface by listing a series of Solovyov's accomplishments and explicitly embracing him as poet, thinker and mentor.

Despite the fact that Ivanov ultimately rejected it, this preface serves as an excellent introduction to a central aspect of Ivanov's mature poetics.[36] The reader is immediately struck by the text's overtly intertextual nature. Ivanov's allusions are not hints or riddles whose solution demands the utmost ingenuity from the reader. For Ivanov's purposes, explicit allusions are clearly preferable. It is *necessary* that the reader recognize the "foreignness" of Goethe and Dante (hence the quotations in German and Italian) as well as Ivanov's debt (both personal and spiritual) to Solovyov. By bringing together the hallowed names of various national literatures, Ivanov emphasizes the continuity of tradition and—equally crucial—lays claim to a spiritual genealogy. As the repeated word "approval" indicates, Ivanov sees his work as being sanctioned by these (deceased) writers and thinkers.

The preface also gives additional insight into Ivanov's ongoing reception of Goethe. While Goethe retains his position of the utmost

---

36. Ivanov rewrote the preface at least twice, but ultimately chose to publish the book without any preface whatsoever. A later version reveals a number of interesting changes. "The poetic harvest of a long and drawn-out series of 'years of study and wanderings' inevitably betrays contradictions of form and interest, and the strictest selection will not transform the collection into a unified whole; but the constant contemplation of transcendent guiding principles is also a form of unity, and this is what has given the collection its overall title which received the blessing of him to whose great memory this book would have been dedicated with reverence, if another more sacred duty had not turned it into an ex-voto offering to the deceased mother of the poet." (This preface was first published by Pamela Davidson, p. 92, whose translation I quote.) In this much-shortened text, Ivanov eliminated the Dante allusion and considerably toned down the references to Goethe. However, it would be incorrect to interpret these changes as a reflection of changing allegiances within Ivanov's personal canon. If this were so, it would be impossible to explain the inordinate number of Goethe and Dante epigraphs within the book itself. (Moreover, using the same faulty logic, one would have to conclude that when he decided to publish the book without any preface at all, Ivanov ultimately rejected Solovyov.) Any number of arguments can be advanced to explain why Ivanov chose not to include the prefaces, from their prolix style to their too "apologetic" tone. In my view, it would be false to see Ivanov's "rejection" of the preface as a reflection of an altered worldview.

authority, he appears to share the spotlight, as it were, with Solovyov and Dante. As a cursory glance into *Pilot Stars* makes evident, this constellation of exemplary figures forms the foundation of Ivanov's spiritual world. Upon opening the book, the reader immediately confronts an epigraph from Dante; turning to the first section, he finds an epigraph from Goethe; glancing at the first poem of the first section, he notes a dedication to Solovyov. Yet to recognize Ivanov's emphatic acceptance of these writers is by no means to understand their role within his larger poetic system. It is not immediately apparent what elements unify these three extremely individual thinkers, except that each was a towering genius in his respective historical epoch. It becomes, in a sense, a challenge to Ivanov's poetics to bring this diverse triumvirate under the banner of a single program.

One is apt to think of turn-of-the-century literature in terms of the "revaluation" of traditional values. According to this scheme, the modernist finds a place for himself by exposing the irrelevance of past platforms for contemporary literature. Ivanov's preface, in this regard a valid reflection of his poetic credo, offers an alternative to the decadent or polemical strains of European modernism by explicitly affirming the unity of the European cultural heritage. A number of subsequent Russian poets shared this view, yet no one developed a poetic system that relied so heavily on explicit quotation.[37]

---

37. One thinks of Tsvetaeva (cf. Ronen [1992], p. 10) or, most obviously, of Mandel'shtam (cf. Taranovsky [1976] and Ronen [1983]).

Chapter 2

Ivanov's Bride of Corinth: Introduction to a Syncretic Poetics

> Нужно техническое чтение — читая, смотреть, как это делает поэт. Например, если знаешь иностранные языки, перелистывая, например, Гете, читать его технически. Вот Пушкин, как большой художник, быстро усваивал чужие приемы, но никак не был под чьим-либо влиянием...[1]
> —Vyacheslav Ivanov's advice to young poets, Moscow, 1920

What sets Ivanov's mature verse apart from the poems of the Berlin years? His "Russian Faust" (1887) shows an almost slavelike devotion to its German model. The characters and larger dramatic structure owe a profound and unmistakable debt to Goethe's masterwork. In *Pilot Stars* (1903), his first collection of poetry, Ivanov continues to affirm his spiritual affinity with Goethe. Most noticeably, he appends strategically selected epigraphs to individual poems or entire sections. Yet in this later work, his treatment of Goethe's texts is markedly original.

Ivanov's creative response to Goethe's "The Bride of Corinth" exemplifies the complexity of his poetic reception. Goethe's poem dates from 1797, known in German literary history as the "ballad year." In a period of a few months, Goethe created a number of ballads that were immediately recognized as masterpieces. With each new ballad, Goethe redefined the genre, broadening its content and refining its formal structure. For all of their diversity, a thematic invariant links these po-

---

1. "It is necessary to read technically—while reading, look how the poet does it. For example, if you know foreign languages, leafing through, for example, Goethe, read him technically. Pushkin, as a great artist, quickly mastered other writers' techniques, yet he was never under anyone's influence..." From F. I. Kogan, "Kruzhok poezii pod rukovodstvom Vyacheslava Ivanova" ("The Poetry Circle under the Supervision of Vyacheslav Ivanov"), TsGALI, f. 2272, op. 1, ed. khr. 33, l. 33.

ems; Goethe's ballads repeatedly describe man's encounter with magical and mysterious forces.[2]

"The Bride of Corinth" tells of a young man from Athens who visits Corinth. His parents have previously agreed with a family there that he should wed their daughter. On the day of his arrival he receives a warm welcome. He goes to sleep exhausted and awakens to find a beautiful woman in his room. Assuming her to be the daughter whom he is to marry, he falls immediately and passionately in love. This incorrect assumption proves fatal. This woman, originally promised to him, has died and now returned as a vampire. (Her younger sister, who never appears in the poem, was to substitute for her.) She sucks the young man's blood and leaves him to die.

Goethe structures his eerie ballad so as to achieve maximum ambiguity. An omniscient narrator begins the poem ("Nach Korinthus von Athen gezogen / Kam ein Jüngling, dort noch unbekannt"—"From Corinth to Athens / Came a young man, as yet unknown there"), yet decreases in prominence as the poem progresses. The central section (stanzas 5–22) is primarily a dialogue between the two main characters, with the narrator filling in sparse details (often mere "stage directions," e.g., "'Bleibe, schönes Mädchen!' ruft der Knabe"—"'Remain, beautiful girl!' cries the boy"). At the conclusion, the authorial voice completely disappears, leaving the final six stanzas as the direct speech of the vampire. This narrative technique allows Goethe to develop the plot carefully while avoiding authorial commentary at the critical moments. By giving the vampire the final word, Goethe neither judges nor explains the poem's supernatural events. As in so many of his ballads, the plot is shrouded in mystery.

In his earlier ballads, Goethe used traditional meters to reflect the genre's popular origin. In the ballads of 1797, he experimented with unusual strophic forms. For the "Bride of Corinth," Goethe devised a stanza unprecedented in German verse.[3] I quote a well-known passage from the vampire's closing monologue; my observations on the formal features can be applied to any of the poem's twenty-eight stanzas:

> Aber aus der schwerbedeckten Enge
> Treibet mich ein eigenes Gericht.
> Eurer Priester summende Gesänge
> Und ihr Segen haben kein Gewicht;
> Salz und Wasser kühlt
> Nicht, wo Jugend fühlt;
> Ach, die Erde kühlt die Liebe nicht! (ll. 162–68)

---

2. See Trunz's commentary (in Goethe [1982], p. 659): "A mysterious relationship stands at the center of Goethe's ballads: higher powers influence man."

3. See Kayser, p. 95.

The stanza is composed of seven lines with the rhyme scheme A-b-A-b-c-c-b.⁴ In the German tradition, this strophic construction appears mainly in folk poetry.⁵ Goethe, aware of this association, had used the seven-line stanza in a number of his earlier ballads.⁶ However, in "The Bride of Corinth," he made a crucial change by truncating the fifth and sixth lines. Against a background of trochaic pentameter, these lines (here: "Salz und Wasser kühlt / Nicht, wo Jugend fühlt") form a couplet in trochaic trimeter. Syntactically and semantically, they begin a new section. Goethe thus created an asymmetrical, bipartite stanza, using the short lines to give the conclusion an additional urgency. The "accelerando" effect of these two short lines is regarded as one of Goethe's brilliant technical innovations.⁷

In his critical essay on Goethe, Ivanov lavishes praise on the ballads ("incomparable ballads... for only in Goethe's ballads does a visionary understanding of nature open up and breathe..."),⁸ placing special emphasis on "The Bride of Corinth":

> The ballad "The Bride of Corinth" combines the ancient with the romantic in order to tell us, in this guise of Greek Romanticism, one of Goethe's deepest insights into nature's secret about love. "The earth cannot cool love,"—this is what Goethe finally discovered. Love is stronger than death. Nature wants to join together the individuals whom it predetermines for conjunction, and the accidental death of one of them is powerless to avert this destiny.⁹

This idiosyncratic account passes over almost all of the poem's distinctive features, including its plot and central motif (the vampire).¹⁰ Instead, Ivanov notes the ballad's synthetic character; it combines elements of antiquity (the Greek setting) with elements of Romanticism (the supernatural). After this single introductory remark, Ivanov turns directly to the poem's "deeper" significance. He apodictically states its fundamental insight, attributing to Goethe the words spoken by the vampire: "Ach, die Erde kühlt die Liebe nicht!" ("Oh, the earth cannot

---

4. Here and throughout this book, capital letters designate feminine rhymes and small letters indicate masculine rhymes.
5. Frank, p. 525.
6. See Hinck, pp. 25–47.
7. Cf. Kommerell, cited in Goethe (1982), pp. 663–64 and Kayser, p. 95.
8. *SS*, vol. 4, p. 146.
9. Ibid.
10. This is particularly striking, given the fact that Ivanov's essay was written as a chapter of a history of Western literature. Either Ivanov assumed that his readers knew the plot, or he did not feel that it was significant enough to be summarized.

cool love!") Ivanov interprets this sentiment "symbolically"—it becomes a philosophical statement of love's power over death.

Ivanov's interpretation exemplifies the mystical view of Goethe characteristic of the time. It recalls an essay on the same poem that Rozanov had written several years earlier.[11] As a scholarly reading of Goethe's ballad, however, it is clearly inadequate, for it reduces a highly ambiguous poem to a single questionable assertion. Since Ivanov does not develop these thoughts elsewhere in his critical or theoretical essays, scholars have traditionally quoted this admittedly unusual evaluation and proceeded to the next explicit Goethe reference.[12] Such treatment relegates Ivanov's view to the status of a literary curiosity.

Ivanov's reading of "The Bride of Corinth" was, however, more subtle and far-reaching than the above-quoted prose passage suggests. To discover the full extent of the poem's significance for Ivanov, one must look beyond his critical essay to his poetic practice. Four poems, composed more than a decade apart, bear testimony to his continued fascination with Goethe's ballad. They also serve as a fine introduction to his extraordinarily varied poetic reception.

In *Pilot Stars*, Ivanov twice alludes to Goethe's ballad. In the more obvious instance, he uses the line "Ach, die Erde kühlt die Liebe nicht!" as the epigraph for "Moonlit Roses" ("Lunnye Rozy"). Ivanov's poem, itself a narrative, relies on a number of formal devices associated with the ballad; interrupted narration, direct speech, refrains, etc. The stanzaic form (four-line anapestic trimeter stanzas with alternating rhyme) bears no resemblance to Goethe's "The Bride of Corinth," but is nevertheless commonly found in Russian literary ballads (e.g., Zhukovsky).[13] In keeping with the balladic tradition (and Goethe's own practice), Ivanov includes supernatural elements in the poem. The opening stanzas set the tone, creating an atmosphere of mystery and uncertainty:

> Из оков одинокой разлуки,
> На крылах упоительных сна,
> К ней влекут его тайные звуки,
> К ней влечет золотая луна ...

---

11. Rozanov also gives special attention to the passage "The earth cannot cool love." He summarizes the basic idea of Goethe's ballad as follows (p. 14): "If love and, in general, the romantic principle in us is a miracle in the sense that it can neither be explained by mechanics nor deduced by logarithms, then it is impossible to doubt that this miracle does not die with the death of our physical body."

12. Cf. Gronicka, vol. 2, p. 197, and Zhirmunsky (1937), p. 591.

13. Gasparov (1984), p. 121.

Все вперед, в бездыханные сени
Лунным сном отягченных древес;
Все вперед, где пугливые тени
Затаил околдованный лес.

Там она, на печальной поляне,
Ждет его над могилой, одна,
Сидючи недвижимо в тумане,—
Как туман, холодна и бледна.

И любви неисполненной пени
Поднялись в безнадежной груди:
"О, зачем мы бесплотные тени?"
— Милый друг! погоди, погоди![14]

In these stanzas (and throughout the poem), Ivanov relies on pronouns, never naming the poem's protagonists. To maximize the uncertainty, he introduces both characters in an oblique case. Because the omniscient narrator chooses not to reveal the poem's "Vorgeschichte," the reader must recreate the plot based on a series of hints. The female protagonist's words ("O, why are we bodiless shades?"), repeated several times in the course of the poem, reveal the central thematic thread: a dead woman yearns for her lover. This refrain expresses a desire as well as an awareness of its futility. Death, the woman implies, has rendered her love powerless.

Yet there is also a suggestion that this "unfulfilled love" will be attained. The woman's mysterious voice clearly has an effect on her beloved—"K nei vlekut ego tainye zvuki" ("Mysterious sounds draw him to her"). A second refrain, "Vse vpered" ("Always forward"), creates the expectation of an imminent meeting. Such expectations prove justified at the end, when the lovers are finally reunited. In describing this passionate moment, Ivanov makes clear his debt to Goethe by introducing the motif of the vampire.[15] This motivic bor-

---

14. "From the bonds of lonely separation / On the intoxicating wings of a dream / Mysterious sounds draw him to her, / A golden moon attracts [him] to her . . . // Always forward, [drawn] by a lunar dream into the breathless covers / Of burdened trees. / Always forward, where the enchanted forest / Concealed frightened shadows. // There she, on the sad clearing, / Waits alone for him above the grave, / Sitting motionless in the mist,— / Cold and pale, like the mist. // And plaints of unfulfilled love / Arose in her hopeless breast: / 'O, why are we bodiless shadows?' / —'Dear friend! Wait, wait!'" *SS*, vol. 2, p. 564.

15. Although mediated by a rose, it is unmistakable: Она ветвь бледной розы срывает: / — "Друг, тебе дар любви, дар тоски!" / Страстный яд он лобзаньем впивает — / Жизнь из уст пьют, зардев, лепестки. // И из роз, алой жизнью налитых, / Жадно пьет она жаркую кровь . . . " "She tears off a branch of a pale rose: / —'My friend, here is a gift of love, a gift of longing!' / He drinks in the

rowing leads, in the poem's final stanza, to a more fundamental thematic similarity:

> Рок любви преклонен всепобедной
> Веет хлад... веет мрак... веет мир...
> И зарей безмятежности бледной
> Занялся предрассветный эфир.[16]

At the denouement, Ivanov's poem becomes explicitly philosophical, exploring the relationship between love and death. The lovers' encounter after death is construed as "fate bowed down to all-triumphant love" ("Rok lyubvi preklonen vsepobednoi"). In Ivanov's own words (from his summary of "The Bride of Corinth"), "Love is stronger than death." "Moonlit Roses" depicts, in symbolic form, this mystical, "all-triumphant" love.

In "Moonlit Roses," Ivanov relies on a relatively simple use of intertextuality. By selecting an epigraph from Goethe, he points the reader toward a specific poem. Knowledge of that poem reveals deeper connections between the two works: generic (various balladic devices, such as dialogue), motivic (the vampire), thematic (love versus death). Ivanov does not hesitate to change aspects of Goethe's poem. The metrics of the "model" are ignored; the setting and the dramatis personae lose their specificity. Yet Ivanov's larger use of Goethe's poem parallels the interpretation he gives in his critical essay; in both places, he emphasizes the elemental, supernatural power of love as a means of overcoming even death. In "Moonlit Roses," Ivanov develops his mystical reading of Goethe's enigmatic ballad.

The seminal poem "Beauty" ("Krasota") reveals a more complicated example of Ivanov's reception of "The Bride of Corinth." It is hardly possible to overestimate this short poem's importance in Ivanov's work. Placed at the beginning of the first section of the first book of poetry, "Beauty" serves as an introduction not only to *Pilot Stars*, but to Ivanov's poetics as a whole.

---

passionate poison with a kiss— / The petals, turning red, drink life from his lips. // And from the roses, filled with scarlet life / She greedily drinks the hot blood." *SS*, vol. 1, p. 565.

16. "Fate is bowed down to an all-triumphant love . . . / Coldness wafts . . . darkness wafts . . . peace wafts . . . / And at the dawn of pale serenity / The predawn ether lit up."

КРАСОТА

Владимиру Сергеевичу Соловьеву

Περί τ'ἀμφί τε κάλλος ἄητο.
Hymn. Homer.

Вижу вас, божественные дали,
Умбрских гор синеющий кристал!
Ах! там сон мой боги оправдали:
Въяве там он путнику предстал . . .
   "Дочь ли ты земли
   Иль небес, — внемли:
Твой я! Вечно мне твой лик блистал".

— "Тайна мне самой и тайна миру,
Я, в моей обители земной,
Се, гряду по светлому эфиру:
Путник, зреть отныне будешь мной!
   Кто мой лик узрел,
   Тот навек прозрел —
Дольний мир навек пред ним иной.

Радостно по цветоносной Гее
Я иду, не ведая — куда.
Я служу с улыбкой Адрастее,
Благосклонно — девственно — чужда.
   Я ношу кольцо,
   И мое лицо —
Кроткий луч таинственного Да".

Beauty
To Vladimir Sergeevich Solovyov
   Beauty spread round about her.
                          Homer. Hymn.

I see you, divine vistas,
The crystal looming blue of the Umbrian mountains!
Ah! there the gods justified my dream:
In reality it [i.e., the dream] appeared to the wanderer . . .
"Whether you are the daughter of the earth
Or the heavens,—Listen:
I am yours! Your visage has been shining to me for eternity."

—"I am a mystery to myself and to the world,
I, in my earthly abode,
Lo, approach along the light ether:
Wanderer, henceforth you shall see like me!
He who has looked upon my visage
Has seen eternally—
The world below is eternally different for him.

> Joyously over flower-bearing Gaia
> I go, not knowing where.
> I serve Adrastea with a smile,
> Beneficently, virginally, alien.
> I wear a ring,
> And my face
> Is the meek light of the mysterious Yes."

In an essay on *Pilot Stars*, Bryusov wrote, "In accordance with the spiritual striving of our entire epoch, Vyacheslav Ivanov is an eclectic."[17] The poem "Beauty" amply supports this claim. The presence of three alphabets (Cyrillic, Greek, Latin) already hints at the poem's remarkable heterogeneity. Even on the formal level, Ivanov creates links with a variety of historical periods and styles. Words like "zret'" ("to behold"), "lik" ("visage"), "gryadu" ("approach"), exclamations such as "se" ("lo") as well as neo-classical epithets like "tsvetonosnaya Geya" ("flower-bearing Gaia") recall the lexicon of Russian eighteenth-century poetry. The predilection for monosyllabic words ("Doch' li ty", "Kto moi lik" or, more noticeably, "Tvoi ya! [Vechno] mne tvoi lik" and "Akh! tam son moi") reflects Ivanov's efforts to apply principles of classical Greek prosody to Russian verse.[18] The poem's distinctive metrical form belongs neither to classical antiquity nor to Russia, but rather to Germany; it is modeled on "The Bride of Corinth."[19]

To understand the significance of Ivanov's metrical allusion, it is necessary to make some preliminary observations about "Beauty." The poem describes a meeting between a male protagonist and an other-worldly female figure. Ivanov sets this encounter in a tradition of epiphanic poetry through two explicit allusions: the dedication and the epigraph. By dedicating his poem to Vladimir Solovyov, Ivanov not only pays tribute to his late mentor, but also calls to mind his poetic world. As numerous critics have noted, the "plot" of "Beauty" parallels one of Solovyov's most celebrated poems.[20] In "Tri svidaniya" ("Three Meetings"), Solovyov depicts his own encounters with a mysterious and beautiful female figure.

For Ivanov and Solovyov, the notion of transformation plays a central role. The beautiful woman *alters* her observers, leading them

---

17. Bryusov (1975), vol. 6, p. 295.

18. See M. L. Gasparov, (1987), p. 115. The use of monosyllabic Russian words as a reflection of Greek verse is most clearly shown in the translation Ivanov did in 1914 of the Greek poet Terpander: "Зевс, ты — всех дел верх! / Зевс, ты — всех дел вождь! / Ты будь сих слов царь; / Ты правь мой гимн, Зевс!"

19. To my knowledge, R. E. Pomirchy was the first to draw attention to this, in his commentary to Ivanov (1976), p. 457.

20. See, for example, Pomirchy's comments. Ibid.

to a higher state of knowledge.²¹ Solovyov and Ivanov both use the verb "prozret'" ("to see [through]/to understand") to signal this transformation. In the short concluding section of his poem, Solovyov writes:

> Еще невольник суетному миру,
> Под грубою корою вещества
> Так я *прозрел* нетленную порфиру
> И ощутил сиянье божества.²² (my emphasis)

Ivanov develops this motif. Beauty tells the wanderer:

> Путник, *зреть* отныне будешь мной!
> Кто мой лик *узрел*
> Тот навек *прозрел* —
> Дольний мир навек пред ним иной.²³ (my emphasis)

The sequence of verbs emphasizes the progression from literal seeing ("zret', uzret'") to figurative seeing ("prozret'"). The latter, as emphasized by the repetition of the word "navek" ("forever") is permanent.

Both poets characterize the woman by her smile, thereby accentuating the joyous nature of the encounter. Solovyov writes: "Stoyala ty s ulybkoyu luchistoi," ("You stood with a radiant smile").²⁴ In Ivanov's poem, the woman identifies herself in terms of a smile: "Ya sluzhu s ulybkoi Adrastee" ("I serve Adrastea with a smile"). This seemingly trivial detail takes on enormous significance in Ivanov's writings, where the smile invariably accompanies visionary experience, the meeting of the divine with the human. The poem "Beethoveniana," for example, ends with such a moment: "I bozhestvennoi ulybkoi / Proyasnilas' pechal' ochei."²⁵ Ivanov also uses the motif in his theoretical writings. In "The Symbolism of Aesthetic Principles," he writes "A smile is inspired mercy. Gracious Beauty smiles."²⁶ At the end of the same essay, a smile symbolizes Aphrodite's contact with

---

21. In a 1905 essay, Ivanov refers to his own poem, calling the figure of Beauty "an archetype and promise of universal Transfiguration . . . " *SS*, vol. 1, p. 827.

22. "[While] still a slave to the vain world, / Beneath the coarse cover of matter / Thus I saw the undying porphyry / And felt the radiance of the divine."

23. "Wanderer, henceforth you shall see like me! / He who looked upon my visage / Has seen eternally— / The world below is eternally different for him."

24. Also after their meeting: "Ulybkoi rozovoi dusha sledy khranila" ("The soul preserved its traces in a rosy smile").

25. *SS*, vol. 1, p. 779. "And, with a divine smile, the eyes' sadness became clear." The motif occurs in the later poetry as well, e.g., in *Tender Mystery* (*SS*, vol. 3, p. 56) and *Vespertine Light* (*SS*, vol. 3, p. 522).

26. "Ulybka—poshchada okrylennaya. Ulybchiva milostivaya Krasota." *SS*, vol. 1, p. 826.

mankind. This symbolic smile, especially prominent in Ivanov's works, draws on a lengthy tradition.[27]

In his epigraph ("Beauty spread round about her"), Ivanov uses classical antiquity to underscore the poem's theme. On the most straightforward level, the connection between the "Homeric" epigraph and Ivanov's poem is obvious: both describe a sudden manifestation of beauty. However, given Ivanov's detailed knowledge of Greek literature, it is unlikely that he would have chosen the epigraph to a crucial poem only because the word "beauty" appeared in it. Two additional aspects should be considered. The first concerns the question of authority: by naming Homer as his source, Ivanov claims kinship to the progenitor of the entire Western literary tradition.[28] In an explicitly programmatic poem like "Beauty," the significance of such claims cannot be overemphasized. The second consideration is intertextual. Ivanov quotes a line from the "Hymn to Demeter" in order to call to mind this specific myth. The passage he selects comes at the turning point of the narrative. Demeter, posing as an ugly old nurse, attempts to give Metaneira's son immortality by throwing him into the fire. Metaneira hears her child's cries and interrupts Demeter. Furious at people's inability to comprehend her actions ("witless are you mortals and dull to foresee your lot ... "), Demeter orders them to build her a temple: "And I myself will teach my rites, that hereafter

---

27. Ivanov's image of the smiling Aphrodite can be found in classical literature (cf. the first Sapphic ode). Numerous poets rely on the smile as a topos. Goethe, for example, uses it in "Zueignung" ("Dedication"), a poem that Ivanov often quoted and that contains numerous parallels to Ivanov's "Beauty." Describing his meeting with "ein göttlich Weib" ("a divine woman"), Goethe writes that her smile "cured" him: "Sie lächelte, da war ich schon genesen ... " ("She smiled, and I was already recovered ... "). In the Russian Symbolist tradition, Voloshin's 1909 poem "She" ("Ona") draws on the epiphanic tradition under consideration. In it, the poet searches for a mysterious woman, whose distinguishing characteristic is her smile. "И я читал ее судьбу / В улыбке внутренней зачатья, / В улыбке девушек в гробу / В улыбке женщин в миг объятья." ("And I read her fate, / In the inner smile of conception / In the smile of young women in the grave / In the smile of women at the moment of an embrace.") The final image (indeed, the final word) of the poem is "smile"—"И тихо светятся уста / Неотвратимою улыбкой." ("And her lips quietly shine / In an inevitable smile"). Voloshin also indirectly evokes the image of a smile by referring to Aphrodite and the Mona Lisa. In Voloshin (1982), vol. 1, pp. 94–95.

28. As a student of classical philology, Ivanov was surely aware that the "Hymn to Demeter" (like all of the so-called "Homeric Hymns") was *not* written by Homer. (Cf. Allen and Sikes, pp. liii–liv). One may assume that Ivanov made this attribution for "strategic" rather than scholarly reasons. For Ivanov's purposes, Homer is far preferable to "anonymous." He thereby extends the direct line of his poetic predecessors, adding the venerable name of Homer to those of Dante, Goethe, and Solovyov.

you may reverently perform them and so win the favour of my heart."²⁹ Directly following this passage comes the section from which Ivanov draws his epigraph: "When she had so said, the goddess changed her stature and her looks, thrusting old age away from her: beauty spread round about her."

A reader unaccustomed to Ivanov's allusive poetics may be confused by the glaring incongruities between the "Hymn to Demeter" and the Ivanov and Solovyov poems. The goddess confronts a woman, not a man; she is not smiling, but furious. Yet despite these differences, the scene has obvious relevance to the epiphanic tradition, for it describes the meeting of the human and the divine. The line that Ivanov uses as an epigraph depicts the transformation from mortal to immortal. Demeter herself embodies this process by shedding her earthly guise (as an old nurse) and assuming divine form (beauty). She also (indirectly) bestows immortality on mankind by promising to teach her "rites." These rites, the Eleusinian mysteries, allow the initiate to conquer death.³⁰ By citing the "Hymn to Demeter," Ivanov subtly evokes these associations.

Goethe's role in "Beauty" must be understood against this complicated background. Victor Terras, noting the poems' common metrical form, has stated that "Beauty" shares the "basic theme and ethos" of "The Bride of Corinth."³¹ His laconic statement requires elaboration. In terms of genre and theme, the poems display no obvious resemblances. Ivanov's essentially philosophical poem is virtually static, while Goethe's mysterious ballad relies on sudden shifts of plot. Vampirism, the most celebrated aspect of Goethe's poem, has no connection to the epiphanic tradition that inspired "Beauty."

Yet the poems have a similar structure; they begin with an omniscient authorial voice that in turn yields to direct speech (a conversation). On the semantic level, they share the constellation of characters; a male protagonist and an other-worldly female figure. In both poems, the woman possesses a supernatural power over the man whom she immediately and ineluctably attracts; through their encounter, she permanently transforms him. In "Beauty," the man's immediate surrender to this woman ("Tvoi ya!"—"I am yours!") parallels the sudden passion that characterizes the behavior of Goethe's protagonist. A

---

29. Hesiod, pp. 307–9.
30. The Homeric "Hymn to Demeter" is traditionally known for its explanation of the origin of the Eleusinian mysteries. These mysteries are symbolized by the myth of Demeter's daughter Persephone. Ivanov himself repeatedly writes about Persephone, e.g., the poem entitled "Persephone" in the 1904 collection *Transparence* or the "Poslanie na kavkaz" ("Epistle to the Caucasus") in *Tender Mystery*.
31. Terras (1986), p. 344.

crucial difference should, however, be noted—Ivanov transfers the physicality of Goethe's ballad to a spiritual plane.

Ivanov's poem thus displays an unusual internalization of Goethe's legacy. In order to comprehend the semantic significance of his metrical allusion, the reader must view "Beauty" and "The Bride of Corinth" not in terms of their myriad differences (e.g., a daytime revelation versus a midnight passion), but as sharing a few key concepts. Both poems focus on a man whose fate is determined by the sudden appearance of a beautiful woman. Ivanov expands on Goethe's ballad, interpreting elemental passion as epiphanic experience. He does not conceive of this woman as an evil or ruthless force, for she initiates man into a higher realm. In this respect, she resembles not the archetypal "femme fatale," but the "eternal feminine."[32]

These considerations suffice to demonstrate a fundamental aspect of Ivanov's poetics—the "layering" of subtextual levels. "Beauty" recalls Solovyov's "Three Meetings," Goethe's "Bride of Corinth," and the homeric "Hymn to Demeter." However, the poem's essential significance cannot be reduced to any one of these subtexts. The title identifies the woman as an incarnation of "beauty" (a word of feminine gender in Russian), yet her deeper significance remains a mystery. She herself states this explicitly: "Taina mne samoi i taina miru."[33] The multifarious allusions serve to elucidate this enigmatic figure. While she is not equivalent to any of the women in the subtexts, she assumes characteristics of all of them. By a simple process of addition, the encounter in "Beauty" gains symbolic weight. For example, while there is no hint of death in "Beauty," the allusion to "The Bride of Corinth" suggests that the woman is both privy to and yet beyond the realm of death. Ivanov's poetics are based on a firm sense of tradition. His allusions demonstrate the continuity that links his work to certain exemplary texts ranging from classical antiquity to Goethe to Solovyov. Ivanov thus uses subtexts to create a mythical foundation for his poetry.[34]

More than a decade after writing "Beauty," Ivanov returned to "The Bride of Corinth," using its distinctive metrical form for a poem in the second part of the lengthy philosophical work entitled "Man."

---

32. In general, the Symbolists were fascinated by the concept of the "eternal feminine" (cf. Kluge, p. 54). Ivanov (*SS*, vol. 4, p. 156) considered it Goethe's "most important and mysterious testament to posterity." Solovyov also used the motif (e.g., his own poem "Das Ewig-Weibliche"), but combined it with Russian Orthodox conceptions. Cf. Knigge, pp. 41-42.

33. "I am a mystery to myself and to the world."

34. In his theoretical writings on poetry, Ivanov repeatedly discusses the central role of mythopoesis. Cf. *SS*, vol. 2, p. 90; *SS*, vol. 3, p. 375; *SS*, vol. 4, pp. 518, 554. See also chaps. 4 (concluding part) and 5.

As in the case of "Beauty," the poem's position within the larger work immediately endows it with special significance. Ivanov constructs the second part of "Man" like a mirror: the metrics of the first poem correspond to those of the last, the second poem's metrics correspond to those of the penultimate poem, and so forth. He designates each of the paired poems by a Greek letter; the first eight poems proceed through the Greek alphabet from "α" to "θ," and the final eight go in reverse order from "θ" to "α." The ninth poem, located at the exact center, is metrically unique. Ivanov labels it not with a Greek letter, but with a Greek word of obvious import: "ακμή" ("acme"—"the highest point"). According to Ivanov's original conception, "Man" consisted of three parts.[35] The poem in question thus served as the "summit" not only of the second part, but of the work as a whole.

In keeping with its central position, the poem treats a subject of crucial importance to Ivanov's entire philosophy. It is devoted to the enigmatic inscription on the ancient temple at Delphi.[36] Except for the superficial similarity of the Greek setting, the poem's semantic connection to Goethe's "Bride of Corinth" is not immediately apparent. It lacks even the basic configuration of the mortal man and other-worldly woman. Nonetheless, the reader acquainted with Ivanov's poetic practice recognizes specific motivic and overarching symbolic echoes that link the poem both to Ivanov's own "Beauty" as well as to Goethe's ballad.

The poem begins with an apostrophe to a pilgrim of antiquity who confronts the mysterious phrase "Ty esi" ("You are") on the gates of Delphi:

> Что тебе, в издревле пресловутых
> Прорицаньем Дельфах, богомол,
> Возвестила медь ворот замкнутых?
> Что познал ты, гость, когда прочел
>   На вратах: ЕСИ?
>   У себя спроси,
> Человек, что значит сей глагол.[37]

---

35. The fourth part and epilogue were written two years after the original "trilogy" and were not part of the initial plan. For the history of composition, see *SS*, vol. 3, p. 737.

36. The subject intrigued Ivanov for years. He already discussed it in the 1904 essay "Kop'e Afiny" ("Athena's Spear"), *SS*, vol. 1, pp. 732–33. It later became the central theme of two religious-philosophical essays, "Ty esi" ("You are") and "Anima." (*SS*, vol. 3, pp. 263–93). For a discussion of the relationship of "You are" to "Man," see West (1988).

37. "In Delphi, famed for its prophesying from the earliest times, what did the brass of the closed gates proclaim to you, pilgrim? What did you learn, guest, when you read on the gates: [YOU] ARE? Ask yourself, man, what this word means." (*SS*,

56   Part One: Ivanov and Goethe

By the end of this first stanza, the protagonist (a nameless pilgrim, or "bogomol") has become a generalized "Everyman" ("Chelovek"). He encounters not a mysterious woman (as in the earlier poems), but a mysterious "word" ("sei glagol"). To the protagonist of "Beauty," the woman appeared both heavenly and earthly ("Doch' li ty zemli / il' nebes...").[38] The origin of the phrase "You are" creates a similar ambiguity in the mind of the beholder: "Ty esi'—poet / S golubykh vysot—Iz glubin li khramovykh?"[39] It is unclear whether these words emanate from the depths or from the world above.[40]

The remainder of the poem offers an explanation of the cryptic phrase "You are." Like "Beauty" and "The Bride of Corinth," it is structured as a dialogue. However, Ivanov dispenses with the symbolic configuration of mortal male and other-wordly female. Instead, he presents a discussion in which Man and God are interlocutors.

> С вечным так о праве первородном
> Спорит, — отрекаясь вновь и вновь
> От преемства в бытии свободном, —
> Человек. Но Бог: "Не прекословь,
>   Ибо ты еси!
>   Царский крест неси!..."
> Состязаясь, спорит их любовь![41]

By the penultimate stanza, no trace remains of the pilgrim who was apostrophized in the poem's opening lines. He has been completely replaced by "Man" (a transformation already foreshadowed in the first stanza). Similarly, the phrase "You are" has changed; it becomes a sentiment voiced by God. The discussion between God and Man is described as a dispute, yet the tone is characterized not by anger, but by love ("Sostyazayas', sporit ikh lyubov'").[42] God's words explicitly

---

vol. 3, pp. 213–14). I quote the final version of this stanza (from the 1937 "Dom Knigi" edition), not the earlier variant (*SS*, vol. 3, p. 738), which shares the interrogative character, but is more distant from its Goethean model.

38. "Whether you are the daughter of the earth / Or the heavens..."

39. "'You are'—does it sing/From the light blue heights—[or] from the temple depths?"

40. Such uncertainty was, for Ivanov, inherent to the process of mythopoesis. Cf. *SS*, vol. 2, p. 556.

41. "Man quarrels with the Eternal about his inborn right, again and again renouncing his succession in free existence. But God [says]: 'Do not disagree, for you *are*! Bear the king's cross...' Thus competing, their love quarrels!"

42. "Thus competing, their *love* quarrels!" (my emphasis).

link the pagan phrase from Delphi⁴³ to Christ's Passion ("Tsarskii krest nesi! ... ").⁴⁴

> Крестное Любови откровенье!
> Отворенье царственных Дверей! ...
> "Ты еси"—вздохну, и в то ж мгновенье
> Засияет сердцу Эмпирей ...
>   Миг—и в небеси
>   Слышу: "ты еси"—
> И висит на древе Царь царей!⁴⁵

In this final stanza, Christian elements dominate: the Greek gods are supplanted by Christ. The closing passage repeats several key elements found in both Goethe's "Bride of Corinth" and Ivanov's own "Beauty"—the encounter and conversation, the themes of love and death. As in "Beauty," Ivanov removes all traces of the demonic side of Goethe's poem (vampirism, physical passion). The poem in "Man" has no physical aspect whatsoever. Goethe's ballad was set in a house in Corinth. Ivanov's "Beauty" described a meeting in the mountains of Umbria. The poem in "Man" is nominally situated in Delphi. Yet, at the conclusion of the poem, this setting disappears. The "action," as it were, moves to a spiritual plane. In this new context, Goethe's dictum that love is stronger than death is applied to the image of Christ on the cross (described not as death, but as love: "Krestnoe *Lyubovi* otkroven'e").⁴⁶ As in the earlier poems, the notion of transformation plays a central role. The poem had begun with a question: what did the mysterious words on the *closed* doors of the temple of Delphi mean ("Chto ... vozvestila med' vorot *zamknutykh*")?⁴⁷ The concluding stanzas, symbolized by the *open* doors of Christ ("*Otvoren'e* tsarstvennykh Dverei! ... "),⁴⁸ supply the "answer." These opened doors signal an epiphany.⁴⁹ Through his encounter with God, Man

---

43. The temple at Delphi was Apollo's. Ivanov refers to this in the third stanza: "To Apollon / Proritsaet Gei temnym chadam!" ("Thus Apollo prophesies to the dark children of Gaia").
44. "Bear the king's cross ... "
45. "The cross' revelation of Love! The opening of the royal Doors! ... 'You are'—I will sigh, and at that very moment the Empyrean realm will shine [into my] heart ... One moment—and in the heavens I hear: 'You are'—And the King of kings hangs on the wood."
46. "The cross' revelation of *Love*."
47. "What did the brass of the closed gates proclaim?"
48. "The opening of the royal Doors!"
49. The "royal Doors" ("tsarstvennye Dveri") refer most obviously to the doors in the iconostasis of a Russian Orthodox church ("tsarskie Dveri"). During transubstantiation, the highest mystery of the Orthodox ritual, these doors are closed

achieves entry into a higher truth: "Ty esi'—vzdokhnu, i v to zh mgnoven'e / Zasiyaet serdtsu Empirei..."⁵⁰ This transformation is reflected on the grammatical level in the progression from the historical past tense of the first stanza to the striking mixture of present and future that characterizes the final stanza.

In obvious ways, the poem in "Man" radically diverges from its Goethean "model." Yet the metrical allusion is not without semantic significance, for Ivanov develops several motifs from "The Bride of Corinth." Most importantly, he reworks the notion of love, bringing the intensely physical, pagan elements of Goethe's ballad to a supremely metaphysical, ultimately Christian plane. This radical revaluation need not be understood polemically. Goethe's poem undergoes the same treatment as Ivanov's own "Beauty"—both serve as the raw material from which the later poem is created.

As the discussion of "Beauty" and "Man" have shown, Ivanov often underscores his kinship with Goethe by nonsemantic means. A further example of this allusive technique can be found in the poem "The Tsar's Departure," from the 1912 collection, *Tender Mystery*. Unlike "Beauty" and the poem from "Man," this poem has no programmatic significance. It was an occasional piece, inspired by his daughter Lidiya's request for a ballad that she could set to music. Lidiya apparently even suggested some of the imagery; a moon, a forest, a wolf.⁵¹ Ivanov responded with a cryptic poem of six stanzas that included the desired imagery as well as some other traditional balladic motifs: a king (here Russianized as a "tsar"), a singer, an unidentified woman, a haunting melody, and a death by drowning.

>   Вошел, — и царь челом поник.
>   Запел, — и пир умолк.
>   Исчез... "Царя позвал двойник", —
>   Смущенный слышен толк.
>   Догнать певца
>   Царь шлет гонца...
>   В долине воет волк.⁵²

(and covered with a curtain). Immediately afterwards, the curtain is drawn, the doors are opened, and the priest emerges, bearing the chalice. The "opening of the royal doors" marks the symbolic and dramatic climax of the Russian Orthodox service.

50. "'You are'—I will sigh, and at that very moment the Empyrean realm will shine to my heart..."

51. Ivanova, p. 47.

52. "[He] entered,—and the tsar bowed his head. / [He] began to sing,—and the festival fell silent. / [He] disappeared... —'The double has summoned the tsar,'— /

This opening stanza uses grammatical obscurity (the subject of the first verb is not named until the fifth line, and even then only obliquely) to create an appropriately mysterious atmosphere. The poem focuses on the tsar who has been "summoned" by this song. In the second stanza, haunted by the melody, he finds himself unable to sleep and wanders outside into the moonlight. The third and fourth stanzas develop the image of the summons, suggesting that nature itself is singing (the singer appears to have merged with the forest) about "her," an enigmatic woman. In the penultimate stanza, the woman herself sings, urging the tsar to cross the river to join her. The search for this woman proves fatal:

> И день угас; и в плеске волн,
> Где лунною игрой
> Спит, убаюкан, легкий челн, —
> Чья песнь звенит порой?
>   Челнок плывет,
>   О н а зовет
> За острой той горой.
>
> На бреге том — мечта иль явь? —
> Чертога гость, певец:
> Он знает путь! — и к брегу вплавь;
> Кидается пловец . . .
>   Тут омут синь,
>   Там сеть закинь —
> И выловишь венец.[53]

In the final stanza, Ivanov uses the bipartite structure to break off the narration. The drowning, the culmination of the plot, occurs during the ellipsis at the end of the fourth line. Only in the final three lines does the poet reveal the quest's tragic outcome: "Where the water's depths are blue, Throw in a net—And you will fish out a crown." Thus Ivanov, giving only the faintest outline of a plot, weaving in magical elements and assiduously avoiding authorial commentary, creates an original ballad.

Went the embarrassed explanation. / To catch up to the singer, / The tsar sends his courier . . . / A wolf howls in the valley."

53. "And the day faded; and in the splash of the waves, / Where lulled to sleep by the play of the moon, / The light skiff sleeps,— / Whose song sounds out at times? / The little skiff sails, / *She* calls, / From behind that sharp-peaked mountain. // On that shore—is it a dream or reality? / —[There is] the singer, the guest of the palace: / He knows the way! / And the sailor rushes across to the shore . . . / The water's depths are blue here, / Throw in a net there— / And you will fish out a crown."

Once again, the poem's strophic construction deserves special attention. Ivanov uses a seven-line stanza in which the first and third lines are iambic tetrameter, the second, fourth, and seventh are iambic trimeter, and the fifth and sixth are iambic dimeter. The rhyme scheme is a-b-a-b-c-c-b, with all rhymes masculine. While the poem's plot cannot be traced to any single source, this formal structure is almost certainly German in origin. Seven-line stanzas are common in the German ballad, whereas they are exceedingly rare in Russian poetry and carry no generic associations.[54] However, Ivanov's distinctive treatment of the stanza suggests that it is yet another variant on the "Bride of Corinth." Goethe's ballad is written in trochees and Ivanov's in iambs, yet they share the unusual effect of the truncated couplet in lines five and six.

It appears that when "commissioned" to write a ballad, Ivanov instinctively turned to Goethe as a model. The asymmetrical seven-line stanza (4 + 3), designed by Goethe to accentuate sudden twists of plot, proved an equally effective vehicle in Ivanov's own poem. In terms of thematics, Ivanov alters the constellation of characters and the motif of meeting characteristic of his other "Bride of Corinth" poems. In "The Tsar's Departure," the protagonist seeks a meeting with an otherworldly woman, but this quest ends in failure.[55] Ivanov also adds an additional character (the singer who mediates between the protagonist and his beloved), thereby setting his ballad yet further apart from that of Goethe. In short, Ivanov alters his "source" both metrically and thematically. Yet this does not entail a rejection of Goethe's legacy. Rather, it confirms Goethe's status as a master ballad-writer and exemplary figure in his pantheon of great poets. "The Tsar's Departure," like "Moonlit Roses" and "Beauty," continues the balladic genre as established by Goethe's "Bride of Corinth." No matter how far Ivanov appears to stray from his "model," his underlying motive is to affirm the continuity of tradition.

Ivanov's poetic responses to "The Bride of Corinth" demonstrate his multifaceted reception of a single text. All four of his poems develop Goethe's motif of the "fateful encounter," but in a variety of ways. Ivanov alternately turns "The Bride of Corinth" into a supernatural tale, a philosophical inquiry, a mystical manifesto, and a religious statement. Moreover, he adds to Goethe's original by blending in other texts (Solovyov's poetry, a "Homeric hymn"), other themes (religious rites of antiquity and Russian orthodoxy), and other charac-

---

54. Cf. Kreid, p. 60, Scherr, p. 243.
55. It is conceivable that Ivanov borrowed certain motivic elements from other Goethe ballads; the singer with the power to move a royal audience with his song (cf. "Der Sänger") or the mysterious death of the protagonist after being "tempted" by anthropomorphized nature (e.g., "Erlkönig" and "Der Fischer").

ters (a pilgrim, a tsar, a singer) and by altering the metrical form (the Russian balladic stanza of "Moonlit Roses," the adapted Goethean strophe of "The Tsar's Departure"). Ivanov wrote these poems over a period of about fifteen years. Yet it would be incorrect to see them as a gradual evolution of Ivanov's interpretation of Goethe's ballad. Each new poem does not "annul" the message of its predecessors. Rather, each one responds to and develops different elements of the original.

Chapter 3

Faust and Ivanov's Conception of the Symbol

> В сфере поэзии принцип символизма, некогда утверждаемый Гете, после долгих уклонов и блужданий, снова понимается нами в значении, которое придавал ему Гете, и его поэтика оказывается, в общем, нашею поэтикою последних лет.[1]
> —Vyacheslav Ivanov, "Goethe on the Border of Two Centuries"

In the previous chapter, I demonstrated the type of reception characteristic of Ivanov's mature poetics. From a single Goethean ballad, Ivanov drew a wealth of creative impulses: formal, motivic, and even philosophical. Goethe's extended works, of course, offer far greater material for development. *Faust*, the traditional touchstone of Goethe reception, fascinated Ivanov throughout his life. Guenther writes of Ivanov: "He knew Goethe by heart, especially *Faust*."[2] Innumerable references to this work, found in all genres of Ivanov's writings (philosophical, poetic, literary-theoretical, letters, diaries, occasional verse), make clear its centrality.

Throughout his essays, Ivanov unambiguously voices his preference for the second part of *Faust*. In his essay on Goethe, he notes: "The second part does not resemble the first and represents its infinite symbolic extension."[3] Such a statement should not be construed as a rejection of the first part, but simply as an emphatic affirmation of the second. Historically speaking, this judgment represents a radical departure from tradition. Nineteenth-century Russian writers and critics had strongly favored the first part, faulting the second for a variety of reasons.[4] Thus, when the young Ivanov took *Faust I* as the model for

---

1. "In the sphere of poetry, the principle of symbolism established long ago by Goethe, after long periods of turns and wanderings, is again understood by us in the meaning Goethe gave to it; and, in general, his poetics turn out to be our poetics of the last years." *SS*, vol. 4, p. 112.
2. Guenther, p. 123.
3. *SS*, vol. 4, p. 148.
4. See Gronicka, vol. 2, p. 99.

his "Russian Faust," he proved himself an inheritor of a nineteenth-century position. By the time of *Pilot Stars*, however, Ivanov's special interest in the second part was already pronounced.⁵

Such an evaluation of *Faust* was unusual, but not without precedent. Vladimir Solovyov, the mentor of many Russian Symbolists, had also given high praise to *Faust II*. In the 1889 essay "The General Meaning of Art," he wrote:

> To see that, in the greatest poetic works, the sense of spiritual life is realized only through a *reflection* of non-ideal human reality, we will take Goethe's *Faust*. The positive sense of this lyrico-epic tragedy becomes directly apparent only in the final scene of the second part and is summarized abstractly in the final chorus: Alles Vergängliche ist nur ein Gleichnis, etc.⁶

Solovyov refers to the last lines of the entire work, emphasizing *not* the notion of the eternal feminine (which is of course implicit), but rather the belief that "everything transient is only a parable" ("Gleichnis"). In this final utterance, Solovyov finds a basic notion of his own dualistic (Neo-Platonic) philosophical system confirmed—the phenomenal world is a "reflection" of the ideal world. Goethe's recognition of this fundamental philosophical truth prompts Solovyov to consider *Faust* one of the "greatest works of poetry." However, he qualifies this praise in the continuation of the same passage:

> But where is the direct link between this apotheosis and the other parts of the tragedy? Heavenly forces and "das ewig Weibliche" ["the eternal feminine"] appear from above, consequently from without, but they do not open up from within the content itself. The idea of the final scene is present in all of *Faust*, but is only a reflection of that partially real, partially fantastic action, of which the tragedy itself consists ... even here the spiritual light of the absolute ideal, reflected through the

---

5. In her memoirs, Margarita Voloshina testifies to Ivanov's fascination with *Faust II*: " ... I also first experienced the second part of *Faust* when he read it aloud. I still remember how he could not control his emotion as he read the words of the Samaritan woman: 'Bei dem Bronn, zu dem noch weiland / Abram ließ die Herde führen, / bei dem Eimer, der dem Heiland / kühl die Lippen durft' berühren' ('By the well, to which Abraham in his time let the herds be led, by the bucket which was allowed to touch with coolness the lips of the Savior.'). He covered his face with his hands and cried. 'And they say that Goethe is a cool Olympian. Here every word is aglow, transfigured by Christian love; even a little bucket is transfigured!'" Woloschin, pp. 184–85.

6. Solovyov (1988), vol. 2, p. 403.

imagination of the artist, illuminates dark human reality, but in no way changes its essence.[7]

Such criticism must be understood in the general context of Solovyov's thought, where the relationship of the real to the ideal is characterized in terms of incongruity.[8] For Solovyov, human existence is but a flawed version of the ideal.[9] Hence, the purpose of beauty (and art, its human expression) is to *change* earthly existence: "That means it is necessary that genuine art be *an important matter*, that means, true beauty must be recognized as the ability to act profoundly and forcefully on the real world."[10] In his interpretation of *Faust*, Solovyov praises Goethe for recognizing the relationship between man's imperfect reality ("neideal'naya chelovecheskaya deistvitel'nost'") and the ideal, but criticizes him for making no attempt to alter this relationship. He deems even the concluding lines of *Faust* unequal to the true task of art—the transformation of reality.

Ivanov frequently invokes Solovyov's authority and, indeed, the two thinkers share a number of fundamental presuppositions. Like Solovyov's, Ivanov's worldview is essentially Neo-Platonic, based on a dualism between the phenomenal and noumenal worlds. Yet Ivanov does not see these two realms as necessarily antithetical. A mystical notion of "symbol" allows him to posit an organic relationship (a system of correspondences) between "realia" and "realiora." Through the symbol, the phenomenal world partakes of the noumena. Ivanov repeatedly expresses this conviction in his poetry, where emissaries of the "realiora" (e.g., the female figure in "Beauty") invariably belong to the terrestrial world *as well as* to the world beyond.[11] This notion of

---

7. Ibid.

8. This point is central not only to Solovyov's philosophy, but also to his poetry: "Милый друг, иль ты не слышишь, / Что житейский шум трескучий— / Только отклик искаженный / Торжествующих созвучий?" ("Dear friend, do you not hear / That the world's vain noise— / Is but a distorted echo / Of triumphant harmonies?") In this often-quoted poem, human existence is viewed not as a pure reflection, but as a "distorted echo" of the harmony of the transcendent world.

9. Zara Mints has noted that Solovyov is not always consistent in this respect. At times, he appears to contradict himself, recognizing in earthly existence a mystical potential. This is, in fact, the line of Solovyov's argument closest to Ivanov. Cf. Solovyov (1974), pp. 23–25.

10. From "Beauty in Nature" Solovyov (1988), vol. 2, p. 351.

11. This idea clearly emerges in the programmatic opening poem of Ivanov's second book of poetry, *Transparence* (1904). The poem is nominally about snow on mountaintops, but as the title ("Poets of the Spirit"—"Poety Dukha") implies, nature in this poem must be understood symbolically: "Не мни: мы, в небе тая, / С землей разлучены: — / Ведет тропа святая / В заоблачные сны." ("Do not think that we,

symbol also explains why the transformation of reality plays a lesser role in Ivanov's theory of Symbolism than in Solovyov's aesthetics.[12] True art, according to Ivanov, is a process of discovery, not invention. He unambiguously rejects the latter tendency, "the artist-tyrant, about whom Nietzsche dreamed, the artist-enslaver, who revalues all aesthetic values and breaks the old tablets of beauty, following only his 'will to power.'"[13]

Ivanov firmly believed in an objective truth that could be perceived by gifted artists. He condemned subjectivity in art, which he felt distorted this fundamental truth. Ivanov phrased his much-debated distinction between realist Symbolism and idealist Symbolism in precisely these terms: "Being in regard to his object purely impressionable, only receptive, the realistic artist sets himself the task of an unalloyed acceptance of the object into his soul and its transmission to another soul. In contrast, the idealist artist either returns things differently from how he perceives them ... or he gives combinations not justified by observation, the progeny of his despotic, capricious fantasy."[14]

When Ivanov speaks of the artist's "unalloyed acceptance of the object," one might erroneously conclude that he is describing a purely mimetic process. It should be remembered that this "object" is not physical, but metaphysical; it is a "hidden truth" that can be grasped only through mystical means.[15] The artist, according to Ivanov, possesses certain extraordinary faculties that allow him to observe the deeper truth concealed within the phenomena of everyday life.

Ivanov's insistence on art as a fundamentally receptive process enables him to embrace as a poetic credo the very lines from Goethe that Solovyov deemed insufficient. He frequently cites the phrase "Alles Vergängliche ist nur ein Gleichnis" ("Everything transient is only a parable") to support his own position on the nature of Symbolism.[16]

---

melting in the sky / Are separated from the earth:— / A holy path leads / To the dreams beyond the clouds.")

12. It does, however, play a role. See, for example, the concluding stanza of the early programmatic poem "Tvorchestvo" ("Creation"). *SS*, vol. 1, p. 537.

13. *SS*, vol. 2, p. 538. Cf. Stepun (1989), pp. 125–26.

14. *SS*, vol. 2, p. 540.

15. Ibid., p. 548.

16. The lines became a rallying cry for the entire younger generation of Symbolists. Andrei Bely (1910, p. 9) maintained, "Goethe's slogan 'Alles Vergängliche ist nur ein Gleichnis' found its justification in Symbolism." Ellis (1910), p. 15, calls the line Goethe's "classic formulation." It is significant that Mandel'shtam (p. 595), in "On the Nature of the Word," begins his celebrated attack on Symbolism by quoting the phrase "Alles Vergängliche ist nur ein Gleichnis."

The concluding paragraph of his 1904 essay on Sologub's stories exemplifies this tendency:

> Yet again we become convinced, upon reading this book about the obvious mystery, that realism, which concealed the mystery, was false, and that true realism reveals it; that the more subtle the observation and the more refined the attention focused on reality, the more significant symbolic reality is, [then] the more transparent is the reflection of the permanent in the ripple of appearances that run past: "Alles Vergängliche ist nur ein Gleichnis."[17]

Like Solovyov, Ivanov speaks of the "reflection" of the permanent in the transient world of appearances. However, Solovyov's perception of this duality emphasizes the incompatibility of the two worlds, while Ivanov stresses their interconnectedness. His insistence on "observation" ("nablyudenie") and "attention" ("vnimanie") makes clear the salient difference between two very different views of the creative process. According to Ivanov, the proper perception suffices to make reality "transparent," i.e., to recognize its essence.[18] At the time this passage was written, Ivanov had not yet elaborated the concept of "realistic Symbolism." However, it is not difficult to detect its presence, albeit in embryonic form. Ivanov attacks traditional realism (i.e., the historical movement), contrasting it to "true" realism (an impulse common to traditions separated both temporally and spatially). His eventual description of the "realistic Symbolist" is phrased in much the same terms:

> ... the realistic Symbolist, who sees the most profound, true reality of things, *realia in rebus*, and who does not reject in relative reality the phenomenal insofar as it contains concealed yet marked within itself the most real reality. "Alles Vergängliche ist nur ein Gleichnis"— "Everything transient is only a symbol."[19]

Even without the familiar Goethean flourish, one notices the continuity between this passage from 1908 and the essay written four years earlier. Ivanov again expresses the conviction that the noumenal can

---

17. In Ivanov, 1904 (*Vesy*), p. 50.
18. Precisely at the time this essay was written (1904), "transparence" was Ivanov's central theoretical concept. It is derived, at least in part, from the medieval concept of "transparentia formae," which Ivanov later (1915) described as the procedure by which "in a work of art, the substance allows light through, becomes transparent, and displays divine nature to view." *SS*, vol. 3, p. 178.
19. *SS*, vol. 2, p. 549.

be found within the phenomenal. He does not dismiss "relative reality" (Goethe's "Vergängliches"), for it contains within itself the "most real" reality. Ivanov essentially labels Goethe a "realistic Symbolist" and equates Goethe's aesthetics with his own.[20] Indeed, there are grounds for such a conclusion, yet Ivanov's terminology begs the question. Ivanov's intentionally inexact translation of the word "Gleichnis" ("parable") as "simvol" ("symbol") claims an identity where there is in fact only a similarity.[21] In this way, Goethe's connection to "Symbolism" appears much more definite than is actually the case. Furthermore, the distinction between "relative reality" and "true reality" is much more strictly defined in Ivanov's theoretical writings than anywhere in Goethe. Yet Ivanov ascribes to Goethe this same hierarchy of "realities" and even the same rhetoric.

In short, in the closing verses of *Faust II*, Ivanov discovers a formula for his own artistic program. These lines frequently recur in his theoretical discussions of the symbol. In "The Testaments of Symbolism" (1910), for example, the first distinctive feature of Symbolist art is defined as a

> parallelism between the phenomenal and noumenal, consciously expressed by the artist; a harmony between what art depicts as external reality (realia) and what it sees through the external, as an internal and higher reality (realiora); the naming of correspondences and interrelationships between the appearance (which is "only a parable," "nur Gleichnis") and its essence (comprehended rationally or mystically), which casts a shadow of the visible event . . . [22]

It is noteworthy that, in this passage, Ivanov synthesizes Goethe's concept of "Gleichnis" with traditional philosophical oppositions (phenomenal/noumenal) as well as with his own idiosyncratic terminology (realia/realiora).

From the standpoint of aesthetic theory, the final lines of *Faust II* serve as the single most important passage in Ivanov's reading of Goethe. In his essay on Goethe, he views this passage as proof of the

---

20. He does so expressly in the 1912 essay on Goethe. *SS*, vol. 4, p. 145.
21. Elsewhere Ivanov renders it more exactly, as "podobie." Cf. *SS*, vol. 2, p. 597. In any case, the mistranslation ("simvol") is not as willful as it may seem. Goethe scholars note that Goethe uses several words ("Abglanz," "Gleichnis," "Symbol") virtually interchangeably. See Trunz, vol. 3, p. 538. Ivanov was not alone among the Russians in rendering Goethe's "Gleichnis" as "symbol." Cf. Voloshin (1988), pp. 59, 428, and Ellis (1910), pp. 14–16. In fact, already in 1892, Merezhkovsky had used this "loaded" translation as the epigraph to his collection "Symbols." Cf. Kuznetsova (1991), p. 8.
22. *SS*, vol. 2, p. 597.

ultimate convergence of Goethe's and Schiller's views on the symbol.[23] In the 1936 essay on "Symbolism," Ivanov states that Goethe "concluded the work of his entire life" with these lines.[24] However, as concerns *poetic* reception, their significance is limited. While Ivanov's poetry often explores the relationship of "realia" to "realiora," the importance of "Gleichnis" is only implicit. Ivanov prefers to incorporate other passages (and images) from *Faust II* into the verse.

The lyric poem "Morning Star" ("Utrennyaya Zvezda") offers a convenient "practical application" of Ivanov's theory of the symbol and demonstrates the extent to which that theory is linked to Goethe. Not only does Ivanov supply a Faustian epigraph for "Morning Star"; he places the poem in the first section of *Pilot Stars*, which is itself introduced by a Faustian motto. Both the motto and the epigraph come from the opening scene of *Faust II*, where they are separated by a mere thirty lines.

The scene in question figures so prominently in "Morning Star" (and in Ivanov's writings in general) that a brief summary is in order. *Faust I* culminates in Gretchen's madness and death, leaving Faust in a state of physical and emotional exhaustion. In contrast, the second part opens with a scene of serenity and rejuvenation. It is dusk, and various forces of nature work together to revive and restore Faust. Ariel begins by enlisting the help of a group of elves (spirits). The elves comply by singing four stanzas, each representing a period of night. In the first, Faust falls asleep, presumably from the exertions of the first part. In the second, he is bathed in Lethe's stream in order to forget the past. The third celebrates the break of day, and the fourth describes the actual awakening. The epigraph to "Morning Star" comes from the third stanza of the elves' song: "Fühl' es vor! Du wirst gesunden: / Traue neuem Tagesblick!" ("Sense it! You will recover: / Trust the light of the new day"). This peaceful song is followed by an enormous crash that announces the appearance of the sun. Faust awakens, completely refreshed and eager to strive onward. He turns to the earth and exclaims the words that Ivanov uses as the motto for the entire section: "Du regst und rührst ein kräftiges Beschließen, / Zum höchsten Dasein immerfort zu streben." ("You move and stir up a powerful resolution, / To strive constantly to the highest [form of] existence.") Faust's attention is then drawn to the sunrise. However, in attempting to look at the sun, he is momentarily blinded by its rays.

23. Ibid., p. 137. It is curious that Ivanov all but ignores Goethe's own *theoretical* discussion of the symbol, preferring to derive the concept from Goethe's *poetic* works. He justifies this approach by emphasizing the unsystematic nature of Goethe's thought (cf. Ibid., pp. 137, 143).

24. Ibid., p. 655.

Forced to avert his gaze, he turns first to a waterfall and then to a rainbow. The latter becomes emblematic of human existence: "Der spiegelt ab das menschliche Bestreben. / Ihm sinne nach, und du begreifst genauer: / Am farbigen Abglanz haben wir das Leben." ("It [i.e., the rainbow] reflects human striving. / Consider it, and you will comprehend more exactly: / In the colorful reflection we have life.")[25] The rainbow, as a mediated form of the sun, is the closest Faust can get to the absolute. This image of "Abglanz" (reflection) plays a seminal role both in this scene and in Goethe's general worldview. Accordingly, man is capable of experiencing the absolute—but only indirectly, through its reflection in earthly things.[26]

Like its Goethean epigraph, "Morning Star" is written in trochaic tetrameter. Ivanov thereby creates on the formal level a sense of continuity; the rhythm of the epigraph, as it were, flows organically into the poem itself.[27] In addition to this metrical echo, Ivanov makes semantic borrowings from *Faust*. The poem's second stanza begins with the lines:

> Зеленеются поляны;
> Зачернелась сквозь туманы
> Нови крайней полоса.
> Звезды теплятся далече...[28]

Without the Goethean epigraph, the reader would not think to seek a subtext in this nature description. However, since the epigraph points to a specific scene in *Faust*, the attentive reader looks—and discovers direct quotations to this very scene. In their song, the elves use the phrases "Täler grünen" ("the fields become green," which translates exactly into Russian as "Zeleneyutsya polyany") and "[Sterne] glänzen fern" ("stars shine in the distance," which, rendered in Russian, is "Zvezdy teplyatsya daleche"). The importance of context should be emphasized; these verses are not found in the actual epigraph, but

---

25. These final verses of Faust's monologue are among the most celebrated lines in *Faust*. Among the Russian Symbolists, Ellis (1910, p. 15), especially emphasized their importance: "It is hardly possible to find a more beautiful and exact expression of the fundamental idea that we inescapably find in every serious attempt to define the goal and the meaning of artistic contemplation."

26. Cf. Trunz's commentary, vol. 3, pp. 537–38.

27. The stanzaic forms are of course different—Goethe divides his verse into eight-line stanzas while Ivanov uses six-line stanzas. However, since only two German lines are quoted, the reader has no sense of these larger structural differences. The immediate impression is one of continuity.

28. "The fields turn green; through the haze the strip of extreme virgin soil begins to show darkly. Stars shine in the distance."

rather in the passage from which the epigraph is taken. There are, however, also echoes from the epigraph itself; in the fourth stanza, the repeated imperative "Ver'!" ("Trust!"), uttered once by the morning star and once by the rays of morning, is clearly related to Goethe's "Traue neuem Tagesblick" (literally: "Trust the glance of the new day"). Even the "glance" in the word "Tages*blick*" is reflected in Ivanov's apostrophe to the morning star: "Ty odna, v ventse rassveta, / Klonish' *vzory* . . . "[29] (my emphasis).

Despite these numerous similarities, Ivanov's poem departs noticeably from the scene of *Faust* alluded to in the epigraph. The focal point and fundamental symbol of Goethe's scene is the sun. As the title of Ivanov's poem suggests, the central image is not the sun (although it does appear), but rather the morning star itself. The poem consists of eight stanzas, which divide logically into two sections of equal length. Taken together, these two parts exemplify the ascent/descent paradigm so fundamental to Ivanov's thought.[30] The first part describes the "ascension" of the morning star; in the course of the initial four stanzas, its presence is increasingly felt. The second concerns its "descent" into invisibility.

The poem's opening stanza introduces several crucial motifs:

> Над опаловым востоком
> В легионе светлооком
> Блещет вестница Зари.
> Ранних пастырей отрада,
> Утра близкого лампада,
> Благовестная, гори! . . .[31]

---

29. "You alone, in the crown of dawn, / Turn your *glances* . . . " (my emphasis). To this list of echoes, one might add the image of a "tent" of air (the "vozdushnyi shater" of the third stanza), for it recalls another passage from the second part of *Faust* (ll. 11997-12000): "Höchste Herrscherin der Welt! / Lasse mich im blauen, / Ausgespannten Himmelszelt / Dein Geheimnis schauen." ("Highest sovereign of the world! Let me see your secret in the extended blue sky-tent.") Serman (pp. 199–200) considers Ivanov's "tent of air" an allusion to Lomonosov's translation of Psalm 103: "Ty zvezdy rasproster bez scheta / Shatru podobno pred toboi." ("You spread out the stars without number / Like a tent before you.") Such an interpretation is no doubt justified, given Ivanov's predilection for eighteenth-century images. However, in the context of numerous Goethe allusions, it seems equally plausible that the "sky tent" should refer to *Faust*, especially since the lines in question are among the most well-known in the entire work.

30. Ivanov discusses this subject in depth in "The Symbolism of Aesthetics Principles" (*SS*, vol. 1, pp. 823–30). For an account of his predecessors, see Terras (1986), p. 337 and Terras (1983).

31. *SS*, vol. 1, p. 524.

> Above the opal east
> In a light-eyed legion
> Shines the herald of Dawn,
> The joy of early shepherds,
> The icon-lamp of the nearby morning,
> Blessed one, shine!

Among the "legion" of stars, Ivanov singles out the morning star. The fact that the entire book is entitled *Pilot Stars* (a reference to Dante's guiding stars in *Purgatory*, XXVII) suggests that the present poem is more than a simple nature description. Even without knowledge of the larger context, Ivanov's specific lexical choices make the reader immediately aware that the star is to be understood "symbolically." Following Goethe's model (the elves' song contains the oft-quoted line "Schließt sich *heilig* Stern an Stern"—"*Sacredly*, star joins star"), Ivanov endows the star with religious associations. The first instance of sacred imagery is found in the metaphor of a "lampada" (an "icon lamp," a word explicitly connected to Russian Orthodox ritual).[32] The basic trope involved is metonymy; an icon lamp is important not in and of itself, but rather because of that which it stands beside and illuminates (the holy image). In the phrase "Utra blizkogo lampada," the morning thus assumes the role of icon. The word "blizkogo" ("near") can be understood spatially or temporally, but in either case accentuates the element of contiguity. The same principle informs the image "vestnitsa Zari" ("herald of Dawn"). A "herald" is significant by virtue of the person or thing whose arrival it announces. By capitalizing the word "Dawn," Ivanov gives the image a religious connotation. While the Russian "vestnitsa" ("herald") does not have sacred associations, it obtains them when, in the stanza's final line, the star is addressed as "Blagovestnaya," a word with distinctly biblical overtones.[33] Once again, the notion of metonymy is central; these words are linked by the notion of "announcing" something else. Their religious connotations are bestowed on the neutral word "vestnitsa" by means of

---

32. In eighteenth and early nineteenth-century usage, "lampada" could mean any sort of lamp. Thus, in the celebrated hymn to Petersburg in "The Bronze Horseman," Pushkin describes how, during the white nights, he reads without a lamp ("lampada"). However, by the twentieth century, the word had strong religious connotations. Ivanov's direct source for the comparison of a heavenly body with a "lampada" was probably Lomonosov's "Morning Meditation on the Greatness of God." "O kol' presvetlaya lampada Toboyu, Bozhe, vozzhzhena . . . " ("Oh, what a radiant lamp is lit up by you, God . . . ").

33. In the New Testament, "blagovestie" and "blagovestit'" occur frequently in the sense of "spreading the word of God." They are related to "blagoveshchenie" (the Annunciation) and "blagovest" (the bell that marks the beginning of worship).

paronomasia ("*Bl*eshchet *vestn*itsa" and "*Bl*ago*vestn*aya"), made especially prominent by graphic parallelism (both phrases are in initial position in their respective lines). The stanza closes with a hortatory imperative: "gori! . . . " In the context of a heavenly body (i.e., the morning star), it obviously means "Shine!" However, the word also connotes fire ("Burn!"), a meaning which becomes increasingly significant as the poem progresses.

The second stanza, in addition to the already mentioned Goethean echoes, develops the imagery of the opening. As if in compliance with the imperative that closed the first stanza, the morning star gains in prominence. Whereas the morning star was initially one of a "legion," in the second stanza it comes into the foreground: "Zvezdy teplyatsya daleche, / Dnya siyayushchei predteche / Ustupaya nebesa . . . "[34] However, even as the central image, the morning star continues to play its metonymic role. It is the "forerunner of the shining day." The motif of a "forerunner" recalls the "herald" of the opening stanza. Yet there is additional significance in the choice of the word "predtecha" for "forerunner." In Russian, "Ioann Predtecha" is John the Baptist; this image thus has a much more specific religious referent than the numerous sacred connotations of the first stanza.

The third and fourth stanzas introduce a new opposition. Whereas the earlier stanzas had concentrated on the morning star either in contrast to the other stars or as the harbinger of day, the star now becomes a representative of a higher world. The resulting contrast is that of the heavens versus the earth, the dualism that forms the basis for Ivanov's (and virtually all Neo-Platonic) philosophy.

> Ты одна, в венце рассвета,
> Клонишь взоры, чадо света,
> К нам с воздушного шатра,
> Бедных снов утешный гений,
> Средь немеркнущих селений
> Мира дольнего сестра!
>
> Над мерцающим бореньем
> Ты сияешь увереньем:
> "Жизни верь, и жизнь вдохни!"
> И летящих по эфиру
> Ты лучей ласкаешь лиру:
> "Верь, и виждь!" поют они . . .[35]

---

34. "Stars shine in the distance, / Leaving the heavens / To the forerunner of shining day."
35. "You alone, in the crown of dawn, / Turn your glances, child of light, / To us, from the tent of air, / [You are] the consoling genius of poor dreams, / Among the unfading settlements / The sister of the earthly world! / Above the glimmering battle /

The most radical change between these and the preceding stanzas can be seen in the new dominant trope: personification. The morning star is given a face ("Klonish' *vzory*"—"[You] turn your glances") and is called by turns a child ("*chado* sveta"—"child of light") and a sister ("Mira dol'nego *sestra*"—"sister of the earthly world"). This final personification is particularly revealing, as it posits a kindred relationship between the earth and the heavens. In these stanzas, the morning star becomes a kind of guardian angel of the sleeping earth ("Bednykh snov uteshnyi genii"—"the consoling genius of poor dreams"). Pronouns are used for the first time, setting up an opposition between the "ty" (familiar "you," the morning star) and the "nas" ("we," presumably mankind). The contrast between the heavens and the earth is stark: "Nad mertsayushchim boren'em / Ty siyaesh' uveren'em."[36] The brightness of the star ("siyat'") stands out against the tentative, flickering light of earth ("mertsat'"). Moreover, earthly existence is portrayed as a battle ("boren'e") as opposed to the "musical" spirit that pervades the heavens (cf. the "lyre" of lights that "sing"). Despite their obvious differences, these two realms are connected; the heavens "speak" to the earth. The words attributed to the heavens contain two crucial concepts: life and faith (the imperative "ver'" and the word "zhizn'" both occur twice). The poem's first half concludes on this life-affirming note.

The fifth stanza, an obvious counterpart to the first, describes the morning star as it fades from view ("gasnet sputnitsa Zari").[37] The textual echoes are unmistakable, since numerous words recur (including three of the rhymed words). Against the background of such repetition, several changes stand out: "Ugasai, lileya neba! / Ty zhe, vozhd' krylatyi Feba, / Alym polymem gori!"[38] Ivanov again uses the verb "goret'," meaning "to shine," but also having the connotation of "to burn." He combines it with a new verb that contains a similar ambiguity ("ugasat'"—"to fade away," but also "to burn out"). While the context of a star suggests the "shine/fade" reading, the stanza's final trope ("Alym polymem"—"like a red flame") makes clear that the "burn/burn out" distinction is nevertheless present. Finally, the reference to Phoebus (i.e., Phoebus Apollo, the sun god) adds a classical dimension to a poem that had heretofore been characterized by Christian imagery. (In the next stanza, the Roman goddess Aurora continues this classical line.)

You shine with the assurance: / 'Trust life, and breathe in life' / And you caress the lyre of the rays that fly along the ether: / 'Believe, and see!' they sing . . . "

36. "Above the glimmering battle / You shine with assurance."

37. "The companion of the Dawn fades."

38. "Fade, lily of the sky! / You, the winged leader of Phoebus [Apollo], / Burn with a dark red flame!"

The sunrise of the sixth stanza is in many ways the climax of the poem:

> Вспыхни, Солнце! Бог, воскресни!
> Ярче, жаворонка песни,
> Лейтесь в золото небес!
> День грядет, Аврора блещет,—
> И твой тихий луч трепещет,
> И твой бледный лик—исчез...[39]

The opening line, composed of two short imperatives, is a point of arrival for much of the poem's imagery. The chiasmic structure places the two key nouns side by side and in the center of the line: "Vspykhni, *Solntse*! *Bog*, voskresni!" (literally: "Blaze up, *Sun*! *God*, be resurrected!"). Both the sun and the divinity have repeatedly been implicit in the imagery, yet the words themselves appear for the first time. In a similar way, the frequent suggestions of burning find their ultimate justification in the verb "Vspykhni," the primary meaning of which is "to burst into flame." The final verb, "voskresni" ("be resurrected") also develops earlier imagery. In the fourth stanza, the morning star, as harbinger of the sun, had urged loyalty to life. In the sixth stanza, the sun's appearance is parallel to "resurrection."[40]

The arrival of the sun, accompanied by tremendous din, was the symbolic and thematic center of the scene in *Faust* alluded to in the poem's epigraph. In Ivanov's poem, the sunrise is equally dramatic. However, in contrast to Goethe, Ivanov does not focus his attention on the sunrise. Having proclaimed the arrival of day, he returns to the theme of the morning star: "I tvoi tikhii luch trepeshchet, / I tvoi blednyi lik—ischez..." ("And your quiet ray flickers, / And your pale face—has disappeared..."). In the course of a single stanza, the tone changes radically. The uncertainty expressed in these tentative final lines presents a marked contrast to the enthusiastic imperatives of the opening. The morning star has diminished to a single ray of light (in contrast to the "blaze" of the sun). The personification of the earlier stanzas remains, but the "face" of the morning star is now "pale." The final verb in the stanza adds a particularly expressive touch. Broken off from the word before it by a dash and the following stanza by an ellipsis, it also stands out because of a sudden shift in verb tense. It forms the final, distant link in a series of verbs in word-final posi-

---

39. "Blaze up, Sun! Be resurrected, God! / Songs of the lark, / Flow more brightly into the gold of the heavens! / Day approaches, Aurora shines,— / And your quiet ray flickers, / And your pale face—has disappeared..."

40. These two imperatives ("Blaze up and be resurrected") are conceivably an echo of Goethe's own double imperative: "Stirb and werde!" ("Die and become!"). The importance of this paradigm is treated in chap. 5.

tion: "bleshchet" ("shines"), "trepeshchet" ("flickers"), "ischez" ("disappear*ed*").

Yet the visual disappearance of the morning star does not correspond to its disappearance from the poem:

> Но, незримая, над нами,
> За лазурными волнами,
> Чистым гением пребудь!
> Как сестра пред братней битвой,
> Дольний мир твоей молитвой
> Проводи в тревожный путь!
>
> И, когда для жертвы мирной
> Ночь раздвинет храм эфирный,
> Снова светоч твой яви—
> И, предтеча слав нетленных,
> Отблеск тайн богоявленных
> В грезе зрящей оживи![41]

The most striking element of these closing stanzas is the way they rework earlier imagery. Most of the poem's central images recur: the morning star is again called a "genii" ("genius"), a "sestra" ("sister") of the "dol'nii mir" ("earthly world"), a "predtecha" ("forerunner"). The new simile, "Kak sestra pred bratnei bitvoi" ("like a sister before her brother's battle"), synthesizes two earlier images: the morning star was called the sister of the earthly world (final line of the third stanza), while the earth was described as a battle (first line of the fourth stanza). In addition, several of the new words indirectly recall earlier ones: the "greza" ("dream") was anticipated by the "sny" ("dreams") in the third stanza, the imperative "ozhivi" ("revive") is related to the noun "zhizn'" ("life"), the notion of prayer ("tvoei molitvoi") was suggested by numerous sacred references.

Such correspondences are characteristic of Ivanov's poetic method. However, they should not draw attention from the significant differences that set these final stanzas off from those that preceded. The penultimate stanza begins with the crucial word "No" ("But"), implying a turn in the poetic argument. Ivanov unexpectedly follows the progress not of the sun, but of the morning star. Rather than continuing with a magnificent visual description of sunrise, he opts for

---

41. "But, invisible, above us, / Beyond the azure waves, / Remain a pure genius! / Like a sister before her brother's battle, / See the earthly world off with your prayer / On its troubled path! // And when for a peaceful sacrifice / Night spreads its ether temple, / Again display your torch— / And, as a forerunner of imperishable glories, / Revive the reflection of epiphanic mysteries / In a visionary dream!"

the realm of invisibility. The star can no longer be seen ("nezrimaya"), yet this invisibility is by no means construed as absence. The poet posits direct and uninterrupted communication between the morning star and the earth. During the day, he asks the star to "pray" for the earth's welfare. During the night, he urges it to participate in what is clearly a religious ritual: "I kogda dlya zhertvy mirnoi / Noch' razdvinet khram efirnyi / Snova svetoch tvoi yavi—" ("And when for a peaceful sacrifice / Night spreads its ethereal temple, / Again display your torch—"). In the final imperative, Ivanov offers his most explicit explanation of the morning star's significance. It is the "forerunner of imperishable glories," and it revives in man the "reflection of epiphanic mysteries." Once again, the carefully chosen images of a "reflection" and a "forerunner" denote not the thing in itself, but a mediated version of that thing. In both cases, the "thing" is a metaphysical truth, what in Ivanov's terminology would be termed the "realiora." Earlier the "forerunner of shining day," the morning star is now the "forerunner of imperishable glories." Furthermore, whereas the dreams of the third stanza were considered "poor," the final "visionary dream" is linked to "epiphanic mysteries."

The precise role that the Goethe quotations play in Ivanov's poem has yet to be established. On a basic level, certain "correspondences" come readily to mind. The motto ("Du regst und rührst . . . ") suggests the interrelationship between the earthly and heavenly realms: the earth inspires man to strive "to the highest [form of] existence." The morning star, by connecting man to the transcendent, has a similar function. The epigraph, specific to "Morning Star," ("Fühl'es vor! Du wirst gesunden: Traue neuem Tagesblick!—"Sense it! You will recover: Trust the light of the new day") contains several motifs: anticipation ("Fühl'es vor"), recovery ("gesunden"), belief ("Traue"), and daybreak ("Tagesblick"). To a greater or lesser extent, all of these concepts recur in Ivanov's poem.

However, there is another element to these epigraphs: their source in *Faust*. In this respect, the epigraphs point "beyond" themselves. Both Goethe quotations come from the same crucial scene, one of the seminal symbolic passages in the German literary tradition. In "Morning Star," Ivanov does not employ Goethe's central image (the rainbow), yet he repeatedly emphasizes Goethe's fundamental concept—nature as a signal of the transcendent. Throughout the poem, he praises the morning star in its relation to something else: as a "herald" ("vestnitsa"), an "icon lamp" ("lampadka"), a "companion" ("sputnitsa"), a "forerunner" ("predtecha"). In the penultimate line, Ivanov introduces yet another term—"otblesk." This word is a direct translation of the German "Abglanz," composed of the prefix "ot" ("away from," German "ab") and the noun "blesk" ("brightness," German "Glanz"). Like Goethe's "Abglanz," Ivanov's "otblesk" has metaphysical significance; it is a reflection of divine mysteries ("Otblesk tain bogoyavlennykh"). The reflection in *Faust* is conjoined with life ("Am farbigen *Abglanz* haben wir das *Leben*"—"In the colored *reflection* we have *life*"). Ivanov also connects these two central concepts in the poem's closing lines: "*Otblesk* tain bogoyavlennykh / V greze zryashchei *ozhivi*!"[42] The morning star's function is to make this reflection "come alive." Ivanov alters Goethe's dictum, yet the underlying philosophical conviction remains the same. Man, incapable of grasping the totality of life, must depend on symbols to understand his relationship to the absolute.

"Morning Star," with its numerous echoes from the first scene of *Faust II*, expresses a fundamentally Goethean worldview by means of a Goethean motif. Ivanov's morning star fulfills the function of Goethe's rainbow. Both are natural phenomena that reflect a higher reality. However, "Morning Star" is no mere paraphrase of Goethe. The passage in *Faust* is based on a moment of insight inspired by the physical presence of the symbol (the rainbow). Ivanov's poem follows the symbol (in this case, the morning star) from its ascent to its disappearance and beyond. In the final stanzas, the poet urges the now invisible star to continue to perform its intermediary function between man and the transcendent. The implication is obvious and important—the symbol can function independently of physical presence. Even when imperceptible to the human eye, it acts as a bond linking mankind to the eternal.

---

42. "*Revive* the *reflection* of epiphanic mysteries / In a visionary dream!"

Chapter 4

Faustian Allusions in *Pilot Stars*, *Transparence*, and *Tender Mystery*

> Всякое дальнейшее творчество обусловлено преодолением уже достигнутого; преодоление же не значит отрицание, но раньше — полное овладение пережитым и органическое его усвоение.[1]
> —Ivanov, "Goethe on the Border of Two Centuries"

The poem "Morning Star" reveals several elements characteristic of Ivanov's Goethe reception in *Pilot Stars*. In this poem, as in the preface that he ultimately rejected, Ivanov uses direct quotation to draw attention to his source. He actively invites the reader to understand his verse as an extension of Goethe's. However, whereas the verses cited in the preface were not significant from an ideological or poetic standpoint, the epigraph to "Morning Star" carries substantially greater weight. The quotation comes from a scene in which Goethe states one of his fundamental philosophical beliefs, and as a careful reading of the poem indicates, Ivanov accepts and develops this idea. Thus, the epigraph is not merely a means of laying claim to Goethe's authority, but also a sincere confirmation of his worldview.

The fact that three of the five Goethean epigraphs in *Pilot Stars* are taken from this single scene in *Faust* makes clear the central importance that Ivanov attributed to it. The short section entitled "Oready" ("Oreads") begins with the laconic epigraph: "Sie dürfen früh des ewigen Lichts geniessen, / Das später sich zu uns hernieder wendet." ("They are allowed to enjoy the eternal light early, / That later turns downward toward us.") Taken out of context, the passage is incomprehensible, since it contains two pronouns whose antecedents are unnamed. An examination of Goethe's text is not only helpful, but necessary. The lines come from Faust's monologue, at the point when he first looks upward:

> Hinaufgeschaut!—Der Berge Gipfelriesen
> Verkünden schon die feierlichste Stunde;

---

1. "All further creative work is dependent on overcoming that which has already been achieved. Overcoming does not mean rejection, but rather the full mastery of that which has been experienced and its organic assimilation." *SS*, vol. 4, p. 111.

> Sie dürfen früh des ewigen Lichts genießen,
> Das später sich zu uns hernieder wendet,
> Jetzt zu der Alpe grüngesenkten Wiesen
> Wird neuer Glanz und Deutlichkeit gespendet,
> Und stufenweis herab ist es gelungen;—
> Sie tritt hervor!—und leider schon geblendet,
> Kehr' ich mich weg, vom Augenschmerz durchdrungen.
> (ll. 4695–4703)
>
> Look up!—The giant peaks of the mountains
> Already announce the most solemn hour;
> They are allowed to enjoy the eternal light early,
> That later turns downward toward us,
> Now new sparkle and clarity is granted
> To the lowered green meadows of the Alps,
> And it has reached downward by steps;—
> It comes forward!—and unfortunately, already blinded,
> I turn away, my eyes pierced with pain.

The first thing Faust sees are "Der Berge Gipfelriesen"—the colossal mountain peaks. These mountaintops, then, are the subject of the epigraph. Because of their proximity to the heavens, the mountain peaks are the first to receive the sun's rays, the "eternal light." Afterwards, the light gradually ("stufenweis") descends "toward us." In terms of Ivanov's philosophy, it is important to remember the ubiquitous paradigm of ascent and descent. This passage represents movement downward ("hernieder/herab"), a direction Ivanov often associates with divinity (here, the eternal light). It complements movement upwards, which Ivanov sees as the aspiration of mankind and finds expressed in another of Faust's lines from the same scene: "Zum höchsten Dasein immerfort zu streben" ("to strive constantly to the highest [form of] existence").[2]

Knowing this context, one begins to understand the motivic organization of the "Oreads" section of *Pilot Stars*. As soon as one realizes that the "they" in the epigraph refers to mountains, the title "Oreads" (*mountain* nymphs) obtains a certain logical cohesiveness.[3] The section, composed entirely of nature poetry, draws mainly on classical myth and Tyutchev.[4] Goethe's role, while not always so prominent, is

---

2. Cf. *SS*, vol. 1, p. 823.
3. "Oread" is etymologically derived from the Greek "oros" ("mountain").
4. To cite two characteristic examples: lines from Ivanov's "Pred grozoi" ("Before the storm") strongly recall Tyutchev's "Yarkii sneg siyal v doline" ("Bright snow shone in the valley"). When Ivanov writes, "I uzhas vysei snegovykh / Vnezapnoi blednost'yu bledneet" ("And the horror of the snow heights / Pale with a sudden paleness") he expects the reader to recall Tyutchev's "No kotoryi vek *beleet* tam, na *vysyakh snegovykh* . . . " ("But how long does it stay white there, on the

nevertheless present. Throughout the section, numerous symbols (the rainbow, the waterfall) and themes (ascent and descent, reflection) of *Faust II*, scene 1, recur. The opening poem, for example, is entitled "Na kryl'yakh zari" ("On the Wings of Dawn"). Dawn, while not necessarily associated with Oreads, is crucial in the scene from *Faust*. Ivanov's poem concerns an imaginary nocturnal ascent to the heavens. It concludes with the new dawn:

> И когда в святыне зрящей дрогнет вспыхнувший эфир
> И по лествице горящей вниз метнется трубный клир, —
> Я бы чело моей царицы дымкой облачной обвил,
> Я бы первый луч денницы, упредив, благословил![5]

These lines are admittedly distant from the Faustian epigraph. Yet the description of dawn as motion downwards ("vniz," cf. "herab"), by steps ("po lestvitse," cf. "stufenweis"), combined with the emphasis on the first ray of daylight ("früh des ewigen Lichts genießen"), all resonate with the passage from *Faust*.

The scene in *Faust*, despite its broadly symbolic character, takes place in a specific location: the Alps.[6] The last of the nature poems in the "Oreads" section of *Pilot Stars*, is entitled "The Alpine Horn." This poem has traditionally been viewed as a reworking of Pushkin's "The Echo" ("Ekho").[7] Such an interpretation, based on intertextual references, can hardly be disputed. Both Pushkin and Ivanov apply the concept of "echo" first to nature and then to the poet. In Pushkin's version, everything creates an echo *except* the poet. Ivanov, however, extends the notion of echo to the poet, viewing it as a precondition for artistic creation.

Several aspects of Ivanov's poem suggest, however, that it is a reworking of Pushkin informed by Goethe. While the opening scene of *Faust II* is primarily visual (the rainbow, the waterfall), it nevertheless has a significant aural component. To begin with, the scene opens

---

snowy heights . . . "). The poem "Two Glances" ("Dva Vzora"), contains a more explicit reference to tradition: Ivanov includes a note pointing the reader to the myth of Silene as retold by Plutarch.

5. "And when, in the visionary holy place, the ether, having flared up, flickers / And along the glowing steps the trumpeting holy host rushes downwards / I would entwine the forehead of my queen in a cloudy haze, / [And,] having anticipated it, I would bless the first ray of morning!"

6. "Jetzt zu der Alpe grüngesenkten Wiesen . . . "—"Now to the lowered green meadows of the Alps . . . " (l. 4699)

7. Cf. Ivanov (1976), p. 458, where R. E. Pomirchy notes: "The poem is linked to Pushkin's 'Echo,' bringing to Pushkin's treatment of the eternal question of the role of the poet a 'correction' on behalf of modern art."

with song, first by Ariel and then by a chorus of spirits. An "ungeheures Getöse" ("enormous din") announces the sun's appearance. This din is, however, inaudible to humanity. As Ariel explains, "Tönend wird für Geistesohren / Schon der neue Tag geboren" ("For spirits' ears the new day is born with sound.") In short, Goethe draws a distinction even on the level of sound between the human and the divine. Mankind is incapable of perceiving the "sound" of the new dawn. Yet Goethe does not develop this notion any further, as he does with light, for example, where the sun (direct light) cannot be seen, while the rainbow (mediated light, yet emblematic of this higher light) is accessible.

In "The Alpine Horn," Ivanov applies to sound this relationship between the earthly and the transcendent. He recasts the concept of "ot*blesk*" ("reflection," Goethe's "Abglanz") in terms of "ot*zvuk*" ("echo"). The poem is based on a series of echoes, from the lexical level (the anagrammatic key words "rog" and "gor")[8] to the motivic (earthly and heavenly music), to the symbolic (the echo as the goal of artistic creation). In the first stanza, the poet describes a meeting with a shepherd who plays an Alpine horn. The horn's purpose is not simply to produce a pleasant sound, but rather to create an "echo" in the mountains:

> Приятно песнь его лилась; но зычный,
> Был лишь орудьем рог, дабы в горах
> Пленительное эхо пробуждать.[9]

The echo is itself so beautiful that the sound no longer seems earthly:

> Что мнилося: незримый духов хор,
> На неземных орудьях, переводит
> Наречием небес язык земли.[10]

The song of an "invisible choir of spirits" as well as the distinction between heavenly and earthly music go far beyond anything in Pushkin's poem, yet are clearly relevant to the opening of *Faust II*.

---

8. "Rog" is a horn, while "gor" is the genitive case of the word "mountains."
9. "The song streamed forth pleasantly. But the loud horn was merely an instrument to awaken a captivating echo in the mountains."
10. "It seemed that an invisible choir of spirits, on heavenly instruments, was translating the language of earth into heavenly speech."

In Ivanov's poem, as in Goethe, these motifs must be understood symbolically. In the final lines, a voice from "beyond the mountains" speaks in reply to the poet's own thoughts:[11]

> Природа — символ, как сей рог. Она
> Звучит для отзвука; и отзвук — Бог.
> Блажен, кто слышит песнь, и слышит отзвук.[12]

Ivanov presents a parable; just as the Alpine horn sounds in order to produce an echo, so nature exists for the sake of *its* echo—God. Ivanov's symbolic interpretation of sound parallels Goethe's use of reflection. Both images characterize the relationship between the phenomenal (nature) and the transcendent (God). The two planes are viewed as distinct, yet related. Their relationship is not one of identity, but rather of correspondence. Ivanov produces variations on a Goethean theme by applying this insight to the artist, who is embodied in the musical shepherd of the first stanza and, more obviously, in the "genius" of the second stanza. Through his song, the artist awakens "another song" in the hearts of his audience. In "The Alpine Horn," Ivanov freely combines central images from Pushkin with certain key notions of Goethe. These latter parallels would go unnoticed if the poem were not part of a section of verse introduced by a quote from *Faust II*.

A related passage serves to corroborate the closeness between Ivanov's conception of "otzvuk" ("echo") and Goethe's notion of "Abglanz" ("reflection"). In "The Poet's Mysteries" ("Misterii poeta"), another poem in *Pilot Stars*, Ivanov thematizes the act of poetic creation. The poem has two epigraphs, the first of which comes from *Faust II* (l. 9626): "...dem die ewigen Melodieen / Durch die Glieder sich bewegen..." ("...through whose body the eternal melodies move...").[13] These lines describe Euphorion, in Goethe's words

---

11. This "otzyvnyi glas" ("responsive voice") is yet another of the poem's myriad echoes.

12. "Nature is a symbol, like this horn. It sounds for an echo; and the echo is God. Blessed is he who hears the song and hears the echo."

13. The second epigraph comes from Ovid: "Phoebus adest: sonuere lyrae, sonuere pharetrae." ("Phoebus arrives: let the lyre and the quiver sound.") Ivanov's use of this epigraph is uncharacteristic, since the larger context of the passage (the "Remedia Amoris," l. 705) is ignored. A knowledge of Ovid's lighthearted verses tends, if anything, to minimize their effect in Ivanov's poem, where these words are invested with high seriousness. Yet Ovid's line is more than a flourish, for Ivanov carefully develops the imagery. His poem begins with the arrival of Phoebus Apollo (with lyre in hand) and concludes with the metaphor of poetry as an arrow.

"poesy incarnate."[14] In Ivanov's version, the poet is likewise depicted as an instrument for "eternal melodies."

> И, полна движеньем стройным, грудь певца звучит согласно;
> Мощной мере горних хоров вторит отклик уст земных . . .[15]

> And, full of ordered motion, the singer's breast sounds in concert;
> The echo of earthly lips repeats the powerful measure of celestial choruses . . .

Ivanov again conceives of poetry as the earthly echo (here: "otklik") of heavenly melody. In "Epirrhema," the companion poem to "The Poet's Mysteries," Ivanov demonstrates that the converse also holds; true poetry cannot exist where this echo is lacking. He devotes "Epirrhema" to the plight of the bad poet:

> Лишь немногих кликов отзвук, уловлен, поет в ушах . . .
> Вызвать чары горних звуков ищет он бессильной лирой,
> Но небес не воскрешает косных струн неверный звон.

> The echo of only a few sounds [that he has] caught sings in his ears . . .
> With his powerless lyre he seeks to summon the charms of celestial sounds,
> But the false ring of sluggish strings cannot resurrect the heavens.

In these poems, the notion of "echo" is not so carefully elaborated as in "The Alpine Horn." Yet it is undeniably present as a metapoetic concept. The epigraph from *Faust II* strongly suggests that the notion derives from Goethe.

The echo becomes one of Ivanov's central theoretical concepts. Ivanov quotes "The Alpine Horn" as an epigraph to his 1912 essay "Thoughts on Symbolism." In this programmatic essay, Ivanov elaborates on the poem's basic imagery by describing the entire Symbolist enterprise in terms of an echo. "I am not a Symbolist, if my words . . . do not awake an echo in the labyrinth of souls."[16] It is telling that in the essay's final paragraph, Ivanov refers to Goethe as "the distant father of our Symbolism."[17]

To read Ivanov's "Alpine Horn" without an awareness of its connection to Goethe does not distort the poem's meaning. In bringing the notion of "symbol" from the visual to the aural, Ivanov extends the

---

14. "die Poesie personifiziert." From the conversation with Eckermann on 20 December 1829. Cited in Friedrich and Scheithauer, p. 229.
15. *SS*, vol. 1, p. 579.
16. *SS*, vol. 2, p. 609.
17. *SS*, vol. 2, p. 612.

potential of Goethe's symbolic worldview. Characteristically, he uses intertextuality to affirm his ties to tradition rather than to rupture them.

In *Pilot Stars*, Ivanov consciously and emphatically draws attention to the writers and artists whose work has inspired him. Through numerous epigraphs and overt references (i.e., direct naming), the reader is introduced to a pantheon of Symbolists and proto-Symbolists. Although the precise connections between their work and Ivanov's own may be elusive, even the most casual reader recognizes the book's profoundly "literary" stance. In *Transparence*, Ivanov's second book of poetry, the intertextual level is less obvious. Except for a lengthy footnote on dithyrambs, Ivanov rarely draws attention to his sources.

In keeping with this more restrained tone, Ivanov never names Goethe explicitly. In the absence of direct quotation (either in a particular poem or as an epigraph), it is often difficult to do more than identify a general resemblance between the two poets. However, when Ivanov, writing on a distinctly Goethean theme, uses a distinctly Goethean meter, it seems fair to assume a conscious connection. Ivanov's "Ganymede," for example, treats a theme that had supplied Goethe with the subject of one of his most celebrated hymns (also called "Ganymede") from the "Sturm-und-Drang" period. In both cases, the poet does not directly describe the mythical event (an eagle seizing the hero and carrying him to heaven), but rather allows the protagonist to speak for himself. Goethe's poem, written in free verse, uses extremely short lines and brief, elliptical constructions to reflect the speaker's excitement and confusion:

> Ich komm, ich komme!
> Wohin? Ach, wohin?
>
> Hinauf! Hinauf strebt's.
> Es schweben die Wolken
> Abwärts, die Wolken
> Neigen sich der sehnenden Liebe.
> Mir! Mir!
> In euerm Schoße
> Aufwärts![18]

---

18. "I'm coming, I'm coming! / Where, o where? // Upwards, upwards it goes. / The clouds float / Downwards, the clouds / Bend to the yearning love. / To me! To me! / In your lap / Upwards!"

Goethe, seeking to create a spontaneous, unpremeditated effect, uses unrhymed lines in an irregular stanzaic structure. The protagonist's speech consists primarily of exclamations and questions, with many repeated words.

Ivanov's Ganymede also speaks in lengthy, unrhymed stanzas of unusually short lines. This monologue is written in a form of free verse (extremely rare in Russian poetry) that is remarkably reminiscent of Goethe's poem:

> Но могучие лапы
> Тесно нежат,
> Подъемлют,
> Подъемлют...
> Орел, орел!
> Как весело мне
> Лететь над долом!
> Куда ты взнесешь меня!
> Сильный орел?[19]

Such metrically irregular, short exclamations (with numerous word repetitions)—particularly when used in the identical thematic context—are surely derived from Goethe.

Nonetheless Ivanov alters Goethe's model by adding two choruses (of the valley and of the heights), which interrupt the protagonist's monologue. Written in four-line logaoedic verse, they function as commentary on the scene, for they lament Ganymede's disappearance from the world below.

> О, Ганимед! в добычу
> Птице Зевса, тайный наш цвет, был ты Весной взлелеян!
> Небу первина Дола,
> Цвет наш — плачьте, души дубрав! — сорван влюбленным небом![20]

Such an addition is distinctly foreign to Goethe's poem, which owes its emotional effect to the unimpeded flow of the monologue. It is likely that Ivanov includes the chorus in accordance with the theories of drama that he was developing at the time. For his purposes, the measured chorus adds an element of classical solemnity and returns the myth to its origins in antiquity. In short, Ivanov borrows from Goethe

---

19. "But powerful claws / Hold me tightly / Raise [me] up / Raise [me] up ... / Eagle, eagle! / How happy I am / To fly above the earth! / Where are you carrying me / Powerful eagle?" *SS*, vol. 1, p. 792.

20. "O Ganymede! as prey / For Zeus's bird, our secret flower, you were coddled by Spring! / The firstling of the Earth to the sky, / Our flower is torn away by the enamored heaven—lament, spirits of the groves!"

a theme and its poetic expression (in this case, metrics and syntax), but supplements it with his own notions of choric art.

The same type of intertextuality can be found in Ivanov's *Faust* reception. Johannes Holthusen has drawn attention to the short dactylic lines in certain poems in *Transparence* ("Rainbows" and "The Beautiful is Good"), noting their connection to the famous chorus of angels in the conclusion of *Faust II*. "Rosen, ihr blendenden, / Balsam versendenden! / Flatternde, schwebende, / Heimlich belebende . . . "[21] In fact, Ivanov's use of dactylic dimeter differs slightly from that of Goethe. Ivanov uses only fully-realized dactylic dimeters, while Goethe often truncates the final foot.[22] Yet when this unusual metrical form is combined with highly suggestive Goethean imagery, it seems probable that an intertextual association was intended.

Faust's epiphanic vision of nature occurred in a rather specific natural setting, consisting of the sun, a waterfall, and a rainbow. The rainbow, exemplifying the symbolic nature of the universe, ultimately became the center of attention. In "Rainbows" Ivanov combines these same natural phenomena and interprets them in a strikingly similar fashion. In terms of formal features, the poem is unusual. Each of the ninety-six lines ends with a dactylic rhyme (the poem is a tour-de-force in this respect). Since the lines are so short (always six syllables, rarely composed of more than two words), the insistent rhyming is extremely noticeable. Ivanov avoids a monotonous effect by varying the rhyme scheme.[23] The content of the poem is purely lyrical—as the first verb ("slavyat"—"celebrate") implies, it is essentially a hymn to the rainbows. Despite the absence of narrative qualities, there is a clear development over the course of the poem, reflected in the verbal forms: from present indicative (first two stanzas), to future indicative (penultimate stanza) to hortative imperative (final stanza).

Throughout, the poem takes the form of an apostrophe to the rainbows:

> Горы с долинами
> Вы сочетаете;
> Вздохами таете
> В горних селениях,
> В буйных стремлениях
> Дольними чадами

---

21. In Ivanov (1967), pp. x–xi. Cf. Potthoff, p. 196.

22. This tendency can be noted even in the continuation of Holthusen's exemplary passage: "heimlich belebende, / zweigleinbeflügelte, knospenentsiegelte,— / *eilet zu blühn*!" (my emphasis).

23. For example, the first line rhymes with the fifth, the seventh, and the twenty-third lines.

Над водопадами
Вы расцветаете.²⁴

The highly figurative poetic language makes clear that the poem is not attempting to create a visual impression of a natural scene. Ivanov understands the rainbows as emblems of a higher reality. Already in this first section, they are explicitly symbolic, conceived of as the link between the earth and the heavens. The almost gratuitous reference to waterfalls in this passage seems to be present for the sole purpose of recalling *Faust*. The second section discusses the rainbows' salutary effect on mankind:

О мимолетные,
Души бесплотные,
Мир улегчите вы,
Мир научите вы,
Как растворяется
Тайна в явлении...²⁵

This passage not only addresses the problem of the relationship of the noumenal and the phenomenal worlds (the "mystery in the appearance"); it also identifies the rainbows as the teachers of these universal secrets. In the final section (the imperatives), the source of this mystery is named: "Tainu povedaite / Solntsa prekrasnogo..." ("Disclose the secret of the beautiful sun..."). As in Goethe, the sun is the symbolic "center" and the rainbow its mediated form.

While using Goethe's basic symbols (rainbow, sun, waterfall), Ivanov does not hesitate to invest them with additional significance. He includes numerous motifs that have no recognizable connection to Goethe's "farbiger Abglanz." One notes, for example, the application of Ivanov's ubiquitous ascent/descent paradigm to the rainbows:

Вас, нисхождения
Отсветы бледные,
И восхождения
Двери победные!²⁶

At the poem's conclusion, Ivanov includes another favorite image:

---

24. "You connect / The mountains with the valleys; / You melt with sighs / In the celestial settlements, / In wild stirrings, / Like earthly children / Above the waterfalls / You bloom." *SS*, vol. 1, p. 751.

25. "O fleeting, / Incorporeal souls, / You will unburden the world, / You will teach the world, / How the mystery/ Dissolves in the appearance..."

26. "You, pale reflections of descent, and victorious doors of ascent!"

> Как улыбается
> Светлость под тучами;
> Как нагибается
> Легкость над кручами;
> Как упиваются
> Светами зыбкими,
> Осияваются
> Цвета улыбками
> Мглы окрыленные.[27]

The smile, often signifying the meeting of the human and the divine in Ivanov's poetry and theoretical writings, is perfectly in keeping with the poem's theme. It is, however, unrelated to Goethe's *Faust*.

It is characteristic that Ivanov returns to the rainbow theme in a poem written almost a decade later. "Raduga" ("The Rainbow"), from the 1912 collection *Tender Mystery*, exemplifies another step in Ivanov's appropriation of Goethean imagery.

> Та, что любит эти горы,
> Та, что видит эти волны
> И спасает в бурю челны
> Этих бедных рыбаков, —
> От земного праха взоры
> Мне омыла ливнем струйным,
> Осушила ветром буйным,
> Весть прислала с облаков.
>
> В небе радуга сомкнулась
> Меж пучиной и стремниной.
> Мрачный пурпур за долиной
> Обнял хаос горных груд.
> Ткань эфира улыбнулась
> И, как тонкий дым алтарный,
> Окрылила светозарный
> Ближних склонов изумруд.
>
> И тогда предстала радость
> В семицветной Божьей двери —
> Не очам, единой вере, —
> Ибо в миг тот был я слеп
> (Лишь теперь душа всю сладость
> Поняла, какой горела!), —
> Та предстала, что согрела
> Розой дня могильный склеп.

---

27. "How lightness smiles under storm clouds; How weightlessness bends above the cliffs; How the inspired haze revels in the vascillating lights; How they become illuminated with smiles of color."

Золотистый, розовея,
Выбивался в вихре волос,
И звучал мне звонкий голос:
"Милый, приходи скорей!"
И виссон клубился, вея,
И бездонной глубиною
Солнце, ставшее за мною,
Пили солнца двух очей.

She, who loves these mountains,
She, who sees these waves
And, in the storm, saves the ships
Of these poor fishermen,—
With a shower of streams
She cleansed my glances from the dust of earth,
[She] dried [them] with a fierce wind,
And sent a message from the clouds.

In the sky a rainbow formed
Between the abyss and the precipice.
The dark purple beyond the valley
Embraced the chaos of mountain heaps.
The layer of ether smiled
And, like the thin smoke of an altar,
Inspired the shining emerald
Of the nearby hills.

And then joy stepped forward
In God's seven-colored door—
Not to the eyes, [but] to belief alone,—
For at that moment I was blind
(Only now has my soul understood
The complete sweetness with which it shone!),—
That which had warmed
The sepulchral crypt with the rose of day, stepped forward.

A gold-colored hair, turning rose-colored
Kept appearing in the whirlwind,
And a sonorous voice spoke to me:
"My dear, come quickly!"
And the thin cloth swirled, wafting,
And the suns of two eyes
Drank into their bottomless depths
The sun that rose behind me.

Once again, Ivanov's theme is the communication between divine and earthly realms. As in *Transparence*, the rainbow plays a mediating role between man and a higher reality. In this case, however, Ivanov supplements the rainbow with the image of a divine female figure. These two functionally-equivalent symbols are further connected by their common grammatical gender (feminine). Indeed, Ivanov uses this linguistic feature for poetic purposes, deliberately obscuring the points where one ends and the other begins. (The first and fourth stanzas appear to describe the woman while the second and third more obviously concern the rainbow. Upon closer examination, however, a number of passages are fundamentally ambiguous, e.g., much of the first and third stanzas.)

Although there is no metrical similarity ("The Rainbow" is written in trochaic tetrameter), a number of motifs suggest that the poem should be understood in the context of Ivanov's ongoing reception of Goethe. In addition to the general use of the rainbow as a manifestation of divinity accessible to man, the poem contains specific lines that recall Faust's celebrated monologue (part II, scene 1), to which Ivanov so frequently alludes throughout his works. In stanza three, Ivanov exclaims, "Ibo v tot mig byl ya slep" ("For at that moment I was blind"), recalling the exclamation "Sie tritt hervor!—und leider schon geblendet, Kehr ich mich weg, vom Augenschmerz durchdrungen" ("It [the sun] comes forward!—and unfortunately, already blinded, I turn away, my eyes pierced with pain"). In the final stanza, Ivanov refers to the "solntse, stavshee za mnoyu" ("the sun that rose behind me"). Faust had expressed the same thought as he turned from the sun to the rainbow: "So bleibe denn die Sonne mir im Rücken" ("Then let the sun remain behind me" [literally, "at my back"]). In this Goethean context, the enigmatic woman (who clearly represents salvation, cf. stanza 1) can be understood as an embodiment of another central symbol of *Faust II*: the eternal feminine, who leads man upwards. It is clearly her voice that urges the poet to "come quickly." The woman's transcendent status becomes especially apparent in the poem's striking closing image, in which her two eyes (metaphorically described as "suns") swallow up the sun itself. These concluding lines are, of course, distanced from Goethe's text, yet they are linked by a principle of extension. As in Goethe, man cannot confront the sun directly, but is shown the divine way by the rainbow. His ultimate salvation occurs through the intercession of the eternal feminine.

The fact that Ivanov was thinking of Goethe's *Faust* at the time of his work on *Tender Mystery* is evident from two other poems in this uncharacteristically slender collection. "V al'bom studenta-esteta" ("Into the album of a student-aesthete") is a rather unserious effort, yet its Faustian epigraph makes clear that, even in minor poetry, Ivanov looked to Goethe.[28] The title already calls to mind a genre of light poetry popular in early ninetenth-century Russia. "Album poetry" generally implied "impromptu" poems written upon request for the albums of young ladies. However, the epigraph from *Faust* draws attention to a more specific subtext. In the first part of Goethe's masterpiece (ll. 1868–2072), a would-be student comes to visit Faust and is greeted by Mephistopheles, who proceeds to confuse the young man with witty and unsavory advice. At the end of their discussion, at the young man's urging, Mephistopheles makes an entry in his album: "Eritis sicut deus, scientes bonum et malum" ("You will be like god, knowing good and evil"). Ivanov takes this line, slightly altered, as his epigraph, giving the source as *Faust II*.[29] In the poem itself, he briefly summarizes the scene from *Faust* in the first stanza, discusses his own position (neither that of Faust, nor of Satan) in the second and offers a "modernized" variant of the same statement in the third:

> Мораль сообразую с веком
> И чужд, ей-ей, бесовских злоб:
> "Добро (по Канту) вспомни, сноб,
> И станешь просто — человеком".
>   Eritis sicut homines,
>   scientes bonum et malum.

> I form my moral in accordance with the age
> And of course [I] am free of demonic malice:
> "Remember Good (according to Kant), [you] snob,
> And you will become simply . . . a man.
>   Eritis sicut homines,
>   scientes bonum et malum.

In the post-Kantian world (i.e., a world in which man cannot know the transcendent), a knowledge of good leads one to become not like a god, but simply a man.[30] Ivanov thus concludes the poem with an un-

---

28. The poem is found in the book's second part, which, according to Ivanov's own introduction, contains poems written "for personal, modest purposes, or simply as a joke." *SS*, vol. 3, p. 7.

29. Goethe alters the biblical "eritis sicut dei" ("you will be like gods") to read "eritis sicut deus" ("you will be like a god"). Ivanov, who was undoubtedly quoting from memory (in the Russian tradition) uses the biblical original rather than Goethe's slightly altered version. "Eritis sicut dei" is, moreover, the title of a poem in *Pilot Stars* that is connected to the Bible, not to Goethe (cf. *SS*, vol. 1, pp. 572–74). Ivanov errs in his epigraph, attributing these lines to *Faust II* (rather than *Faust I*), presumably because he confuses the scene with its parallel scene in *Faust II*, which he quotes in another poem in the same collection (*SS*, vol. 3, p. 56).

30. For more on Kant's "godlessness," see *SS*, vol. 3, p. 391.

expected reversal: "You will be like *men*, knowing good and evil" (my emphasis).

The final Faust-oriented poem of *Tender Mystery*, entitled "Сон" ("The Dream"), is one of the collection's darkest and most perplexing texts. In this poem, the poet relates a nightmare: under cover of darkness, he steals into a house to ask forgiveness from a woman whom he loved but subsequently abandoned. During their meeting, he becomes aware that her grief has driven her mad.

"The Dream" is written in highly unusual five-line iambic stanzas (a-b-b-b-a, all masculine rhymes), using lines of dimeter (l. 1), tetrameter (ll. 2 and 4) and trimeter (ll. 3 and 5). In many respects, this stanzaic form recalls the ballad "The Tsar's Departure," which immediately precedes it in *Tender Mystery*. That poem, it will be recalled, combines lines of iambic dimeter, trimeter, and tetrameter and also uses exclusively masculine rhymes. "The Dream" can in certain ways be considered a companion piece to "The Tsar's Departure," for both are tragic, plot-oriented poems that rely on hints rather than detailed narration. However, "The Dream" contains a pathos completely foreign to "The Tsar's Departure" and a psychological dimension rarely found in Ivanov's verse.

> Я дверь, как вор,
> Приотворил. Ко мне, бледна,
> Метнулася она,
> Смертельным ужасом пьяна,
> Вперив в убийцу взор . . .
>
> Есть, Фауст, казнь:
> В очах возлюбленной прочесть
> Не гнев, не суд, не месть —
> Но чудный блеск — безумья весть —
> И дикую боязнь.
>
> "Сгинь!" слышу крик:
> "Еще ль тебе мой сладок плач,
> Полунощный палач?
> Ты, знаю, дьявол, — как ни прячь
> Рога в е г о двойник! . . ."

I opened the door slightly, like a thief
Toward me, pale,
She hurled herself,
Drunk with deathly horror,
Fixing her glance on the murderer . . .

There is murder, Faust:
To read in the eyes of one's beloved
Not anger, not judgment, not revenge,—

> But a foreign gleam—the sign of madness—
> And a wild fear.
>
> "Disappear!" I hear [her] scream:
> "Is my cry still sweet to you,
> Midnight executioner?
> You, I know, are the devil—however you may hide
> Your horns in *his* double! . . . "

The poem's effect depends largely upon the reader's ability to interpret the single word "Faust." In the concluding scene of *Faust I*, Faust returns with Mephistopheles to rescue Gretchen from prison under cover of night. She refuses his entreaties to escape, and, after observing her with anguish and horror, Faust hurries away without her. The scene's parallels to "The Dream" are numerous and unmistakable: a protagonist, aligned with the devil, attempts to "rescue" his mad beloved, only to have her identify him as a murderer. In Ivanov's poem, the protagonist asks for forgiveness, but it is already too late:

> А я крещу
> Ее рукой, моля: "Прости!
> Меня перекрести!
> Я сам пришел. Ты ж не грусти,
> Как по тебе грущу . . . "
>
> В мой взор глядит
> Чужого неба бирюза . . .
> Застылая слеза
> Пустые стеклянит глаза . . .
> Глядит. Молчит. Глядит . . .

> But I cross
> Her with my hand, entreating: "Forgive [me]!
> Cross me again!
> I myself have come. Do not lament,
> As I lament for you . . . "
>
> Into my glance looks
> The turquoise of an alien sky . . .
> A frozen tear
> Makes the empty eyes glassy . . .
> [She] looks. [She] is silent. [She] looks . . .

Ivanov's conclusion differs in emphasis from that of Goethe. *Faust I* ends with action (the protagonist's hurried departure), while "The Dream" concludes with stasis (the mad glance of the beloved). As the insistent repetition of the word "glyadit" ("looks") indicates, the beloved stares at the protagonist and recognizes nothing. This final stanza depicts a fundamental lack of communication; the direct speech of the two previous stanzas yields to silence. For Ivanov, who conceived of love based on mystical recognition, this conclusion represents a moment of utter despair.[31]

Why is Ivanov's "nightmare" oriented on this particular scene from Goethe? Even in terms of Ivanov's general *Faust* reception, the choice of scenes is striking, since Ivanov expressly states his preference for the second part.[32] The answer appears to be linked to Ivanov's strong sense of archetypes. The final scene of *Faust I* depicts what for Ivanov is the ultimate failure of love. It will be remembered that in the correspondence of 1895, it was precisely this scene that Ivanov used to depict his own guilt. Decades later, Ivanov would again refer to this scene in his German essay on "Anima." That work, which Ivanov considered one of his major accomplishments of the emigration period, discussed religious experience in erotic terms as the meeting of two elemental forces.[33] The female aspect (anima) waits for the masculine aspect (animus) in order to be saved. As Ivanov notes, "Numerous myths and fairy-tales about the captive, transformed, sleeping virgin, about the enchanted rose and her saviour repeat the same motif of the 'anima' in need of salvation."[34]

In this unabashedly myth-oriented essay, the final scene of *Faust I* figures prominently.

> If, instead of the one whom the "anima" fervently awaits, a stranger appears who arbitrarily tries to pass himself off as her saviour, she is capable of rousing herself for a moment in order to repulse him decisively; but soon all of her life strength and consciousness nonetheless break down. She must fall victim to the demon of enmity towards God that has taken power over the faithless spirit. Gretchen does not recognize her Faust, who through Mephisto's arts penetrates into the prison to free her: she is horrified by him, she refuses to follow him or be saved by him. Had he called her in God's name, she would have followed.

---

31. For Ivanov, love was connected to the mystical notion of recognizing something foreign within oneself and addressing it as "you." This principle serves as the basis for all religious awareness (cf. the essay "You Are" of 1907, *SS*, vol. 3, pp. 262–69) as well as the basis for love between two people. Cf. *SS*, vol. 3, pp. 211–12 (a crucial poem in "Man") or Ivanov's own statement about Lidiya in the "Autobiographical Letter" (*SS*, vol. 2, p. 20): "Through each other we both found ourselves and more than ourselves: I would say, we discovered God."

32. *SS*, vol. 4, p. 148.

33. In a letter to Herbert Steiner of 11 March 1935, Ivanov wrote that "Anima" was "the most important [thing] that I have written in the last years." (Deutsches Literaturarchiv, Marbach am Neckar.)

34. *SS*, vol. 3, p. 274.

In Dostoevsky's *The Devils*, a similar stance can be found in the feeble-minded but nonetheless clairvoyant cripple's attitude toward her beloved who has rebelled against God. Full of horror, loathing, and despair, she sees in him the assassin and servile imitator of her "sun falcon."[35]

Goethe's scene provides Ivanov with a powerful negative archetype—a paradigm of failed love. As Ivanov argues elsewhere, it is not by chance that Dostoevsky's *The Devils* recalls *Faust*: "Thinking to base his novel on the symbolism of the interrelationship between the Earth Spirit, the human ego, daring and creating, and the forces of Evil, Dostoevsky naturally had to look back to a depiction of the very same symbolic structure of the myth as it had already appeared in the world's poetry—to Goethe's *Faust*."[36] This passage is perhaps less valuable as literary criticism (i.e., a description of Dostoevsky's novel) than as a reflection of the Symbolist approach to creativity. Ivanov contends that a writer, in seeking to express a certain theme, *naturally* looks for models in previous works of art. Because myth, according to Ivanov, is objectively true, it serves as the wellspring for artistic creation.[37] Artistic power thus lies less in pure inventiveness than in an ability to incorporate myth into the creative process.[38] For these reasons, Ivanov declared mythopoesis to be the goal and natural extension of Symbolism.[39] A passage from the book on Dostoevsky (again with characteristic references to Goethe) neatly summarizes this credo:

> The more the writer has the feeling for *realiora in realibus*—that pathos which breaks out in Goethe's "All that is transient is but a parable"—the more naturally, of course, does he meet and conform with the original imaginative patterns of the essential train of thought that lives on in the obscure memory of the ancient myth. Conversely, the more deeply the poetic conception is rooted in the native soil of the myth, the more

---

35. *SS*, vol. 3, p. 290.
36. Cf. *SS*, vol. 4, pp. 440–41.
37. *SS*, vol. 2, p. 90.
38. Once again, a passage from Ivanov's work on Dostoevsky is revealing: "Dostoevsky does not abide by his chosen literary example. With poetic intuition he examines the innermost essence of the type personified in his hero; and, as usually happens before the growth of a great poetic conception, he finds its native soil—which never denies its strengthening sustenance to any truly original work—in obscure memories of ancient myth." Ivanov (1966), pp. 88–89. I quote from Norman Cameron's English translation, as the Russian version of the text has been lost. For the complicated history of publication, see *SS*, vol. 4, pp. 757–70.
39. *SS*, vol. 2, p. 554.

significant and intrinsically true does it seem to us—that is, if we have not yet lost the sense of its magnetic force, so that Goethe's words "the truth was discovered long ago" can still be fully applied to poetic truth.[40]

"The Dream" represents a direct application of Ivanov's theoretical precepts. The poem describes not simply an isolated moment, but an archetype and, as such, a recurring theme in world literature and human experience. It is at once highly personal (Deschartes, Ivanov's close friend and posthumous editor, insists on locating the poem's origin in an actual dream)[41] and, as mythical repetition, universal. Finally, it testifies to Goethe's role not only as personal model and poetic authority, but as a direct mythopoetical source.

---

40. Ivanov (1966), p. 52.
41. *SS*, vol. 1, p. 181; *SS*, vol. 3, p. 700. Given Ivanov's tendency to perceive the world through literary models, there is little reason to doubt her claim.

Chapter 5

Goethe's Poetry in the Mythology of *Cor Ardens*

> Мне кажется, что никто из моих современников так не живет чувством мифа, как я. Вот в чем моя сила, вот в чем я человек нового начинающегося периода. Если, по Огюсту Конту, человечество в своем развитии прошло через три фазы: мифологическую, теологическую и научную, то ныне наступают сроки новой мифологической эпохи. И тогда, когда она настанет, меня впервые должным образом оценят.[1]
> —Vyacheslav Ivanov, Conversation with M. S. Al'tman of 20 December 1921

The discussion of Ivanov's Goethe reception has thus far neglected Ivanov's lengthiest and most complex poetic achievement—*Cor Ardens*. Rather than drawing on *Faust*, this collection looks back to the poem "Selige Sehnsucht" ("Blessed Yearning"), in which Goethe uses the image of a butterfly consumed by flame to symbolize death and resurrection. Ivanov invokes this brief and enigmatic text throughout his writings. In the essay on Goethe, it is the only poem that he translates in its entirety.[2] Within the context of the essay "On the Russian Idea," it represents the yearning of the Russian people.[3] In the 1921 *Correspondence from Two Corners*, it becomes emblematic of Ivanov's philosophy of culture.[4] In "Anima," Goethe's

---

1. "It seems to me that none of my contemporaries lives by myth to the extent that I do. This is where my power lies, this makes me a man of the new age that is only now beginning. If, according to Auguste Comte, humanity has gone through three phases of development (the mythological, the theological, and the scientific), then today a new mythological epoch is dawning. And when it arrives, I will be properly appreciated for the first time." In Al'tman, p. 321. Ivanov makes a curious and telling error in this passage. Comte (in his *Cours de philosophie positive*) actually spoke of metaphysical (*not* mythological), theological, and scientific phases.
2. *SS*, vol. 4, p. 140. In contrast to his usual practice, Ivanov gives a prose translation.
3. *SS*, vol. 3, p. 332.
4. Ibid., p. 387.

imagery exemplifies the soul's "mystical death."[5] In the poetry, particularly in *Cor Ardens*, it becomes firmly integrated in Ivanov's larger symbolic system.

Ivanov's fascination with "Blessed Yearning" is directly linked to his conceptions of mythopoesis and creativity. According to Ivanov, the artist seeks to express a mystical truth that is not apparent to ordinary individuals. This activity, it will be remembered, is essentially receptive (cf. the discussion of theurgy in chap. 3). However, at rare moments (most notably in the 1912 essay "Manner, Personality, and Style"), Ivanov himself acknowledges a certain unavoidable degree of subjectivity in the creative process. Such an admission, of course, opens a Pandora's box of theoretical problems. How is the poet a mouthpiece for objective truth if, in fact, he is expressing his own individual perception? For this reason, Ivanov qualifies the extent of subjectivity that is admissible.

> One cannot agree with the right of the subjective lyric poet to pervert reality ["dannost'" (literally: "what is given")] to the point of unrecognizability or to swallow it up so that the depiction of the external world turns into a disconnected nightmare. One cannot allow him the right to name things with names inappropriate to those things and to attribute to them inappropriate characteristics. One cannot allow the rape of reality ["dannosti"] by lyrical subjectivity.[6]

In short, Ivanov conceives of an essential universal order that even the "subjective" poet must respect.

However, the very possibility of subjectivity in art forces Ivanov to reconsider his assumptions and confront the problem of ontological relativity:

> It is true that the very conception of reality ["dannost'"] is only conditionally objective; it is that which is subjectively perceived as given ["dannoe"]. "Darum pfuscht er auch so: Freunde, wir haben's *erlebt*" (Goethe, Venz. Epigr. 33).[7] Thus we are deprived of the possibility of checking the honesty of the utterances of the perceiver about the perceived; as concerns the ability to follow the perceiver along the paths of his subjective perception, then this ability is in turn

---

5. Ibid., p. 284.

6. *SS*, vol. 2, p. 625.

7. Ivanov quotes from Goethe's "Venetian Epigrams," No. 15 (not 33), which is directed against the Germans' refusal to learn to write poetry. "That's why he (i.e., the German) does it so badly; We, friends, have *experienced* it." (The emphasis is Ivanov's, not Goethe's.) Cf. Goethe (1982), p. 177.

> subjective. Here it seems we lose a reliable criterion—if we did not have numerous indirect means of determining the degree of trustworthiness of that person who bears witness to his own experience.[8]

In all of Ivanov's theoretical writings, this passage is perhaps the closest he comes to expressing doubt. However, after what seems like incontrovertible arguments against his own fundamental beliefs, Ivanov avers—without elaborating—that there are numerous "indirect" methods of determining artistic fidelity.

It is precisely at this juncture where myth (as well as the "formal canon" of literary masterworks) fits into Ivanov's theoretical model. Repeated assertions make clear that Ivanov considered myth a most reliable standard of evaluation. In myth, the modern artist had at his disposal a means of attaining universal truth.[9] "For myth is the depiction of realities.... A new myth is a new discovery of those same realities."[10] It should be emphasized that Ivanov did not mean that a new myth revived an "urmyth." Rather, he advocated using myth freely, arguing that all forms of a given myth have validity.[11] Historically speaking, a myth had a secret religious origin and was known only to the initiated. However, with the passage of time the myth would be discovered by the masses and disseminated in various forms. All of these, *regardless of contradictions and innovations*, were for Ivanov genuine.[12] Their very acceptance proved their ultimate validity.[13]

Ivanov's early efforts to recreate ancient tragedy on the modern Russian stage represent the most straightforward practical application of his theory. In ancient theater, there was no distance between the audience and the actors; the audience participated as in a religious ritual. In attempting to recreate these circumstances, Ivanov sought to achieve a timelessness that would unite the modern viewer with the actors, with the audience, and with the past. As he wrote in a preface to his projected dramatic trilogy: "The author set himself a task neither archeological nor scholarly, but universal and atemporal and therefore in its essence always ancient and new together.... In its es-

---

8. *SS*, vol. 2, p. 625.
9. Already in his 1895 correspondence with Lidiya, Ivanov had written, "The myth of Eros's shot, like all myths, is true." RGB, f. 109, k. 9, ed. khr. 37.
10. *SS*, vol. 2, p. 555.
11. Cf. *SS*, vol. 2, p. 168; Gerasimov, p. 186.
12. *SS*, vol. 2, p. 560.
13. Cf. Ibid.

sential features, the form of Attic tragedy seemed to the author the form of the revived people's theater of the future."[14]

To what extent Ivanov's own stylized dramas fulfilled their utopian mission is a secondary concern. More important is their explicit orientation on myth, for, in less obvious ways, the same orientation can be found in all genres of Ivanov's writings. Lyric poetry, more "subjective" (in Ivanov's sense of the word) than drama and therefore more closely linked to personal experience, nevertheless draws its power from myth. By rooting his own experience in archetypes, the poet moves from the individual to the universal. (One may think of Ivanov's own poetry, e.g., "Beauty" or "The Dream.") For an example of the unity of myth and individual experience that underlies lyric poetry, Ivanov refers the reader to Solovyov: "In the case of Vladimir Solovyov, internal experiences of his personal life, understood 'cosmically' (to use the language of astrologists and alchemists) serve as the subjects of his poetic inspiration, so that he only paints that which has happened as a real myth of his personality."[15] In great poetry, it follows, the individual level represents an instance of the mythical; the "subjective" in actuality coincides with the objective.

Numerous contemporaries and subsequent literary historians have characterized Ivanov as "the herald of Dionysus."[16] Indeed, Ivanov's attitude toward Dionysus is one of the most frequently mentioned and misunderstood aspects of his worldview. His initial interest in the subject can be traced to studies he began before the turn of the century and which he articulated most clearly in *The Hellenic Religion of the Suffering God*. In this work, Ivanov demonstrated how the myth of Dionysus contained a powerful paradigm: "Only in the religion of Dionysus did the ancient Greek find the god who suffered and died like himself, the god with the face of a mortal man, the god who was reborn, who promised resurrection."[17] Because Ivanov saw myth as an essentially repetitive phenomenon, he recognized the same pattern of suffering and resurrection in numerous cultures, including Christianity. However, as the work's penultimate chapter makes clear, he spoke of analogy—not identity—when comparing Dionysus and Christ.[18] He never suggested that modernity believe in Dionysus *per se*; in Ivanov's words, Dionysus was a "how," not a "what."[19]

---

14. In Gerasimov, p. 185.
15. *SS*, vol. 2, p. 557.
16. The phrase is from Berdyaev, p. 156.
17. *Ellinskaya religiya*, in *Novyi put'*, 1904, No. 2, p. 73.
18. *Ellinskaya religiya*, in *Voprosy zhizni*, 1905, No. 7, p. 134.
19. *SS*, vol. 1, pp. 723–24. In this regard, Ivanov criticizes Nietzsche's notion of a "superman."

Dionysus becomes ubiquitous in Ivanov's work, both as a mythical personage, and—more importantly and indirectly—as a symbol of the universal belief in death and resurrection. More a spiritual condition than an historical entity, the Dionysian paradigm recurs in numerous forms. Ol'ga Deschartes has written, "Always, and always in a different way, V[yacheslav] I[vanov] announces one and the same Dionysian myth. Whether he sings of spring or love, of Persephone or Orpheus, he inevitably celebrates the unity of suffering and rejoicing, of dying and rebirth."[20] Such mythical recurrences form the basis of Ivanov's art. In his poetry and prose, Ivanov thinks in terms of homologies, relying on parallels between myths that are separated both temporally and spatially.[21] Johannes Holthusen has illuminated Ivanov's poetry by means of two "Dionysian topoi": the phoenix and the seed that must die in order to give birth (John 12:24).[22] While these topoi are neither historically nor culturally related to Dionysus, both express its mythic essence. It is characteristic of Ivanov's worldview that the biblical parable coexists with and affirms the pagan symbol.

The butterfly and the flame, the fundamental image of "Blessed Yearning," should be understood as yet another instance of the same mythical construct. Its source, as Ivanov was well aware, is not in Goethe, but in ancient myth. In "Psyche" (*Pilot Stars*), the speaker describes a dream in which he meets three gods: Nemesis, Hope, and Eros. All watch in horror as Psyche approaches the "altar of burning love":

> ... И мотылек — все отвратили лица —
> Вблизи порхал ...
>
> Уж он в перстах божественных ... Привольно
> Ему гореть! ...
> Так сладко зреть мне было казнь, — так больно! ...
> Метнись — и встреть! ...[23]

The image of a butterfly burning at the altar of love strongly recalls Goethe's poem. Yet "Psyche" stops at the moment of death: the final lines read "Dusha v grudi zabilas'... i vdokhnula.../ I—umerla..."

---

20. Ibid., p. 66.
21. On these grounds, N. V. Braginskaya (p. 299) questions the validity of Ivanov's classical scholarship. She demonstrates how, in his fervor to reconcile all oppositions, Ivanov loses his ability to see *differences*.
22. Holthusen (1982), pp. 16–17.
23. "And a butterfly—all averted their faces—fluttered nearby . . . It is already in divine fingers . . . it can burn freely! . . For me it was so sweet to watch the execution,—so painful! . . . 'Rush off—and meet!'" (*SS*, vol. 1, pp. 701–2).

("The soul began to beat in the breast... and inhaled.../ And—died!..."). In this poem, the possibility of resurrection is only implicit, suggested in the speaker's ambiguous attitude toward the immolation: "Tak sladko zret' mne bylo kazn',—tak bol'no!..." ("For me it was so sweet to watch the execution,—so painful!..."). Yet Ivanov subtly alludes to Goethe's butterfly by means of a curious phonetic and syntactic echo: "Metnis'—i vstret'" ("Rush about—and meet!'"). This combination of two short imperatives mimics Goethe's famous formula "Stirb und werde!" ("Die and become!"); the resemblance even extends to the stressed vowels "i" and "e."[24]

The poem "Psyche" concentrates on the "fiery death," playing down the resurrection that Goethe demands. In a footnote, Ivanov locates the poem's source in ancient sculpture.[25] Nevertheless, the reader cannot help but notice the Goethean echoes. That "Psyche" should be understood in terms of "Selige Sehnsucht" is supported indirectly by Ivanov's own comments in his 1912 essay on Goethe. After translating "Blessed Yearning," Ivanov himself draws the parallel between Goethe's poem and the myth of Psyche's immolation in the presence of Eros: "Thus, the living imprints its life by seeking an exit to a new life from the fullness of its vitality; the transition is death; the fire is God; the butterfly is the soul; death is the marriage of man with God. The ancients already depicted Psyche in the form of a butterfly, flying into the flame of a torch held by Eros."[26] In the essay "Anima," Ivanov again emphasizes the close relationship of Goethe's poem to Greek myth: "In its fear of death the soul must fulfill the command 'Die and become': how else could it realize the rebirth, so longingly awaited, that could also be called resurrection? Already in antiquity mystical initiations were considered a way of anticipating death."[27] In both of these passages, Ivanov stresses continuity, according Goethe's poetry the same status as ancient myth.

Ivanov's desire to connect disparate traditions is nowhere so evident as in *Cor Ardens*. In the collection's title, the heart, traditional symbol

---

24. Such use of a double imperative (as an allusion to Goethe) occurs in another poem in *Pilot Stars*. In the fourth stanza of "Sphinx," a long poem in terza rima, Ivanov includes the image of moths flying into a flame. A few stanzas later, the scene is described with a double imperative: "Se zhertva: vstan', pozhri!" ("Behold the victim: arise, consume!"). *SS*, vol. 1, pp. 644–45.

25. "[The image of] Psyche the Butterfly, burned by Eros on the flame of a torch in the presence of Nemesis and Hope, with all three of them compassionately averting their gaze from the sight of the execution—was inspired by ancient statues." *SS*, vol. 1, p. 861.

26. *SS*, vol. 4, p. 140.

27. *SS*, vol. 3, p. 284.

of life, is conjoined with flame, an image suggestive of death and destruction.[28] Characteristically, Ivanov immediately introduces two epigraphs that resonate with these basic motifs, thereby supplementing the Latin title with German and Russian quotations. The first epigraph is the opening quatrain of Goethe's "Blessed Yearning":

> Sagt es Niemand, nur den Weisen,
> Weil die Menge gleich verhöhnet:
> Das Lebend'ge will ich preisen,
> Das nach Flammentod sich sehnet.
>
> Tell no one, only the wise [ones],
> Because the rabble will immediately scoff:
> I want to praise the living
> That yearns for death by flame.

Goethe's words create an atmosphere of mysterious expectation. It is not difficult to recognize that, in this new context, Goethe's lines realize the symbolic potential of Ivanov's title. The symbolic significance of the "heart" ("cor") is spelled out in "the Living" ("das Lebend'ge") while the notion of "burning" ("ardens"), with its suggestion of death, finds expression in the death by flame ("Flammentod"). The second epigraph also echoes the title by drawing on motifs of fire and light: "Ty—moi svet; ya—plamen' tvoi" ("You are my light; I am your flame").

Ivanov does not select these passages purely for their motivic significance. As usual, the sources of the epigraphs are as significant as their direct semantic import. Goethe's verses come from the "West-östlicher Divan" ("West-easterly Divan"), one of the most celebrated masterworks of his late period. In this collection of poems, Goethe sought to combine the symbolism and spirit of Eastern poetry with that of the West. This synthetic principle plays a central role in Ivanov's own undertaking. The second epigraph, which Ivanov attributes to Lidiya Zinov'eva-Annibal (his by then deceased second wife), draws attention to the autobiographical aspect of *Cor Ardens*. In this book, more than any of the previous ones, Ivanov's personal experiences are reflected in his poetry. The theme of death and resurrection, abstract and philosophical in the earlier work, comes to have a very specific referent in the poems composed after Lidiya's death. This is not to suggest, however, that the poetry becomes *primarily* autobiographical. Rather, the personal becomes another manifestation of the mythical.

---

28. For a discussion of Ivanov's sources, see Davidson, p. 198.

To a reader unfamiliar with Ivanov's creative method and theoretical assumptions, such a combination of epigraphs is incomprehensible. In this regard, Robert Stacy's reaction is instructive: "Goethe's lines have depth and public content: we think of a 'Heldenleben' seeking transfiguration, of the phoenix theme, and an 'Empedoclean' death. The words attributed to Ivanov's second wife, however, are somewhat inane. They have merely private content and are akin to much of the actual language of women (or of men, for that matter) in love, in that, to others than the beloved, it is apt to seem nonsensical."[29] Recognizing the myriad differences between the epigraphs, Stacy unambiguously rejects Ivanov's mixture of "public" and "private." Yet precisely this conflation of biographical and literary sources supplies the key to the poetics of *Cor Ardens*.

Already in the book's dedication, biography and poetry are inextricably linked:

> БЕССМЕРТНОМУ СВЕТУ
> ЛИДИИ ДИМИТРИЕВНЫ
> ЗИНОВЬЕВОЙ-АННИБАЛ
>
> Той, что, сгорев на земле моим пламенеющим сердцем
>   Стала из пламени свет в храмине гостя земли.[30]

> TO THE IMMORTAL LIGHT
> OF LIDIYA DIMITRIEVNA
> ZINOV'EVA-ANNIBAL
>
> To her, who, having burned up on the earth in my flaming heart,
>   Became light from flame in the temple of the guest of the earth.

Ivanov phrases his dedication to Lidiya in the easily recognizable form of an elegiac distich. He thus announces its *poetic* nature, consciously integrating the personal with the literary. In this context, the distich's syncretic semantics should be noted. Ivanov conjoins a burning heart ("plameneyushchim serdtsem"—the "cor ardens" of the work's title) with key words from the epigraphs. The "svet" ("light") and "plamen'" ("flame"), taken from Lidiya's epigraph, here refer to Lidiya herself. Ivanov also invokes "Blessed Yearning" through an allusion to fiery death ("sgorev moim plameneyushchim serdtsem"—"having been burned up by my flaming heart"), which in turn leads to a new state of

---

29. Stacy, p. 84.
30. *SS*, vol. 2, p. 225.

"becoming" ("*stala* iz plameni svet"—"*became* light from flame"). The unusual phrase "gost' zemli" ("guest of the earth") makes the connection to Goethe yet more emphatic. While these words do not appear in the Goethe epigraph, they recall the well-known *final* quatrain of "Blessed Yearning."

> Und solang du das nicht hast,
> Dieses: Stirb und werde!
> Bist du nur ein trüber Gast
> Auf der dunklen Erde.
>
> And as long as you do not have
> This: 'Die and become!'
> You are only a sad guest
> On the dark earth.

Goethe's poem concludes with an appeal to the audience in which he relegates the uninitiated to the status of a "sad guest on the dark earth." In his own dedication, Ivanov omits the epithet "sad," presumably because he himself (the referent of "guest") knows well the mystical lesson of "Die and become!" Most of *Cor Ardens* (particularly the fourth book, "Love and Death") concerns this very theme, i.e., Ivanov's personal understanding of the immortality of the soul.

In innumerable ways, Ivanov weaves the paradigm of death and resurrection into the poetry of *Cor Ardens*. A close analysis of a single passage from the sonnet cycle "Spor" ("The Dispute") makes evident how Goethe's "Blessed Yearning" participates in this complex undertaking. "The Dispute" is found in the second section of "Love and Death." In terms of genre, it has its roots in medieval and Renaissance literature. Like most of "Love and Death" it strongly recalls, both formally and thematically, Petrarch's sonnets and canzones on the death of Laura.[31] Yet it also brings to mind the mystery plays of the Middle Ages, in which the characters were allegorical figures. In Ivanov's "dispute," the interlocutors are Man (grieving over the death of his wife) and Death. In German literature, one could find several works of this type, of which Johannes von Tepl's "Der Ackermann aus Böhmen" ("The Farmer from Bohemia") is perhaps the most celebrated example. However, the tradition was widespread and, given Ivanov's idiosyncratic treatment of the genre, it would be futile to seek a specific model.

In "The Dispute," the allegorical Man represents a version of Ivanov himself. "Proof" of this assertion is not merely the highly autobiographical nature of all of the verse in "Love and Death." More

---

31. Cf. Davidson, pp. 192–94.

importantly, the sonnets that comprise "The Dispute" contain several direct quotations from Ivanov's earlier verse. Ivanov conjoins these autobiographical subtexts with literary and biblical allusions, ranging from the veil of Isis (introductory sonnet) to the pale horse of the apocalypse (final sonnet).

For present purposes, the sixth sonnet is of particular interest. The poetic "argument" up to this point can be briefly summarized. The cycle begins with the appearance of Death, who explains to the grieving poet that she (the word "death" is feminine in Russian)[32] represents love. In the second sonnet, the poet disputes this assertion, praising Eros as the true god of love, and contrasting Eros (a force of unification) with Death (a force of separation). Death replies (third sonnet), swearing that she is telling the truth. Eros, she explains, is subservient to her. In the fourth sonnet, she equates herself with passion, which she defines as an essentially divisive force. By referring to specific events, Death convinces the poet that she has accompanied the poet and his beloved from the very beginning. The fifth sonnet belongs to the infuriated poet, who calls Death an envious spy and a thief. If Death had been kind, he explains, she would have taken the lives of the two lovers together:

> И на костре б одном сердца сгорели;
> И две руки единого креста
> В борении одном закостенели.
>
> And [our] hearts would have burned up on a single bonfire;
> And the two arms of a single cross
> Would have hardened in a single battle.

In this final tercet, the poet imagines such a simultaneous death. In the line "And our hearts would have burned up on a single bonfire," one immediately recognizes the ubiquitous image of the burning heart. The next line is a self-quotation; Ivanov repeats the concluding verse of his own poem "Love" ("Lyubov'"). This poem, inspired by Lidiya, had immense significance for Ivanov. He wrote it while she was alive, and returned to it after her death, using it as the so-called "magistral" of a garland of sonnets.[33] The poem itself repeatedly depicts love as a process of unification. It consists of a series of im-

---

32. Because of grammatical gender, a Russian naturally conceives of death as a woman. This of course differs from the German tradition, where death ("der Tod") is invariably portrayed as a man. Cf. Jakobson, pp. 433–34.

33. It first appeared in *Pilot Stars* (*SS*, vol. 1, pp. 610–11). The garland of sonnets is found in the "Love and Death" section of *Cor Ardens* (*SS*, vol. 2, pp. 411–19). For a commentary on its "dialogical" nature, see Venclova, p. 212.

ages in which two things converge into one. The "two arms of a single cross" closes the series, at once invoking death and resurrection. Through self-quotation, Ivanov carries these same associations into the new context of "The Dispute." The imagery of this final tercet relies on the same principle—the poet yearns for a death that makes two into one ("on *one* bonfire," "in *one* battle").

In the sixth stanza, Death responds to the poet's rage:

> Гляди: мой свет — палит.
> Я — пламенник любви. Твоя Психея
> Вперед, святой купели вожделея,
> Порхнула в мой огонь. Он утолит
> Желанье душ, которым Дух велит
> Светить Земле, светясь и пламенея.

> Look: my light burns.
> I am the torch of love. Your Psyche,
> Longing for the holy font,
> Fluttered forward into my fire. It [i.e., my fire] will satisfy
> The desire of souls, whom the Spirit,
> Shining and blazing, orders to illuminate the Earth.

Death's words again invoke the epigraphs to *Cor Ardens*. The insistent repetitions of the words "svet" ("light") and "plamen'" ("flame") recall the epigraph from Lidiya. The image of Psyche fluttering into the fire has its source in the fiery death of Goethe's "Blessed Yearning." Death, in short, identifies Lidiya as the butterfly ("Das Lebend'ge") that seeks immolation ("Flammentod").

Implicit in the Goethe allusion is the dictum "Stirb und werde" ("Die and become"), the notion of death as a passage to new life. A few lines later, Ivanov calls to mind this famous dictum through a double imperative: "Zhelai i zhdi" ("Desire and wait"). In the final tercet of the stanza, these hints become yet more explicit when Death herself suggests the possibility of resurrection:

> Живых мне не дано расторгнуть уз.
> Что́ жить должно, смеется над забвеньем.
> В день третий я — вожатый в Эммаус.

> I am not allowed to dissolve living bonds.
> What should live laughs at oblivion.
> On the third day I am the guide to Emmaus.

In the Bible, the resurrected Christ meets two of his disciples on the road to Emmaus. This passage is of central importance to Ivanov:

among other things it is one of the sources of the "cor ardens" (cf. Luke 24:32).[34] These hints of resurrection receive yet greater subtextual support in the following stanza. Relying on a metaphor derived from Solovyov's aesthetic theory, Ivanov describes the transformation of a "dead coal" ("mertvyi ugol'") into a diamond, symbolically realizing the potential resurrection already alluded to in the previous stanza.[35]

This passage from "The Dispute" must be understood in terms of Ivanov's layering of allusions. The cycle is at once general (the archetypal argument between Man and Death) and extremely personal (as the self-quotations demonstrate, "Man" is an extension of the poet Vyacheslav Ivanov). The theme of resurrection, first suggested through "Blessed Yearning" (in the reference to Psyche and the double imperative that followed it), develops by means of a biblical allusion (the road to Emmaus). The long anticipated rebirth occurs in the next sonnet by means of Solovyovian imagery. Characteristically, Ivanov uses intertextuality as a means of syncretizing writers and thinkers from numerous traditions. Goethe's "Blessed Yearning," as Ivanov himself emphasizes, is based on ancient Greek myth. In "The Dispute," he blends this pagan myth of resurrection with a biblical account of Christ's resurrection. Undisturbed by the incongruities involved in such a synthesis, he relies on a common archetype to unite his sources. This procedure, fundamental to his general poetic system, is directly relevant to the question of Goethe reception. One cannot speak of "Blessed Yearning" as the subtext of "The Dispute," for Ivanov incorporates Goethe's image into a texture already saturated with allusions. Goethe's parable for death leading to another form of life is one of many myths that Ivanov affirms and combines.

---

34. Cf. Davidson, p. 198.
35. The image of coal becoming diamond, originally from Solovyov's "Beauty in Nature" (see Solovyov [1988], vol. 2, pp. 357–58) recurs throughout Ivanov's poetry as the quintessential image of transformation. It can be found in "Almaz" ("The Diamond," *SS*, vol. 1, p. 754) as well as the celebrated "Yazyk" ("Language," *SS*, vol. 3, p. 567).

PART II

IVANOV AND NOVALIS

Preliminary Remarks

In discussing Ivanov's reception of Goethe, I focused primarily on Ivanov's own poetry, using his essays and, to a lesser extent, his letters for purposes of clarification. Given the wealth of material, I chose to exclude Ivanov's translations from consideration. The lengthiest of these, a rendering of the verse drama "Prometheus," displays an extraordinary degree of faithfulness to the semantics and rhythms of the original. However, it reveals little of Ivanov's *creative* interest in Goethe. The specific circumstances in which he undertook this work ensured that even had he wished to, he could not risk departing from the letter of Goethe's text.[1] Ivanov's only other complete and published poetic translation from Goethe appears in the 1943 essay "Thoughts on Poetry," where he quotes the lyric "Dauer in Wechsel" ("Permanence in Change") to illustrate his theory of "forma formans" and "forma formata."[2] As occurs so often, Goethe's verses serve as Ivanov's exemplary text. In the rather specialized context of that essay, the translation deserves attention, but in terms of Ivanov's larger conception of Goethe, it cannot be considered a central document.

In the case of Novalis reception, the situation is quite different. Ivanov's Novalis translations occupy a unique position in his entire oeuvre. Completed in a mere two months during a time of personal crisis, they served as a defining moment in Ivanov's poetic and spiritual development.[3] Ivanov's renderings of Novalis force the reader to broaden his conception of poetic translation. A close comparison of two texts, normally the foundation for critical analysis, is valuable—but insufficient—for grasping the full significance of this work. These translations intersect with numerous planes of Ivanov's creative activity: the semantics and stylistics of both his previous and subsequent poetry, his mystico-philosophical worldview, his theory of

---

1. In August 1929, Ivanov was commissioned to translate "Prometheus" as part of the multivolume Soviet anniversary edition of 1932. Since he had experienced little success in publishing his works in the U.S.S.R. and was leading a somewhat precarious existence in Italy, one can imagine the eagerness with which he accepted the commission. Drafts of a letter of 21 December 1929 that he sent to A. G. Gabrichesky, the editor of the relevant volume, can be found in the Rome archive. They indicate Ivanov's frustration with the Soviet publishing establishment as well as the extent to which Ivanov had to defend the specific lexical and metrical choices he made in his Goethe translation.

2. *SS*, vol. 3, pp. 671–72.

3. Recognizing their importance, the editors of the *Collected Works* place them with the original poetry, rather than in the volume of translations. Cf. their comments in *SS*, vol. 4, p. 724.

poetics and translation (metrical semantics), and even his personal life. Needless to say, these planes are not easily detached from each other. In the chapters that follow, I attempt to keep them separate. However, as Ivanov himself did not distinguish form from content or personal life from spiritual life, a certain degree of overlap is unavoidable.

Chapter 6

Novalis in Russia

> *Новалис* является тем *живым*, что связывает нас с романтизмом.[1]
> —Vyacheslav Ivanov, from the lecture "The Blue Flower" (1909)

Friedrich von Hardenberg (1772–1801), known to posterity by his pseudonym Novalis, is today widely recognized as the central figure of German Romanticism. In poetry, novelistic prose, and philosophy, Novalis contributed seminal texts. So secure is his present reputation that one is apt to forget the lengthy and complicated oscillations that marked his literary fate. To understand Novalis's significance for turn-of-the-century Russian culture, however, it is necessary to reconstruct this larger historical context. A number of seemingly tangential issues become crucial: the circumstances of his life and death, the publication history of his works, and—particularly for our purposes—the details of their reception.

In contrast to Goethe, who achieved international renown early in his career and witnessed its steady growth until his death in 1832, Novalis attracted a large readership only posthumously. Indeed, at the time of his death, the majority of his writings existed only in the form of scattered manuscripts. The first publication of most of the central works was left to Novalis's friend Ludwig Tieck. A poet, not a scholar, Tieck approached his task in a most capricious fashion. Using principles that remain unclear to the present day, he selected a number of Novalis's religious poems and turned them into a "cycle."[2] Since he vehemently objected to the views expressed in Novalis's essay "Die Christenheit oder Europa" ("Christendom or Europe"), he refused to

---

1. "*Novalis* is that *living element* which connects us with Romanticism." SS, vol. 4, p. 740.
2. Novalis clearly intended his "Sacred Songs" ("Geistliche Lieder") to form a cycle. However, he did not indicate precisely which poems were to comprise it and what their order should be. These decisions were apparently made by Tieck, who never explained his methodology (or lack thereof). In fact, the very title "Sacred Songs" may not be Novalis's own. For the complicated history of composition, see Seidel, pp. 11–46.

print it.[3] Tieck inflicted almost irreparable textological damage on the "Fragments," Novalis's most significant philosophical statements. By choosing the ones that appealed to him and rejecting the others, he confused generations of readers.[4]

However, Tieck's most influential decisions concerned less the work than the image of his friend. For the edition of 1815, Tieck added a brief biographical sketch intended to satisfy those inquisitive readers who wished to know more about Novalis's life. A Romantic himself, Tieck knew the expectations of these readers—and did not disappoint them. Indeed, Novalis's short life contained all the elements traditionally associated with a Romantic poet: a handsome, brilliant youth with mystical inclinations; a beautiful and enigmatic beloved; her sudden death from a mysterious illness; the poet's inexpressible grief followed by his own premature and tragic death; posthumous fame. By embellishing these motivic strands, Tieck created a minor masterpiece in a genre one might term "fictionalized memoir."

Tieck prefaced his account by stating that "there are few books in which the author's spirit is reflected so clearly and purely as in his."[5] These words set the tone for the rest of the biography, which seeks to explain how Novalis transformed his tragic personal experiences into magnificent poetry. Tieck's technique consisted in fully exploiting the "romantic" aspects of his subject while playing down (or ignoring) the "prosaic" details. He exaggerates Novalis's love for Sophie von Kühn to the point of absurdity, adding a fateful "love-at-first-sight" motif to their initial encounter.[6] He then attempts to sidestep the peculiar circumstances of this passionate attraction—namely, that Novalis met Sophie (and, several months later, became engaged to her) while she was still twelve years old.[7] Tieck waxes poetic about Novalis's grief over Sophie's death, but glides quickly over the fact

---

3. Tieck defended his decision in a "Foreword to the fifth edition" (1837), reprinted in Novalis (1988), pp. 175–78.

4. Tieck paid no attention to chronology or to context when selecting the "Fragments" for publication. It is largely for this reason that until recently, Novalis's philosophical works were treated as secondary to his poetic works. For the history of reception of the "Fragments," see Hiebel, *Novalis*, pp. 119–21.

5. From "Novalis' Lebensumstände" ("The Circumstances of Novalis's Life"), in Novalis (1977), p. 219.

6. "The first glimpse of this beautiful and wonderfully charming figure decided his entire life . . . " Ibid., p. 221.

7. Apparently recognizing potential problems, Tieck adds a year to her age at the time of their meeting and, by noting that they were engaged more than half a year afterwards, implies that the engagement took place when Sophie was fourteen. Ibid.

that Novalis became engaged a second time, little more than a year later.[8]

From a modern perspective, such details seem trivial and even humorous. However, Tieck's approach to biography was fully in keeping with the Romantic spirit.[9] Historical reception testifies to the fact that his essay possessed an undeniable appeal for general readers *and* scholars, for the Novalis myth that Tieck created was accepted wholesale and lasted well into the twentieth century.[10] It was essentially this image that Vyacheslav Ivanov inherited when he turned to Novalis's works in 1908–9.

In nineteenth-century Russia, Novalis was virtually unknown. Even the Russian Romantics, who eagerly read Goethe, Schiller, and Schelling, tended to overlook Novalis. Exemplary in this regard is Vasily Zhukovsky (1783–1852), considered to be "the father of the 'German' school of Russian poets."[11] Perhaps the finest and most prolific translator from German in the history of Russian literature, Zhukovsky never translated a single line of Novalis.[12] This fact is es-

---

8. Tieck uses a subtle technique in this regard, suggesting that only those truly close to Novalis could understand how this might have happened: "Here he met Julie von Charpentier and it may perhaps seem peculiar to anyone except his intimate friends that he became engaged to her in 1798. As we see from his works, Sophie remained the center of his thoughts." Ibid., p. 223.

9. A passage from a letter of 1810 (i.e., before Tieck's version was written) by the minor poet Justinus Kerner typifies the Romantic approach to biography. Wishing to read Novalis's life as an aesthetic whole, Kerner expressed indignation upon discovering some of its less appealing aspects—as well as satisfaction with certain more appropriate elements: "But it has a strange and disturbing effect if one thinks of Novalis as a civil servant or an assessor of salt-mines. It's horrible!! I had imagined Novalis's life very differently. Also, that young lady Charpentier so disturbs the poesy. But his death is beautiful and much else is beautiful." Cited by Mähl in Novalis (1981), p. 655.

10. Haussmann, p. 403, notes that: "It was mainly due to Tieck that a 'romantische Legende' about Novalis was formed and spread. The poet was considered a gloomy, melancholy mystic, a poetic dreamer, reveling in remote spiritual realms of fancy, a ghost-seer and visionary enthusiast, brooding over his loss, living only for his grief. . . . There is certainly a bit of truth in this characterization of Novalis, but unfortunately this has become the entire truth." It is a tribute to the appeal of Tieck's version that the author of this scholarly essay (written in 1913) still finds it necessary to discredit it.

11. See Zhirmunsky (1937), pp. 97–98. This sobriquet has its source in Ivan Kireevsky's "Survey of Russian Literature for 1829."

12. Zhukovsky did at one point intend to translate of some of Novalis's *prose*. In a letter (presumably from 1817) to Dashkov, he sketched out a plan (never realized) of an entire book of translations from German literature. While the majority of the volume was to be devoted to Schiller and Goethe, the list of prose includes "Novalis:

pecially startling in view of the obscure German Romantic poets (e.g., Johan Peter Hebel and Christoph August Tiedge) whom Zhukovsky *did* find worthy of his efforts. Moreover, Zhukovsky's library seems not to have included any volumes of Novalis.[13] Fyodor Tyutchev (1803–73), another major Russian Romantic poet who was fluent in German, translated Schiller, Goethe and Heine—but again, not Novalis. While it is a commonplace of Russian criticism to speak of Novalis's influence on Tyutchev, there is little evidence to suggest that Tyutchev had even read the verse of his German "counterpart."[14]

Two letters of the poet Wilhelm Kyukhel'beker provide a revealing comparison of the relative stature of Goethe and Novalis in the perception of a Russian Romantic. In 1820, Kyukhel'beker had the opportunity to travel to Germany. During his meeting with Tieck in Dresden, the topic of Novalis came up:

> I visited Tieck this morning; he is extraordinarily entertaining and remarkable for his manner of thinking. To begin with, I mentioned the works of the late Novalis, which Tieck had published, and regretted that Novalis, in spite of his great gifts and unusually fervid imagination, did not try to be clear, and completely drowned in mystical hair-splitting. Tieck calmly and quietly told me that Novalis *was* clear, and did not consider it necessary to corroborate this with any proof . . . [15]

Kyukhel'beker's opinion of Novalis combines respect with thinly-veiled criticism: Novalis was indisputably gifted, yet his mysticism rendered his writings incomprehensible. The complaint that Novalis

---

Der Poet. Erzählung" (Novalis: The Poet. [Short] Story"), followed by a parenthetical "prekrasno" ("beautiful"). However, since this title does not correspond to any of Novalis's works, one must assume that Zhukovsky had read his Novalis in anthologized form. The letter can be found in Alferov, vol. 1, pp. 516–18.

13. See *Biblioteka V. A. Zhukovskogo v Tomske* (Tomsk, 1984), vol. 2, p. 143. Zhukovsky's library was immense and his knowledge of German literature excellent. The absence of Novalis's works is therefore all the more significant.

14. Ivanov himself (*SS*, vol. 2, p. 591) notes the similarity between the poetic worlds of Novalis and Tyutchev. Following Ivanov's lead, the young Zhirmunsky (1915, p. 96) states the connection apodictically: "The 'night' poems of Tyutchev were formed under the influence of Novalis's hymns." I remain unconvinced by such claims, as they are invariably "supported" by broad thematic resemblances (e.g., the "theme of night") common to a multitude of Romantic poets. Toporov is the only scholar to look beyond the critical commonplaces and examine Tyutchev's connections to German literature on the basis of genuine textual echoes. Curiously, as regards Novalis, he avoids the poetry completely, limiting his discussion to a single prose work, *The Apprentices of Sais*. Cf. Toporov, pp. 67–77.

15. In Kyukhel'beker, p. 15.

"did not try to be clear" well illustrates the gulf that separated German Romanticism from its Russian counterpart. Tieck, himself a major representative of the Jena Romantics, becomes in Kyukhel'beker's narration a source of amusement rather than awe.

Shortly afterwards, Kyukhel'beker traveled to Weimar, where he visited Goethe. His account of this meeting differs sharply from the bemused detachment with which he described the encounter with Tieck:

> Yesterday evening we arrived in Weimar,—Weimar, where the greats once lived: Goethe, Schiller, Herder, Wieland; Goethe alone has outlived his friends. I saw the immortal one. . . . Goethe is of medium height, his dark eyes are lively, fiery, full of inspiration. I had imagined him to be a giant even in appearance, but was mistaken. In conversation he speaks slowly: his voice is quiet and pleasant; for a long time I could not imagine that before me was standing the giant Goethe . . .[16]

Kyukhel'beker paints a portrait of Goethe that is less human than mythical. Awed by Goethe's grandeur, he uses the word "giant" twice (a particularly striking epithet for a man "of medium height"). The details of his physical description—eyes that are "fiery" and "full of inspiration"—derive more from clichés than from actual observation. Indeed, Goethe's exact words and opinions are not even reported; they become secondary to his aura.[17]

Throughout Europe, Novalis's posthumous reputation was slow to develop. In most European countries, it was only the advent of the Symbolist movement that brought genuine interest in Novalis.[18] And in Russia, always somewhat behind Western Europe in its cultural enthusiasms, the first serious efforts to bring Novalis to the attention of the reading public date from the beginning of the twentieth century. In 1901, in conjunction with the centenary of the poet's death, the influential journal *Russkaya mysl'* (*Russian Thought*) carried a lengthy essay on Novalis by the scholar P. S. Kogan.[19] The following month the same journal reviewed a Russian translation of Thomas Carlyle's 1829 essay on Novalis. Both these accounts make clear the extent of

---

16. Cited in Durylin, p. 376.
17. Shortly after the meeting, Kyukhel'beker gave this hero worship its fullest expression in a poem he wrote to Goethe. Entitled "To Prometheus" and written in Russian elegiac distichs (with a German interlinear translation for Goethe), Kyukhel'beker sought to put his awe into poetry. The text is given in Durylin, pp. 383–84.
18. Cf. Haussmann, p. 399.
19. Kogan (1901), pp. 102–14.

Novalis's obscurity. Kogan's essay is designed not as an interpretation, but rather as an introduction. It consists of a biographical sketch (loyally reflecting Tieck's distortions), followed by summaries of the "Hymns to the Night" and *Heinrich von Ofterdingen*. The nameless reviewer of Carlyle praises the book for quoting large passages from Novalis's works: "The translations of these excerpts are especially valuable for the Russian reader, unacquainted with the writings of Novalis, since, to our knowledge, nothing has been translated into Russian from the works of the author of the 'Hymns to the Night.'"[20] The reviewer was unaware that two Novalis poems had appeared, poorly translated, in N. V. Gerbel's 1877 anthology of German poetry.[21] Nonetheless, his assumption that most Russian readers knew nothing of Novalis's writings was certainly correct.

In keeping with the European trend, Russian Novalis reception reached its height in the Symbolist period. While Novalis never commanded the readership of other German writers (e.g., Goethe or Nietzsche), the Symbolists mentioned him with some regularity. In 1897, Bryusov had already noted in his diary: "I am reading Weber, Maeterlinck, the Bible, Sumarokov. I [still] need to read: Kant, Novalis, Boileau."[22] In 1904, Bryusov's journal *Vesy (Libra)*, the leading journal of Russian Symbolism, considered Novalis significant enough to note the publication of several new German books on him.[23] The first Symbolist to take a serious interest in Novalis seems to have been Ivan Konevskoi, who undertook translations of the "Hymns to the Night" but died before completing them.[24] Emil Metner, one of Russia's most fanatic Germanophiles, was also an ardent admirer of Novalis. According to Bely, Novalis was one of the names Metner used in his attempt to inculcate impressionistic young Muscovites with the grandeur of German culture: "He fills your ear

---

20. *Russkaya Mysl'*, no. 6 (1901), p. 182.
21. Cf. Engel-Braunschmidt, pp. 107–8, 207–8.
22. Bryusov (1927). Bryusov's interest in Novalis was surely inspired by his readings in Maeterlinck, whose French Novalis translations had appeared a few years earlier. Since the same diary entry contains a host of plans that were never realized, it is doubtful that Bryusov actually read Novalis. His reference nevertheless indicates that the general European Novalis renaissance was beginning to reach Russia.
23. *Vesy*, no. 11 (1904), pp. 79–80.
24. Konevskoi, the pseudonym of Ivan Ivanovich Oreus (1877–1901), was hailed by Bryusov as the most promising young poet of his day, an opinion that Ivanov seems to have shared. See Yampolsky, pp. 80–81. Konevskoi's notebooks (TsGALI, f. 259 op. 1) contain drafts of translations of the first two "Hymns to the Night" as well as the German text (in Konevskoi's hand) of the "Hymn" (in free verse) from the "Geistliche Lieder." His translation of the first "Hymn to the Night" was first published in *Zolotoe pero* (Moscow, 1974).

with Novalis, Hölderlin, Richard Wagner, Simmel and Christiansen."[25] In a letter of 18 May 1905, Metner quotes Novalis's poem "Ich sehe dich in tausend Bildern" ("I see you in a thousand images") in its entirety and proceeds with unqualified praise of the Germans:

> How is this not Bugaev or Blok? Everything that is good in Russia is also [found] in Germany, but one cannot yet say that the opposite is true. The impossible, the eternal, the tender, the dear, the old, the new forever . . . The German Romantics of the end of the eighteenth and beginning of the nineteenth century (the Schlegels, Tieck, the monk Wackenroder, Novalis, etc., etc.) are terribly reminiscent of our "new" [poets]; among them are both Balmont and Bryusov, both Bugaev and Blok: all types. Stefan George (the contemporary German decadent or Romantic), who in poetic craftsmanship rivals Balmont and in mystic depth Bugaev, with good reason considers Novalis the forefather of the most recent poets.[26]

Metner's ideas cannot be considered typical. Nevertheless, a general interest in German Romanticism was characteristic of the Symbolists, as a letter from Sergei Solovyov to Bryusov (of March 10, 1905) demonstrates: "I want to study Schlegel, Tieck, and Novalis. Apparently they are the decadents of the beginning of the nineteenth century, and all the harshness [rezkosti] and effects that so infuriate our ignorant public are not at all new. . . . It seems to me that decadence is, on the one hand, simply the renaissance of Romanticism."[27] Both Metner and Solovyov emphasize the similarities between Romanticism and Symbolism, without, however, suggesting any direct influence. They view the Germans as important precursors of Russian modernism.

For similar reasons, Novalis's works also found an appreciative audience in theosophical circles. Rudolph Steiner, for example, turned to Novalis in his lectures of 26 October 1908 ("Novalis and his 'Hymns to the Night'") and 22 December 1908 ("Novalis the Visionary"). Through people like Anna Rudolfovna Mintslova, word of Steiner's lecures reached Russia without delay. In this instance,

---

25. Bely (1930), p. 343.
26. In *Literaturnoe nasledstvo*, vol. 92, book 3, pp. 223–24. The letter is to A. S. Petrovsky. The line "the impossible, the eternal, the tender, the dear, the old, the new forever..." is a quotation from Bely's "Second Symphony." Bely, 1969, p. 210.
27. GBL, f. 386, k. 103, ed. khr. 23. It must be remembered that at this point in Russia, the terms Symbolism and Decadence were frequently treated as synonyms.

Mintslova appears to have anticipated Steiner; she was already at work on Russian translations of Novalis in 1905.[28]

Of all the Russians, no one took more serious steps to propagandize Novalis than Vyacheslav Ivanov.[29] The first explicit indication of his interest can be found in the 1908 essay "Two Elements in Contemporary Symbolism," where Ivanov lauds Novalis as a Romantic who exemplifies "realistic Symbolism."[30] On 25 June 1909, Ivanov noted in his diary: "In bed at night I am sampling here and there Novalis's verse, which I would like to translate."[31] In the course of the next two months, Ivanov rendered into Russian the complete "Hymns to the Night," the complete "Sacred Songs," almost all of the poetry from the novel *Heinrich von Ofterdingen*, and selections from the miscellaneous verse.[32] In a public lecture on 23 November 1909, Ivanov first brought this work to the attention of a large audience. The lecture notes, which have survived, indicate that Ivanov's central strategy consisted in emphasizing Novalis's relevance for Russian Symbolism. Applying his own Symbolist slogans to the work of this German Romantic, he explained that "Novalis, a true realist, goes 'a realibus ad realiora' . . . "[33]

Contemporary responses indicate that the lecture was greeted enthusiastically. Sergei Auslender, in a two-page summary in "Apollon," concluded with the following unqualified endorsement:

> When Vyacheslav Ivanov read the "Sacred Songs" and
> "Hymns to the Night" in his own translations, which

---

28. In the literary almanac of *Grif*, no. 3 (1905), there appeared an advertisement for future publications that included "Novalis. *Die Lehrlinge zu Sais*. Translation by Mintslova." This book never appeared.

29. Cf. Gronicka (vol. 2, p. 162), who asserts, correctly, that Ivanov was "the first among Russian poets who . . . recognized the true greatness of Novalis in all his many-sided originality and creative power."

30. *SS*, vol. 2, p. 546, and especially p. 549.

31. *SS*, vol. 2, p. 773.

32. The exact number of Novalis poems Ivanov actually translated is unknown. Because of the enormous lag time between composition and publication (more than seventy years), it is quite likely that certain translations were lost. Ivanov's 1909 diary strongly suggests that he had translated Novalis's poetry in its entirety; in an entry from 22 August, he wrote: "I am translating the last poems from 'Misc[ellaneous verses]'" and on 23 August, "Novalis is essentially finished." (*SS*, vol. 2, p. 794). In searching through materials in the Rome archive I located one complete poem ("M. und S.") that was not included in the Complete Works edition, one almost complete draft (of "Das Gedicht"), and one fragment (the opening of "Astralis"). The first two poems are from the miscellaneous verse and the last from *Heinrich von Ofterdingen*.

33. *SS*, vol. 4, p. 741. "A realibus ad realiora" was, of course, one of Ivanov's most celebrated formulas for Russian Symbolism.

> achieve to the highest degree the embodiment of one poet in the mystery of the work of another, it seemed that this strange youth, almost a boy, perhaps not understood by everyone, with his hair covering his forehead, with his tender lips, his pale expression, his friendly and sad glance, was with us again. And the mysterious "Blue Flower" bloomed in these unexpected inspired-improvised words about Novalis, lost for centuries and again discovered, necessary and close to us.[34]

Since this effusive praise was written by one of Ivanov's friends and appeared in a journal closely associated with Ivanov, it must be treated circumspectly.[35] However, similar observations can be found in a more sober, private account of the same event. The passage comes from the diary of S. P. Kablukov, who was at the time the secretary of the Petersburg Religious-Philosophical Society:

> November 23, 1909 in the great hall of Solyany Gorodok (Panteleimovskaya Street, No. 2), V. I. Ivanov read a public lecture on the subject of "The Blue Flower." Novalis and his work ... The hall was full ... During the first half the lecturer spoke rather pallidly; the subject was Romanticism and Novalis's relation to it: "The high priest of Romanticism" and a short biographical sketch of his life. In the second part, much more animated, Vyacheslav gave a short account of Novalis's worldview, calling it idealistic realism and noting its essentially mystical and religious character. The lecturer supported these assertions by reading Novalis's poems in his own translation. Nine of the 'Sacred Songs' were read and many of his 'Hymns of Night' [sic]. The translations were done magnificently ... The hall was full.[36]

This reaction is valuable because it was not intended for publication.[37] Kablukov does not hesitate to criticize aspects of Ivanov's lecture; however, the general impression is positive, and especially the assessment of the translations. Moreover, in repeating the phrase "the hall was full," Kablukov suggests substantial public interest in Novalis.

---

34. Auslender, p. 42.
35. Auslender may even have had access to the text of Ivanov's lecture, since his summary closely resembles the lecture notes. *SS*, vol. 4, pp. 739–41.
36. GPB, f. 322, No. 7, l. 158.
37. Like Auslender, Kablukov was a friend of Ivanov's. He had visited Ivanov during the work on Novalis and expressed interest in the translations. Cf. *SS*, vol. 2, pp. 783–84.

In 1910, a few of these translations were printed in "Apollon," prefaced by a short introduction in which Ivanov made known his intention to publish an entire book *(Novalis's Lyre)*. Although this plan was never realized, it advanced to the point where Andrei Bely composed a paragraph to announce its imminent publication. Bely used the opportunity to stress, like Ivanov before him, the organic link between German Romanticism and Russian Modernism (in both its purely artistic and mystical components):

> The interest in Novalis, as one of the most talented representatives of Romanticism, has a twofold cause: the representatives of Romanticism, still little known in Russia, are linked with the most interesting currents in modern art; contemporary Symbolists are in many respects only a continuation of the Romantics; for this reason Novalis's lyre is close to us; on the other hand, in Novalis's poetry, deeply rooted in the people, one hears motifs common to the most important mystics; at the present time, interest in these mystics has awakened; Novalis combines an enormous poetic talent with a deeply and strongly emphatic intimate religious pathos.[38]

This announcement, dating from May or June, 1910, never appeared in print. While the somewhat hyperbolic tone can be attributed to its function (it was essentially an advertisement), the statement nevertheless appears to reflect Bely's own ideas. In that same year, Bely had written in *Symbolism* that the Romantics were "related by spirit to the Symbolists."[39]

In 1912, a second phase of the Russian reception of Novalis began with the publication of a landmark *History of Western Literature*, edited by F. D. Batyushkov. This work contained a lengthy chapter on Novalis by F. A. Braun, a distinguished Petersburg professor of German literature. Braun had consulted the most recent Western research and produced a carefully balanced account of Novalis's life and work. He viewed Novalis as the central figure of the Jena Romantics and argued for a reappraisal of Romanticism in general. Shortly after, Braun's student, Viktor Zhirmunsky, published his first book, *German Romanticism and Contemporary Mysticism*. Zhirmunsky was certainly aware of the parallels between Romanticism and Russian modernism; in addition to his training as a Germanist, he was well acquainted with Russian Symbolism. He had read Ivanov's essays, attended his lectures, and even sent his own poetry to Ivanov

---

38. RGB, f. 109, k. 12, ed. khr. 29.
39. Bely (1910), p. 457.

for evaluation.⁴⁰ Yet despite its intriguing title, Zhirmunsky's book barely touched on contemporary Russian culture. Its significance lay in its serious and sympathetic account of German Romanticism.

Not surprisingly, the very title *German Romanticism and Contemporary Mysticism* was sufficiently suggestive to galvanize a debate on the literary and spiritual heritage of Russian Symbolism. Numerous critics seized the opportunity to comment on contemporary literature.⁴¹ Dmitri Filosofov, in an article entitled "German Romanticism and Russian Literature," drew impassioned conclusions that went far beyond anything in Zhirmunsky's book:

> And if our contemporary criticism wishes to approach objectively the works of the Russian "Symbolists," such writers as A. Blok, Andrei Bely, not to mention Tyutchev, Sologub, Merezhkovsky, Vyach. Ivanov, and many, many others, then it must understand the link of cultural succession between early German Romanticism and our contemporary Symbolists.... Books like Zhirmunsky's study should wean our criticism away from such a superficial treatment of Symbolism. Criticize it, treat it negatively, but at least know with whom you are dealing; understand that this is not a casual, fashionable "decadentism" [dekadentshchina], but a serious phenomenon that is linked by succession to an enormous cultural movement.⁴²

In 1914, Ivanov again turned his energies to Novalis, delivering another lecture⁴³ and devoting a lengthy critical essay to his life and work. He began this essay by emphasizing the extraordinary change in awareness that had occurred in Russia since his 1909 lecture.

---

40. In a letter of 21 November 1910 (RGB, f. 109, k. 18, ed. khr. 49), Zhirmunsky wrote, "I would like to hear an evaluation of my verses from someone whom I believe and respect as I believe and respect you, having read your essays *By the Stars* and heard your words in the Academy." On 26 March 1910, Zhirmunsky had attended Ivanov's lecture on "The Testaments of Symbolism" and, a week later, participated in a heated discussion about it (with Ivanov himself, Gumilev, Gorodetsky, V. V. Gippius, and other leading Petersburg literati). See Kuznetsova (1990), p. 206.

41. In the course of fifteen months, the book was reviewed eleven times. For a complete list of reviews, see *Materialy k bibliografii uchenykh SSSR: Viktor Maksimovich Zhirmunskii* (Moscow, 1965), pp. 28–29.

42. Filosofov, p. 3. Filosofov's own expertise in the matter is, however, called into question when he complains that "No one in Russia reads Novalis's *Hans Efterdinger*" (sic!).

43. *SS*, vol. 4, p. 728. The lecture was entitled "Novalis, Singer and Magus."

> When, several years ago, before a large audience in Petersburg, I lectured for the first time about the Blue Flower as a mystical symbol and about its great singer, I knew that for the vast majority of my listeners this information was in fact new and spiritually significant. A few had detailed knowledge about the author of "The Disciples of Sais," "Sacred Songs," and *Heinrich von Ofterdingen*, but since their knowledge was based on old historico-literary studies, they necessarily had a narrow and false conception of this poet and thinker. Since then much has changed; the study of Novalis has deepened and broadened, his glory has grown and his inner meaning for contemporaneity is keenly felt. One can say with a feeling of satisfaction that, in understanding and evaluating Novalis, Russian thought was at the avant-garde of the movement, as it has been recently in all questions of high spiritual interests.[44]

In this introduction, Ivanov praises Zhirmunsky and even more so Braun. In other sections of the essay (particularly parts five, six, and seven), Ivanov borrows liberally, particularly in his choice of quotations, from their writings. This factor must be considered, lest one overestimate the extent of Ivanov's own research. For example, it would be unwise to assume that Ivanov had thoroughly studied Novalis's fragments; with rare exceptions, his numerous citations coincide with those found in Braun's study.[45] While the essay contains Ivanov's most detailed account of Novalis, it reflects a later phase (more indebted to scholarly research and less idiosyncratic) of his reception. It does not always correspond to the spirit in which Ivanov had undertaken the translations five years earlier.

At approximately this time—and in spite of the inception of war with Germany[46]—Ivanov's zeal in popularizing Novalis began to extend far beyond Symbolist circles. Nikolai Aseev, a leader of the Futurists, testifies to this in his memoirs:

---

44. Ibid., p. 252.
45. The fact that the German quotations are consistently translated in the identical way strongly suggests that Ivanov was reading Braun, not the original. On the same evidence, it appears that Ivanov's sole quotation from Schlegel's *Lucinde* comes from Zhirmunsky, not from the German original. Cf. *SS*, vol. 4, p. 269, and Zhirmunsky (1914), p. 88.
46. In 1914, presumably after Ivanov's lecture, a Russian translation of *Heinrich von Ofterdingen* appeared. The time was not auspicious for the reception of German literature on Russian soil, but Russian critics generally applauded the novel, seizing the opportunity to contrast the greatness of Germany's past with its morally bankrupt present. Cf. Kogan (1915), pp. 266–67.

> Vyacheslav Ivanov urgently recommended that I read Swedenborg, Jakob Boehme and other mystics, for whom I did not have any particular inclination. But out of respect for him, I carefully went through the endless pages of "Aurora" or diligently studied the rules of marriage for various ranks of angels. Starry-eyed Vyacheslav was enthralled and hoped to make a believing mystic out of me. But I do not regret those boring hours. Thanks to them, I was introduced to the writings of Novalis, that wisest of Romantics and most subtle poet, in whom, if one does not seek only mystical confusion, one can already detect all the petals of the future splendid flower of modern European literature, still closed up in a complicated, faint-smelling, tender bud. Thus Vyacheslav tormented me with the "Flowers of Saint Francis" and his rapture over them. But with his own translation of "The Apprentices of Sais" (not published anywhere, it seems) he compensated [me] for my torture.[47]

Despite their extremely divergent artistic and philosophical outlooks, Ivanov succeeded in convincing Aseev of Novalis's value. It seems probable that, through Aseev, Ivanov's literary tastes and enthusiasms reached lesser-known Futurists. Such a link would provide the most plausible explanation for the interest in this otherwise still obscure German Romantic by members of Aseev's immediate circle. Grigory Petnikov did the first Russian translations of a selection of Novalis's "Fragments" and "The Apprentices at Sais."[48] Sergei Bobrov wrote a number of poems that used epigraphs and imagery from Novalis.[49]

Even after the Revolution, Ivanov continued to proselytize on behalf of Novalis. In 1920, he read from his translations and lectured on Novalis to a circle of young poets and, afterwards, for the more official "Lovers of Russian Literature" ("Lyubiteli russkoi slovesnosti").[50] In Baku, Ivanov taught a seminar on German Romanticism. When he left the Soviet Union in 1924, the Novalis translations and essay were among the relatively few papers he brought with him.

---

47. Aseev. According to Parnis's introduction to the 1992 reprint, the meetings took place in the fall of 1914.

48. His edition of the "Fragments" was published in 1914 in Kharkov (although, for purposes of prestige, the publishers claimed that it was printed in Moscow). "The Apprentices at Sais" appeared in 1920 in the Kharkov journal *Puti Tvorchestva* (nos. 6–7).

49. See especially his 1913 collection "Gardeners above the Vines." In this case it is possible that his interest preceded Aseev's, since Bobrov, before his Futurist incarnation, had been closely affiliated with the Symbolists.

50. This information is from the memoirs of a participant (F. I. Kogan) in the poetry circle. TsGALI, f. 2272, op. 1, ed. khr. 33, 1. 26–27.

In sum, Ivanov's reception of Novalis differed substantially from his reception of Goethe. Ivanov was not the type of writer who avoided mentioning his spiritual precursors, and while numerous documents attest to his early fascination with Goethe, there is no evidence to suggest that he had even read Novalis until 1908. Numerous explicit references in his earliest published essays reveal a personal "canon" of German writers that includes not only Goethe, but also Schiller, Schopenhauer, and Nietzsche. In this context, Novalis's absence is particularly striking. Beginning in 1908, however, Novalis received a privileged place in Ivanov's "proto-Symbolist" pantheon. After that, virtually every statement on the nature and goals of Symbolism included an obligatory reference to Novalis. This association became so strong that, in 1910, Bely characterized Ivanov by saying that "the breath of Novalis's lyrics and of old Romanticism flows out from behind the mask of a scholarly professor of philology."[51]

What was so attractive about Novalis? How did he suddenly emerge from obscurity to become "exemplary" in 1908? There can be little doubt that his mystical worldview appealed to Ivanov, yet this alone cannot explain the timing. Another factor, central to Ivanov's general approach to literary reception, must be considered: biography. It will be remembered that Goethe provided the young Ivanov with a revered model and justification for his own behavior as he courted Lidiya.[52] In 1908, matters were significantly different, but the basic need for a model remained. Lidiya had died in October of 1907 and Ivanov was attempting to come to terms with his fate. In brief (the situation is elaborated in the following chapters), Ivanov discovered in Novalis's biography a mirror of his own recent experiences. And in Novalis's poetry, he found a reflection of his innermost convictions. As in the case of Goethe, the chosen model influenced all aspects of Ivanov's existence, from personal behavior to personal writings, from poetry to aesthetic theory.

When Ivanov turned to Novalis in 1908–9, he essentially "discovered" a poet known to only a handful of Russian readers. Given the dearth of translations and secondary literature, he was in a position to *create* a Russian image of Novalis (in contrast to adjusting a prior image, e.g., his Goethe reception). As the Russian proselytizer of

---

51. Bely (1971), p. 473. Elsewhere Bely unwittingly confuses the work of Ivanov and Novalis. See Wachtel (Lewiston, 1991), p. 37.

52. See chap. 1. It should be emphasized that Ivanov's biographical orientation toward Goethe, while most pronounced in the early period, continued throughout his life. His so-called "conversations" of 1921 with M. S. Al'tman were obviously modeled on Goethe's own conversations with Eckermann; in both cases, a venerable master pronounces his views on a variety of subjects to his amanuensis, who sets them down for the edification of posterity.

Novalis, Ivanov occupied a position similar to that of Tieck a century earlier. Of course, temporal, spatial, and linguistic distances all left their mark. The "Russian Novalis" was a translation in every sense of the word. Yet the result, the most palpable bridge between German Romanticism and Russian Symbolism, is one of Ivanov's greatest poetic achievements. A detailed investigation of this reception reveals the fundamental principles of the Symbolist creative process.

Chapter 7

Ivanov's Translations from Novalis: Stylistic and Semantic Preconceptions

> Русский язык имеет единственную в своем роде привилегию свободной расстановки слов — зачем же отказываться от нее? Прятать драгоценные кубки и пить из оловянных кружек?[1]
> —Vyacheslav Ivanov

When Ivanov commenced work on the Novalis translations, he was already a mature poet and thinker, possessing a carefully articulated poetic system and extremely strong artistic and philosophical convictions. If Ivanov's early Goethe reception (the creative works from the Berlin period) was marked by its derivative nature, then, somewhat paradoxically, his renderings of Novalis's verse stand out for their boldness and originality. A translator ordinarily aims for maximum fidelity to the semantics and formal elements of the original. However, Ivanov consciously approached Novalis with a degree of stylistic and semantic freedom unprecedented in his other translations. In a diary entry of 25 August 1909, Ivanov described the reaction of an acquaintance of his, the minor poet Petr Potemkin: "He was horrified by the freedom of my translations, which indeed often seems unpardonable."[2]

In a review of the second part of *Cor Ardens* (the book that directly followed the Novalis translations), Nikolai Gumilev concisely characterized the peculiarities of Ivanov's poetic style: "Who does not know Vyacheslav Ivanov's style, with its solemn archaisms, sharp enjambements, emphatic alliterations, and an arrangement of words which assiduously obscures the general meaning of the phrase?"[3] In a review of the first part of *Cor Ardens* (which directly preceded the Novalis translations), Gumilev had noted, "It seems that there is not a single very difficult technique that he does not know."[4] Virtually all of Ivanov's contemporaries joined Gumilev in drawing attention to the

---

1. "The Russian language has the unique privilege of free word order—why should one renounce it? [Why should one] hide precious goblets and drink from tin mugs?" As reported by F. I. Kogan, TsGALI, f. 2272, op. 1, ed. khr. 33, l. 21.
2. *SS*, vol. 2, p. 795.
3. Gumilev, p. 297.
4. Ibid., p. 268.

sheer difficulty of Ivanov's verse in general and, more specifically, *Cor Ardens*. D. S. Mirsky called *Cor Ardens* "the high-water mark of the ornate style of Russian poetry."[5]

Novalis's poetry, albeit with the notable exception of the "Hymns to the Night," represents another extreme. To recognize the difference, one need only consider a typical description of Novalis's "Sacred Songs": "In spite of their metrical variety, the style of the 'Songs' is smooth, marked by a simple choice of words and artless rhyme."[6] Efim Etkind accurately describes some of this verse as "intentionally infantile."[7] It is, in fact, difficult to imagine two poets as stylistically opposed as the Novalis of the "Sacred Songs" and the Ivanov of *Cor Ardens*.

In spite of his outspoken admiration for Novalis the lyric poet, Ivanov was fully cognizant of the stylistic gulf that separated them. In the short introduction he wrote for the publication of a few translations in "Apollon," he interrupted a paean to Novalis (as "a colossal event of modern European—or more precisely—Christian culture")[8] to hint at some of Novalis's weaknesses as a craftsman: "Novalis, the creator of songs and ballads, at once simple in spirit and intricately allegorical, romantically fanciful and symbolically exact, *not very demanding and not always stylistically consistent*, but nevertheless musically well-constructed and showing unexpectedly new possibilities of verbal melody..."[9] (my emphasis).

This admittedly veiled criticism is neither thematic nor ideological. It reflects an archaist's confrontation with a foreign, far less ornamental, poetic idiom. It is therefore curious that Ivanov, in his essay of 1914, singles out the uncomplicated "Sacred Songs" (rather than the "Hymns to the Night") as Novalis's greatest poetic achievement. To understand this evaluation, one must recognize extra-textual evidence—historical reception. Ivanov points out that while most of Novalis's work had been consigned to oblivion, the "Sacred Songs" had found their way into church services and therefore survived.[10] The "people" had recognized the songs' greatness. This historical fact completely supports Ivanov's contention (in the theoretical essays, e.g.,

---

5. Mirsky, p. 450.
6. Kurt Grützmacher, "Toward an Understanding of the Works" in Novalis (1977), p. 248.
7. Etkind, p. 161.
8. *SS*, vol. 4, p. 182.
9. Ibid.
10. "The circle of Stefan George, we would add, for the first time appreciated Novalis as one of the greatest representatives of German lyric poetry. Before this, only the 'people' had sensed it, when they included the 'Sacred Songs' in their religious practice." Ibid., pp. 253–54.

"The Poet and the Mob" ["Poet i chern'"]) that the poet must link himself to the the people. (The fact that a complicated style precludes the possibility of widespread acceptance seems not to have troubled Ivanov in regard to his own poetry.)[11]

While Ivanov admired the "Sacred Songs" on a theoretical level, his translations clearly show that he could not accept them as poetry. Their willed simplicity was completely alien to his own poetics. The fundamental alteration that takes place in the translations is mirrored in the very title: the German "Geistliche *Lieder*" ("Sacred *Songs*") become in Russian "Dukhovnye *Stikhi*" ("Sacred *Verses*").[12] Novalis conceived of these religious poems as songs in the most literal sense, and the history of their reception shows that they were indeed sung.[13] In his renderings, Ivanov deliberately transforms simple melodies into weighty statements.[14]

---

11. Cf. Holthusen (1982), p. 22, and West (1970), p. 144. Georgy Chulkov (p. 75), who recognized this problem when writing on Ivanov, solved it in a most ingenious fashion: "This poet, inaccessible to large circles of our intelligentsia, in essence asserts his direct link to the nation and embodies in his lyrics national experiences. Such is the irony of history: until a certain time the people do not recognize their singer, so that at the appropriate time they can recognize him as the mouthpiece of their aspirations."

12. It is curious that Ivanov originally referred to them as "pesni" (songs), but ultimately opted for "stikhi" (verses). Cf. *SS*, vol. 2, p. 776 (the first mention of them in the diaries). "Dukhovnye Stikhi" ("Sacred Verses"), a traditional genre of Russian poetry, intrigued Ivanov throughout his life. In a letter of 25/12 April 1900, he wrote to M. M. Zamyatina, thanking her for an engraving she had sent (RGB, f. 109, k. 9, ed. khr. 33): "That you, my dear friend, by sending me this dear present hit the very nerve of my mood, you will see from the poem I am enclosing with this letter—from the 'sacred verses' I composed in March." This poem was probably the "Stikh o svyatoi gore" ("Verse[s] about the Holy Mountain"), later included in *Pilot Stars* (see the note in *SS*, vol. 1, p. 858). On the other hand, "Dukhovnye pesni" ("Sacred Songs") are also a traditional genre. In any case, Ivanov's decision to translate "Lieder" ("Songs") as "stikhi" is striking. It obviously caught Andrei Bely by surprise. When, in 1910, Bely wrote the announcement for the publication of Ivanov's *Novalis's Lyre*, he twice mentioned that the collection was to include Novalis's "dukhovnye pesni" ("sacred songs"). The word "pesni" ("songs") was later crossed out (in Bely's handwriting) and corrected to read "stikhi" ("verses"). RGB, f. 109, k. 12, ed. khr. 29.

13. Although it remains uncertain whether the title "Geistliche Lieder" was Novalis's own, there is no doubt about their songlike nature. In a letter to Friedrich Schlegel, Novalis refers to them as an "attempt at a new, sacred book of song" ("Probe eines neuen, geistlichen Gesangbuchs"). Novalis (1981), pp. 582–83. Hiebel (p. 255) describes how, within a few years of Novalis's death, some of these songs were incorporated into collections of traditional hymns and sung in churches.

14. In Etkind's fine observation (p. 177): "The style of the translation is not simply different, but opposite. Instead of simplicity—complexity, instead of trans-

The following passage, from Novalis's "Ich weiß nicht, was ich suchen könnte" ("I do not know what I could seek") exemplies these stylistic alterations:

> Hat er sich euch nicht kund gegeben?
> Vergaßt ihr, wer für euch erblich
> Wer uns zu Lieb' aus diesem Leben
> In bittrer Qual verachtet wich?
>
> Habt ihr von ihm denn nichts gelesen,
> Kein armes Wort von ihm gehört?
> Wie himmlisch gut er uns gewesen,
> Und welches Gut er uns beschert?
>
> Но *Он* — ужель вы не постигли,
> Иль вы забыли, кто был Он?
> Кого на крест за нас воздвигли?
> Кто древо нес на Лобный всклон?
>
> Склоняли ль взор ваш к оным книгам,
> Хоть эхо вняли ль вы Словес,
> Под чьим вошли мы легким игом
> В свободу царствия небес?[15]

In certain respects, the translation is faithful. Ivanov retains the meter (iambic tetrameter), the rhyme scheme (alternating feminine and masculine), as well as the interrogative character. Even the straightforward syntax of the original is preserved, although the concluding lines of the translation are admittedly more complicated than the corresponding lines of the original.

The most salient differences are on the lexical level. In Novalis's text, the story of Christ's suffering is told simply, as if by a child. References to the Passion are present, but muted. Ivanov's translation, reveling in the rich Old Church Slavonic lexicon, teems with archaisms

---

parence—darkness, instead of direct meanings of words—a concatenation of figural meanings . . . and, most important, instead of a confidential whisper—declamatory rhetoric."

15. German text: "Did he not announce himself to you? / Did you forget who became pale for you / Who left this life out of love for us / In bitter torture scorned? / Have you read nothing of him / Heard not a single poor word? / How heavenly good he was to us / And what good things he gave to us?" Russian translation: "But He—is it possible that you have not comprehended / Or that you have forgotten who He was? / Whom they raised onto the cross for us / Who bore the tree to Golgotha? // Have you inclined your gaze to those books, / [Have you] perceived even an echo of the Words / Under whose light yoke we entered / Into the freedom of the kingdom of heavens?"

(e.g., "drevo," "vsklon," "onyi"). Not only is "He" (Christ) capitalized (the first time even italicized), but also a number of words related to Him ("Lobnyi," "Sloves"). Novalis's "armes Wort" ("poor word") becomes the imposing and archaic "Slovesa," Words. The biblical references become specific ("Lobnyi" refers to Golgotha in the Russian Bible, the "Lobnoe Mesto," cf. John 19:17, Matthew 27:33, Mark 15:22, and Luke 23:33), and the "legkoe igo" ("light yoke") harks back to Matthew 11:30.[16] The carrying of the cross (referred to metaphorically as "drevo,"—"tree" or "wood") is absent in Novalis's text. Furthermore, in Ivanov's version, the crucifixion precedes the carrying of the cross, producing a hysteron proteron (a complicated trope unthinkable in Novalis's poem).

Ivanov's translation, not merely a random concatenation of archaic words, is structured as carefully as Novalis's original. His method becomes apparent through an examination of the poem's phonological level. In keeping with a poetics of maximum simplicity, Novalis does not concern himself with the poem's sound beyond the necessities of meter and rhyme. The lines "Wie himmlisch *gut er uns* gewesen / Und welches *Gut er uns* beschert?" reveal additional organization of the phonological material. In the context of the adjective "gut" ("good"), the noun "Gut" (ordinarily meaning "possessions") takes on an added connotation of "goodness." One might even go so far as to include "*g*ewesen" and note an alliteration. Such basic sound repetitions are the furthest Novalis goes toward developing the phonological level.[17] Ivanov, in contrast, relies heavily on paronomasia, using the phonological level to underscore the semantics.

The passage centers on Christ, who is never referred to by name, but rather as "He." In Russian versification, pronouns are not ordinarily stressed. Since "He" is of primary importance, Ivanov's task as translator is to see that the pronoun receives sufficient emphasis. For this reason, Ivanov italicizes "On" ("He") the first time it appears.[18] He arranges the word's second occurrence to coincide with the final foot of the line, a position which is always accented in Russian prosody.

---

16. It is a favorite image of Ivanov's, appearing frequently in his poetry and prose, e.g., "Tvorchestvo" ("Creation"), (*SS*, vol. 1, pp. 536–37) or the "Correspondence from Two Corners" (*SS*, vol. 3, p. 387). According to the autobiographical letter (*SS*, vol. 2, p. 12), Ivanov was "captivated" by this biblical passage from the age of seven.

17. For another example of the same phenomenon, see, in the preceding stanza, "Wer uns zu *Lieb*' aus diesem *Leben* . . ."

18. The fact that it is also capitalized is not poetic license. In the Russian tradition, it would simply be heretical *not* to capitalize "He" when it refers to Christ. In Novalis's time, German orthography was extremely free. It is therefore not surprising that he does not capitalize pronouns referring to God.

Hence, the pronoun demands stress both times. This second occurrence, as a rhyme, assures that the syllable "on" will recur in the stanza's final word (in this case "vsklon"—"incline"). This word clearly refers to Golgotha and thus, by metonymy, to "On" ("He," i.e., Christ).

Ivanov's wordplay extends beyond the stanzaic boundary. The following stanza begins with an apostrophe to the "audience" ("Sklonyali l' vzor vash?"—"Have [you] inclined your gaze?"). "Sklonyali," the first word, is grammatically governed by the understood "you" (plural). Yet through paronomasia (as an anagram), it also refers back to "vsklon" and therefore to Christ. Finally, the syllable recurs in the archaic "onyi." While "onyi" ordinarily means "those," the recurring emphatic "on" of the previous stanza creates a new association. "Onyi" here, through phonological association and false etymology, is connected to "On" ("He"); it thereby obtains the meaning "pertaining to Christ." "Onye knigi" are not simply "those books," but also "the books about Christ" (the gospels).

What is the source of this intricate wordplay? It is worth remembering Ivanov's *original* poetry. In *Pilot Stars*, he had used the identical device in a very similar semantic constellation:

Ах! не земля, — дети, вам мать — Голгофа
С *оного* дня, как умер *Он*!
С ним умерла, дети, Земля! *О*, дети![19] (my emphasis)

In his translations, Ivanov brings his own highly rhetorical intonation and archaic lexicon to bear on Novalis's songlike originals. Equally importantly, he draws on the imagery of his own poetry. He often chooses a specific expression or motif not for its fidelity to the German original, but because of its associations within his own corpus. In this way, the translations *forge* numerous intertextual links between Ivanov and Novalis. A few examples suffice to demonstrate the way the introduction of a single word or phrase can make Novalis's poetry sound like a manifesto of Russian Symbolism.

Novalis's "Sacred Songs" conclude with two poems addressed to the Virgin Mary. The first celebrates Mary's power to help and protect her "children." It begins with the words:

---

19. *SS*, vol. 1, p. 551. Ivanov uses the same device in the fifth of the "Hymns to the Night," in the famous and much-disputed passage where Christ gives his "spirit" to a singer from the Orient. In Novalis, "Von ferner Küste, unter Hellas heiterm Himmel geboren, kam ein Sänger nach Palästina und ergab sein ganzes Herz dem Wunderkinde: 'Der Jüngling bist du...'" In Ivanov's version: "I s dal'nikh beregov prishel pevets, / Pod yasnym nebom ellinskim rozhdennyi, / I *ot*roku vsyu dushu *ot*dal *on*. / Ty *on*yi yunosha..." (my emphasis).

> Wer einmal, Mutter, dich erblickt
> Wird vom Verderben nie bestrickt . . .
>
> Whoever has seen you once, Mother
> Will never be stricken by ruin . . .

In rendering these verses into Russian, Ivanov remains true to their semantic import, but exercises certain freedoms in his stylistic and lexical choices:

> О Мать, кто раз Твой лик узрел,
> От пагубы пребудет цел.
>
> Oh, Mother, whoever has looked upon your visage,
> Will be safe from ruin.

Several changes can be noted, but the word "lik" ("visage") is surely the most striking, since it has no correspondence in the German text. Curiously, this word is absent in a draft of the translation, where Ivanov wrote:

> Кто, Мать, Тебя однажды зрел,
> От пагубы пребудет цел.
>
> Whoever has seen you once, Mother,
> Will be safe from ruin.[20]

The existence of this earlier version, which retains the same meter and rhyme syllable, indicates that Ivanov was fully capable of translating the first line without making significant changes. His decision to depart from Novalis's semantics was thus dictated not by linguistic necessity, but by poetic conviction.

The addition of the word "lik" can be explained in terms of cultural translation. "Lik" means "visage," yet it is also the common term for the face of an icon. This strictly religious connotation obtains obvious significance in the context of the Virgin Mary. In this respect, Ivanov's lexical choice appears motivated by a desire to bring the foreign text into a more familiar context. Indeed, his translation of the second of Novalis's poems to Mary lends credence to this hypothesis. In this case, the explicit theme is the pictorial depiction of Mary. Novalis writes: "Ich sehe dich in tausend Bildern, Maria, lieblich ausgedrückt" ("Mary, I see you lovingly depicted in a thou-

---

20. This translation is also closer to the original in terms of intonation. Because it omits the introductory "O," the tone is less odic and more "songlike." The draft is unpublished and can be found in the Rome archive.

sand images"). Ivanov renders the lines: "Tvoi lik napechatlelsya ten'yu, Mariya, v tysyachakh ikon" ("Mary, your visage has imprinted itself as a shadow on thousands of icons").[21] The words "lik" and "ikona" ("icon"), appearing in the same line of text, signal a "religious conversion." Ivanov unambiguously places the German poem in the tradition of Russian Orthodoxy.

One can thus explain Ivanov's departure from the original in terms of his presumed addressee. In his desire to make a German text speak "directly" to a Russian audience, Ivanov adapts the poem to the Russian religious and cultural context. Yet this explanation ignores a crucial factor: the wider context of Ivanov's own poetry. The line "O Mat', kto raz Tvoi lik uzrel" ("Oh, Mother, whoever has looked upon your visage") echoes a passage in the programmatic poem "Krasota" ("Beauty"), where Beauty addresses an unnamed wanderer with the words:

> Кто мой лик узрел,
> Тот навек прозрел —
> Дольний мир навек пред ним иной.[22]

In "Beauty," the word "lik" has no connection to icons, but is semantically equivalent to the modern Russian "litso" ("face"). Purely stylistic considerations determine the lexical choice; in accordance with his larger poetic system, Ivanov selects the archaic word to lend gravity to his utterance. For the same reason, he emphatically repeats the uncommon verb "zret'."[23]

The expression "lik uzret'" is utterly improbable in ordinary Russian usage. The striking similarity between the phrase "kto moi lik uzrel" (from Ivanov's master text "Beauty") and "kto raz tvoi lik uzrel" (Ivanov's "free" translation from the German) can therefore hardly be attributed to chance. Ivanov willfully creates an intertextual connection between his own poetry and Novalis's "song." Once the reader notices this technique of self-quotation, he is in a position to recognize larger parallels between the two poems. Both describe a meeting between a mortal man and a mysterious, "other-worldly" woman. In both the notion of "looking upon a visage" is directly connected to an

---

21. *SS*, vol. 4, p. 214.

22. "He who has looked upon my visage / Has seen eternally— / The world below is eternally different for him."

23. One can find an interesting parallel in Ivanov's critical writings. In an essay on Pushkin's "The Gypsies," he defends Pushkin's use of the archaic verb "rek" ("said"), against Belinsky's well-known criticism (that it provides an unrealistic lexical context for describing a gypsy's language), by emphasizing how the word "prepares the listener for something extremely solemn and holy." *SS*, vol. 4, p. 314.

epiphany. Like the female figure of Ivanov's "Beauty," Novalis's Virgin Mary permanently changes the existence of the man who beholds her. In his translation of Novalis, Ivanov realizes, as it were, the religious possibilities inherent in his depiction of Beauty. According to Ivanov's reading of his own poem, the appearance of Beauty is a "promise of universal transfiguration."[24] The term transfiguration ("preobrazhenie") is borrowed from religious discourse. The inclusion of the Virgin Mary among the hypostases of "Beauty" (i.e., Goethe's "Bride of Corinth," Solovyov's mysterious female figures in "Three Meetings," Demeter from the "Homeric Hymns") thus represents the extension of Symbolist doctrine from the aesthetic and mythical sphere to the overtly Christian. It this context, one can understand Ivanov's contention that Novalis ushers in the knowledge of the final mystery, which "will show the link between Beauty and Religion."[25]

Through the process of transfiguration, the noumenal world ("realiora") becomes evident within the phenomenal ("realia"). In his own writings, Ivanov frequently designates the "realiora" with the term "inoi mir" ("other world") or, at times, "inye miry" ("other worlds"). In the dark poetry of "Love and Death" *(Cor Ardens)*, this "other world" serves as a beacon of hope: "Tesna lyubvi edinoi gran' zemnaya, / I v mir inoi ona rastet iz t'my" ("The earthly border is too constricting for the single love, / And it [i.e., the love] grows from darkness into the other world").[26] Ivanov thus avers that the earth is insufficient for true love, which always strives to transcend it.

The dualism between "this world" and a much desired "other world" is, of course, hardly unique to Ivanov. One can find a similar opposition in the works of Novalis (and the German Romantics in general). However, Ivanov is not satisfied with likeness; in his translations, he often "clarifies" Novalis's points, using a vocabulary so steeped in Russian Symbolism that the reader perceives similarity as identity. The expression "inoi mir" ("other world"), so central to Ivanov's writings, exemplifies this tendency. In the first "Hymn to the Night," for example, Novalis addresses the night as the "Verkündigerin heiliger Welten" ("herald of holy worlds"). Ivanov renders the phrase as "*Inykh* mirov veshchun'ya" ("announcer of *other* worlds").[27] Ivanov's translation remains true to the spirit of the original, since night in Novalis is the time when a higher existence becomes apparent. However, in his inexact word choice, Ivanov removes Novalis's individuality, stressing instead his fundamental closeness to the

---

24. *SS*, vol. 1, p. 827.
25. *SS*, vol. 4, p. 740. From the 1909 lecture on Novalis.
26. *SS*, vol. 2, p. 443. For another example, see Ibid., p. 510.
27. *SS*, vol. 4, p. 184.

Symbolists. The same phenomenon can be found in Ivanov's rendering of a passage from the essay "Die Christenheit oder Europa" ("Christendom or Europe"), where the phrase "Sinn des Unsichtbaren" ("sense of things invisible") becomes the "chuyanie inykh mirov" ("sense of other worlds"). Such a change is particularly instructive in prose, where Ivanov was not constrained by necessities of rhyme and meter.[28]

Ivanov's translation of "Es färbte sich die Wiese grün" ("The meadow became green") presents a more complicated instance of the same technique. In this poem, Novalis personifies spring as a woman and describes her arrival as an epiphanic event. It is easy to recognize the appeal that this poem held for Ivanov. Once again, one finds the familiar thematic constellation of a "meeting" between an otherworldly woman and a man. Small wonder, then, that Ivanov interprets Novalis's poem in terms of his own paradigmatic "Beauty."

The German original contains a refrain in which the astonished speaker expresses the incomprehensibility of the events he observes:

> Ich wußte nicht, wie mir geschah,
> Und wie das wurde, was ich sah.
>
> I did not know what was happening to me,
> And how what I saw was taking place.

Ivanov renders these lines:

> А я не знал ни что со мной,
> Ни почему весь мир иной.
>
> And I knew neither what was happening to me,
> Nor why the whole world was different [literally: "other"].

On first glance, this change appears innocuous enough, since it does not significantly alter the semantic import. Yet the context of Ivanov's poetry and theory gives the Russian refrain an added significance. The phrase "ves' mir inoi" recalls Beauty's words about the wanderer who glimpses her ("dol'nii *mir* navek *pred nim inoi*")—especially in view of the coincidence of vowel sounds in the final three words.

Further confirmation that "Beauty" has supplied the impetus for Ivanov's changes can be found in the personification of spring. Novalis writes, "Ein freundlich Mädchen kam gegangen" ("A friendly young woman came walking [toward me]"). Ivanov renders the line

---

28. *SS*, vol. 4, p. 257. In introducing his translation of this particular passage, Ivanov specifically emphasizes his fidelity to the original. Cf. Ibid., p. 256.

as "Navstrechu deva shla s ulybkoi" ("A young woman walked toward [me] with a smile"). One could argue that with the smile, Ivanov merely concretizes the German adjective "freundlich" ("friendly"). However, in Ivanov's poems and essays, the smile repeatedly signals a moment of mystical initiation. It is an image that Ivanov frequently adds when translating Novalis.[29] In this case, the phrase "s ulybkoi" ("with a smile") again recalls Beauty's words: "Ya sluzhu *s ulybkoi* Adrastee" ("I serve Adrasteia *with a smile*").

Like "Beauty," Novalis's poem describes a scene in which a man confronts a woman who embodies the transfiguration of the earth. This overarching thematic connection allows Ivanov to use his own poem as a "source" for the Novalis translation. "Beauty" again serves as the master text that determines Ivanov's lexical choices. For the Russian reader familiar with Ivanov's poetry but not with Novalis, such intertextual echoes must appear striking indeed. In Ivanov's careful renderings, German Romanticism coincides with Russian Symbolism.

Immediately before undertaking the Novalis translations, Ivanov was at work on "Love and Death," a poetic memorial to his recently deceased wife. This book consists of variations on a single theme: a protagonist who seeks to rejoin his dead beloved. The poems are at once transparently autobiographical and extremely stylized. To express his personal sense of grief, Ivanov includes biographical references (e.g., to the Coliseum in Rome, where he and Lidiya had had a crucial meeting)[30] as well as a number of cryptic phrases whose significance can be understood only in the context of writings not intended for publication (e.g., diaries, letters).[31] Ivanov also includes "personal" literary references in the form of direct quotations and epigraphs from his own and Lidiya's published works. Yet the book is explicitly modeled on Petrarch, whose presence can be felt thematically in epigraphs and generically in the form of sonnets and canzones. In Petrarch, Ivanov appears to have sought (and found) a kindred spirit. Just as Petrarch's grief over the death of Laura becomes a source of

---

29. Cf. *SS*, vol. 4, pp. 205 (several times) and 235.

30. See Davidson, pp. 158–64.

31. A single example will suffice: the Italian phrase "ora e sempre" ("now and always") appears in Ivanov's correspondence with Lidiya as early as 1897 (cf. Ivanov's letter of 13/1 January 1897, f. 109, k. 9, ed. khr. 41). These words, used by Ivanov and Lidiya in the context of love, have a religious association, for they can be found in various Italian prayers (e.g., the "Prayer of Morning" in *Messale dell' Assemblea Cristiana*, Torino, 1973, p. 1491). After Lidiya's death, these words are ubiquitous in Ivanov's diaries and other personal writings, where they signal his mystical communication with his deceased wife. Thus, when this same phrase is integrated into the allusive texture of "Love and Death," (e.g., "The Blue Veil" *SS*, vol. 2, p. 424), the connection of personal and literary become inextricably linked.

poetic inspiration, so Ivanov's profound sense of personal loss becomes the raw material for the poetry of "Love and Death."

Novalis provided a logical extension of Petrarch. According to most biographical accounts, Novalis's fate was inextricably linked to that of his beloved. Her death, which inspired the "Hymns to the Night," was a defining moment in Novalis's existence. In keeping with his profound sense of continuity, Ivanov saw in Novalis a precursor in both biographical and literary terms. He regarded his own fate, and consequently, his own work, as being intimately related to that of his German Romantic counterpart. For this reason, he frequently turned to his own "Love and Death" as a source of imagery when translating the "Hymns to the Night," using his own texts as a gloss on those of Novalis.

In a crucial passage at the end of the first "Hymn to the Night," Novalis describes a visionary moment: "Preis der Weltkönigin, der hohen Verkündigerin heiliger Welten, der Pflegerin seliger Liebe—sie sendet mir dich—zarte Geliebte—liebliche Sonne der Nacht,—nun wach ich—denn ich bin Dein und Mein—du hast die Nacht mir zum Leben verkündet—mich zum Menschen gemacht..." ("Praise to the queen of the world, the high herald of holy worlds, the nurse of blessed love—she sends you to me—tender beloved—dear sun of night,—now I awake—for I am yours and mine—you have brought the night to life for me—[you have] made me a man...").

In these lines, a mystical union of the poet and his beloved takes place. Reversing the traditional relationship of day and night, Novalis relies on a series of unexpected oppositions: he associates the night with sun, waking, and life. Ivanov renders the passage as follows:

> Тебе хвала, владычица вселенной,
> Иных миров вещунья, Ночь-пестунья,
> Блаженств любви Богиня, мне вернула
> Возлюбленная, нежная, тебя;
> Мне солнцем ты полуночным сияешь,
> Я ныне бодрствую: я твой и свой;
> Ты жизнью ночь творишь и в ней меня
> Впервые человеком...[32]

The previously discussed "inye miry" ("other worlds") represents the most obvious, but not the sole, departure from the original. In one of the most celebrated images of the entire cycle, Novalis uses the

---

32. "Praise to you, sovereign of the universe / The announcer of other worlds, Night-mentor, / Goddess of the bliss of love, [who] returned to me / You, tender loved one; / You shine to me like the midnight sun, / Now I am awake: I am yours and mine; / You make night into life and make me in it / A person for the first time."

oxymoronic metaphor "sun of night" ("Sonne der Nacht") to describe his beloved. Ivanov renders this image as "*mid*night sun." Moreover, he puts the phrase into the instrumental case, thereby changing the metaphor into a simile: "Mne solntsem ty polunochnym siyayesh'" ("You shine to me *like* the midnight sun" rather than "you *are* the midnight sun"). The change seems to have little semantic import, yet one wonders what might have motivated it.

The poetry of "Love and Death" supplies the missing link. The concluding sonnet of the cycle "Snows" contains Ivanov's own "hymn to the night":

> Нисходит ночь. Не в звездных письменах
> Ищи звезды. Склонися над могилой:
> Сквозит полношным Солнцем облик милой.³³

Like Novalis's passage, this final tercet is based on a mystical reversal of ordinary nature imagery. Ivanov contrasts the stars in the sky with the star in the grave (i.e., the dead beloved). This "star" shines through like the midnight sun (once again, the instrumental case implies a simile). The striking image of the dead beloved shining like a midnight sun, combined with the overarching common theme of night as the time of supernatural visions, strongly suggests that Ivanov's own "Love and Death" has influenced the translation.

The Russian rendition of the last of the "Hymns to the Night" offers a particularly vivid illustration of the interference between Ivanov's own poetry and his translations. Novalis's poem begins by describing a symbolic boat journey: "Hinunter in der Erde Schoß / Weg aus des Lichtes Reichen" ("Down into the earth's womb / Away from light's realms"). Ivanov reorganizes this basic imagery: "Khochu soiti v mogil'nyi mrak, / I grud' zemli raskryt' ya." ("I want to descend into the grave's darkness, / And open the earth's breast."). The phrase "mogil'nyi mrak" ("grave's darkness") stands out, since it replaces the fecund image of a womb with that of a grave. This alliterative substitution seems to have its source in "Love and Death," where Ivanov uses the identical phrase to describe the whereabouts of his beloved. Moreover, one finds a common intertextual rhyme; in both poems, the phrase "mogil'ny mrak" rhymes with "znak" ("sign").³⁴

---

33. "Night descends. Do not look for the star in the starry letters. Lean over the grave: the face of the beloved shines through like the midnight Sun." *SS*, vol. 2, p. 440.

34. Cf. *SS*, vol. 2, p. 424. "No ne votshche v svinets togo zatvora, / Chto plot' tvoyu unes v mogil'nyi mrak, / Ya vrezal stal'yu nash zavetnyi znak." ("But not in

As the vehicle from one plane of existence to another, the ship is a permanent fixture of Ivanov's symbolic world. Novalis's central image of a ship thus fits neatly into Ivanov's own poetics. Yet Ivanov again seeks identity rather than similarity. In rendering the passage, he turns to the epilogue of his own "Love and Death." This cycle, written in the rare verse form of the "glosa," consists of a four-line motto followed by four ten-line stanzas that expound on the original theme: an apocalyptic boat journey. As in Novalis's hymn, the boat departs from worldly existence and arrives in another world, where the poet is united with his beloved and, ultimately, with God. In both poems, the direction of this mystical journey is at once downward and upward. In Ivanov's rendering of Novalis's second stanza, these general similarities lead to specific intertextual references.

> Gelobt sey uns die ewge Nacht,
> Gelobt der ewge Schlummer.
> Wohl hat der Tag uns warm gemacht,
> Und welk der lange Kummer.
> Die Lust der Fremde ging uns aus,
> Zum Vater wollen wir nach Haus.[35]

> О, Ночь навек, тебе хвала!
> Тебе, дрема глухая!
> Цвела любовь и отцвела,
> Под солнцем иссыхая.
> Гостины стали нам тюрьмой:
> Пойдем к отцу, спешим домой![36]

Ivanov makes several changes when translating this stanza. In the original, the adjectives "warm" and "welk" ("warm" and "withered") refer to humanity. Since "withered" implies a plant, Ivanov supplies an organic metaphor; he compares love to a flower that blooms and wilts beneath the sun ("Tsvela lyubov' i ottsvela / Pod solntsem issykhaya"—"Love bloomed and wilted, / Drying up under the sun."). Novalis writes of having lost interest in the joys of earthly existence. Ivanov renders this more forcefully: earthly existence ("gostiny"—"a guest's stay") becomes a "prison" ("tyur'ma").

---

vain did I cut with steel our secret sign into the lead of the cell that carried your flesh away into the darkness of the grave.")

35. Let us praise the eternal night / Praise the eternal slumber. / The day made us warm, / And the long sorrow [made us] withered. / The joy of a strange place has finished, / We want [to return] to father's house."

36. "O, eternal Night, praise to you! / [And] to you, dull sleep! / Love bloomed and wilted, / Drying up under the sun. / Our stay became a jail for us: / Let us go to father, [let us] hurry home!"

It is particularly interesting that this stanza (the second in Novalis's final "Hymn to the Night") should be intertextually linked to the second stanza of Ivanov's "Boat of Love" (the final poem of "Love and Death"). Like Novalis, Ivanov discusses the inadequacy of "this" world. The stanza begins with the assertion: "Ya znayu: zdes' lyubov'—tsvetok tyur'my" ("I know: here love is a prison's flower").[37] This single line concisely synthesizes *all* the elements in the translation that are absent from Novalis's original (love as a flower, earthly existence as a jail). These two metaphors, which might otherwise simply be understood as "freedoms" of translation, thus have a very specific source. Such subtle intertextual relations indicate the extent to which Ivanov understood Novalis through the prism of his own poetic practice and philosophical convictions.

---

37. *SS*, vol. 2, p. 443.

Chapter 8

Zhiznetvorchestvo: The Conflation of Art and Life

> Переводы из Новалиса производят на всех большое впечатление, но одним они далеки, другим невыразимо близки. "Уж не знаю," говорит Вячеслав Иванов, "конечно, лучше — близки, потому что тут много ясновидения, в этой мистике, просто правда, но опасно потому что из борца можно превратиться просто в тоскующего человека..."[1]
> —F. I. Kogan, "The Poetry Circle under the Supervision of Vyacheslav Ivanov"

In a retrospective examination of the Symbolist movement, erstwhile participant Vladislav Khodasevich summarized what he considered its essence:

> The Symbolists did not want to separate the writer from the person, the literary biography from the personal. Symbolism did not want to be merely an artistic school or literary movement. It constantly attempted to become a method of creative life.... It was a series of attempts, at times truly heroic, to fuse life and art.[2]

In Khodasevich's view, the Symbolists actively sought to merge literature with life. This does not simply mean that the personal experiences of a given poet become the raw material for his works. Rather, it suggests a reciprocal movement between these two usually distinct realms. Just as biography is reflected in the creative works, so the creative works influence the biography.

---

1. "The translations from Novalis make a great impression on everyone, but some find them distant, others [find them] inexpressibly close. 'I just don't know,' Vyacheslav Ivanov says, 'Of course it's better for them to be close, for there is much clairvoyance here, in this mysticism there is simply truth, but it is dangerous because it can turn a fighter into a person who is simply miserable.'" TsGALI, f. 2272, op. 1, ed. khr. 33, 1. 26.

2. Khodasevich (1976), p. 8.

The Symbolists frequently designated their fervently desired ideal with the neologism "zhiznetvorchestvo." This concept, essential for understanding the movement's aspirations, was invoked in spirit if not in name by virtually all the Symbolists. Formed by combining two traditionally distinct words—"life" ("zhizn'") and "[creative] work" ("tvorchestvo")—the resulting term is untranslatable and tantalizingly vague. It suggests both a synthesis of the two constituent elements (creation *and* life) as well as the creation *of* life (that is, divine creation). A further ambiguity concerns the very notion of "life." Does it refer to "life" in general (human existence) or to the individual life of the poet? On the level of Symbolist theory, of course, such fine distinctions were not important, since the poet's life was considered to be a microcosm of human existence. In terms of actual practice, however, the "life" in question tended to be the poet's own, since it provided the most convenient laboratory for experimentation.

Each Symbolist responded to the challenge of "zhiznetvorchestvo" in his own way. For example, the relationship of the poet to the people ("the poet and the rabble," in Pushkin's oft-quoted formulation) was the subject of extensive Symbolist discussion. It would be hard to think of a Symbolist who did not urge the poet to interact, and ultimately merge, with the masses. Aleksandr Dobrolyubov's solution brought this theoretical tenet to its most literal realization. Dobrolyubov left the world of literature altogether, living among religious sects and redirecting his poetic interests to folklore. He wrote letters to many of the Symbolists, urging them to follow his example.[3] However, despite their obvious respect for his actions, the Symbolists were in general unwilling to repudiate their art.[4] Rather than changing themselves in accordance with reality, they chose to change reality in accordance with themselves.

The idea behind "zhiznetvorchestvo" did not arise with the Symbolists. A similar belief can be found in numerous national literatures, particularly during the Romantic period.[5] However, the most direct source for the Russian Symbolists was unquestionably Solovyov. As has been noted, Solovyov viewed aesthetics not as a self-contained sphere, but rather as a force capable of acting on and changing reality. Rejecting traditional ideas of art as reflection in favor of a theory of art as transformation, he came to believe in "theurgic art."[6] It should, however, be emphasized that, according to

---

3. The text of one such letter is given in Azadovsky (1979), pp. 138–39.
4. Cf. *SS*, vol. 2, p. 599, for Ivanov's approving reference to Dobrolyubov.
5. Cf. Tomashevskii, p. 51, Ginzburg, p. 20, Boym, pp. 5–6.
6. Cf. Losev's statement: "Thus art is not a reflection of reality, not a reflection of the ideal, but a real transformation of man and society and, so to speak, a genuine

Solovyov, theurgic art was a goal to be realized by future generations.[7] He neither defined the concept in detail nor suggested how to attain it. It was left to the younger generation of Symbolists to elaborate its theory—and practice.

With few exceptions, the Symbolists wholeheartedly embraced the notion of theurgic art.[8] However, they lacked consensus on the way it could be achieved. This elusive process became the challenge (or, in Khodasevich's words, the "philosopher's stone") of Russian Symbolism. Programmatic statements like "Let the poet create not his books, but his life"[9] (Bryusov) and "Symbolism did not wish to be and could not be 'only art'"[10] (Ivanov) were understood as being not so much theoretical as hortatory, urging the application of Solovyovian theory to quotidian existence.

Ivanov's notion of theurgy differed from that of Solovyov. For Ivanov, theurgy was based less on the artist's transformation of reality than on his ability to discern the noumenal within the phenomenal world. The difference between these two theories of artistic creation (invention versus discovery) is immense. However, in typical fashion, Ivanov accepts both. The first, based on a theory of reflection ("Am farbigen *Abglanz* haben wir das Leben") is central to his reading of Goethe. The second, a theory of transformation, becomes the crux of his Novalis interpretation. In his lecture of 1909, Ivanov speaks of Novalis's "aspiration to transform the world by means of the human spirit . . . "[11] In the essay of 1914, he articulates this more explicitly, using theurgy as the concept that sets Novalis apart from Goethe:

> Goethe called for pure contemplation; Novalis needs to solve the problem of cosmic movement. Goethe limits himself to cognition; for Novalis cognition is an act of universal creation. Poetry for Goethe is contemplation

---

transformation of the one and the other into the ideal." In Solovyov (1988), vol. 1, p. 20.

7. See his conclusion to "The General Meaning of Art," in Solovyov (1988), vol. 2, p. 404.

8. The later Bryusov was of course the significant exception. By 1910, he insisted that theurgy had no direct relevance to poetry. Cf. Bryusov (1975), vol. 6, p. 179, where he polemicizes with Ivanov and Blok. Bely, in turn, attacked Bryusov's essay, stating—with some justification—that it represented a rejection of Bryusov's own artistic program, as articulated in the earlier programmatic essays. Bely's own essay, "Venok ili venets," appeared in *Apollon*, no. 11 (1910).

9. Bryusov (1975), vol. 6, p. 99.

10. *SS*, vol. 2, p. 599.

11. *SS*, vol. 4, p. 741.

independent of will (as Schopenhauer said); for Novalis genuine poetry is theurgy.[12]

Ivanov thus lauds Novalis, all the while recognizing that this philosophy is not consistent with Goethean notions.

Ivanov again takes up the comparison of Goethe and Novalis in a series of highly revealing notes:

> Romanticism is thus . . . the idea of a complete unity of spiritual activity which destroys the borders between its separate spheres: life, poetry, cognition, religion are one. Religion is the highest principle. Symbolism preached the same thing. Andrei Bely; "the mystery," "poetic and prosaic language," Merezhkovsky, Blok. The artist must be a person.
>
> Goethe is different. Poetry out of life, as its ideal reflection. Science and poetry are different spheres. Distance from religion. The self-limitation of the artist.
>
> The Classical: distinguo, divido, circumscribo, coerceo.
> The Romantic: confundo, iungo, solvo, libero.[13]

Ivanov's telegraphic style makes it impossible to interpret this text fully. However, his main idea stands out clearly: Goethe, as a representative of the classical, creates strict boundaries, whereas the Romantics—and the Symbolists after them—seek to annul them.[14] Ivanov's primary example of such a boundary is the distinction between "the artist" and "the person." In short, in their drive to connect life and art, the Symbolists were following an essentially Romantic impulse. One may conclude that when Ivanov himself attempted this synthesis, he was consciously leaving behind the world of Goethean aesthetics.

Discussions of theurgy and "zhiznetvorchestvo" become especially frequent and impassioned in Ivanov's theoretical essays of 1908–1910. In the "Testaments of Symbolism," Ivanov describes the "thesis"

---

12. Ibid., p. 264. The Schopenhauer citation comes from *The World as Will and Idea*, book 2, section 51.

13. Rome archive. From an untitled sheet beginning "Istoriko-literaturnye skhemy i zhivoi opyt" ("Historico-literary schemes and living experience"). The subject matter suggests that these notes were related to Ivanov's work on Novalis, yet Novalis is never explicitly named.

14. When Ivanov speaks of the "classical," he means the literary-historical period called "Klassik" (i.e., Goethe and Schiller after the Sturm-und-Drang period), as Goethe himself used the term and as is usual in German literary criticism to this day.

of Russian Symbolism in terms of theory *and* practice: "Artists were confronted with the problem of completely incarnating in their life as well as in their work (absolutely in the 'agon' of life as in the 'agon' of work!) the worldview of 'mystical realism' or (according to Novalis) the worldview of 'magical idealism.'"[15] In "Two Elements in Contemporary Symbolism," he defines the first condition of mythopoesis as the "agon of the artist himself" ("dushevnyi podvig samogo khudozhnika")."[16]

Ivanov's work on Novalis thus coincides with the height of his fascination with problems of "zhiznetvorchestvo" and theurgy. The years from 1908 to 1909 were for him a time of personal crisis and mystic expectation. Ivanov's detailed diary from this period allows one to reconstruct his concerns (both day-to-day and existential) with unusual thoroughness. The diary serves as a chronicle of the progress made on the Novalis translations, yet it offers far more than such strictly factual information. In many ways the quintessential Symbolist text, it amply illustrates the conflation of life and literature characteristic of the Russian Symbolist movement. In its pages, the realms of real life, the individual psyche, and art become inextricably linked. Details of quotidian reality mix freely with dreams, visions, and personal intrigues.

The overall tone of the diary is bleak. It records a spiritual low point in Ivanov's existence. In the entry of 26 August 1909, Ivanov comments on his own persistent unhappiness: "I am bewildered: is it possible that I—having never been unhappy for a long period of time and irrevocably—am now truly and permanently unhappy?"[17] The immediate source of Ivanov's misery was the death of his wife (Lidiya Dimitrievna Zinov'eva-Annibal) in October, 1907. As the diaries indicate, the intervening time had only deepened the poet's profound sense of loss. The infrequent happy moments recorded in the diaries are connected to Lidiya, who appears to Ivanov in dreams and visions. At times she even makes her own entries in the diary (these are signaled by a change of handwriting). She often speaks Latin, a language that had occult associations for Ivanov.[18]

---

15. *SS*, vol. 2, pp. 598–99.
16. Ibid., p. 558.
17. Ibid., p. 796.
18. Latin was the language in which the world beyond communicated with Ivanov. Such supernatural meetings seem to have been frequent in the period after Lidiya's death. In *Cor Ardens*, the section "Love and Death" (written mainly in 1908) begins with a Latin poem. In an undated letter to Mintslova (RGB, f. 109, k. 10 ed. khr. 20) Ivanov quotes the first stanza of the poem and writes "Dear teacher, here is a Latin poem in medieval style, which I just heard from Her during midnight prayer,

148   Part Two: Ivanov and Novalis

In a variety of ways, Ivanov treats his own personal condition in terms of mythological archetypes, philosophical theories, and even specific literary texts. For example, Ivanov records his own condition in terms of familiar literary works. On 25 June 1909, he writes:

> I would like to mich bergen in jugendlichsten Schleier [hide myself in the youngest veil], perhaps to decipher life im farbigen Abglanz [in the colorful reflection]. Of course, it will seem a reaction, it is "menschlich, allzu menschlich" [human, all-too-human] natural ressentiment?[19]

This passage is a virtual quilt of allusions. In the first sentence, Ivanov combines two quotations (in German) from *Faust II*, scene 1, where Faust ultimately recognizes that the visible world is a reflection of the divine. In the second, he uses two central Nietzschean concepts (one German and one French).

Ivanov's syncretic nature allows him to interpret everyday events as part of a larger, "symbolic" system. Virtually every detail of the diaries could be profitably analyzed from the point of view of Symbolist theory. Knowing, for example, the central role that Beethoven's "Ode to Joy" played in Ivanov's philosophy of art, one cannot be surprised at the effect it produces in the diaries. On 10 August 1909, Ivanov writes, "Kuzmin continues to play the ninth symphony. During the last movement one could feel the closeness and almost the voice of Lidiya."[20] According to Ivanov's theory, already articulated in his 1904 *The Hellenic Religion of the Suffering God*, the final movement of Beethoven's ninth symphony (i.e., the setting of Schiller's "Ode to Joy") recreated for modern times the spirit of the Dionysian dithyramb.[21] For Ivanov, the fundamental significance of the Dionysian myth is that of death and resurrection—death not as an end, but as a means to rebirth. It is logically consistent that Ivanov, upon hearing the modern equivalent of the dithyramb, should "feel

---

when I was speaking with Her . . . " It is curious that Lidiya, during her own life, appears not to have known Latin (cf. the letter from Ivanov to her from 6 January 1897, RGB, f. 109, k. 9, ed. khr. 41, where he translates simple Latin phrases for her). For another example of Ivanov's belief that the world beyond communicated with him in Latin, see "Ein Echo" ("An Echo") *SS*, vol. 3, pp. 646, 648, which describes an incident that, according to the memoirs of Gertsyk (pp. 53–54), must have taken place in the summer of 1908.

19. *SS*, vol. 2, p. 774. Ivanov does *not* translate the German.
20. Ibid., p. 787. Kuzmin was living in "the Tower" at this point. In his diaries, Ivanov frequently notes what Kuzmin was playing (as a rule, the standard German nineteenth-century repertoire).
21. Ivanov, *Ellinskaya religiya*, in *Novyi put'*, no. 2, 1904, p. 62.

Lidiya's closeness and almost her voice." His association is preconditioned by his philosophical convictions.

In the diaries, Ivanov conceives of music less as an abstract form of art (as it was for Schopenhauer and Bely)[22] than as the bearer of specific meaning. On 13 August, he notes that Gluck's "Orpheus" is "inextricably connected to thoughts about one thing, about one person," i.e., about Lidiya.[23] Once again, he interprets music (or, more precisely, the myth on which it is based) as a direct commentary on his own fate. On 26 August, the motif recurs, this time without any reference to Gluck. Ivanov hopes for the "miracle of Orpheus," "the concrete miracle that will bring happiness and restore everything that my dark soul organically desires and naturally demands."[24] Through an allusion to the quintessential poet-theurgist of Greek myth, Ivanov expresses his eagerness to assume the role of the poet who enters the realm of the dead to claim his beloved.[25] This thematic complex links the diaries to the poetry that preceded them. In "Love and Death," Ivanov consistently portrayed a lyric protagonist who sought to overcome the separation caused by the death of his beloved.

The remarkable degree to which the symbolic world of "Love and Death" is carried over into the diaries and translations can be concisely demonstrated through a single image.[26] In the third cycle of canzoni, the protagonist uses the image of an orphan to emphasize his solitariness: "Ya voproshal poludennye volny: / K vam, volny, prikhozhu osirotelyi"—("I asked the midday waves, / 'To you, waves, I come orphaned'") and "Podlunnye tak v polnoch' peli volny / Svoyu tosku dushe osiroteloi"—("So at midnight the sublunar waves sang / Their yearning to an orphaned soul").[27] In the diaries, this image recurs. In the entry of 25 June 1909, Ivanov writes: "My enormous orphanhood is the orphanhood of a warrior alone in the field.... In my soul there is a feeling of enormous orphanhood."[28] In the translations, the word "orphanhood" becomes a synonym for "loneliness." In his version of "Der Sänger geht auf rauhen Pfaden" ("The singer goes along rough paths"), Ivanov renders the phrase "einsam und pfadlos" ("alone and pathless") as "sirym iz sirot" ("[most] orphaned of orphans").[29] In the third "Hymn to the Night," he translates "einsam,

---

22. Cf. Alexandrov, pp. 27–28; Keys, especially pp. 26–35.
23. *SS*, vol. 2, p. 789.
24. Ibid., p. 796.
25. In his essay on Scriabin, an exemplary artist, Ivanov explicitly discusses Orpheus in terms of theurgy. *SS*, vol. 3, p. 176.
26. Cf. Dimitri Ivanov's commentary, *SS*, vol. 4, p. 726.
27. *SS*, vol. 2, pp. 431–32.
28. Ibid., p. 773.
29. *SS*, vol. 4, p. 219.

wie noch kein Einsamer war" ("lonely as no lonely person has ever been") as "I byl odinok, / Kak nikto ne sirotstvoval" ("and was lonely as no one ever was an orphan"). One thus notes a remarkable degree of interpenetration between usually distinct genres. The fact that a word marked by usage in personal and literary writings also appears in translations (with little semantic justification) indicates the degree to which Ivanov understood Novalis's poetry as an extension of his own symbolic world.

The "cor ardens" (or "burning heart") furnishes a more complicated example of an image that crosses personal and literary genres. It serves as the title of Ivanov's lengthiest collection of poetry, and appears repeatedly as the book's central image. Its most obvious intertextual association is biblical (Luke 24:32), where it connotes religious fervor.[30] When he chose the image as the title of his book in 1906, Ivanov seems to have had primarily this meaning in mind. However, in the period after Lidiya's death, the burning heart takes on additional significance. In a diary entry from 15 June 1908, Ivanov records a dream: "I saw Lidiya with giant swan's wings. In her hands she held a burning heart, from which we both partook..."[31] This vision parallels to a remarkable extent a dream recounted by Dante in the *Vita Nuova* (a work that Ivanov greatly admired), in which a burning heart serves as a link between Dante (the poet) and Beatrice (his dead beloved).[32]

The parallel of Dante and Beatrice (joined by a burning heart) fits neatly with the pairing of Ivanov and Lidiya, also joined by a burning heart. Such an interpretation of the diary entry is supported by other writings of this period. In the dedication to *Cor Ardens*, written after Lidiya's death, Ivanov depicts both himself and Lidiya in terms of burning hearts. He speaks of his own "plameneyushchee serdtse" and Lidiya's "ognennoe serdtse," thereby emphasizing the biographical elements of this image.[33]

Additional confirmation of the biographical significance Ivanov attributed to this symbol can be found in extremely obscure extra-literary writings. Among the archival materials at the Russian State Library, there are eighty-three pages of texts written in Ivanov's hand

---

30. The passage concerns the "journey to Emmaus," when, after his resurrection, Christ meets and speaks with two apostles. "And they said to one another: did not our hearts burn within us (in Latin: "nonne cor nostrum ardens erat in nobis?"), when He spoke with us on the way and explained to us the Scriptures?"

31. *SS*, vol. 2, p. 772.

32. For a thorough discussion of this scene (as well as the biblical uses of this image), see Davidson, pp. 195–200.

33. *SS*, vol. 2, p. 225.

(mainly in Latin), and dating from this period.[34] These texts are clearly connected to the automatic writing found in the diaries, often repeating key words and phrases. Like the diaries, they record communication between Ivanov and Lidiya. In the entry from 7 August (the year is either 1908 or 1909), we find the phrase: "ardor cordis signum victoriae nostrae" ("the heart's flame is the sign of our victory"). The phrase "ardor cordis," obviously related to "cor ardens," indicates that a literary symbol has obtained personal significance. It is now a "sign of *our* victory," presumably over death.

The burning heart, ubiquitous in Ivanov's work of this period, gains symbolic weight with each appearance. Particularly instructive is the way this image finds its way into the Novalis translations. Although the image of a burning heart is not found in Novalis, it creeps into Ivanov's translations five times.[35] In the concluding stanzas of the fifth "Hymn to the Night," for example, Novalis writes of the path to eternal life: "Von innrer Glut geweitet / Verklärt sich unser Sinn." ("Broadened by an inner glow / Our sense is transfigured.") These lines, admittedly obscure, would challenge any translator. Yet Ivanov sidesteps the difficulties by substituting his own imagery. He writes "I serdtsa plamen' tlennyi / Gryadushchego zalog." ("And the smoldering flame of the heart / Is the pledge of the future.") In this case, the utmost ingenuity is required to discover any connection between "translation" and original. While Novalis's text might allow for an image of an internal fire ("Von innrer Glut"), there is simply no suggestion of a heart. In Ivanov's "flame of the heart" ("serdtsa plamen'") one immediately recognizes the "cor ardens." Furthermore, Ivanov interprets his own addition, stating that the burning heart is a pledge of the future ("Gryadushchego zalog"). Novalis's poetry is thus subsumed as part of Ivanov's own personal symbolic system. The burning heart, first an image of religious fervor, then a sign of personal victory, now becomes a promise of immortality. These significations are not mutually exclusive, but neither are they identical.

Because Ivanov wrote very little original poetry during the summer of 1909, his diary and Novalis translations functioned as his primary artistic outlets. The interference between these two genres became part of Ivanov's creative method. For example, in the diary entry of 26 June 1909, Ivanov writes: "Ya *ochen'* toskuyu. Ya ne idu, a vlachus' po zemle. Es giebt so bange Zeiten, / Es giebt so trüben

---

34. RGB, f. 109, k. 8, ed. khr. 25. In 1989, I was refused access to these documents. I am therefore extremely indebted to K. M. Azadovsky, who was kind enough to examine them and take notes for me. In 1991, I received access and was able to confirm his readings.

35. SS, vol. 4, pp. 194, 196, 198, 214, 238.

Muth, / Wo alles sich von weiten / Gespenstisch zeigen thut."[36] The German text is a quotation—the opening stanza of one of Novalis's "Sacred Songs." The context indicates that Ivanov uses Novalis's words to depict his own spiritual condition. It is therefore particularly instructive to see what happens to this stanza when Ivanov renders it in Russian. (The translated version does *not* appear in the diary entry.)

> О, немощных мгновений
> Унылая печаль!
> Мир светлых откровений —
> Как призрачная даль.[37]

As usual, Ivanov retains Novalis's meter (iambic trimeter) and rhyme scheme (alternating feminine and masculine). However, he blurs the metrical resemblance by obscuring the rhythm.[38] Novalis's lines regularly alternate a stressed and an unstressed syllable. Ivanov's verses (with the exception of line 3) have only two stresses, separated by three unstressed syllables. The third line, the only one with three stresses is, however, even more distant from Novalis's original, for it begins with a spondee, i.e., a hypermetrical stress.[39] Ivanov's translation contains two hypermetrical stresses (in the first and the final stanzas), which have no corresponding rhythmic shift in the original. While the other rhythmic differences could conceivably be explained through differences inherent in the German and Russian languages (e.g., the frequency of pyrrhic feet in Russian versification, which is preconditioned by the lack of secondary stress in the Russian language), the use of spondees makes clear that Ivanov actively seeks to alter the rhythmic flow of the original.

Yet the differences are not limited to the rhythmic level. Novalis's stanza is intentionally simple—lexically, syntactically, and semantically. It contains three phrases, none of which differs syntactically from ordinary spoken German. Ivanov's rendition bears little resemblance to the spoken language. He uses the opening "O" to suggest

---

36. "I yearn terribly. I don't walk on the earth; I drag myself along it. There are such fearful times, / There is such a sad spirit, / When from afar everything / Shows itself in ghostly fashion." *SS*, vol. 2, p. 775.

37. "Oh, gloomy sadness / Of feeble moments! / The world of light revelations / Is like a ghostly vista." *SS*, vol. 4, p. 207.

38. I use "rhythm" to refer to the specific realization of the more general concept "meter."

39. Such stresses appear in Novalis's poem, but *only* in the penultimate stanza, where they serve a specific semantic function, emphasizing the thematic shift from misery to salvation ("*Géh* zu dem Wunderstamme, / *Gíeb* stiller Sehnsucht Raum / Aus ihm *géht* eine Flamme . . . "). Ivanov reflects this striking rhythmic shift by opening his own penultimate stanza with a spondee ("*Krést vídish'* chudotvornyi?").

the traditional literary "high style."[40] The first two lines give the genitive before the nominative, deliberately complicating Novalis's syntax. A further difficulty arises from the lack of verbs in the translation (there are four in the original). Most importantly, Ivanov alters the semantic level. "Alles" ("everything") is rendered as "mir svetlykh otkrovenii" ("the world of light revelations") and, through a simile that Ivanov introduces, is then compared to a "prizrachnaya dal'" ("ghostly vista"). This last image is freely synthesized from the prepositional phrase "von weiten" ("from afar") and the adverb "gespenstisch" ("ghostly").

Curiously, the words "dal'" ("vista") and "svet" ("light") reappear in the final stanza of the translation, again without any direct correspondence in the original.

>   Ein Engel zieht dich wieder
>   Gerettet auf den Strand,
>   Und schaust voll Freuden nieder
>   In das gelobte Land.[41]

>   Вождь, светом осиянный,
>   Берет тебя на брег!
>   В дали обетованной
>   Ты видишь свой ночлег.[42]

This stanza demonstrates the identical rhythmic freedoms (complete with spondee) that have been noted as characteristic of the first stanza. By comparing the first and last stanzas, it becomes apparent that the spondee serves not merely to complicate the simple flow of the poem's melody, but also is semantically motivated. Like any hypermetrical stress, it slows the reader, thereby drawing extra attention to the words it falls on (in the first stanza "Mir svetlykh" and in the final stanza "Vozhd', svetom"). These two spondees share a common lexeme, the word "svet" ("light"). This word is completely foreign to Novalis's poem. Whereas "dal'" ("vista") is suggested in the original (in the first stanza, at least), there is not even a vague reference to light in Novalis's entire poem.

Yet by repeating the words "light" and "vista," Ivanov brings out the structure that underlies the entire poem. The poem is, after all,

---

40. Ivanov often inserts an "O" when translating moments of exceptional pathos in Novalis's "Hymns to the Night." Cf. *SS*, vol. 4, pp. 183, 194, 195, 196.

41. "An angel brings you again / Saved onto the shore, / And you joyously look downward / Into the promised land."

42. "The Leader, radiant with light, / Brings you to the shore! / In the promised vista / You see your resting place."

composed of two sections. The first part (four stanzas) depicts a situation of hopelessness. The second (the last three stanzas) introduces the figure of Christ as the solution to the misery of the opening. Ivanov's translation converts the "negative" light of the opening (which he likens to a "ghostly vista") into a "positive" light of the last stanza, the light of Christ, which in turn leads to the "promised vista." In this sense (i.e., the link between the first and last stanzas), the translation proves to be as carefully organized as the original.[43]

One can thus account for certain aspects of Ivanov's liberties in translation by recourse to poetic principles. Yet this does not explain the *specific* additions that Ivanov chose to make. In the present case, the larger context of the diary entry considerably enriches a "text-immanent" reading of the poem. After the direct quotation from Novalis (the first, "problem" stanza), the entry appears to switch directions. Ivanov records Lidiya's first visitation from the realm of the dead: "Ee golos: 'Ty dolzhen videt' dali, ty dolzhen volit' Dal'. Ego svet tebya vedet ko mne. Ya tam, gde vidim Ego otrazhennyi lik. On tebya vedet verno ko mne ...'" ("Her voice: 'You must see the vistas, you must will the Vista. His light leads you to me. I am there, where we see His visage reflected. He leads you unfailingly to me ...'")[44]

This visionary moment is by no means a digression. A familiarity with Ivanov's version of Novalis's poem allows one to recognize the connection between this visitation and specific liberties taken in the translation. Most noticeably, the words "svet" ("light") and "dal'" ("vista") appear in the semantic context of salvation. Ivanov's wife distinguishes between "*d*ali" ("*v*istas") and "*D*al'," ("*V*ista") apparently suggesting that the former must be overcome in order to reach the latter. Furthermore, she unambiguously identifies Christ (the capital letter in "Ego"—"His"—makes this obvious) with light, and maintains that it is Christ himself who will bring them together again. Thus, the insistent "svet" ("light") of the translation is explained.

The central role of Christ explains yet another ambiguity in the translation. In the original, Novalis clearly refers to Christ in the fifth stanza ("Wer hat das Kreuz erhoben / Zum Schutz für jedes Herz? / Wer wohnt im Himmel droben, / Und hilft in Angst und Schmerz?").[45] However, in the final stanza, he introduces an angel to bring man to

---

43. It is, however, structured *differently*. In Novalis's poem, the fifth stanza acts as a transition from the "problem" to the "solution." The questions of the fifth stanza are followed by the imperatives of the sixth stanza. Ivanov's version, in which the questions spill over into the sixth stanza and the answer ("Khristos!"—"Christ!") already appears in the fifth stanza, makes no attempt to follow Novalis.

44. *SS*, vol. 2, p. 775.

45. "Who raised the cross / To protect every heart? / Who lives in the heaven above, / And helps in [times of] fear and pain?"

salvation. Ivanov's translation dispenses with the angel. The final stanza begins with the previously discussed spondee "Vozhd', svetom." In the context of Ivanov's translation the word "Vozhd'" ("leader") strongly implies Christ, since there is no other antecedent. Without the benefit of Novalis's original, it is highly unlikely that a reader would interpret the "Vozhd'" as an angel. Furthermore, the word "vozhd'" ("leader") is itself etymologically related to the verbs "vodit'/vesti" ("to lead") and therefore recalls Lidiya's promise that "Ego svet tebya *vedet* ko mne" ("His light *leads* you to me"). These connotations become even more explicit in a passage from the diary entry of the next day. Lidiya "writes": "On tebya vodit vozhatyi.... Morem vedet v dal' obetovannuyu tebya, gde My vmeste budem..." and "On tebya vedet v obetovannuyu dal'."[46] The emphasis on forms of the word "to lead" ("vodit," "vozhatyi," "vedet"), the image of travel by water ("morem" ["by sea"] recalls Novalis's "auf den Strand" ["onto the shore"] and Ivanov's own "na breg"—["to the shore"]), as well as the repeated "obetovannuyu dal'" ("promised vista") make abundantly clear the links between diary and translation.

It is impossible, and ultimately unnecessary, to determine whether the diary entries preceded the translation or vice-versa. What is important is the phenomenon of interference between personal life (diary) and literary life (translation). The diary entries and the poetic translation complement each other.

In a discussion of German Romanticism, Viktor Zhirmunsky notes a similar phenomenon:

> The letters of the Romantic poets bear a remarkable resemblance to their creative works. [This is] not only because their works are characterized by psychological naturalism and not simply because these poets wish their works to be a poetic diary of their experiences, but also because in their letters, experience is already stylized in accordance with a literary model. Life and poetry come together; the poet's life resembles his verses . . .[47]

The dissolution of boundaries between life and work, as Zhirmunsky implies, leads to a conflation of "private" and "public" genres. Letters,

---

46. "He, the leader, leads you. . . . By sea he leads you to the promised vista, where We will be together . . . " and "He leads you to the promised vista."

47. Zhirmunsky (1919), p. 7. Zhirmunsky unabashedly projected his knowledge of Russian Symbolism onto his reading of German Romanticism. When he states in his introduction (p. 7) that "Romantic poetry does not want to be 'only art,'" he consciously paraphrases Ivanov's celebrated slogan (*SS*, vol. 2, p. 599): "Symbolism did not want to be and could not be 'only art.'"

ordinarily intended for a single addressee, are—in the Romantic period—based on the same principles as works intended for publication.

In the case of Vyacheslav Ivanov, the diary (a genre which, strictly speaking, is intended solely for the writer himself) parallels a poetic translation from Novalis. Such a productive interaction between personal and literary can be found in the writings of Novalis himself.[48] Scholars have long noticed the remarkable closeness between the third "Hymn to the Night" and Novalis's diary entry of 13 May 1797.[49] However, in this case, the "interference" is limited to two texts: an original "experience" (the diary), which is then reworked as poetry. In Ivanov's works, the process is significantly more complicated. In the instance examined above, it is impossible to determine which text has "priority" (i.e., which is the "original"). In the example of the "cor ardens," the same image runs through a host of different texts and genres, subtly changing meanings as it goes. Thus, even if the reader can identify the "original" usage, he has by no means comprehended its full significance.

In short, Ivanov not only brings together his own life and work; he also incorporates into this synthesis the life and work of his German Romantic precursor. In Novalis's tragic fate, the Russian Symbolist finds a paradigm of his own experience. Just as Novalis's loss of Sophie prefigures Ivanov's loss of Lidiya, so Novalis's mystical poetry anticipates Ivanov's own. In Ivanov's writings of this period, one can observe how generic and temporal boundaries blur, be they personal and public, art and life, Romantic and Symbolist. All of this work forms a single intricate and heterogeneous—yet fundamentally indivisible—Symbolist text.

---

48. In one of his fragments, Novalis writes: "The true letter is, according to its nature, poetic." Novalis (1981), p. 447.

49. See Grützmacher, in Novalis (1977), pp. 242–43.

Chapter 9

Beyond Translation: Novalis as a Source for Ivanov's Poetry

> Am Ende ist alle Poësie Übersetzung.[1]
> —Novalis, letter to A. W. Schlegel of 30 November 1797

In his renderings of Novalis, Ivanov creates a German Romantic in his own image. The original texts, often serving as a convenient point of departure, intersect with Ivanov's poetics as well as his personal experience. The result is less a translation than a conflation of German Romanticism and Russian Symbolism. Although Ivanov completed this work in the brief interval of two months, his fascination with Novalis's verse continued to grow. The translations, fully integrated into Ivanov's poetic and spiritual world, would in turn become the raw material for "new" poems. In other words, the same German lyric can inspire two poetic responses: a "translation" and an "original" poem. A distich of Novalis provides a brief example of this phenomenon:

> Einem gelang es—er hob den Schleyer der Göttin zu Sais—
> Aber was sah er? Er sah—Wunder des Wunders—sich selbst.

> One [man] succeeded—he raised the veil of the goddess at Sais—
> But what did he see? He saw—wonder of wonders—himself.

The myth of Isis, the veiled Egyptian goddess whose secrets are hidden from man, was well-known in the German literary tradition before Novalis. In Schiller's "Das verschleierte Bild zu Sais" ("The Veiled Image at Sais"), a zealous youth who thirsts for knowledge is punished for his attempt to look at the mysterious goddess. Novalis, in this distich as well as in the fragmentary novel *Die Lehrlinge zu Sais (The Apprentices at Sais)* reworks and reevaluates Schiller's version of this myth. In the distich, the hero raises the veil and—rather than falling senseless upon confronting divine secrets—sees himself. In the context of Novalis's writings, such self-discovery represents a crucial step toward understanding the universe.[2] Novalis thus attacks the implicit

---

1. "Ultimately all poetry is translation."
2. See, for example, his poem "Kenne dich selbst" ("Know thyself").

"moral" of Schiller's poem—that man should not attempt to know the divine.

There can be no doubt that Ivanov was aware of the polemical background to Novalis's distich. On 29 August 1909, less than a week after completing the Novalis translations, Ivanov noted in his diary, "I wrote a poem about Death, an ironic poem, which I want to dedicate 'To The Reader' of the book 'Love and Death' ... "[3] In this poem, which eventually served as the introduction to the sonnet sequence "Spor" ("The Dispute"), Schiller's version of the Isis myth serves as the target for Ivanov's irony.

> Таит покров пощады тайну Божью:
> Убил бы алчных утоленный голод.
> Безумит постиженье ...[4]

> A cover of mercy hides God's secret:
> Sated hunger would kill those who crave.
> Understanding makes insane ...

The situation described in these opening verses closely parallels Schiller's poem. Ivanov appears to accept the notion of a necessary barrier (veil) that separates mankind from the truth. However, the poem continues with the words: "Pust' zhe molod / Zabven'em budet vetkhii mir—i lozh'yu!" ("Let the old world be young by oblivion—and falsehood!"). In these lines, Ivanov's rhetorical strategy becomes evident: rather than advocating oblivion and falsehood, he simply voices a view with which he disagrees. His poem is thus "ironic" in the most straightforward sense of the word.

Perhaps because he was so completely in agreement with Novalis's distich, Ivanov's translation is remarkably faithful to the original:

> Был в Саисе смельчак: покрывало скрытой богини
> Поднял ... Что ж он узрел? Диво! Себя самого.[5]

> In Sais there was a daring one: the veil of the hidden goddess
> He raised ... What did he see? Wonder!—Himself.

Ivanov retains the distinctive metrical form as well as the question/answer intonation. His changes fall into two categories: semantic

---

3. *SS*, vol. 2, p. 797. This is a rare case in which the precise date and circumstances of composition are known. On 23 August 1909, Ivanov had written: "Novalis is essentially finished." *SS*, vol. 2, p. 794.
4. Ibid., p. 401.
5. *SS*, vol. 4, p. 250.

clarification and stylistic embellishment. The former simply give necessary information to the Russian reader unfamiliar with the German tradition of Sais poems. For example, Ivanov calls the hero ("he" in Novalis's version) a "smel'chak" ("daring person") and adds the implicit adjective "skrytoi" ("hidden") to his description of the goddess. Other changes reflect a greater degree of interpretative freedom. Thus, the ordinary German verb "sah" ("saw") is rendered not by the standard Russian "uvidel" but by the more archaic "uzrel." As will be recalled, this verb has visionary associations in Ivanov's own poetic usage.[6] Moreover, by placing the crucial verb "raised" at the end of the phrase, Ivanov subtly alters the syntax: "pokryvalo skrytoi bogini / Podnyal" (literally: "the veil of the hidden goddess / [He] raised"). This syntactic difference coincides with the most noticeable change: the addition of an enjambement.[7] This enjambement, in conjunction with the syntactical inversion, serves to emphasize the word "podnyal." Since the raising of the veil is traditionally associated with death, Ivanov thus heightens the dramatic effect of the original.

Ivanov's creative interest in the Sais myth does not end with his translation. After finishing work on Novalis, Ivanov returned to his own poetry, writing the fifth and final book of *Cor Ardens*. In a group of fifteen distichs, the following verses appear under the title "Isis":

> Мнил ученик покрывало поднять сокровенной богини.
> В тайную целлу проник: роза в пустынной цвела.[8]

---

6. Cf. "Beauty": "Kto moi lik uzrel / Tot navek prozrel / Dol'nii mir navek pred nim inoi." ("He who has looked upon my visage / Has seen eternally— / The world below is eternally different for him.") This poem's "plot" bears an unmistakable resemblance to Novalis's distich. Once again, Ivanov appears to have recourse to "Beauty" while translating Novalis. For yet another example with striking semantic and lexical parallels to Novalis's distich ("strannik," "zret'," "pokryvalo"—"pilgrim," "to see," "veil"), see Ivanov's translation of "Wenn ich ihn nur habe" ("If only I have Him"), especially the second and fourth stanzas. *SS*, vol. 4, p. 203.

7. Ivanov frequently adds enjambements to Novalis's verses. This occurs in several of the "Sacred Songs," which— in the originals— very rarely use enjambement. In this respect it is instructive to compare the draft with the final version of Ivanov's translation of the second "Hymn to the Night." The opening line "Muß immer der Morgen wiederkommen?" ("Must the morning always return?") is first rendered by Ivanov as "Vechno l' budet utro vozvrashchat'sya?" ("Will morning eternally return?") and, in the final version, as "Vechno l' budet, v mig svoi obychainyi, / Den' svetat'?" ("Will eternally, at its usual moment, / Day shine?"). It is apparent that, for Ivanov, the enjambement is a conscious and preferable alternative. *SS*, vol. 4, pp. 185, 729.

8. *SS*, vol. 2, p. 501.

> An apprentice thought to raise the veil of the secret goddess.
> He penetrated into the mysterious shrine: a rose bloomed
> in the solitude.⁹

The connection of these verses to those previously discussed is immediately recognizable. Ivanov retains the metrical form (a distich) and repeats numerous words ("pokryvalo," "podnyat'," "boginya"—"veil," "to raise," "goddess"). The title refers to the Egyptian goddess traditionally associated with the mystery cults of Sais, and the phrase "sokrovennoi bogini" ("secret goddess") clearly recalls the "skrytoi bogini" ("hidden goddess") of Ivanov's translation. The "uchenik" ("apprentice") appears neither in the original nor the translation, yet its obvious source is Novalis's unfinished novel, *The Apprentices at Sais*. The unusual word "tsella," borrowed from Latin, refers to a part of a pagan temple. Since it is phonologically equivalent (and etymologically related) to the German "Zelle" ("Cell") it also points to the German tradition. Yet Ivanov's concluding phrase—the image of the rose—radically departs from the previously discussed distichs.

It should be remembered that Novalis treats two different versions of the Isis myth. In the first (the distich), the protagonist discovers himself behind the goddess' veil. In the second (as related in the second chapter of *The Apprentices at Sais*), the myth is related as a fairytale in which the hero Hyazinth leaves his beloved Rosenblütchen to search for the goddess. When he finally reaches the goddess and raises her veil, he rediscovers his beloved. In Ivanov's image of a rose in the process of blooming ("roza v pustynnoi tsvela"), one finds a concrete realization of the name "Rosenblütchen" (literally: "rose blossom").¹⁰ In this subtle way, understandable only to those acquainted with Novalis, Ivanov recalls another version of the Isis myth: the removal of the veil leading to love. In short, Novalis offers a paradigm for the appearance of a rose in the Sais myth. Ivanov's own "Isis" thus conflates Novalis's two versions, taking the concise form from the distich while borrowing the concluding image from the unfinished novel.

Ivanov's poem clearly draws on Novalis's polemic with Schiller, yet it ultimately forms part of a larger context. "Isis" appears in a book of poetry entitled "Rosarium," in a section called "Anthology of the Rose." As these titles suggest, the book reveals Ivanov's fascination with rose symbolism. The term "rosarium" refers not only to a wreath

---

9. I understand the word "pustynnoi" ("empty") as an adjective modifying "tsella" ("shrine"). In the translation, I take the liberty of rendering this adjective as a noun ("solitude") in order to make the English coherent.

10. Ivanov paraphrases the fairytale in his essay on Novalis, where he calls Rosenblütchen "alaya roza" ("the red rose") or, at times, "roza" ("the rose"). *SS*, vol. 4, pp. 272–73.

of roses, but also to the rosary. These Roman Catholic devotions, begun in the Middle Ages, consist of the recitation of a series of prayers (usually either 50 or 150) to the Virgin Mary. The symbol of the rose, however, goes back to antiquity. In his footnotes to the book, Ivanov quotes at length from A. N. Veselovsky's "From the Poetics of the Rose." This brief essay uses literature of antiquity, Christian legend, folklore, etc., to trace the development of rose symbolism. For Ivanov, always a syncretic thinker, the rose offered the opportunity of unifying numerous traditions and significations. To assign a single meaning to the rose goes against Ivanov's whole enterprise.[11] It also runs contrary to his theory of a multivalent symbol: "If a symbol is a hieroglyph, then it is a mysterious hieroglyph, since it has many meanings and can be understood many ways."[12] Ivanov summarizes his own approach in the metapoetic "Rosa Centrifolia," where he writes "I sang the rose in a hundred keys."[13] For Novalis, the rose may symbolize love, but Ivanov combines it with many other notions: death, suffering, sacrifice, knowledge, salvation. In Veselovsky's formulation, "The rose blooms for us more fully than for an [ancient] Greek. It is not only the flower of love and death, but also of suffering and mystical revelations."[14]

Although "Rosarium" postdates the Novalis translations by almost a year, the symbol of the rose was clearly in Ivanov's mind throughout. Careful comparison reveals that the rose has a way of slipping into the translations without any correspondence in Novalis's originals.[15] Equally important, the rose possessed personal (extraliterary) associations for Ivanov. It often appears in the diaries, always linked to Lidiya. Ivanov describes one of his graveside visits as follows: "It

11. In his poetry seminar in 1920, Ivanov criticized Balmont on precisely these grounds: "[He] took from the rose only one side— love." From F. Kogan's memoirs, TsGALI, f. 2272, op. 1, ed. khr. 33, l. 30.
12. *SS*, vol. 2, p. 537.
13. "Ya rozu pel na sto ladov." *SS*, vol. 2, p. 487.
14. Veselovsky, p. 133.
15. See, for example, the translation of "Der Sänger geht auf rauhen Pfaden" (from *Ofterdingen*), where the lines "Er sinkt im Grase nieder / Und schläft mit nassen Wangen ein" ("He sinks down into the grass / And sleeps with moist cheeks") are rendered "V trave gustoi ustalyi dremlet / I *rozy blednye* lanit / Eshche vlazhny" ("In the thick grass the tired one dozes / And the pale roses of his cheeks / Are still moist"). *SS*, vol. 4, p. 220. Here one should also note the typical addition of an enjambement. Another striking example can be found in the "Hymns to the Night" (Ibid., p. 192): Ivanov renders "Einsam entfaltete das himmlische Herz sich zu einem Blüthenkelch allmächtger Liebe" ("The heavenly heart grew into a flower-cup of all-powerful love") as "Nebesnoe v uedinen'e serdtse / Goryashchei rozy venchik raskryvalo" ("In solitude, the heavenly heart revealed a corolla of a burning rose"). This passage is also interesting because it suggests a burning heart ("cor ardens").

seemed to me that she was saying that my present [i.e., a rose] was a delight, that there should be roses on her grave, because her gift to me was like the Rose."[16] At another point, Lidiya says to him, "Two roses, you and I."[17] In the ubiquitous symbol of the rose, one finds yet another example of the way Ivanov's biography, poetry, and translations intersect. Thus, Ivanov's distich "Isis" points back to Novalis and simultaneously outward, toward a vast number of literary and personal significations.[18]

Ivanov's treatment of Novalis's "Liebeszähren, Liebesflammen" ("Tears of Love, Flames of Love") offers a "tour-de-force" of intertextual relations. As in the case of Novalis's "Isis" distich, Ivanov first translates the poem, then develops the material further and more freely in an original poem written in the same metrical form. However, in this case, the poem is much longer and less easily isolated from the corpus of Novalis's writings.

> Liebeszähren, Liebesflammen
> Fließt zusammen;
> Heiligt diese Wunderstätten,
> Wo der Himmel mir erschienen,
> Schwärmt um diesen Baum wie Bienen
> In unzähligen Gebeten.
>
> Er hat froh sie aufgenommen
> Als sie kommen,
> Sie geschüzt vor Ungewittern;
> Sie wird einst in ihrem Garten
> Ihn begießen und ihn warten,
> Wunder thun mit seinen Splittern.
>
> Auch der Felsen ist gesunken
> Freudentrunken
> Zu der selgen Mutter Füßen.
> Ist die Andacht auch in Steinen
> Sollte da der Mensch nicht weinen
> Und sein Blut für sie vergießen?

---

16. *SS*, vol. 2, p. 786.

17. Ibid., p. 777. This line is strikingly reminiscent of a Cretan love poem ("You are a rose and I am a rose") that Veselovsky cites in his essay (p. 133) and that Ivanov uses as an epigraph for his "Rose of Union" (*SS*, vol. 2, p. 453).

18. Among these it is worth emphasizing an image in a crucial poem of the cycle "Man" (written in 1914) that is surely derived from the distich "Isis": "Tvoi posev v glukhoi krovi, / Bog lyubvi, / Rozy vyrastil v pustyne!" ("God of love, / Your sowing in mute blood, / Grew roses in the wilderness!"). *SS*, vol. 3, p. 211.

Die Bedrängten müssen ziehen
Und hier knieen,
Alle werden hier genesen.
Keiner wird fortan noch klagen
Alle werden fröhlich sagen:
Einst sind wir betrübt gewesen.

Ernste Mauern werden stehen
Auf den Höhen.
In den Thälern wird man rufen
Wenn die schwersten Zeiten kommen,
Keinem sey das Herz beklommen,
Nur hinan zu jenen Stufen.

Gottes Mutter und Geliebte
Der Betrübte
Wandelt nun verklärt von hinnen.
Ewge Güte, ewge Milde,
O! ich weiß du bist Mathilde
Und das Ziel von meinen Sinnen.

Ohne mein verwegnes Fragen
Wirst mir sagen,
Wenn ich zu dir soll gelangen.
Gern will ich in tausend Weisen
Noch der Erde Wunder preisen,
Bis du kommst mich zu umfangen.

Alte Wunder, künftige Zeiten
Seltsamkeiten,
Weichet nie aus meinem Herzen.
Unvergeßlich sey die Stelle,
Wo des Lichtes heilge Quelle
Weggespült den Traum der Schmerzen.[19]

Tears of love, flames of love,
Flow together;
Sanctify these places of miracles,
Where heaven showed itself to me,
Swarm around this tree like bees
In innumerous prayers.

He happily accepted them
As they came,
Protected them from storms;
She will at some point in her garden

---

19. Novalis (1981), pp. 371–72.

Water it and wait for it,
Make miracles with its splinters.

Even the rock has come down
Full of joy
To the feet of the blessed Mother.
When there is reverence even in stones,
Should man not cry
And shed his blood for her?

The sufferers must come
And kneel here,
All will recover here.
No one will complain any longer
All will say joyously:
Once we were sad.

Earnest walls will stand
On the heights.
In the valleys men will cry out
When the most difficult times come,
No one should be faint of heart,
Only onwards to those steps.

God's Mother and Beloved
The sad one
Now wanders from here transfigured.
Eternal goodness, eternal indulgence,
O! I know you are named Mathilde
And [you are] the goal of my senses.

Without my asking boldly
You will tell me,
When I will reach you.
Gladly will I in a thousand ways
Still praise the earth's miracles,
Until you come to encompass me.

Old miracles, future times
Strange things,
Never escape from my heart.
Let this place be unforgettable,
Where the holy source of light
Washed away the dream of woes.

"Liebeszähren, Liebesflammen" comes from "The Fulfillment" (the second part of the novel *Heinrich von Ofterdingen*), where it is carefully woven into the surrounding narrative fabric. The poem, sung by Heinrich himself, marks a turning point in the novel. After a period of suffering and even despair, Heinrich has just had a visionary experience. His poem, a hymn to the place where this epiphany occurred, includes a number of physical details from the preceding scene. Thus, at the beginning of the scene, Novalis writes of Heinrich, "As he was thinking to himself, the tree began to shake. The rock resounded dully..." In the poem, these details are reflected in the tree of the first two stanzas and the rock of the third. The scene's climax occurs when a ray of light penetrates through the branches of the tree, granting Heinrich a vision, presumably of life after death. This "holy ray" ("heiliger Strahl") is referred to in the poem's final stanza ("des Lichtes heilge Quelle"—"the light's holy source"). The name Mathilde (stanza six) also has meaning only in the larger context of the novel; she is Heinrich's beloved. A familiarity with the prose context thus makes the poem far less mysterious than it is when read in isolation, as in Ivanov's translation:[20]

Песнь пилигрима[21]

Liebeszähren, Liebesflammen,
Fließt zusammen.

Вас любви пролили грозы,
Перлы Розы!
Оросите, слезы, долы,
Где раскрылось небо взорам!
Пламя-слезы! рейте хором
Окрест Древа, Божьи пчелы!

Примет Он, гостеприимный,
Эти гимны,
Этих слез родник нагорный!
Пересадит это Древо
В тихий рай Святая Дева,
Ствол взлелеет чудотворный!

Вот утес лежит обрушен:
Он, послушен
Грозовым Осаннам, никнет.
Служит Ей, молясь, и камень...

---

20. It should be noted that Ivanov was not the first to treat the poems independently of the novel. Such practice was common in German editions of the period.

21. The title, "The Pilgrim's Song," not in Novalis's text, is nonetheless traditional. Because the last two stanzas of this translation were inadvertently omitted from the Brussels edition (cf. *SS*, vol. 4, p. 234), and because the Soviet version (in Ivanov [1976], pp. 419–21) is corrupt, I base my version on the poem's first publication (in "Apollon," no. 7, 1910), modernizing the orthography.

Человека ль этот пламень
Жизнь отдать Ей не подвигнет?

В путь, о сонм обремененных!
Здесь склоненных
Осенит вас мир целенья.
Здесь умолкнут ваши пени;
Словно сонной грезы тени,
Вы воспомните томленья.

Долам крепкое подспорье —
То нагорье
Увенчают стен твердыни.
В злую слышат вас годину:
Доступ есть с горы в долину;
Вам — ступени до святыни.

Богоматерь! Молчаливо,
Терпеливо
Твоего я жду призыва.
Медлишь ты меня избавить —
Дива мира буду славить
Твоего дождуся Дива.

Давних дней и дней грядущих
В этих кущах
Буду помнить озаренья.
Это место незабвенно,
Где забил в душе мгновенно
Ключ целебного прозренья.

The Pilgrim's Song

> Liebeszähren, Liebesflammen,
> Fließt zusammen!

Storms of love shed you,
Pearls of the Rose!
Tears, moisten the vales
Where heaven opened to [my] glances!
Flame-tears! Hover in a choir
Around the Tree, God's bees!

He, hospitable, will accept
These hymns,
The mountain spring of these tears!
The Holy Virgin will transplant this Tree
Into quiet paradise,
[She] will tend its miracle-working trunk!

> There lies the fallen cliff:
> It bows down, obedient
> To the storm's hosannas:
> The stone, praying, also serves Her:
> Does that flame not move man
> To give up his life to Her?
>
> O host of burdened ones, be on your way!
> Here the peace of healing
> Will shade you who are bent down.
> Here your reproaches will become silent;
> Like reveries of a dreamy shadow
> You will remember [your] trials.
>
> A strong support for the vales
> Fortresses of walls will crown
> This hilltop.
> In an evil time they hear you:
> There is access from the mountain to the valley;
> For you there are steps to the sacred place.
>
> Mother of God! Silently,
> Patiently
> I await your summons.
> If you are slow to save me—
> I will praise the wonders of the world,
> As I await your Wonder.
>
> I will remember the illuminations
> Of days of yore and future days
> Amidst this foliage.
> This place is unforgettable,
> Where the spring of healing vision
> Suddenly began to flow in my soul.

Ivanov gives a characteristically free translation of the German text. Most of the stylistic preconceptions that mark Ivanov's general approach to Novalis can also be found here. For example, the last two lines of the third stanza demonstrate a conscious effort to complicate the syntax ("Cheloveka l' etot plamen' / Zhizn' otdat' Ei ne podvignet?").[22] Ivanov uses another technique for slowing down the flow of Novalis's lines at the end of the first stanza (" ... nebo vzoram! / Plamya-slezy! reite khorom / Okrest Dreva, Bozh'i pchely"). The constant correspondence between word boundary and metric foot

---

22. "Does that flame not move man to give up his life to Her?" It is not possible to reproduce the syntax and still produce a grammatical sentence in English.

(i.e., every word is a trochee and the meter is trochaic) creates an insistent rhythmic pulse without any pyrrhic feet. Ivanov thereby gives additional weight to each individual word.

One aspect of the translation deserves special emphasis. Ivanov's frequent use of capital letters turns the poem into an explicitly religious statement. Novalis's original contains religious elements (the "blessed Mother," the oblique reference to the cross in the second stanza), but it combines them with a strongly personal dimension ("God's Mother *and* beloved," "Mathilde") that disappear in the translation. (Ivanov solves the problem of Mathilde by omitting the entire sixth stanza.) In the emphatically religious context that Ivanov creates, the adjective "nagornyi" ("mountain"), appearing twice without a corresponding word in the original (cf. stanzas two and five), takes on a special connotation. In Russian, the word recalls Christ's "Sermon on the Mount" ("nagornaya propoved'") and thus adds a specifically religious nuance to the general theme of revelation.[23]

The translation is remarkable for its semantic liberties, particularly in the first two stanzas. In the opening lines, Ivanov introduces three wholly unexpected images—the storm, the pearl and the Rose. The storm of love, a traditional metaphor, can frequently be found in Ivanov's own writings.[24] The pearl combines two notions: rain (from the storm) and tears (of love, "Liebeszähren"). In Russian poetry, the word "pearl" can be a synonym for dew or rain (Tyutchev's "Spring Storm" ["Vesennyaya groza"], to name a single example). Furthermore, it is not unusual for tears to be equated with pearls.[25] These two connotations, both of which are clearly present in Ivanov's poem, have only a tangential relation to Novalis. The Rose is yet more mysterious. The fact that it is capitalized suggests that it refers to the Virgin Mary. (It should be recalled that the rosary is performed using a string of beads *or* pearls.)[26] However, there is no rea-

---

23. "Nagornyi" is one of the words that Ivanov often adds when translating Novalis. Cf. the "Hymns to the Night." *SS*, vol. 4, pp. 186, 189.

24. Cf. "Love" ("Lyubov'"): "We are two trunks set aflame by a thunderstorm" ("My dva grozoi zazhzhennye stvola"). *SS*, vol. 2, p. 411. In the "Autobiographical Letter," he compares his love for Lidiya to a storm. "The meeting with her was like a powerful spring, Dionysian thunderstorm . . . " Ibid., p. 20.

25. See, for example, Ivanov's own "Under the Birch" ("Pod berezoi"): "And she called the little grave a casket, and the touching tears a round pearl." ("I lartsom nazyvala malyi grobik, / Skatnym zhemchugom—umil'nye slezy.") *SS*, vol. 2, p. 318. Cf. Taranovsky (1976, p. 165): "The comparison of tears with pearls is a commonplace in poetry in general (in Russian poetry it goes back to Lermontov's 'sleza— zhemchuzhina stradan'ya'— 'the tear is the little pearl of suffering')."

26. See "Rosenkranz" in *Die Religion in Geschichte und Gegenwart* (Tübingen, 1961). Decades later, in a poem in which he discusses his conversion to Roman

son to restrict the signification of the Rose. Its presence indicates that the poem is mystical, concerned with religious and metaphysical truths. In this context it is worth noting that Ivanov transforms Novalis's simile ("wie Bienen"—"like bees") into a metaphor ("Bozh'i pchely"—"God's bees"). The image of God's bees swarming around a holy tree ("Drevo," an archaic and religiously colored rendering of Novalis's neutral "Baum") recalls Dante's depiction in *Paradiso* of angels as bees flying around a heavenly rose.[27] Ivanov calls to mind an analogy between Dante and Novalis, thereby continuing a long critical tradition.[28]

Another new and significant motivic constellation can be found in the first stanza: the combination of the rose and the cross. In his essay on Novalis, Ivanov writes: "It was his fate... to plan the first steps of a mystical awareness, that... forces one to believe that, if only at individual, special moments, the mystical Rose will light up on the Cross of the Earth."[29] The combination of rose and cross is absent from Novalis's poem (the rose, as has been noted, is Ivanov's addition).[30] Yet the link between the tree and the cross is certainly present (in the second stanza, "Make miracles with its splinters"). In his translation of the "Sacred Songs," Ivanov had used "drevo" ("tree" or "wood") as a metaphor for the cross.[31] In Ivanov's version of "Liebeszähren, Liebesflammen," the concluding lines of the second stanza ("Peresadit eto *Drevo...Stvol* vzleleet *chudotvornyi*"—"[She] will transplant that *Tree...* [she] will cherish its *miracle-working trunk*") recall another passage from the "Sacred Songs" that unambiguously describes a cross: "*Krest* uvidish' *chudotvornyi* / Skhvatis' za etot *stvol*" ("When you see the *miracle-working cross* / Take hold of its *trunk*").[32]

Catholicism, Ivanov writes of the "rose-beads of tender 'Ave Marias'" ("Nezhnykh Ave rozy-chetki"), *SS*, vol. 3, p. 591.

27. It is a recurring image in Ivanov's "Rosarium" (cf. *SS*, vol. 2, pp. 453, 454, 461) as well as in his diaries. "And you will look joyously at the world, because roses spring forth from its wounds, and bees fly out from its decay..." *SS*, vol. 2, p. 807.

28. In his own essay, Ivanov explicitly compares Novalis and Dante. *SS*, vol. 4, p. 278. This comparison probably has its origin in Tieck's sentimental biography of Novalis. Cf. Novalis (1977), p. 228. Ivanov had certainly come across it in Braun, pp. 298–99.

29. *SS*, vol. 4, p. 265.

30. *After* Heinrich sings his song, a girl appears: she "stepped under the tree, looked up with an inexpressible smile and shook from her apron many roses onto the grass." However, the link between rose and cross in this passage is tenuous at best. If this connection is in fact present, Ivanov was the first (and, apparently, the only) person ever to notice it.

31. Cf. "Kto drevo nes na Lobnyi vsklon"—"Who bore the 'tree' to Golgotha" *SS*, vol. 4, p. 208.

32. Ibid., p. 207.

170 Part Two: Ivanov and Novalis

However, one need not rely on such intertextual associations to identify the tree with the cross. Ivanov's archaisms serve a poetic function: the preposition "okrest" (literally meaning "around," but containing the word "cross") brings out the connection, for the phrase "Okrest Dreva" contains both elements. The fact that the rose ("Roza") and the cross ("Drevo") appear in parallel position in the same stanza is more than a coincidence. Ivanov consciously introduces a mystical theme common to Russian Symbolism but absent from Novalis's poetry.[33]

These remarks, by no means exhaustive, suffice to prepare the reader for the next step of Ivanov's creative process, "Vesti" ("Tidings"). Since this poem appeared in *Tender Mystery*, one may assume that it was written during the summer of 1912, i.e., three years after the Novalis translations and two years after "Rosarium."[34] As a whole, *Tender Mystery* consists of extremely optimistic poetry, much of it reflecting the recent turn of events in Ivanov's personal life. After years of grieving over Lidiya's death, Ivanov had entered into a new relationship with his stepdaughter, Vera Konstantinovna Shvarsalon. In the summer of 1912, she gave birth to their son. These joyous events appear to have influenced the thematics of Ivanov's verse; the new collection praises the continuity of life. The influence extended even to the stylistic level; after the semantic and syntactic complexity of *Cor Ardens*, the poetry of *Tender Mystery* is striking for its relative simplicity.

Despite such differences, the new collection has numerous links to its predecessor. The title poem "Tender Mystery" concludes with the lines:

> Тайна, о братья, нежна: знаменуйте же Тайное Розой,
> Тихой улыбкой могил, милой печатью любви.[35]

> The mystery, o brothers, is tender: call the Mysterious a Rose,
> [Call it] the quiet smile of graves, the dear stamp of love.

These verses have their origin in a distich of "Rosarium," which they repeat almost verbatim:

---

33. One of the central symbolic constellations of *Cor Ardens* and *Tender Mystery* is the rose and cross. Cf. *SS*, vol. 2, pp. 469, 493, 494, 533 (the final image of the entire book) and *SS*, vol. 3, pp. 18, 839. It appears prominently in the work of other major Symbolists, e.g., Blok's drama "The Rose and the Cross." For more on Ivanov's connection to Rosicrucianism, see Wachtel (1990), pp. 124–26. For Bely's interest in Rosicrucianism, see Szilard.

34. For the chronology, see the commentary in *SS*, vol. 3, pp. 694, 696.

35. Ibid., p. 30.

Sub Rosa

Тайна, о братья, нежна: знаменуйте же тайное — розой,
Нежной печатью любви, милой улыбкой могил.³⁶

The mystery, o brothers, is tender: call the mysterious a rose,
[Call it] the tender stamp of love, the dear smile of graves.

In both poems, the "tender mystery" concerns the relationship between love ("lyubov'") and death ("mogila"—"the grave"). As this instance of self-quotation indicates, the "secret" (the Latin phrase "sub rosa"— literally "under the rose"—means "in secret") so central to the poetry of *Cor Ardens* also informs *Tender Mystery*. In fact, the basic images found in this distich (the mystery, the rose, the smile, the grave, etc.) recur in numerous poems of the later collection, including "Tidings." This same fundamental theme, of course, links *Cor Ardens* and *Tender Mystery* to Novalis. Ivanov himself emphasizes the significance of Novalis's "link to the mystery of love and death."³⁷ Moreover, he suggestively refers to Novalis's "blue flower," that most traditional emblem of German Romanticism, as a "mysterious and tender symbol."³⁸

The poem "Vesti" illustrates the extent to which Ivanov's "new" poetry (*Tender Mystery*) draws directly on his earlier work.

ВЕСТИ

> Liebeszähren, Liebesflammen,
> Fließt zusammen!
> Novalis.

Ветерок дохнет со взморья
   Из загорья;
Птица райская окликнет
Вертоград мой вестью звонкой. —
И душа, как стебель тонкий
Под росинкой скатной, никнет . . .

Никнет, с тихою хвалою,
   К аналою
Той могилы, середь луга . . .

---

36. *SS*, vol. 2, p. 504. This last phrase ("miloi ulybkoi mogil"— "the dear smile of graves") is a paraphrase of Novalis's words about Sophie von Kühn's grave ("moya milaya mogila"— "my dear grave"— as cited by Ivanov, *SS*, vol. 4, p. 269). For more on this phrase, see my discussion of Ivanov's "Mogila" ("The Grave") at the conclusion of this chapter.

37. *SS*, vol. 4, p. 271.

38. Ibid., p. 264. The passage comes from the essay on Novalis, which postdates *Tender Mystery*.

Луг — что ладан. Из светлицы
Милой матери-черницы
Улыбается подруга.

Сердце знает все приметы;
   Все приветы
Угадает — днесь и вечно;
Внемлет ласкам колыбельным,
И с биеньем запредельным
Долу бьется в лад беспечно.

Как с тобой мы неразлучны;
   Как созвучны
Эти сны на чуткой лире
С той свирелью за горами;
Как меняемся дарами, —
Не поверят в пленном мире!

Не расскажешь песню струнной:
   Облак лушый
Как просвечен тайной нежной?
Как незримое светило
Алым сном озолотило
Горной розы венчик снежный?[39]

TIDINGS

> Liebeszähren, Liebesflammen,
> Fließt zusammen!
>   Novalis.

A breeze blows from the seaside,
From behind the mountains;
A heavenly bird hails
My garden with a resonant tiding.
And [my] soul, like a thin stem
Under a pendulous dewdrop, bows down ...

Bows down, with silent praise,
Toward the lectern
Of that grave amid the meadow ...
The meadow is like incense. From the front room
Of the dear mother-nun
[My] friend smiles.

The heart knows all the signs;
[It] divines all greetings
Today and forever;

---

39. *SS*, vol. 3, pp. 32–33.

It perceives the caresses of the cradle,
And with an other-worldly pulse
It beats without concern in harmony to the vale.

How you and I are inseparable;
How harmonious
Are these dreams on a sensitive lyre
With that reed pipe beyond the mountains;
How we exchange gifts,—
They will not believe it in the captive world!

Will you tell by the song of your stringed [instrument]:
How the moon's cloud
Is illuminated by a tender mystery?
How an invisible heavenly body
Has gilded with a red dream
The snowy corolla of a mountain rose?

The revelation of Novalis's "Pilgrim's Song" concerned the relationship of love and death. "Tidings," through its epigraph of "Liebeszähren, Liebesflammen," immediately recalls this context. Not surprisingly, it uses the same distinctive meter and rhyme scheme as Novalis's poem. The Russian word "vesti" ("tidings") clearly recalls the "blagaya vest'," the "good news" of Christ. This Christian element stands out in the lexicon of the first two stanzas ("raiskaya," "analoi," "ladan," "chernitsa"—"heavenly," "church lectern," "incense," "nun"). However, the specific biblical references that characterized Ivanov's translation are absent.

Most of the allusions to "Liebeszähren, Liebesflammen" refer not directly to Novalis, but rather to Ivanov's own Novalis translation. For example, Ivanov had introduced the phrase "v tikhii rai" ("into quiet paradise") in the second stanza of Novalis's poem. In "Tidings" both adjective and noun recur, albeit in different contexts. Similarly, the verb "niknet" ("bows down," a loose rendering of Novalis's "ist gesunken" in stanza three) appears prominently in the new poem (as both the last word of the first stanza and the first word of the second). Here the connotation of reverence is retained. In his translation, Ivanov had introduced the phrase "Gde zabil v dushe" ("where began to flow [literally: 'to beat'] in the soul") in the last stanza, without any corresponding image in the original. In "Tidings," both the "dusha" ("soul") and the notion of beating ("bien'e" and "b'etsya" in stanza three) are developed. Most noticeably, the symbol of the rose reappears, this time as the poem's final image.

Closer examination reveals other, more subtle connections. On the phonological level, the poem's opening rhyme ("vzmor'ya"/"zagor'ya") echoes the first rhyme of the translation's fifth stanza ("podspor'e"/"nagor'e"). The use of internal rhymes (cf. "slezy"/"slezy" in the first stanza of the translation) can also be found in "Vesti" (where "znaet"/"ugadaet" in stanza three recalls "ulybaetsya" of the last line of the second stanza). On the semantic level, the new poem develops images that were introduced in the translation. The phrase "pod rosinkoi skatnoi" ("under a pendulous dewdrop") is incomprehensible without reference to Ivanov's translation. The dewdrop is modified by "skatnoi" (here: "pendulous") because it is substituting for the pearl that Ivanov added to Novalis's poem. ("Skatnyi" is a word specifically used in reference to pearls.)[40] However, a process of miniaturization has occurred. The pearls ("Perly-Rozy"—"Rose-pearls") become a single dewdrop ("pod rosinkoi skatnoi"—"under a pendulous dewdrop"). Similarly, the tree trunk ("stvol") shrinks into a flower stem ("stebel'").

The new poem also contains elements that come neither from Novalis's poem nor from Ivanov's translation, but rather from Ivanov's own poetics. The harmony of the lyre and the reed pipe (stanza four) refers to the reconciliation of Apollo and Dionysus.[41] The "smile" (stanza two), familiar from Ivanov's essays and original poems, signifies the meeting of the divine and the earthly. In this context, Ivanov's rendering of one of the "Sacred Songs" adds an additional intertextual dimension:

> Если здесь Его не встречу,
> Я улыбкой не отвечу
> Всем улыбкам дольних дней.
> Нет о Нем под солнцем вести:
> С Ним я умер.[42]

> If I do not meet Him here,
> I will not answer with a smile
> To all of the smiles of days in the vale [i.e., on earth].
> If there are no tidings of Him under the sun,
> Then I have died with Him.

---

40. Ivanov himself uses the phrase "zhemchug skatnyi" in "Rosarium" (*SS*, vol. 2, p. 461), in a poem that shares many of the central images of "Tidings."

41. Ivanov discusses this reconciliation in *The Hellenic Religion of the Suffering God*. "In Delphi the two gods celebrate their reconciliation. . . . They exchange attributes. . . . Dionysis plays on the lyre, while Apollo (the 'flutist') draws a double-flute to his lips." Ivanov, *Ellinskaya religiya*, in *Voprosy zhizni*, no. 7, 1905, p. 129.

42. *SS*, vol. 4, p. 205.

In Novalis's original, neither the smile nor the notion of "vesti" ("tidings") appears.[43] One must conclude that this lexical combination had a particular attraction to Ivanov.

The poem's basic theme is the reconciliation of opposites. Whether the Dionysian pipe is paired with the Apollonian lyre, light with dark (subtly signaled by the rhyme pair "*svet*litsy/*chern*itsy"),[44] heart with soul, or death with life (paronomasically present in the combination of "mo*gil*a" and "*lug*"—"grave" and "meadow"), Ivanov creates a picture of the utmost harmony. This spirit of synthesis is nowhere so clear as in the poem's closing lines:

> Не расскажешь...
> Как незримое светило
> Алым сном озолотило
> Горной розы венчик снежный?

> Will you not tell . . .
> How an invisible heavenly body
> Has gilded with a red dream
> The snowy corolla of a mountain rose?

Ivanov combines an unusual mixture of colors (red, gold, snow-white) with the distinctive image of a mountain rose. These lines are reminiscent of "Saturnia Regna," a distich in "Rosarium":

> Будет времен полнота и Сатурново царство настанет,
> Братья, когда расцветут алые розы в снегах.[45]

> There will be a fullness of time and Saturn's reign will dawn,
> Brothers, when red roses bloom in the snow.

They also recall a Novalis distich, "Alpenrose" (Ivanov did not translate it, but one may safely assume that he knew it):

> Selten haftet auf Höhn ein Funken himmlischen Lebens,
> Aber, als Königin, blüht, dann auch die Rose des Bergs.

---

43. Ibid., p. 205. The translation (of "Weinen muß ich, immer weinen"—"I must cry, always cry") is, even by Ivanov's standards, unusually free. Novalis writes, "Nirgend kann ich hier auf Erden / Jemals wieder glücklich werden, / Alles ist ein düstrer Traum / Ich bin auch mit ihm verschieden / Läg ich doch mit ihm in Frieden . . ." ("Never can I again on this earth / Become happy, / Everything is a dark dream / I am even separated from him / If I could only lie with him in peace . . .")

44. In Russian, the words in question contain the roots "light" and "black."

45. *SS*, vol. 2, p. 504.

> Seldom does a spark of heavenly life cling to the heights,
> But then, like a queen, even the rose of the mountain blooms.

While these poems may not be direct sources for Ivanov's closing lines, a certain resemblance in imagery and portent is unmistakable.[46] Both poems describe unusual, if not impossible, situations—red roses in snow (Ivanov) and a mountain rose (Novalis)—which are unambiguously associated with a golden age or a heavenly visitation. In his final lines, Ivanov seems to appropriate the miraculous connotations of these distichs. However, he complicates the imagery. The word "venchik" undoubtedly refers to the corolla of a flower. Yet the word has a second meaning; as a band put on the head of a corpse, it belongs to the traditional funeral rites of Russian Orthodoxy. Given the general context of Ivanov's poem (which has wavered between images of life and death), as well as the web of significations associated with the rose, it seems likely that this final image connotes palingenesis. It is the last of a series of "signs" ("primety") around which the poem is structured.

Looking back to the poem's epigraph—"Liebeszähren, Liebesflammen / Fließt zusammen"—one recognizes that, in its *specific* imagery, "Tidings" has only an indirect connection to Novalis's original poem. Ivanov refers to the German text through the lens of his own Russian translation. Yet he retains the larger theme of revelation, of life after death, that is so fundamental to Novalis's poem. Ivanov thus uses an epigraph to recall a meter which in turn calls forth a particular theme. In the course of the poem, this theme is developed freely. This sort of intertextuality, characteristic of Ivanov's approach to his chosen precursors, is not polemical, but associative.

Throughout his poetry, Ivanov expresses his most profound convictions by means of parallels and models. When Ivanov attempted to convey his grief over Lidiya's death, he consciously turned to a series of exemplary couples: Dante and Beatrice, Petrarch and Laura, Novalis and Sophie. These pairings became archetypes with direct relevance to Ivanov's own condition.

For this reason, Ivanov could not approach Novalis's writings dispassionately. When immersing himself in Novalis's poetry, he was reenacting a story of tragic loss and mystical initiation. The transla-

---

46. The image of roses in snow obviously appealed to Ivanov. In his 1912 essay "Thoughts on Symbolism," he quotes from Tyutchev's "Yarkii sneg siyal v doline" ("Bright Snow Shone in the Valley"): "A kotoryi vek beleet tam, na vysyakh snegovykh, a zarya i nyne seet rozy svezhie na nikh!" "But however long it shows white there on the snowy peaks, the dawn even now is sowing fresh roses on them!" Ibid., p. 611.

tions, in which Ivanov does not hesitate to alter the original text in favor of his own personal imagery, are surely the most obvious reflection of this tendency. The original poems that use Novalis translations as a point of departure represent another instance of this same technique.

Ivanov subsequently wrote a number of poems that borrow central imagery from the Novalis translations. One example of this phenomenon can be found in the first stanza of "Mladenchestvo" ("Infancy"), where Ivanov describes his own birth:

> Мать разрешения ждала, —
> И вышла из туманной лодки
> На брег земного бытия
> Изгнанница — душа моя.[47]

> Mother waited for the delivery—
> And from a foggy ship emerged
> Onto the shore of earthly existence
> An exile—my soul.

Dimitri Ivanov has pointed out that this passage recalls the first stanza of Novalis's final "Hymn to the Night."[48] In Ivanov's translation, the relevant lines read:

> Несет нас тесная ладья
> На брег иного бытия.

> The narrow boat carries us
> To the shore of another existence.

In the common context of a boat journey between two worlds, the phonetic, lexical, and metrical (iambic tetrameter) correspondences between the lines "Na breg inogo bytiya" (Novalis translation) and "Na breg zemnogo bytiya" ("Infancy") stand out. These lexical echoes are striking enough to allow one to posit a link between the two passages, semantic differences notwithstanding. (In "Infancy," Ivanov describes the journey *into* earthly existence, whereas the "Hymn" concerns a departure *from* earthly existence.) Yet it must be emphasized that, when one examines the German original, the intertextual similarities all but disappear. Novalis writes: "Wir kommen in dem engen Kahn / Geschwind am Himmelsufer an." ("We quickly arrive on heaven's shore in the narrow boat.") In his rendering of this passage, Ivanov

---

47. *SS*, vol. 1, p. 232.
48. Cf. *SS*, vol. 4, p. 692. He does not, however, emphasize the crucial mediating role played by the translation.

substituted the expression "other existence" ("inogo bytiya") for "heaven's shore" ("Himmelsufer"). Precisely this phrase provides the weightiest intertextual link to "Infancy." The passage from "Infancy" is thus connected *primarily* to Ivanov's own translation and only *indirectly* to Novalis's original. This phenomenon again makes clear the extent to which Ivanov's translations from Novalis form an organic, independent part of his poetic world.

The short poem "Mogila" ("The Grave"), from the collection *Svet Vechernii (Vespertine Light)*, demonstrates yet another way in which the work on Novalis left its mark on Ivanov's original poetry. Written in January, 1917, "The Grave" treats a theme that was predominant in "Love and Death" and "Rosarium" as well as in Novalis's "Hymns to the Night"—the death of the beloved. Like so much of this poetry, "The Grave" can be understood as a meditation on Lidiya's death. Yet the tone is no longer agitated, but philosophical. Ivanov's highly emotional attempts to "overcome death," so characteristic of the earlier period, are replaced by a sense of tranquility and reconciliation. Moreover, in the ten years that had elapsed, Ivanov's poetic means changed noticeably. Whereas *Cor Ardens* represents the height of the ornamental style in Russian poetry, "The Grave" relies on extreme stylistic and lexical simplicity. The poem is written in iambic tetrameter, that most traditional of Russian meters, without enjambement or hypermetrical stresses:

МОГИЛА

Тот в праве говорить: "я жил",
Кто знает милую могилу;
Он в землю верную вложил
Любви нерасточенной силу.

Не оскудеет в нем печаль,
Зато и жизнь не оскудеет;
И чем он дольше сиротеет,
Тем видит явственнее даль.

Бессмертие ль? О том ни слова.
Но чувствует его тоска,
Что реет к родникам былого
Времен возвратная река.[49]

---

49. *SS*, vol. 3, p. 518.

The Grave

He who knows the dear grave
Is entitled to say "I lived";
He has placed into the loyal earth
The strength of his unspent love.

In him, sadness will not lessen,
But neither will life lessen;
And the longer he is orphaned,
The clearer he sees the vista.

Immortality? Not a word about that.
But his yearning feels,
That the returning river of time
Flows gently toward the springs of the past.

These verses are dedicated less to the deceased (who is only mentioned in the first stanza) than to the survivor.

In the Russian poetic tradition, the image of a river of time ("reka vremen") immediately calls to mind Derzhavin's laconic final poem, in which the poet asserts that oblivion is the unavoidable fate of all things. In "The Grave," Ivanov quite literally reverses this dictum. His "river of time" goes in reverse, bringing together rather than sundering. Poetically, this reunification is underscored by the careful sound repetitions of the final lines: "Chto re*et k r*odnikam by*logo / Vr*emen vozv*ratnaya re*ka."

The notion of time moving backwards can be found in Ivanov's previous poetry.[50] One is therefore justified in reading "The Grave" as an application of this general mystical principle to Ivanov's personal condition. In the absence of other explicit intertextual markers (whether in the form of an epigraph, a mythological reference, or an unusual stanzaic construction), the poem seems simply a reversal of the bleak worldview presented by Derzhavin.

Yet a knowledge of Ivanov's work on Novalis leads to a much richer reading of the poem. The "milaya mogila" ("dear grave"), which serves as the focal point of the first stanza, has a specific referent: Novalis repeatedly used this phrase to designate the tomb of Sophie von Kühn.[51] Ivanov had drawn attention to this in his essay of 1914: "Her grave—'my dear grave, my kind grave,' as Novalis

---

50. Cf. "Melampus' Dream" as well as Ivanov's own note to that poem, *SS*, vol. 2, pp. 296–300. See "Iov" ("Job") for another instance of mystical return. *SS*, vol. 3, p. 18.

51. Cf. Grützmacher, in Novalis (1977), p. 242. "Novalis's diary after Sophie's death speaks of almost daily visits to the 'dear grave'" ("an dem 'lieben Grab'").

writes,—is found in Grüningen."⁵² Moreover, the second stanza draws on central images from Ivanov's writings of the period that directly followed Lidiya's death. The image of the orphan, as has been shown, recurs in the poetry and the Novalis translations.⁵³ Similarly, the idea of "seeing the vista" can also be traced to the writings of 1909. Occupying a position at the intersection of the translations and diaries, this image directly concerned the possibility of overcoming alienation through reunification with Lidiya.⁵⁴ In "The Grave," these two central concepts of 1909 are linked in the passage: "And the longer he is orphaned, / The clearer he sees the vista."

"The Grave" once again demonstrates the extent to which Ivanov experienced Novalis's loss as his own. The "dear grave" of Sophie von Kühn intersects with a lexicon familiar from Ivanov's 1909 diary (and from its "reflection" in the Novalis translations). Yet these references (and the Derzhavin allusion) notwithstanding, Ivanov's poem remains a deeply felt personal statement. "The Grave" exemplifies his seemingly paradoxical tendency to use other texts to give voice to extremely personal sentiments. Unlike "Tidings," where a knowledge of the subtext is obligatory, "The Grave" communicates to the reader unaware of the numerous allusions. However, a familiarity with these subtexts makes clear that the wellsprings of Ivanov's art are both literary and personal. Even in expressing his innermost convictions, Ivanov thinks in terms of paradigms: "The Grave" demonstrates how, following Lidiya's death, Ivanov found a positive model for his own life and work in that of Novalis while turning away from the negative image offered by Derzhavin.

---

52. "Ee mogila,—'moya milaya mogila, moya dobraya mogila', kak pishet Novalis,—nakhoditsya v Gryuningene." *SS*, vol. 4, p. 269. This appears to be another example of Ivanov's indebtedness to Braun, who had written on page 295 of his own essay: "Her grave—'my dear grave,' 'my kind grave,' writes Novalis—was located in Grüningen." ("Ee mogila,—'moya milaya mogila,' 'moya dobraya mogila', pishet Novalis,—nakhodilas' v Gryuningene.") The phrase "dear grave" can already be found in "Sub Rosa" *(Cor Ardens)* in the "miloi ulybkoi mogil" ("dear smile of the grave").

53. See the discussion of this word in chap. 8.

54. See the discussion of "Es giebt so bange Zeiten" in chap. 8.

Chapter 10

Metrical Semantics and the "Hymns to the Night"

> Nur dann zeig ich, daß ich einen Schriftsteller verstanden habe, wenn ich in seinem Geiste handeln kann, wenn ich ihn, ohne seine Individualitaet zu schmälern, übersetzen, und mannigfach verändern kann.[1]
> —Novalis, *Vermischte Bermerkungen*

Every national literature evolves its own distinct poetic tradition, bringing with it certain assumptions about meter, genre, and poetic language. To some extent, these assumptions are determined by the natural character of a given language. For example, the preference for feminine line-endings in Polish poetry can be explained by the obligatory penultimate stress of the Polish language. However, differences between various national traditions depend less on inherent linguistic qualities than on the particular literary-historical circumstances of their development. In this regard, individual poets exert an enormous influence on their successors. When Pushkin conceived of the Onegin stanza for his novel in verse, he created a new set of expectations for the Russian reader. So powerful is this association that any subsequent Russian poet who uses this form invites and expects his audience to search for his work's connection(s) to Pushkin's masterpiece. Were an English poet to use the same stanzaic form, there would be no "shock of recognition."[2] In short, there is a semantic element to a poet's choice of metrical form that is not inherent to that form (synchronic), but rather created in a given historical context (diachronic).[3]

---

1. "Only then do I show that I have understood a writer when I can act in his spirit, when without detracting from his individuality, I can translate and change him in numerous ways." Novalis, *Miscellaneous Remarks*. In Novalis (1981), p. 436.
2. Vladimir Nabokov, whose Russian novel *The Gift* ends with a passage in the Onegin stanza, finds it necessary to point out this connection in his foreword to the English translation.
3. Taranovsky (1963) did the pioneering work in this area. It has since been developed by Gasparov in a series of articles, e.g., Gasparov (1982).

Only rarely is an individual poem so influential that its metrical associations cross national boundaries. Perhaps as a result of its easily recognizable graphic form, the "terza rima" calls Dante's *Divine Comedy* to the mind of any educated reader. One need only look at Shelley's "The Triumph of Life" or Blok's "Song of Hell" to recognize that this association spread beyond the Italian tradition. However, Dante's masterpiece represents the exception, not the rule. Generally speaking, the strophic, metrical, and generic associations of one tradition are lost in another. Thus, in the Russian tradition, one would not expect a Romantic poet to write an ode. In the Russian context, this genre calls to mind a specific period (eighteenth-century neoclassical) and, often, a specific strophic pattern. The Russian Romantics rejected eighteenth-century poetics and, consequently, the ode, its defining genre.[4] In contrast, an English reader, relying on associations with Shelley and Keats, correctly considers the ode a high Romantic genre. Once again, there is nothing inherently romantic (or unromantic) about the ode. In different literary traditions, it simply assumed different roles.

One might expect that translation would bridge the gap between national literatures. Yet translation follows its own mysterious and unpredictable paths. Minor poets often attain enormous reputations in foreign countries (cf. the virtual cult of Parny among the Pushkin pleiad or Verhaeren among the Russian Symbolists), while major poets fail to cross linguistic boundaries (the fate of Hölderlin and Keats in Russia). Even when translations do exist, the eternal question of their adequacy arises. As concerns subtle relationships between meter and genre, translation has proven to be an unreliable mediator. There being no established "codex" for translation, practitioners have frequently ignored the form of the original. (French and, increasingly, English translators have preferred to render verse as prose.) Even in Russia, with its rich tradition of poetic translation, translators have often removed distinctive features of the original *precisely because* these features were foreign to their own poetic tradition.[5] Thus, the irregular stress patterns of Heine's poetry were systematically rooted out by Russian nineteenth-century translators, much as Turgenev "corrected" the inaccuracies of Tyutchev's German-influenced verse. Because the prosody of ancient Greek sounds peculiar to an ear accustomed to modern languages, translators rarely made an effort to reproduce the cadences of the original. It is noteworthy that Gnedich, before decid-

---

4. I am speaking of the main line of Russian Romanticism (i.e., Zhukovsky, the Pushkin after "Freedom", Lermontov, etc.). One does find odes in the work of the backward-looking "archaists" (e.g., Kyukhel'beker's "On the Death of Byron" was originally called an ode), but poems of this type are exceptional.

5. Cf. Zhovtis, p. 511, Gasparov (1984), p. 261.

ing on a translation of the *Iliad* in hexameters, completed a large portion of the work in iambs.[6] He and Zhukovsky, the acclaimed Russian translators of Homer, simplify their hexameters by virtually eliminating trochaic substitutions.[7] In the English tradition, Alexander Pope translated Homer into the rhyming couplets of his own poetic repertoire.

Translators who attempt equimetrical translations of unfamiliar verse forms confront the difficult task of creating an association in the mind of the reader. Thus Ivanov, in his renderings of the poetry of Pindar, Alcaeus, Sappho, and the plays of Aeschylus, sought to teach the Russians the *sound* of ancient Greek verse. In his introduction to the projected 1926 edition of Aeschylus, Ivanov noted that he gave special attention to preserving the "rhythmical movements and metrical structure" of the Greek.[8] Likewise, Bryusov, in his final version of the *Aeneid*, willingly sacrificed even readability in his attempt to recreate the Latin text. Such examples, however, are few and rarely successful; they demand erudition and talent from the translator and extreme patience on the part of the reader, unaccustomed to such unusual metrics and syntax.

The recent controversy over an English translation of Lermontov's complete poetry raises an important question about the very desirability of such equimetrical translation.[9] If it is true that meter carries semantic weight only within a national tradition, then what is the value of an equimetrical English edition of Lermontov's poems? After all, a knowledgeable English reader is apt to have a completely different association to these meters than his Russian counterpart. In principle, then, such an edition would be justified only as a first step in the English equimetrical translation of *all* Russian poets. Alternately, one might propose English translations of Lermontov done in the "equivalent" (not necessarily the *identical*) meters, if such a thing could be determined.[10] Both of these solutions are of course utopian.

---

6. Scherr, pp. 130–31.
7. Cf. Burgi, pp. 133–35.
8. Eskhil, p. 197. Already in 1904, in his "Note on the Dithyramb" in *Transparence*, Ivanov writes: "A poetic interpreter of a foreign poem who changes its meter and rhythm replaces its musical soul with another, foreign one." *SS*, vol. 1, p. 818.
9. See Liberman and also Smith.
10. Here one finds an example in Zhukovsky's translations of Grey's "Elegy Written in a Country Churchyard." In 1802, Zhukovsky used an equimetrical translation (iambic pentameter) and then, in the version of 1839, turned to dactylic hexameter. While unrelated to Grey's metrical choice, the Russian hexameter had a certain epic solemnity (thanks to Zhukovsky's own prior experiments) that helped convey the underlying pathos of the English poem.

However, the lack of a definitive answer does not lessen the essential problem that all serious translators must confront.

While Ivanov never devoted an essay to the theory of translation, his general approach can be deduced from his large body of renderings from poets as diverse as Pindar, Aeschylus, Alcaeus, Sappho, Dante, Petrarch, Michelangelo, Baudelaire, Byron, Goethe, Novalis, and George. For all of their idiosyncracies, Ivanov's translations are characterized by a fanatical interest in preserving the metrics of the original.[11] Only in exceptional cases does Ivanov allow himself the liberty of departing from a poem's metrical form.[12] This premise holds true even in the Novalis translations; regardless of the sometimes flagrant semantic and stylistic liberties, Ivanov retains the meter and rhyme scheme.

Such fidelity to the metrics of the original is not a sign of pedantry, but rather a statement about the nature of poetry. According to this view, the "dominant" of poetry (to borrow a term from Formalism) lies less in its specific imagery than in its aural component. A belief in equimetrical translation was not unique to Ivanov; it formed a basic principle of Symbolist translation. Bal'mont, for example, preferred to render a poem in prose rather than violate its metrical form.[13] Bryusov's career as translator was marked by a steady progression toward an ideal of literal (and equimetrical) translation.[14] In supervising a Russian Heine edition, Blok urged a faithfulness to the text so extreme that he deemed all previous translations (which were legion) to

---

11. That this was indeed Ivanov's basic orientation is confirmed by a letter of 1912 from Henry von Heiseler, the German translator of Ivanov's drama *Tantalus*. After consulting with Ivanov, Heiseler reported to his wife: "Ivanov places great importance on retaining the exact Greek meters. I had intentionally translated more freely in the choruses, more according to my ear. And now I am attempting to bring into harmony the demands of my ear with those of the Greek meter, which is no easy task." In Heiseler, p. 69.

12. Such freedoms occur with regularity *only* in the "self-translations" of the 1930s, that is, when Ivanov rendered his own Russian verse into German. The lengthiest example is the German version of the first part of "Man" (first published in Doubrovkine, pp. 319-25), but other examples can be found in the essays, e.g., the "lyrical intermezzo" in "Anima" (*SS*, vol. 3, p. 280). A word is in order about the 1943 essay "Thoughts on Poetry," where Ivanov, using Lermontov's notoriously free rendering of Goethe's "Wanderers Nachtlied" ("Wanderer's Night Song") as his sole example of great translation, apparently advocates extreme metrical (and semantic) license. It should be emphasized that such an approach (at least as concerns *metrics*) does not correspond to Ivanov's actual practice—with the exception of his self-translations.

13. See Orlov's description of the Shelley translations, in Balmont, p. 71.

14. See Gasparov (1971).

be unacceptable.[15] His own translations reveal an extraordinary faithfulness to the rhythms of the original.[16]

Ivanov favored equimetrical translation not simply for reasons of euphony. There is considerable evidence that he attributed semantic associations to metrical forms. In his seminars for young poets in 1920, he would often explain the appropriate content for a given poetic form, e.g., "the triolet is light ... it cannot bear seriousness ... the seven-footed iamb is characteristic of ballads ... the ballad is romantic, full of sentimentalism, lunar qualities, while the triolet is penetrated by the sun."[17] Moreover, such a belief can be directly traced to his poetic practice. I have repeatedly shown the frequency with which Ivanov's poetic reception of Goethe and Novalis relied on metrical allusions. The meter provides the link between Goethe's "The Bride of Corinth" and three of Ivanov's poems. "Morning Star" is written in the same meter as its Faustian epigraph. "Tidings" refers to Novalis's "Pilgrim's Song" through its epigraph, imagery, *and* metrical form. Further examples of this technique can be found throughout Ivanov's creative work. The Onegin stanza supplies a Pushkinian backdrop for the idyllic "Infancy."[18] The first eleven lines of a Petrarchian canzone (on the death of Laura) serve as epigraph *and* metrical model for the canzoni in Ivanov's own "Love and Death" (to commemorate the death of Lidiya).[19]

In this context, Ivanov's translations of Novalis's "Hymns to the Night" deserve special attention. On first glance, Ivanov seems to ignore completely the formal aspects of Novalis's poems. In contrast to the original, the translations use a variety of meters, sometimes changing within a single poem. Such a departure from the metrics of the original would appear to contradict one of Ivanov's fundamental principles of translation. It is particularly puzzling in view of the fact that Ivanov without exception carefully reproduces the large variety of stanzaic forms of Novalis's "Sacred Songs."

An examination of the publication history of the "Hymns to the Night" helps to resolve this paradox. Of all Novalis's major works,

---

15. See Blok, p. 116.
16. See Bailey. A contemporary recalled Blok tapping out the rhythms of Heine's verse with a pencil as an aide to translation. See Knipovich (1980), p. 38.
17. Cf. F. I. Kogan, TsGALI, f. 2272, op. 1, ed. khr. 33, l. 37–39.
18. It is noteworthy that Ivanov criticized Blok's "Retribution," where an attempt is made to apply Pushkinian metrics (a traditional iambic tetrameter) to a non-idyllic childhood. "Pushkinian form is inappropriate for contemporary complexity; it seems like a golden raiment on a corpse." Cf. F. I. Kogan, TsGALI, f. 2272, op. 1, ed. khr. 33, l. 25. Also cited in *Literaturnoe nasledstvo* (1982), vol. 92, book 3, p. 496.
19. *SS*, vol. 2, p. 396.

only the "Hymns to the Night" were published during the poet's lifetime. This cycle of six hymns appeared in the Schlegels' journal "Athenaeum" in August, 1800. Written in rhythmical prose with a few interpolated iambic poems, this version soon became canonical. When Tieck prepared his Novalis edition, he included precisely this text. However, among Novalis's papers another, earlier variant existed. This so-called "manuscript version" was written in free verse ("freie Rhythmen," according to traditional German terminology), again with interpolated iambic poems. Because of its representation on the printed page, the "manuscript version" is immediately perceived by the reader as poetry. In contrast, the "Athenaeum" text, despite its strongly rhythmical qualities, resembles prose. While the two versions differ most obviously in their graphic representation, they also contain occasional semantic discrepancies.

In the only study of Ivanov's Novalis translations, Efim Etkind expresses surprise at the fact that Ivanov chose not to render the "Hymns to the Night" in the free verse of the "original."[20] However, Etkind does not consider the state of Novalis scholarship at the beginning of the twentieth century. While acknowledging that two variants of the "Hymns" exist, he dismisses the prose as being contrary to Novalis's original intention. Etkind's preference is by no means as obvious as he suggests.[21] For the present purposes, and for the sake of historical accuracy, it should be emphasized that the version in free verse was printed *for the first time* in 1901. For many years thereafter, the Tieck edition (prose) remained more available and more accepted. It is unknown what Novalis edition(s) Ivanov consulted for the translations. However, all evidence suggests that he favored the traditional Tieck edition over the more recent scholarly texts that introduced and propagandized the free verse.[22] Most importantly, a comparative

---

20. Etkind, p. 181.
21. Standard editions now print the versions side by side.
22. In his library in Rome, Ivanov had "Hempels Klassiker-Ausgabe" of Novalis. The book bears the dedication: "To Vyacheslav Ivanov, as a sign of love, friendship, and admiration, from Guenther. Saint-Petersburg 11/XI MCMIX." According to the diaries, Ivanov finished work on the Novalis translations in August, 1909. Thus, he most likely did not translate from the book that Guenther presented to him. Nonetheless, it stands to reason that Ivanov thought highly of this edition, a somewhat modernized version of the Tieck, in which The "Hymns to the Night" appear in prose with the earlier text included in an appendix. This editorial decision is explained as follows: "Our edition gives the 'Athenaeum' version. Given the editorial freedoms of the Schlegels it is not certain, *but nevertheless probable*, that Novalis originally desired it this way" (part 4, p. 164, my emphasis). Furthermore, in a list of library requests compiled *after 1910* (probably in 1913), Ivanov specifically asks for the Tieck edition. (RGB, f. 109, k. 4, ed. khr. 14.) He does *not* ask for the Heilborn (who, dismissing the traditional "Athenaeum" prose version as a

textual analysis makes clear that Ivanov's translation follows the prose. Virtually every time there is a semantic discrepancy between the two texts, Ivanov opts for the "Athenaeum" (prose) variant.[23]

Thus, in translating the "Hymns to the Night," Ivanov did not disregard one verse form in favor of another (as Etkind suggests), but rather gave metrical form to those sections which, in Novalis's text, appeared as prose.[24] It should be emphasized that Ivanov *always* renders the *interpolated* poetry in the meter of the original. Whenever Novalis uses a recognizable verse form (i.e., not rhythmic prose), Ivanov retains it.

Another factor should be considered: if Ivanov was aware of the existence of both texts (a likely supposition), why did he decide not to follow the free verse? Such a question leaves the purely textological realm and introduces a fundamental issue of historical poetics. In the German literary tradition, Novalis's use of free verse aligns his "hymns" with a specific genre. Introduced by Klopstock and canonized by Goethe in his "Sturm und Drang" period, "freie Rhythmen" are associated with strong emotions, high-style, and philosophical

---

creation of the Schlegels, relegates it to an appendix) or the Minor (who offers both texts side by side).

23. A few examples make this clear. In the first hymn, the prose text is divided into three distinct paragraphs separated by numerous blank lines. The verse, however, is one continuous passage. Ivanov's translation, taking its cue from the prose, is also divided into three stanzas. In the interpolated poem at the conclusion of the fourth hymn, the manuscript version (sanctioned by Etkind) consists of six stanzas. In the "Athenaeum" (prose) variant, the verses contain an additional stanza, as does Ivanov's translation. The sole exception occurs at the end of the third hymn, where Ivanov uses the image of the "sun of night" rather than the "light of night." This suggests that Ivanov was nonetheless acquainted with the manuscript version.

24. Etkind seems unaware of these textological problems. He accuses Konevskoi (who obviously modeled his translations on the prose, since he died the year the "manuscript" version was first published) of "ignoring" the free verse of the original (Etkind, p. 182). Etkind himself seems not to be terribly concerned by textological fine points. The very title of his article (which also serves as the basis of his concluding paragraph) is based on a mistranslation (the German word is "mythisch," which should be rendered "mificheskii" and not "mifologicheskii"). In fact, his entire exegesis is based on a misreading of the text; Etkind would have us believe that Novalis's "theory of translation" (which, he explains, is a part of that writer's general aesthetic theory) distinguishes between *two* types of translations. Novalis actually differentiates among *three* types of translations. (The relevant fragment can be found in the collection *Blüthenstaub*, No. 68.) In his discussion of this fragment, Etkind refers at length to what Novalis calls a "changed" ("verändernd") translation, incorrectly identifying this as Novalis's definition of "mythological" translation. Etkind's article, which at times provides valuable insights, is marred by errors of fact and judgment, and must be read with the utmost circumspection.

content. In Russian literary history, free verse is exceedingly rare.[25] Only Ivanov's contemporary Kuzmin, in his "Alexandrian Songs," had succeeded in popularizing it. Ivanov's use of this meter would therefore have created a strikingly "modernist" association inappropriate for Romanticism. Ivanov did render the celebrated "Abendmahl" ("Communion") hymn of the "Geistliche Lieder" in free verse, but that was a single, relatively short poem, deliberately set off metrically from the other poems.[26] In order to preserve the poem's special status *within a cycle*, it was necessary to retain its unusual metrical form.[27]

Textological, poetic, and historical evidence all suggest that Ivanov chose to work with the prose version of Novalis's "Hymns to the Night." The fundamental question therefore concerns Ivanov's poetic realization of what he perceived as a prose text. His ideal was not to remain true to each nuance, but to create poetry that would communicate with the urgency and intensity of the original. To accomplish this task, Ivanov relies to a large extent on what will henceforth be termed the "metrical semantics" of the Russian verse tradition.

Novalis's first "Hymn" introduces the opposition between day and night on which the entire cycle is based. The poet begins by lavishing praise on the day: "Seine Gegenwart allein offenbart die Wunderherrlichkeit der Reiche der Welt" ("Only its presence reveals the wondrous magnificence of the world's realms"). However, after this lengthy introduction, the poet turns his attention "to the holy, inexpressible, mysterious night" ("zu der heiligen, unaussprechlichen, geheimnißvollen Nacht"). When compared to the night, the day's grandeur becomes insignificant: "Wie arm und kindisch dünkt mir das Licht nun—wie erfreulich und gesegnet des Tages Abschied." ("How poor and childish the light seems to me now—how joyous and blessed the day's parting.") Novalis's night is the time of mystical initiation, which he expresses through a series of powerful and paradoxical images. The hymn closes with an ecstatic vision: the poet "awakens" and, seeing the true nature of the universe, comes into contact with his

---

25. Russian nineteenth-century poets had in no way prepared the reception of free verse. Tyutchev, for example, when translating Heine's "Nordsee" poems (written in free verse), simply ignored their unusual form, preferring to render them in traditional Russian meters.

26. In 1929, he also translated the "freie Rhythmen" of Goethe's drama "Prometheus," keeping extraordinarily close to the rhythms of the original. However, this work, done on commission, was conceived and executed under very different circumstances from the Novalis translations.

27. Ivanov read the "Geistliche Lieder" as a cycle, unaware that Tieck (and *not* Novalis) had created the cycle and selected the poems. Cf. Seidel, pp. 11–46.

"tender beloved." He begs for a mystical cleansing by fire, in order that he may be forever united with her.

In a short speech on Novalis to a group of aspiring poets, Ivanov said, "Novalis has a way of throwing out a whole bunch of images and—understand them as you will."[28] In addition to coming to terms with the complicated abstract imagery of the original, Ivanov confronted another significant problem: finding the appropriate meter to express the metaphysical content.

Ivanov chose to render the first hymn in iambic pentameter, without rhyme and without caesura (the "blank verse" of English prosody). To recreate the logic behind his decision, it is necessary to know the meter's semantic associations. Unrhymed iambic pentameter has a rich tradition in Russian poetry, yet it was by no means a natural Russian meter. Zhukovsky had "imported" it from Germany for two 1816 translations from Johann Peter Hebel.[29] (This German lineage is not insignificant in the context of Novalis translations.) As their titles imply ("Tlennost'" and "Derevenskii storozh v polnoch'"—"Perishability" and "The Village Guard at Midnight"), these poems discuss questions of mortality and permanence. Thus, from its very inception in the Russian tradition, the unrhymed iambic pentameter was associated with philosophical content.

Zhukovsky's metrical innovation at first attracted ridicule from contemporary poets, Pushkin among them.[30] However, such negative

---

28. F. I. Kogan, TsGALI f. 2272, op. 1, ed. khr. 33, l. 27.
29. See Gasparov (1984), p. 116. Zhukovsky first introduced the *rhymed* iambic pentameter (in 1811), and then, with the help of Hebel's German model, moved on to the unrhymed iambic pentameter without caesura. The meter can occasionally be found in the translations of Russian eighteenth-century poets (e.g., Lomonosov's version of Horace's "Exegi monumentum"), but these poems were exceptions that never entered the standard repertoire.
30. See the commentary in Zhukovsky, vol. 1, p. 449. In 1819, Batyushkov wrote to Zhukovsky, "I ask you to write to me; how much work can it be, when you have time to write to all the young ladies and still have time to translate some Pindar of Basel into some sort of pentameter verses." Pushkin's critique took the form of parody. "Perishability" begins with a child speaking to his grandfather: "Послушай, дедушка, мне каждый раз, / Когда взгляну на этот замок Ретлер, / Приходит в мысль: что, если то ж случится / И с нашей хижиной?" ("Listen, grandfather, every time / When I gaze at the Röttler castle / The thought enters my mind: what if the same thing also happens / To our little house?"). Pushkin repeats the first two lines verbatim, then, instead of the words that introduce the philosophical theme of the poem (perishability), substitutes his own "verse": "Приходит в мысль: что, если это проза, / Да и дурная? . . " ("The thought enters my mind: what if this is prose, / And bad prose at that? . . "). Years later, Pushkin turned to this very meter to discuss the theme of perishability in one of the masterpieces of Russian poetry, " . . . Vnov' ya posetil" (" . . . Again I visited").

reactions did not prevail; Russian "blank verse" soon became the meter of choice for dramatic works (Zhukovsky's translation of Schiller's "Die Jungfrau von Orleans" and Pushkin's "Boris Godunov")[31] as well as meditative, philosophical lyrics. Etkind has suggested three such poems by Lermontov entitled "Night" (1830) as direct subtexts for Ivanov's choice of meter.[32] This assertion seems forced, as the resemblance stops at the general thematic level. Aside from conventional associations of night and death, there is little reason to see Ivanov's poem as a direct response to Lermontov: the same metrical and thematic constellation can already be found in Zhukovsky's "Perishability." Nevertheless, Etkind correctly notes that the meter carries certain associations. Ivanov invokes the life-and-death subject matter as well as the solemnity of the Russian unrhymed iambic pentameter.

Ivanov's translation of the hymn's last few lines gives a sense of his ability to manipulate the meter. Novalis's text reads: "nun wach ich—denn ich bin Dein und Mein—du hast die Nacht mir zum Leben verkündet—mich zum Menschen gemacht—zehre mit Geisterglut meinen Leib, daß ich luftig mit dir inniger mich mische und dann ewig die Brautnacht währt" ("now I awake—for I am yours and mine—you have announced to me that night is life—[you have] made me a man—consume my body with spiritual fire, that I, like air, may mix myself more intimately with you and then the marriage night will last eternally").

> Я ныне бодрствую: я твой и свой;
> Ты жизнью ночь творишь и в ней меня
> Впервые человеком. Эту плоть
> Сожги огнем духовным, что б воздушней
> Тебя проник — с тобой смешался я,
> И брачной ночью станет ночь на век.[33]

In terms of semantics, Ivanov's text is surprisingly accurate. However, his poetic rendering nonetheless creates its own atmosphere. Novalis's text is composed of short interjections that give a breathless, spontaneous quality to his words. Ivanov's translation is measured, even

---

31. Pushkin's choice of "blank verse" in historical drama may well have been suggested by Shakespeare's powerful example, not by Zhukovsky.

32. Etkind, pp. 181–82.

33. "Now I am awake: I am yours and mine; / You make night into life and make me in it / A person for the first time. This flesh / Burn with a spiritual fire, so that more airily / I would enter you—I would mix with you / And the night will become a wedding night forever."

solemn. The intricate syntax and elaborate constructions slow down the pace. Despite the syntactic complexity, Ivanov creates a sense of urgency through enjambement. The dramatic effect of this passage depends on four consecutive enjambements that end with the penultimate line. This technique sets off the final line, an expression of the eschatological hope to which the entire poem has led. Ivanov gives this crucial statement special solemnity by realizing all five conceivable stresses—"I brachnoi noch'yu stanet noch' navek." He takes advantage of formal features of Russian verse to underscore Novalis's semantics, interrupting enjambement (a device that relentlessly pushes the reader forward) with its formal "opposite" (a line without pyrrhic feet, which forces the reader to slow down).

After the ecstatic mysticism that concludes the first hymn, Novalis's tone changes radically. The second "Hymn," much shorter and far less emotional than the first, opens with a question: "Muß immer der Morgen wiederkommen?" ("Must the morning always return?"). The remainder of the poem answers this question by affirming the ultimate superiority of night. The hymn concludes with a paean to "holy sleep" ("heiliger Schlaf"), which is contrasted to physical (temporary) sleep.

Ivanov renders the second hymn in trochaic pentameter. Once again, our main interest is in determining the poetic "logic" behind his choice. In this case, Novalis himself may have suggested this meter in the hymn's opening questions: "Muß immer der Morgen wiederkommen? Endet nie des Irdischen Gewalt?" With one exception (the word "immer"), this passage, if read as poetry, would scan as two lines of trochaic pentameter. Metrical semantics, however, supplies an additional reason; the Russian trochaic pentameter is historically linked to the German poetic tradition. Russian translators "imported" the meter in order to render German poetry.[34] In the German tradition, it was a standard metrical form, often used for philosophical lyrics, e.g., Schiller's "Die Götter Griechenlands" ("The Gods of Greece") and "Das Ideal und das Leben" ("The Ideal and Life").

Ivanov, extraordinarily faithful to the semantics of the original, uses his command of poetic form to emphasize certain aspects of Novalis's hymn. The translation opens with an octave (rhyme scheme A-b-A-b-A-b-C-C).

> Вечно ль будет, в миг свой обычайный
> День светать? Земного власть вечна ль?
> И должно ль под суетой случайной
> Никнуть ночи вещая печаль?
> И любовный пламень жертвы тайной

---

34. See Gasparov (1984), p. 117.

Угасать, едва зардела даль?
Света срок, и круг его — размерен;
Весь простор вселенной ночи верен.³⁵

As in the original, the passage consists of a series of questions followed by an answer. Ivanov uses the octave to highlight this structure. The first six lines, characterized by emjambement, contain the questions. In these lines the "a" vowel sound is predominant, accounting for eleven of twenty-four stressed vowels, including all six rhymes. The final two lines, set off as a couplet, reveal the "answer." The vowel "e" becomes the dominant sound (five of nine stresses) and the stressed "a" is omitted completely. (The change is most noticeable in the rhymes.)

The central concept of the entire hymn sounds forth in the very first word ("Vechno"—"eternally"). It recurs in parallel position in the passage that follows the octave ("Vechno dlitsya son. O, son svyashchennyi ... ").³⁶ After the octave, Ivanov reverts to unrhymed lines, but retains the trochaic pentameter. He uses only feminine line endings, creating an incessant string of trochaic rhythms for the hymn's remaining seventeen lines. The translation is unusually faithful both to the semantics and syntax of the original. Novalis ends the second hymn with the image of sleep as salvation: "daß aus alten Geschichten du himmelöffnend entgegentrittst und den Schlüssel trägst zu den Wohnungen der Seligen, unendlicher Geheimnisse schweigender Bote" ("that you step forward, opening heaven, from old stories and [you] carry the key to the abode of the blessed, [you] silent messenger of endless mysteries"). Ivanov's faithful translation ends on an exclamatory note:

... что старинной сагой
Ты нас дивам учишь вековечным,
Сон, ключарь обители блаженных,
Тайн бессмертных вестник молчаливый!

... that like an ancient saga
You teach us eternal miracles,
Sleep, sacristan of the abode of the blessed,
Silent messenger of immortal mysteries!

---

35. "Will the day eternally dawn at its usual time? Is the power of earth eternal? And must the prophetic sadness of the night bend under fortuitous bustle? And [must] the love-flame of a secret sacrifice go out as soon as the vista has reddened? The time of light and its orbit are measured; the entire expanse of the universe is true to night."
36. "Sleep lasts eternally. O, sacred sleep ... "

The image of sleep as a "sacristan" is not found in the original. However, Novalis's passage, rich in religious connotations, warrants the addition. In biblical usage, for example, the Russian "obitel'" exactly corresponds to the German "Wohnung" (cf. John 14:2).

In the context of the entire cycle, Novalis's third hymn occupies a position of special importance. In terms of tone and subject matter, it differs radically from its predecessors. While the first two hymns are meditative lyrics, the third is closer to narrative. The metaphysical musings of the first hymns give way to specific memories as the poet recalls a visionary moment at the grave of his beloved. The biographical element, only implicit in the earlier hymns, becomes unmistakable. Novalis employs a lexicon that closely recalls his visits to Sophie von Kühn's grave, as recounted in the diaries of 1797.[37] This textual interference between diary and poetry has caused scholars to designate it as the "Urhymne," the first to be written and the foundation of the entire cycle.[38]

Ivanov reflects Novalis's strikingly new tone in his choice of meter. He uses unrhymed alternating amphibrachic tetrameter and amphibrachic trimeter, dividing the poem into four-line stanzas with masculine cadences in the first and third lines and feminine cadences in the second and fourth. In terms of the entire cycle, this choice of meter unambiguously sets off the third hymn. It is the first ternary meter (the first hymn was rendered in iambs and the second in trochees). However, Ivanov does not choose this meter simply to distinguish this hymn from the others. In the history of Russian verse, amphibrachs have a specific association. They were rarely used until the beginning of the nineteenth century, when they became the meter of choice for rendering German ballads.[39] Zhukovsky, who initiated and canonized this practice, especially favored amphibrachic tetrameter or alternating amphibrachic tetrameter and trimeter (the form that Ivanov uses in the third hymn). This form then began to be used by various Russian poets in original ballads.

Ivanov, with his keen sense of metrical semantics, was surely aware of both of these associations (German poetry and the balladic genre). Yet there was a more specific reason for his choice of meter. Russian

---

37. See Grützmacher, in Novalis (1977), pp. 242–43, for a comparison of the relevant passages.

38. Whether the hymn was actually written the same year as the diary entry is of course unclear. More recent scholars (i.e., after Ivanov's time) have voiced doubts.

39. The German ballads were written in meters resembling what would later be called a "dol'nik" in Russian versification. Since this meter was not in the repertoire of nineteenth-century Russian poetry, a more "natural" meter was chosen to substitute. For an explanation of why the amphibrach was most suitable, see Gasparov (1984), p. 121.

poems in amphibrachs, whether translations or original poetry, were rhymed. Ivanov's translation is not. In the Russian nineteenth-century tradition, only one poem was written in unrhymed alternating amphibrachic tetrameter and trimeter: Zhukovsky's "Teon and Eskhin."[40] In choosing this meter for his translation, Ivanov thus created a set of associations and expectations for a knowledgeable Russian reader.

Zhukovsky wrote "Teon and Eskhin" in 1814, a time when he was first experimenting with amphibrachic ballad forms. In this poem, references to Zeus and Bacchus, as well as the stylized names of the main characters (i.e., Teon and Eskhin), set a tone that is neo-classical rather than Romantic. Nevertheless, the poem has obvious thematic relevance to Novalis's third hymn. Its content can be summarized quickly: Eskhin returns home after a long absence, having experienced disappointment. He meets Teon, a friend of former years, who has suffered a similar fate. Deep in thought, Teon sits at the grave of his beloved. The remainder of the poem is devoted to Teon's plaint. Zhukovsky's poem contains both stylistic and semantic parallels to Ivanov's translation from Novalis:

> Увы! я любил... и ее уже нет!
>   Но счастье, вдвоем столь живое,
> Навеки ль исчезло? И прежние дни
>   Вотще ли столь были прелестны?
>
> О, нет, никогда не погибнет их след;
>   Для сердца прошедшее вечно.
> Страданье в разлуке есть та же любовь;
>   Над сердцем утрата бессильна.
>
> И скорбь о погибшем не есть ли, Эсхин,
>   Обет неизменной надежды:
> Что где-то в знакомой, но тайной стране
>   Погибшее нам возвратится?
>
> Кто раз полюбил, тот на свете, мой друг,
>   Уже одиноким не будет...
> Ах! свет, где *она* предо мною цвела, —
>   Он тот же: всё *ею* он полон...[41]

---

40. I am grateful to M. L. Gasparov for drawing my attention to this poem.

41. "Alas! I loved her, and she is no more! / But the happiness, so alive when we two were together / Did it disappear forever? And were the former days / So beautiful for nothing? / Oh, no, their trace will never perish. / For the heart the past is eternal. / Suffering in separation is the very same love. / Loss is powerless over the heart. /

In this passage, Teon refuses to accept a permanent separation, stating that death cannot triumph over love. He suggests the possibility of a future meeting in a "known, but mysterious land." Finally, he notes that his beloved has left her mark on *this* world, and that she is therefore still with him. The lexicon of Zhukovsky's poem is characteristic of the standard nineteenth-century elegy. Ordinarily, the fact that many of these words ("skorb'", "nadezhda," "odinokii" "bessil'no",— "grief," "hope," "lonely," "powerless") recur in Ivanov's translation would not be particularly significant. After all, the subject of a lamentation requires a specific set of lexical choices. Nevertheless, given the remarkable metrical and thematic resemblances already noted, these specific echoes serve to heighten the poems' similarities.

Ivanov's translation parallels Zhukovsky, but only up to a point. Teon's conclusion is far removed from that of Ivanov (and Novalis). Despite some moments suggesting the possibility of mystical communication with the "other world," Zhukovsky's poem ends in resignation. Teon praises Zeus, asserting that one must become reconciled to one's fate. In short, Zhukovsky's poem discusses various mystical notions (meeting with the dead, the grave as a door to happiness), before reaching its rather staid conclusion ("Khvala zhiznedavtsu Zevesu!"—"Praise to life-giving Zeus!").

Novalis's third hymn and Ivanov's translation are structured differently. Rather than discussing the possibilities of occult experience, they record an actual visionary moment. They trace a path not from grief to resignation, but rather from grief to a mystical union. Ivanov's rendering of this hymn thus creates a complicated intertextual web. Like all of the Novalis translations, it draws on Ivanov's own poetic and symbolic world as reflected in both his poetry and his diary. Additionally, it presents a rewriting of Russian Romanticism, as portrayed in Zhukovsky's poem.

Novalis's hymn depicts the utmost grief and is characterized stylistically by long sentences:

> Einst, da ich bittre Thränen vergoß, da in Schmerz
> aufgelöst meine Hoffnung zerrann, und ich einsam stand
> am dürren Hügel, der in engen, dunkeln Raum die Gestalt
> meines Lebens barg—einsam, wie noch kein Einsamer
> war, von unsäglicher Angst getrieben—kraftlos, nur ein
> Gedanken des Elends noch.—Wie ich da nach Hülfe
> umherschaute, vorwärts nicht konnte und rückwärts

And the grief over the departed, is it not, Eskhin / A promise of immutable hope: / That somewhere in a known yet secret country, / The departed will return to us? / Whoever loved once, my friend, / Will never be alone on the earth . . . / Ah! the world where *she* bloomed before me,— / It is the same: it is still full of *her* . . . "

nicht, und am fliehenden, verlöschten Leben mit unendlicher Sehnsucht hing.⁴²

Ivanov's translation, through polysyndeton, reflects the syntax of the original. The anaphoric "I" ("And"), repeated six times, conveys the unrelenting misery of the poem's opening:

> Однажды, как слезы лились из очей,
> И в скорбь растворялась надежда,
> И я у кургана сухого стоял
> Где жизнь моя тлела в могиле,
>
> И был одинок, как никто никогда
> В глухой не сиротствовал доле,
> Без сил несказанной тоскою гоним,
> Весь, — смертная боль и унынье,
>
> И помощи ждал, а ноги ни вперед
> Не мог ни назад передвинуть,
> И все ж удержать ускользавшую жизнь
> Хотел, а она иссякала . . .⁴³

As in "Teon and Eskhin," the protagonist stands at the grave of his beloved and mourns her death. The unusual metrical form, combined with the common theme of mourning and the appropriate lexicon, makes the resemblance to Zhukovsky's poem unmistakable.

Yet there are elements that can be explained neither by Novalis nor by Zhukovsky. For example, one is immediately struck by Ivanov's idiosyncratic use of sound instrumentation. Particularly notable are lines such as "odi*nok, kak nikto ni*kogda" and "I vse *zh* ud-er*zh*at' *u*skol'zavsh*uiu zh*izn'." Moreover, certain lexical choices (e.g., "sirotstvovat'"—"to be an orphan," as well as "toska"—"yearning") depart from both Zhukovsky and Novalis. Such freedoms must be understood in the more general biographical context of Ivanov himself. The theme of graveside revelations had tremendous

---

42. "Once when I poured bitter tears, when my hope dissolved into pain, and I stood alone on the bare hill, which in narrow, dark space hid the figure of my life—alone, as no lonely person has ever been, driven by unspeakable fear—powerless, a mere thought of misery.—As I looked around for help, could not go forwards or backwards, and hung on to fleeing, extinguished life with endless yearning."

43. "Once, when tears flowed from my eyes, / And hope dissolved into grief, / And I stood at the dry funeral mound, / Where my life decayed in the grave, // And was lonely, as no orphan ever / Had been on the dull earth, / Without strength, driven by unsaid longing, / All extreme pain and dejection, // And I waited for help, but my legs neither backward / Nor forward could move, / And nevertheless to hold onto life as it slipped away, / I wanted, but it [i.e., life] dried up . . . "

significance to Ivanov in 1909. His own diaries of this period contain numerous descriptions of visits to Lidiya's grave, replete with visionary experiences.[44] Specific intertextual echoes strongly suggest that Ivanov identified himself with the poetic "I" of Novalis's poem. In the diaries and the translations, these particular words frequently recur.[45]

While the lamentation of the first stanzas of the translation bears an obvious resemblance to Zhukovsky's "Teon and Eshkin," the semantic similarities become less evident as the poem progresses. Indeed, the crucial theme of "night's inspiration" ("Nachtbegeisterung"—"Naitie Nochi") has no connection to "Teon and Eshkin." Ivanov's poetic language (following Novalis) becomes intentionally obscure, often combining concrete and abstract concepts within a single image. Novalis writes: "da kam aus blauen Fernen—von den Höhen meiner alten Seligkeit ein Dämmerungsschauer—und mit einemmale riß das Band der Geburt—des Lichtes Fessel."[46] The mystical experience is a kind of rebirth, expressed metaphorically as the tearing of an umbilical cord. The translation remains true to the spirit, but not the letter of the original:

> Былого блаженства с нагорных высот,
> Из далей былого лазурных, —
> Как сумерки, облак дохнул ... пелена
> Расторглась — и свет мне родился.[47]

Ivanov makes no effort to reduce the ambiguity of the original. He adds certain favorite words to Novalis's text (e.g., "nagornyi")[48] and substitutes others. For example, to render the German "Band," Ivanov uses "pelena." While the German word suggests an umbilical cord, the Russian does not. However, it is a powerful and appropriate image insofar as it connotes both birth (as "swaddling clothes") and death (as a "shroud"). Its placement (in an enjambement) serves to dramatize the

---

44. See *SS*, vol. 2, pp. 786–87.
45. Cf. Ibid., pp. 774, 775, for a passage in the diaries where the words occur together. In regard to the poetry, see Ivanov's translation of the fifth hymn (*SS*, vol. 4, p. 193), where he renders "Nach dir, Maria, heben / Schon tausend Herzen sich"— "Mary, a thousand hearts raise themselves up to you" as "*Tosku* serdets, Mariya / Beschislennykh vnemli!"—"Mary, listen to the *yearning* of innumerable hearts" (my emphasis). For the crucial image of the orphan, see the discussion in chap. 8.
46. "There came a twilight shower from the blue vistas—from the heights of my old bliss—and suddenly it tore the cord of birth—the light's chain."
47. "Joys of the past from mountain heights / From azure vistas of the past,— / Like dusk, the cloud blew ... the cover / Was rent—and light was born to me."
48. See the discussion of this word in Ivanov's translation of "Liebeszähren, Liebesflammen" in chap. 9.

effect, since the reader must reach the following line to complete the image. This double meaning (death and birth) has obvious relevance in view of the vision itself, which combines images of physical decay ("Staub" or its Russian equivalent "prakh") with those of spiritual rebirth ("mein entbundner, neugeborner Geist" or, in Ivanov's accurate rendering, "Moi dukh vozrozhdennyi i vol'nyi"—"My spirit reborn and free").

In short, by the end of the poem, Zhukovsky's thematics have been left behind and only his metrical form remains. What is the function, then, of the metrical allusion? For the Russian reader, Zhukovsky is virtually synonymous with German literature. For generations, Zhukovsky's numerous poetic translations played the mediating role between the German and Russian traditions. To an enormous extent, Zhukovsky's personal canon of German poets determined the Russians' knowledge and expectations of that tradition. The Russian Symbolists, careful and brilliant translators, were themselves raised on Zhukovsky's renditions of German poetry. As Bryusov wrote, "All of us 'so-called educated people'... know the German language from our childhood, yet I would hardly be mistaken were I to say that the majority of us know Schiller's poetry not from the originals but from Zhukovsky's translations."[49] Ivanov, whose knowledge of German can hardly be questioned, himself pays homage to Zhukovsky's translations in *Pilot Stars*, when he chooses an epigraph from Schiller's "Sehnsucht" ("Yearning"), cites it in Russian and writes below, "Zhukovsky (based on Schiller)."[50] In "Thoughts on Poetry" (1943) Ivanov praises Zhukovsky's renderings of Schiller as an example of translations that sound "sweeter" than the original.[51]

As has been noted, the fact that Zhukovsky never translated Novalis contributed significantly to that writer's obscurity in Russia. In undertaking his own translations, Ivanov was in a sense continuing where Zhukovsky left off. As Ivanov was surely aware, Zhukovsky had created for the Russian reader a horizon of expectations for German Romanticism. Any new translations from the German would be read against a background of Zhukovsky's poetics. In his rendering of the third "Hymn to the Night," Ivanov subtly responds to these expectations, showing a remarkable resemblance (the opening) as well as the profound differences (the conclusion) between Zhukovsky's worldview and that of Novalis.

---

49. Bryusov (1975), vol. 6, p. 105.
50. "Zhukovskii. Po Shilleru." *SS*, vol. 1, p. 568. This extremely rare instance of a foreign epigraph appearing in Russian translation indicates that Ivanov regarded the Zhukovsky's translation as an independent work of art.
51. *SS*, vol. 3, p. 670.

Novalis's fourth hymn consists of three distinct parts. Ivanov uses three widely differing metrical forms to reflect this structure. The first part of the poem is narrative in character. The poet tells of his symbolic journey to the "Grenzgebürge der Welt" ("border mountains of the world"). This symbolic topography separates the realms of day and night. Novalis's text, laden with religious imagery and biblical references, describes a pilgrimage: "Weit und ermüdend ward mir die Wallfahrt zum heiligen Grabe, drückend das Kreuz." ("My pilgrimage to the holy grave became distant and exhausting, the cross [became] heavy.")

Ivanov renders this opening section in unrhymed dactylic hexameter, with occasional spondaic substitutions on the fourth foot. His choice of a ternary meter might have been suggested by the rhythms of Novalis's prose: "Himmlische Müdigkeit fühl ich in mir" (the second sentence) can be read as dactylic tetrameter. More significantly, the third sentence (and the beginning of the truly narrative section) consists of a rhythmical period strongly suggesting a hexameter line. "Weit und ermüdend ward mir die Wallfahrt zum heiligen Grabe ... "

In terms of metrical semantics, the dactylic hexameter has important associations. In the Russian poetic tradition, this meter became popular in the Russian Golden Age. Gnedich (1784–1833) had used unrhymed dactylic hexameter in his translation of the *Iliad* as a modern equivalent to the hexameter of ancient prosody. The meter then developed an aura of antiquity. Zhukovsky, for example, chose it for his version of the *Odyssey*, which Ivanov himself considered a "classic" (i.e., canonic) translation.[52]

By using hexameter, then, Ivanov accentuates the epic nature of Novalis's hymn. Indeed, Ivanov makes a semantic change that appears to be influenced by his choice of meter. In Novalis's hymn, the pilgrimage has a dual nature: it is at once a journey to Christ's grave and to the grave of the beloved. By using the word "Hügel" for the goal of his pilgrimage, Novalis recalls the "Hügel" of the third hymn (the funeral mound of the beloved and site of mystical revelations). Ivanov clearly rejects this ambiguity, carefully removing all references to the beloved. In the third hymn, he had rendered "Hügel" as "kurgan," a traditional Slavic word for a funeral mound. In the fourth hymn, it becomes a "kholm" (the neutral Russian word for "hill"), thus precluding their identification. Ivanov further eliminates Novalis's intentional ambiguity by breaking the opening paragraph into two stanzas. In the first stanza, the poet speaks about himself:

---

52. Zhukovsky used the meter in a variety of poems and translations, but the primary associations remained with the Homeric epics. See Gasparov (1984), p. 126. For Ivanov's high regard of Zhukovsky's *Odyssey* (and of Gnedich's *Iliad*), see Al'tman, p. 311.

200   Part Two: Ivanov and Novalis

> Ведаю ныне, когда и последнее утро настанет . . .
> Ах, я усталостью горней устал . . . (my emphasis)
>
> Now *I* know when the last morning will come . . .
> Oh, *I* am wearied by a lofty weariness . . .

In the second stanza (beginning with the fifth line), Ivanov removes the first-person pronoun. "Weit und ermüdend ward *mir* die Wallfahrt" ("Far and exhausting was *my* pilgrimage") becomes "Dolog i tomen palomnika put' ko Grobu Svyatomu" ("Long and exhausting is the path *of the pilgrim* to the Holy Grave"). This small change transforms personal experience into epic narrative.

The entire hexameter section (twenty lines in Ivanov's text) is characterized by elevated diction and complex syntax. Such verse corresponds to the long, complicated sentences of the original. Novalis often uses archaisms as well as biblical language, and Ivanov reproduces these nuances faithfully. He translates "Oben baut er sich Hütten, Hütten des Friedens"[53] (with its implicit reference to Matthew 17:4 and Mark 9:5) as "Stavit on kushchi svoi na vershine—kushchi pokoya,"[54] retaining the same biblical echoes. Similarly, he renders Novalis's "promised land" ("das neue Land") as "Zemlyu Zaveta" ("Land of the Testament"), the Russian "Zavet" being the standard term for "Testament" (i.e., Old and New Testaments).

After describing the pilgrimage, Novalis changes tone abruptly. From philosophical considerations (the ultimate "victory" of darkness over light) his attention shifts back to the mundane world: "Noch weckst du, muntres Licht den Müden zur Arbeit—flößest fröhliches Leben mir ein—aber du lockst mich von der Erinnerung moosigem Denkmal nicht."[55] Novalis marks this thematic change graphically, separating the first two paragraphs from the third by means of a large blank space. Ivanov also reflects this semantic change graphically.[56]

> Еще, веселый Свет,
> К страде и злобе дней
> Ты будишь усталого,
> Бодрость и силы мне в жилы льешь;

---

53. "He builds himself huts above, huts of peace."
54. "He builds huts above—huts of peace."
55. "Again, lively light, you wake the tired one for work—you pour merry life into me—but you do not lure me from the mossy monument of memory."
56. In the manuscript version, Novalis makes this change even more pronounced by switching from long lines (ten to fifteen syllables) to short lines (three to eight syllables). It is conceivable that in this case, Ivanov responded to the graphical representation of verse in Novalis's manuscript version. (His *specific* metrical choices do not coincide with those of Novalis, but a general similarity can be noted.)

> Но от мшистых камней
> Обветшалого
> Памятника — не отзовешь![57]

Ivanov's new form, unprecedented in the Russian tradition,[58] seems to have been chosen as the metrical opposite of the hexameter. The hexameter is an exacting poetic form—except for trochaic substitutions (the Russian spondee, used sparingly by Ivanov on the fourth foot), the rhythm is an unbroken string of dactyls. Because of its origin (an imitation of classical poetry), it never rhymes. Instead, the line endings reflect the classical cadence of a dactyl and a spondee (or, depending on one's perspective, two dactyls, the second truncated by one syllable). The extremely short lines of Ivanov's new meter stand out against the background of the long verses that preceded them. While each hexameter line contains sixteen or seventeen syllables, the lines of the new form range from five to a maximum of nine syllables. In the context of such short verses, the presence of rhyme becomes especially apparent. One of every three words rhymes, a stark contrast to the rhymeless hexameter introduction. In keeping with the free, unstructured nature of the passage, the rhyme scheme is irregular. The first part has the pattern a-b-c-d-b-c-d, with the "c" rhymes dactylic and the others masculine. The insistent end rhymes are amplified by internal rhyme: "Bodrost' i *sily* mne v *zhily* l'esh'." The metrical level provides another jarring contrast between the two sections. While the hexameter's distinguishing characteristic was its strict rhythm, the new form lacks a steady rhythmic pulse. It cannot even be considered a *dol'nik*, for it varies in stresses per line from one to four.

This unique rhapsodic form ultimately leads to the poem's third and final section, which consists of the first of Novalis's interpolated poems. Set off from the rest of the hymn graphically, the poem nevertheless shares numerous motifs, for it describes a symbolic pilgrimage from day to night. Novalis uses iambic dimeter, with a rhyme scheme of A-b-C-b. The feminine lines do not rhyme, but are connected by consonance (wall ich/Stachel, Zeiten/trunken, Leben/oben, etc.). Ivanov retains the metrics of the original and even takes into account the unusual rhyme scheme by using A-b-A-b, where the feminine rhymes are impure (i.e., kazhdyi/vlazhnoi, dal'nei/opochivan'ya, kipuchii/kruchi, etc.):

---

57. "Again, merry Light, / To everyday toil, / You wake the tired one / You pour cheer and strength into my veins; / But from the mossy stones / Of the decrepit / Monument—you don't call [me] away!"

58. It anticipates the form Bely was to use in his 1918 "Khristos voskres" ("Christ is risen"). Gasparov gives an account of this form in Balashov, pp. 452-53.

Hinüber wall ich
Und jede Pein
Wird einst ein Stachel
Der Wollust sein.

Noch wenig Zeiten
So bin ich los,
Und liege trunken
Der Lieb im Schoß.[59]

Иду, и каждый
Тропы кремень
Сулит мне влажной
Прохлады сень.

Иду: не дальней
Мне светит цель —
Опочиванья
Небесный хмель.[60]

This section develops the pilgrimage theme of the poem's opening. Since Ivanov uses an equimetric translation, the question of metrical semantics does not arise. Nonetheless, a detailed analysis reveals other ways in which Ivanov uses the Russian tradition to give additional meaning to Novalis's verses. To mention only one: for Novalis's image of pain becoming a thorn of joy, Ivanov substitutes the phrase "tropy kremen'" (a "flinty path"), which nevertheless promises a cover of moist coolness. For a Russian reader, these lexical choices recall Lermontov's celebrated "Vykhozhu odin ya na dorogu" ("Alone I go out onto the road"). In the second line of this poem, Lermontov writes of the "kremnistyi put'" ("flinty path"). Moreover, Lermontov concludes by expressing the hope that he will lie peacefully, under the cooling breeze of an oak tree.

The fifth hymn, the most complicated and lengthiest of the entire cycle, is at once a mythopoeic version of the history of man, a treatise on death, and a religious confession. Novalis creates a detailed mythological foundation for the philosophical assertions of the earlier meditative hymns. In view of the hymn's length, the present analysis must limit itself to a few central passages that best illuminate the larger concerns of this chapter, i.e., Ivanov's poetic realization of Novalis's mythical constructs.

---

59. "Thither I make my pilgrimage and every pain will ultimately become a thorn of bliss // A little time yet and I am free, and I lie drunken in the lap of love."

60. "I go and every slate of the path promises me a cover of moist coolness. // I go: from not far my goal shines to me—the heavenly hops of the bed-chamber."

Except for Novalis's interpolated poems (which Ivanov renders in the meter of the original), Ivanov translates the fifth hymn in unrhymed iambic pentameter (without caesura), a metrical form familiar from his translation of the first hymn. However, these poems belong to different genres. The first was a philosophical meditation, while the fifth is a narrative. In this case, the rhythmical period of the German original, which suggests a ternary meter, cannot explain Ivanov's decision to use iambs.[61] The answer to this problem must be sought in the history of Russian verse. In the Russian tradition, unrhymed iambic pentameter was used not only for philosophical lyrics, but also for epic tales. Once again, Zhukovsky played the pioneering role by writing numerous narratives in this form.[62] Within the apocalyptic context of the fifth hymn, it should be recalled that Zhukovsky had also used this meter in translations from "Revelation," written in 1851–1852.

Novalis's poem opens on an extremely somber note: "Ueber der Menschen weitverbreitete Stämme herrschte vor Zeiten ein eisernes Schicksal mit stummer Gewalt. Eine dunkle, schwere Binde lag um ihre bange Seele..."[63] Ivanov's rendition of this passage exemplifies a striking disregard for the letter of Novalis's poetry:

> Глухонемой пастух, жезлом железным
> Пас древле Рок земные племена.
> Был робкий ум слепою пеленой
> Ополонен.[64]

The nightmarish vision of a "shepherd" (a reversal of standard biblical imagery—for example, Psalm 23, "The Lord is my Shepherd") with a "zhezl zheleznyi" ("iron rod") has no connection to Novalis, yet is familiar from "Revelation" (2:27, 12:5, 19:15). In Zhukovsky's rendering, Ivanov had a biblical model in unrhymed iambic pentameter:

> ... И из уст Его меч острый
> На казнь народов исходил; Он их
> *Пасет жезлом железным* ...[65]

---

61. The latter part of the first line is clearly dactylic. "Ueber der Menschen weitverbreitete Stämme *herrschte vor Zeiten ein eisernes Schicksal mit stummer Gewalt*" (my emphasis). The second line is in a binary meter, but it is trochaic, not iambic: "Eine dunkle, schwere Binde lag um ihre bange Seele..."

62. Cf. Gasparov (1984), p. 119.

63. "Long ago an iron fate ruled with silent force over the widespread clans of men. A dark, heavy band lay around their fearful soul..."

64. "Fate, a deaf and dumb shepherd, / Of old tended the tribes of earth with an iron rod. / The timid mind was by a blind band / Imprisoned."

65. "And from His lips a sharp sword / Was extended for the execution of nations; / He tends them with an iron rod" (ll. 606–8).

Ivanov's version synthesizes these biblical references with images loosely derived from Novalis's text. From Novalis's "mit stummer Gewalt," Ivanov selects the word "stumm" (normally "mute" or, in Russian, "nemoi") and then adds the modifier "deaf." This "deaf and dumb" despot is complemented by the "blind" bond that enslaves man. The semantic choices are clearly made in accordance with the poem's sound fabric. In addition to the alliterative pairs "pastukh/pas," "zhezlom/zheleznym" one is struck by the repeated "p," "l," and "n" sounds. Thus the words "*pl*eme*n*a, s*l*e*p*oyu, *pel*e*n*oy, and o*p*o*lon*e*n*" become related through paronomasia.

The fifth hymn contains a number of Novalis's most crucial philosophical insights. His treatment of the relationship between the ancient Greek and Christian worlds deserves special attention, for this theme had obvious importance for Ivanov. Novalis describes the birth of Christ as the beginning of the "new world." "In der Armuth dichterischer Hütte—Ein Sohn der ersten Jungfrau und Mutter— Geheimnißvoller Umarmung unendliche Frucht. Des Morgenlands ahndende, blütenreiche Weisheit erkannte zuerst der neuen Zeit Beginn—zu des Königs demüthiger Wiege wies ihr ein Stern den Weg. In der weiten Zukunft Namen huldigten sie ihm mit Glanz und Duft, den höchsten Wundern der Natur."[66] Without direct quotations or even proper names, Novalis clearly draws on the biblical account of Christ's birth.

Ivanov's rendering of these lines is semantically faithful. He follows Novalis's lead, not hesitating to make the biblical allusions explicit. In the translation one finds the "yasli" ("manger") in Luke 2:7, the "zvezda na vostoke" ("star of the east") from Matthew 2:2, and the "zoloto," "ladan," and "smirnu" ("gold, incense, and myrrh") of Matthew 2:11.

> Под нищим кровом, Девы Сын, объятий
> Таинственных неизреченный плод.
> Востока тайну виденье встречало
> Времен иных священное начало:
> К смиренным яслам шла звезда в ночи.
> Несли Царю волхвы ливан и злато
> И смирну — все, чем естество богато,
> Грядущих тайн пророки — толмачи.[67]

66. "In the poetic hut of poverty—a son of the first virgin and mother—the unending fruit of secret embrace. The orient's anticipatory, blossoming wisdom first recognized the beginning of the new age—a star showed it the way to the king's humble cradle. In the distant future they paid homage with light and fragrance to him, to the highest miracles of nature."

67. "Beneath a poor roof, the Son of the Virgin, the ineffable fruit of mysterious embraces. The vision met the East's mystery, the holy beginning of other times: the

Ivanov's most radical change occurs on the formal level. In rendering this passage about the birth of Christ, he turns to rhymed verse. Novalis, who gives the whole passage in rhythmic prose, in no way suggests such a striking stylistic change. For Ivanov, the birth of Christ forms the hymn's climax and, as such, must be given special emphasis. The sudden application of rhyme should be understood as part of Ivanov's poetic interpretation. He reflects Christ's birth, an ordering of the universe, in the poetic material—in rhyme, the most obvious way to structure verse. The "new world" is thus set apart from the "old world."[68]

The rhyming section, continuing for twenty lines, is interrupted by three unrhymed lines that announce the arrival of a mysterious singer. Scholars of Novalis's work have long disputed the identity of this figure.[69] For present purposes, it is sufficient to recognize that he in some way represents the classical world: "Von ferner Küste, unter Hellas heiterm Himmel geboren, kam ein Sänger nach Palästina und ergab sein ganzes Herz dem Wunderkinde." ("From a distant coast, born under the joyous sky of Hellas, a singer came to Palestine and gave his entire heart to the miraculous child.") Ivanov renders the passage faithfully:

> И с дальних берегов пришел певец,
> Под ясным небом эллинским рожденный,
> И отроку всю душу отдал он.
>
> And from distant shores came a singer,
> Born under the clear Hellenic skies,
> And he gave his whole spirit to the youth.

With this strong emphasis on the "o" vowel sound, Ivanov introduces a new rhymed passage. In this case, the change to rhymed verse is dictated by Novalis, who uses an octave to render the singer's words. As

---

star in the night went to the humble manger. The magi, interpreters, prophets of future mysteries, brought to the Tsar incense, gold, and myrrh—everything with which nature is rich."

68. One finds a curious parallel to this technique in the second part of Goethe's *Faust*, where Faust's meeting with Helen of Troy is depicted on the level of poetic material as a change from unrhymed hexameter (ancient Greek versification) to rhyme (modern German versification).

69. For an overview of the relevant scholarship, see Balmes, in Novalis (1987), vol. 3, pp. 81–82. In his essay on Novalis (*SS*, vol. 4, p. 277), Ivanov identifies the singer as Orpheus.

usual when rendering the interpolated poems, Ivanov follows the metrics of the original.⁷⁰

> Ты — оный юноша, чей лик печальный
> Мы зреть привыкли на камнях могильных.
> Он был нам дан как Твой прообраз дальний,
> Первиною даров Твоих обильных.
> В руке держал он светоч погребальный
> Он ныне брачный светоч <2 нрзбр.>
> Желанна смерть — святых блаженств начало.
> Ты — смерть, и Ты ж у Смерти отнял жало.⁷¹

Keeping Novalis's semantics largely intact, Ivanov applies an extremely personal poetic style. Once again, the stressed "o" obtains semantic weight: from "*o*troku vsyu dushu *o*tdal *on*" to "Ty—*on*yi yunosha," where "onyi" clearly refers to "on."⁷² In the crucifixion scene, fifteen lines later, Ivanov includes the final touch, raising "on" to "*On*." The semantic constellation of "lik" ("visage") and "zret'" ("to see") provides another link to Ivanov's poetry; these two words occur together frequently in a context of mystical knowledge.⁷³ Yet another detail should be noted: in the phrases "On byl nam dan kak Tvoi ..." and "Ty—Smert', i Ty zh u Smerti ...", monosyllabic words dominate. To an extent, Novalis himself suggests this technique (cf. "Du bist der Tod und machst uns erst gesund"). However, such a phenomenon is much less striking in German than in Russian, which severely limits the possibility of consecutive monosyllabic words.⁷⁴ In his poetic practice, Ivanov favors such constructions as a means of adding emphasis. The historical *source* of this device is ancient Greek prosody, for monosyllabic words serve as the Russian equivalent to the Greek

---

70. Uncharacteristically, Ivanov uses only feminine rhymes, while Novalis alternates.
71. "You are that youth, whose sad visage / We have grown accustomed to see on tombstones. / It [i.e., the visage] was given to us as Your distant archetype, / As the first of Your abundant gifts. / In his hand he held a funeral torch: / Now he [two words are illegible in the manuscript] a wedding torch. / Death is desired as the beginning of holy bliss. / You are Death, and it is You who took the sting away from Death."
72. Cf. the discussion of Ivanov's translation of ""Ich weiß nicht, was ich suchen könnte" in chap. 7.
73. Cf. the discussion of "Wer einmal, Mutter, dich erblickt" in chapter 7.
74. Cf. Averintsev (1975), p. 154. "In German, not to mention English, there are many more monosyllabic words [than in Russian] and their brevity is therefore not so striking as it was already in Derzhavin's line: 'I am a tsar,—I am a slave—I am a worm—I am a god.' ('Ya tsar',—ya rab,—ya cherv',—ya bog!') Ivanov's verse gives monosyllabic words special semantic power."

spondee.[75] In the context of the present passage—the only point thus far in the entire course of the "Hymns to the Night" where Ivanov uses strings of monosyllabic words—it can hardly be coincidental that the speaker of these lines is a Greek. Ivanov describes the meeting of Christ and antiquity both semantically and formally.

From the point of view of metrical semantics, the final hymn needs no discussion. Novalis writes a poem in iambic tetrameter (with lines two and four in trimeter). As always in the interpolated poetry, Ivanov translates in the meter of the original. Nonetheless, Ivanov's specific treatment of Novalis's meter deserves a brief commentary.

In the hymn's final stanza, Ivanov departs from Novalis's text in tone and substance:

> Hinunter zu der süßen Braut,
> Zu Jesus, dem Geliebten—
> Getrost, die Abenddämmrung graut
> Den Liebenden, Betrübten.
> Ein Traum bricht unsre Banden los
> Und senkt uns in des Vaters Schooß.[76]

> К невесте снидет в глуби недр,
> В сень смерти к Иисусу!
> Посул зари вечерней щедр:
> Последнему искусу,
> О скорбь любви, покорна будь!
> В Дом отчий, Ночь, — крылатый путь.[77]

In keeping with his general tendency, Ivanov heavily "orchestrates" the translation. Where Novalis uses sound repetitions (for example, "*süß*en" and "*Jesus*"), Ivanov not only follows the original, but also develops it: e.g., "V *sen' s*merti k I*isusu* / Po*sul* . . . " More importantly, he alters the rhythmic flow of Novalis's original. Ivanov twice adds a spondee to Novalis's verses, augmenting this expressive effect by re-

---

75. Cf. Ibid. "A preference for monosyllabic words is characteristic of Vyacheslav Ivanov. In this respect the logical end of his poetry is the experimental translation he did of the 'untranslatable' lines of the Greek lyric poet Terpander, which consist exclusively of long syllables . . . " Cf. the discussion of "Beauty" in chap. 2.

76. "Downwards to the sweet bride, / To Jesus, the beloved— / Consolingly, the dusk becomes grey / To those who love, to those who are troubled. / A dream breaks our bonds / And sinks us into father's lap."

77. "It [apparently the "zagrobnyi vzdokh" or "breath from beyond the grave" of the previous stanza] will descend into the depths to the bride, / Into the cover of death to Jesus! / The promise of evening twilight is generous: / To the final test, / O grief of love, submit! / Night is the winged path to father's House."

peating the same vowel sound in both syllables: "V s*e*n' sm*e*rti" and "V D*o*m *o*tchii." The translation's weighty, declamatory effect results from an unusually high incidence of fully realized lines (none of the tetrameter lines contain pyrrhic feet). Through formal means, Ivanov maximizes the oratorical effect of the conclusion. In the middle of the stanza, a modulation occurs: from "light" vowels ("i" and "e" account for eight of eleven stresses in the first half of the stanza) to "dark" vowels (where "o" and "u" dominate, with nine of eleven stresses). In the fourth line, Ivanov realizes only two of the possible three stresses. In the next line, all four possible stresses are realized. And, to mark the culmination of the stanza, the hymn, and the cycle, Ivanov places *five* stresses in the final line—a remarkable achievement in a Russian tetrameter.

In addition to these rhythmic variations, Ivanov departs radically from the semantics of the original. Novalis describes the evening as a consolation to the loving and troubled. Ivanov complicates this statement, converting the loving and troubled people into an abstract metaphor that he proceeds to address directly (apostrophe, absent in the original, is a device that recalls the highly rhetorical odic style): "O grief of love" ("O skorb' lyubvi"). The "final test" ("Poslednemu iskusu") that Ivanov envisions also has no basis in the original, where consolation is assured. Novalis's poem ends with motion downward ("Und senkt uns in des Vaters Schoß"), the fulfillment of the stanza's first line ("Hinunter zu der süßen Braut") and the hymn's first line ("Hinunter in der Erde Schooß"). Ivanov once again changes Novalis's basic imagery. Rather than sinking into the father's lap (the earth), he uses an image of motion upward, a *winged path* into the father's *House* (the heavens). The imagery of the translation combines descent (the first line) with ascent (the final line). The change, consistent with Ivanov's own philosophy, is compatible with the larger context of Novalis's hymn, which contained the same ambiguity in its first stanza. Yet it clearly departs from the specific passage it ostensibly translates.

The most salient changes are not Ivanov's additions, but rather, his omissions. Novalis depicts death as a religious and *erotic* experience. In the imagery of the final stanza, he appears to conflate his beloved with Christ: "Hinunter zu der süßen Braut, / Zu Jesus, dem Geliebten"[78]

---

78. Scholars disagree as to whether Novalis intended such a reading. Mähl (in Novalis [1981], p. 582) glosses "Downwards to the sweet bride" with the apodictic assertion: "Here, in accordance to Pietism, it refers only to Christ and not (in a second meaning) to the beloved of the opening hymns." Balmes (in Novalis [1987], vol. 3, p. 83), while accepting Mähl's contention about the topos of Pietism, qualifies his conclusion: "The passage thus refers only to Christ, who as the central mediating figure contains within himself both the beloved of the first hymns as well as

("Downwards to the sweet bride, / To Jesus, the beloved"). Throughout the stanza, Ivanov emphasizes the religious aspects and minimizes the eroticism. He removes the adjective "sweet" from the bride, omits the phrase "the beloved," and transforms the physicality of the "Vaters Schoß"[79] into "father's House." In Ivanov's rendering, love is an abstract concept ("grief of love"), a stark contrast to the ardent eroticism of the original.

The fact that Ivanov makes such significant changes in Novalis's final stanza, the symbolic culmination of the entire cycle, indicates that he was not simply translating Novalis, but was "creating" him for a Russian audience. Through the encounter with Russian Symbolist poetics, Novalis's text "gains" specific images (the most striking example being the "cor ardens" that appears three times in six hymns), but loses some of its specific mystical conception. The ultimate gain, however, is a cycle of *Russian* poems, complete with the formal and semantic organization associated with an original work of poetry. Ivanov thus firmly situates Novalis within the Russian poetic tradition; German Romanticism becomes one with Russian Symbolism.

Mary of the fifth hymn." Although Ivanov never commented in any depth on the "Hymns," his essay on Novalis makes clear that he recognized the central role that eros played in Novalis's worldview. Cf. *SS*, vol. 4, p. 274.

79. The German "Schoß" can mean "womb" (as it surely does in the hymn's first line, since German "Erde" ["earth"] is feminine in gender) or "lap," the more logical sense in regard to "father."

Conclusion

> Was man liebt, findet man überall, und sieht überall Ähnlichkeiten.[1]
> —Novalis, "Glauben und Liebe oder der König und die Königin"

What was "Symbolism"? The reader of Russian Symbolist critical writings is invariably impressed and often bewildered by the breadth and diversity of this term. In "The Problem of Culture," Andrei Bely writes:

> The principles of modern art crystallized in the Symbolist school of the last decades: Nietzsche, Ibsen, Baudelaire, [and] later in Russia, Merezhkovsky, V[yacheslav] Ivanov and Bryusov articulated platforms of an artistic credo; at the basis of this credo lie the individual statements of geniuses of the past about the meaning of artistic creation; Symbolism only summarizes and systematizes these statements.[2]

As a definition of a twentieth-century literary movement, Bely's statement is curious and telling. The criterion of originality that proved so central for the Romantics and would peak in the Futurists and Formalists in the 1910s and 1920s, seemed to be temporarily in abeyance. Indeed, the Symbolists return to an earlier, platonic and time-honored definition of "originality"—as a return to origins. These origins are conceived of as timeless essences that both inform and enrich the present. In contrast to most other past-oriented aesthetics, Symbolist theorizing about predecessors is remarkably free of rivalry, jealousy, anxiety, or "patricide."[3] Rather than laying claims to innovation, Bely emphasizes how the Symbolist school looks backward, celebrating and "systematizing" past achievement. It is particularly striking that Bely should include Nietzsche, the arch-iconoclast, among his exemplary Symbolists. In "The Emblematics of Meaning,"

---

1. "What one loves, one finds everywhere, and everywhere one sees similarities." Novalis, "Faith and Love or The King and the Queen." In Novalis (1981), p. 488.
2. Bely (1910), pp. 7–8.
3. Cf. Ivanov's comment to Al'tman: "I honor my literary ancestors. And he who honors his father and mother will live many years on the earth, that is, in the present case, will achieve glory. Genius cannot but appreciate its precursors if only because it loves them extraordinarily." In Al'tman, p. 310.

Bely himself admits that his reading of Nietzsche is based on the spirit, not the letter:

> But it is in this unwavering urge to combine the artistic methods [priemy] of a variety of cultures, in this impulse to create a new outlook on reality through a reexamination of a whole series of forgotten world views that the entire strength, the futurity of the so-called new art lies. This is the source of the peculiar eclecticism of our era. I do not know if Nietzsche was correct when he so completely condemned the Alexandrian period of ancient culture. After all, this period, intersecting so many paths of thought and contemplation, is up to this very day a firm base for us, when we gaze into the depths of past ages. By mixing Alexandrianism together with Socraticism into one big illness, one big, degenerate mass, Nietzsche was subjecting his own path of development to a cruel, Nietzschean judgment. For what Nietzsche himself created, and what we like so well in him, is neither more nor less than Alexandrianism. If he had not himself been an Alexandrian to the core he would never have been able to pronounce such prophetic words about Heraclitus, about the mysteries, about Wagner. Moreover, he would never have been able to write *Zarathustra*. In creating something new he always returned to the old.[4]

With the phrase "I do not know," Bely introduces a reading of Nietzsche that utterly contradicts Nietzsche himself. Rather than the "philosopher with a hammer" (destroying in order to create), Bely sketches a kinder, gentler Nietzsche, oriented entirely toward the achievements of the past.

Of course, a firm belief in tradition does not condemn a writer to repetition.[5] As Bely's "strong misreading" suggests, Symbolist reception contained a marked creative component. Only a highly idiosyncratic interpretation of Nietzsche could bring him into the Symbolist canon. In general, the Symbolists prized the facility for seeing—or creating—similarities. It is characteristic that Bely gives the epithet "eclectic" a laudatory connotation ("the peculiar eclecticism of our

---

4. Bely (1910), p. 50. Translated in Cassedy, p. 112.

5. In this respect, Bely's first letter to Blok (from 4 January 1903) contains a telling evaluation of Blok's poems: "In them one sees succession in the positive sense. As if ordained by Lermontov, Fet, Solovyov, you continue their paths, illuminate and reveal their thoughts. An extraordinary present-day-ness, I would say even before-one's-own-time-ness, nonetheless coexists with a *succession by blood* [Neobychainaya sovremennost', skazhu, dazhe prezhdevremennost', tem ne menee uzhivaetsya *s krovnoi preemstvennost'yu*]." In Blok and Bely, p. 7.

era"). Bryusov, it will be remembered, had made a similar comment about *Pilot Stars*: "In accordance with the spiritual striving of our entire epoch, Vyacheslav Ivanov is an eclectic."[6] Only a Symbolist (Ivanov) could state that "genius is a power that unites to the highest degree, and for this reason it selects as its dwelling-place and implement a soul that yearns to unite with everything, that responds to everything, that encompasses everything . . . "[7]

Much has been made of Ivanov's role as "master," of his attempts to educate younger poets. Such activity represents a consequent application of Symbolist cultural philosophy. Ivanov considered it imperative for the young artist to acquaint himself thoroughly with the "formal canon" (the body of traditional masterworks):

> [The formal canon] has a cleansing effect on art; it reveals the inelegance and falseness of innovations that are not internally justified; it sweeps aside everything accidental, temporary, alluvial; it cultivates strict taste, artistic severity, a sense of responsibility and a careful restraint in the treatment of old and new; it places the Symbolist poet face to face with his true and ultimate goals,—and finally, it develops in him the awareness of a live succession and of an inner connection with past generations . . . [8]

According to Ivanov, the "new" art should do essentially the same thing as the "old" art: namely, unify.[9] The same basic principle can be found in all aspects of Ivanov's teaching and practice, whether on the level of specific poetic devices, motifs, or entire mythological systems. The great artist remembers (rediscovers) and synthesizes; he does not invent.[10]

It is ironic that a movement so obsessed with continuity and synthesis should have constantly been beset by internal dissension. Although unified in their ideals, the Symbolists rarely coincided in specifics. One of the most contentious subjects was the very concept of Symbolism and, consequently, the meaning of tradition. In this regard, the development of the relationship between Ivanov and Bryusov

---

6. Bryusov (1975), vol. 6, p. 295.
7. *SS*, vol. 3, p. 190.
8. *SS*, vol. 2, p. 600.
9. One may recall Goethe's conception of "das alte Wahre" ("the old truth"), to which Ivanov often alluded (e.g., *SS*, vol. 3, p. 94; *SS*, vol. 4, p. 518) and which ultimately served as the title of a German collection of his essays. (The book materialized several years after his death.)
10. Cf. Ivanov's conception of mythopoesis as "finding" ("obretenie"), as opposed to "inventing" ("izobretenie"). *SS*, vol. 2, p. 556.

is particularly instructive. In the formative period of Russian Symbolism, the two worked closely together, overlooking disagreements for the sake of a common cause.[11] As Ivanov expressed it in a letter of 1904, "in necessariis unitas."[12] However, with the passage of time, their differences became increasingly pronounced and, ultimately, irreconcilable. While both agreed on the importance of tradition, the two differed on where to locate Symbolism in relationship to the past.

Bryusov objected to a conception of Symbolism, "according to which Aeschylus and Goethe not only could be called, but would have to be called Symbolists."[13] To counter this tendency, he called on traditional literary history:

> "Symbolism," like "Romanticism," is a definite historical phenomenon, connected with definite dates and names. Having arisen at the end of the nineteenth-century in France (not without English influence), the "Symbolist" movement found followers in all the literatures of Europe, fertilized other arts with its ideas, and of necessity was reflected in the worldview of the epoch.[14]

In contrast, Ivanov came to view Symbolism not as a strictly defined historical movement, but as a creative impulse. France, the birthplace of Bryusov's Symbolism, plays a relatively minor role in Ivanov's scheme. In a particularly pointed formulation, he wrote:

> And so, Dante is a Symbolist. But what does this mean in the sense of the self-definition of the Russian Symbolist school? It means that we annul ourselves as a school. We annul ourselves not because we renounce something and think of setting out on another path. On the contrary, we remain completely true to ourselves and to the activity that we have begun. But we do not want sects; our faith is ecumenical.
>
> Indeed, the real Symbolist, of course, does not care about the fate of that which is ordinarily called a school or a movement, defining this concept by chronological borders and names of its proponents. He cares about firmly

---

11. Ivanov, for example, was never comfortable with "decadence" and "individualism," two concepts that played an enormous role in Bryusov's theory and practice. Bryusov, in turn, felt that Ivanov overestimated the importance of theurgy. Cf. Azadovsky and Maksimov, pp. 267–68.
12. *Literaturnoe nasledstvo* (1976), vol. 85, p. 459.
13. Bryusov (1975), vol. 6, p. 177. This line was, of course, directed at Ivanov.
14. Ibid., pp. 177–78.

> establishing a certain general principle. That principle is the symbolism of all true art.[15]

Such a radically syncretic and consciously ahistorical credo was difficult for many of Ivanov's contemporaries (and most subsequent scholars) to accept.[16]

Ivanov's notion of the Symbolist tradition at times bewildered even Bely. In a lengthy commentary to his own "Sense of Art," Bely discusses Ivanov's celebrated distinction between realistic and idealistic Symbolism. He is not so much bothered by the idiosyncratic use of traditional terminology, but rather by its application.[17] Why, Bely wonders, do all of Ivanov's favorite writers fit neatly within the category of the Realists? "Goethe and the Romantics, according to Ivanov, are Realists; then why did Goethe say that it cost him several years to overcome Romanticism?"[18] From the perspective of literary history, Bely's skepticism is completely justified. As numerous contemporary polemics attest, Goethe was often at odds with the Jena Romantics.[19]

Ivanov's reception of Goethe and Novalis is not as willful as Bely's image of Nietzsche, yet it bears the unmistakable imprint of Symbolist thinking. Ivanov tends to exclude or play down moments of friction between his exemplary Germans, while emphasizing events that suggest their spiritual closeness. He names Goethe as one of the two major influences on Novalis, allowing that Novalis went further than his mentor, but never questioning their basic kinship.[20] Moreover, he places special emphasis on the mutual respect between mentor and student.

> Goethe said of the already deceased Novalis: "He was not yet an emperor, but he could have become one." Where did the mysterious concept and unexpected word "emperor" come from? At that time, Napoleon had become an emperor. What did the young poet-mystic have in common with the titan of historical movement? Napoleon set himself the goal of realizing an unheard-of synthesis: the

---

15. *SS*, vol. 2, p. 613.

16. For a detailed account of the immediate reactions to Ivanov's position, see Kuznetsova (1990).

17. Elsewhere Bely also takes Ivanov to task on terminological grounds, cf. Bely (1910), p. 316.

18. Bely (1910), p. 549. Bely argues that realism and idealism are poles that can be separated only in theory. Both participate, to a greater or lesser extent, in any creative act.

19. Cf. Mähl. He cites Goethe's well-known comment to Eckermann (of 2 April 1829): "I call Classical healthy and Romantic sick."

20. Cf. *SS*, vol. 4, pp. 262–64.

> synthesis of revolution and a universal, newly stratified and religious monarchy. Novalis, verily, conceived of the same thing in the spiritual domain . . ."²¹

According to this interpretation, Goethe not only recognized Novalis's greatness, but even located the source of this brilliance in the ability to conceive of an "unheard-of synthesis." Ivanov uses Goethe's authority to legitimize Novalis in the pantheon of German literature.

In fact, Goethe's comment was meant quite differently. The quotation that Ivanov cites does not occur in Goethe's own writings, but in a book of conversations with Goethe compiled by Johannes Falk. In a section entitled "Goethe's Humor," Falk attributes the following speech to Goethe:

> In the German scholarly republic, things are now going just as colorfully as in the decline of the Roman empire, where Everyone wanted to rule and No One knew any longer who the real king was. At such a time, the great men almost all live in exile and any insolent sutler can become emperor as long as he has the favor of the soldiers and the army or can otherwise enjoy some influence. In such times, it's not important whether there are a few kings more or less. At one point in the Roman empire there were thirty kings simultaneously; why should we have fewer sovereigns in our learned states? . . . What were we talking about? Ah yes, about emperors! Good! Novalis was not yet one; but in time he could have become one. It's only a pity that he died so young, especially since he had done his epoch the favor of becoming a Catholic.²² And as the newspapers reported, flocks of young women and students made the pilgrimage to his grave and threw handfuls of flowers on it. That's what I call a good start, and it gives one high expectations for the future. Since I seldom read newspapers, I entreat my friends who are present to let me know immediately should something of further significance take place along these lines, for example, a canonization.²³

Context makes clear that Goethe's comment was intended as an unambiguous dismissal of Novalis (and, indeed, of the entire Romantic

---

21. Ibid., pp. 259–60. Ivanov also discusses the passage in his lecture. Ibid., p. 740.

22. Although many of the German Romantics converted to Catholicism, Novalis did not. Goethe appears to have confused Friedrich von Hardenberg (Novalis) with his brother Karl von Hardenberg. Cf. Mähl, pp. 193–94.

23. Falk, pp. 98–100.

movement). However, it should be emphasized that Ivanov's interpretation was not a deliberate distortion. Since the comparison of Novalis to an emperor (out of context and without any reference to Falk's rather obscure book) can be found throughout the German secondary literature, one may safely assume that Ivanov was unaware of the original context.[24] Nonetheless, the fact that he should seize on precisely this detail (and endow it with a highly idiosyncratic interpretation) clearly illustrates that a set of syncretic ideals and presuppositions were at work.

In repeated, yet extremely varied ways, Ivanov's reception of Goethe and Novalis represents an essentially agglutinative approach to tradition. For Ivanov, these writers were "classics" not only because they comprehended and expressed certain fundamental truths, but also by virtue of the powerful impulse they gave to future generations. Ivanov responded to this stimulus by selecting and developing specific elements of their poetics and philosophy and, when necessary, reconciling them with his own convictions.

Given the Symbolists' obsession with cultural continuity, it seems only appropriate to conclude with the question of Ivanov's own legacy. Even before the Soviet literary establishment conspired to marginalize Symbolism, the movement had lost its position at the vanguard of Russian poetry and thought. The aggressive manifestoes of the so-called "Cubo-Futurists" called for radical innovation at the expense of tradition. Arguing that "the past is [too] narrow," they developed the notorious slogan: "Throw Pushkin, Dostoevsky, Tolstoy, etc., etc., off the Steamship of modernity."[25] While such proclamations contained the most direct threats to Symbolist hegemony, the Acmeists could also be outspoken in their polemics.[26] Nonetheless, Ivanov continued to exert an influence, sometimes indirectly, on the next generation. Osip Mandel'stam's early work was conceived under Ivanov's aegis, and his celebrated definition of Acmeism as a

---

24. For a detailed and amusing survey of German critics' use of this passage, see Mähl, pp. 190–95. In Russia, even the normally careful Braun (p. 290) fell into the trap of repeating it (without reference, of course!), although, to his credit, he did not offer the detailed "interpretation" that Ivanov gave. In this case, Ivanov must have discovered the passage in the German secondary literature rather than in Braun, since he mentions it already in his 1909 lecture.

25. Both quotes from "A Slap in the Face of Public Taste," by Burlyuk, Kruchenykh, Mayakovsky, Khlebnikov. Reprinted in Markov (1967), 50–51.

26. See Mandel'stam's "The Morning of Acmeism" (especially parts three and five). In "On the Nature of the Word," with a degree of self-criticism, he noted: "Acmeism arose from repulsion: 'Away from Symbolism, long live the living rose.'—such was its original slogan." In Mandel'stam, pp. 298–99.

"yearning for world culture" surely owes much to Symbolist thought. Mandel'stam himself stated: "Not the ideas, but the tastes of the Acmeists were fatal for the Symbolists. The ideas were partially taken from the Symbolists, and Vyacheslav Ivanov himself greatly helped in the creation of Acmeist theory."[27] Recent scholarship has shown both specific and general resemblances (although by no means identity) between Mandel'stam's poetics and those of Ivanov.[28] The allusive quality of Akhmatova's later poetry (e.g., "Poem without a Hero") also displays a certain affinity, although Akhmatova herself strongly denied any such allegiance.[29] Gumilev, the founder of Acmeism and a severe critic of Symbolism, nonetheless recognized his debt to Symbolism in general and to Ivanov in particular.[30] Even the Futurists (both the "Cubo-Futurists" and the less radical "Centrifuge" faction) were to some extent educated on Ivanov's theories.[31]

Curiously, it is in the context of Russian literary scholarship where the Symbolists' views of literary continuity have been most thoroughly dismissed. Even before the forced ascendence of Marxist theory, the Formalists had to a large extent pushed Symbolist concepts from center stage. Portraying the emergence of their movement as a direct response to Symbolism, the Formalists largely succeeded in discrediting their predecessors. Eikhenbaum's "Theory of the Formal Method" exemplifies this bellicose position: "We engaged in battle with the Symbolists in order to wrest poetics from their hands. . . . The revolt of the Futurists (Klebnikov, Kruchenykh, Mayakovsky) against the poetic system of Symbolism, a revolt that had taken definite shape at about that time, lent support to the Formalists and imbued their struggle with an even greater relevance."[32] It is not surprising that Viktor Shklovsky, with his aggressively polemic style, found in Ivanov

---

27. Ibid. See also "The Slump," where he writes: "All contemporary Russian poetry came out of the ancestral Symbolist womb." Ibid., p. 272.

28. In addition to Taranovsky (1976), pp. 83–114, see Malmstad (1986) and Ronen (1983).

29. Akhmatova's own memoirs contain perhaps the most strident attacks on Ivanov and Symbolism. An overview is given in Blinov, pp. 14–17.

30. See Ibid., pp. 19–23.

31. The young Khlebnikov, a complete outsider to literary circles, brought his poetry to Ivanov for evaluation. Cf. Guenther, pp. 209–11. For a study of their subsequent contact, see Parnis. See Aseev for an account of Ivanov's influence on yet another Futurist.

32. Eikhenbaum, pp. 6–7. For a detailed analysis of Ivanov's relationship to Formalist theory, see Obatnin and Postoutenko, who argue that Ivanov occupied a middle ground between the Formalists and the Symbolists they so frequently attacked (Bryusov, Bely).

an appealing target.³³ But even Yury Tynyanov, the Formalists' most systematic and perhaps most enduringly influential thinker, directly challenged the Symbolists' sense of tradition by articulating a theory of literary evolution that canonized change. "If we agree that evolution is the change in interrelationships between the elements of a system—between functions and formal elements—then evolution may be seen as the 'mutations' of systems."³⁴ In his critical writings, Tynyanov generally focused on a writer's polemical or parodic attitude toward his predecessors. His own legacy to literary studies has been the "jagged line" of literary succession, whereby norm-breaking becomes the moving force in the development of a national literature.

Tynyanov had little sympathy for the ideal of continuity that lay at the foundation of Symbolist poetics.³⁵ In an essay devoted to Bryusov's syncretic poetics, Tynyanov writes:

> This was not eclecticism,—it was a necessary enrichment of a tired poetic culture.³⁶ In order to overcome this tiredness and emerge from a flattened circle, a disorderly breadth of traditions was necessary. There are periods when poetry does not need this breadth, when it lives through the power of a limited number of traditions; there are epochs when a national poetry closes up into itself and resolves its own questions. Bryusov's epoch needed the opposite. Broad, even contradictory, traditions were needed,—the door of literature was opened wide to the West.³⁷

Tynyanov allows that Bryusov's method was historically justified, yet he evaluates it negatively: "But such is the unavoidable historical rule: in fighting against tired verse, combining widely different and contradictory traditions, Bryusov's verse, having completed its historical role, unavoidably turns to us with its opposite side and seems for the same reason tired, overburdened with poetic culture, and therefore naked."³⁸

The reactions of Tynyanov and Bely toward the poetry of Vladislav Khodasevich provide an instructive example of the way the-

---

33. In his famous essay "Art as Technique," Shklovsky uses a barely veiled allusion to Ivanov in his dismissal of Symbolism. Shklovsky, p. 7.

34. Tynyanov (1967), p. 46. Translation in Tynyanov (1978), p. 76.

35. His short essay on Blok (Tynyanov [1967], pp. 512–20) marks a notable exception. Tynyanov recognizes the "long-known, traditional images" (p. 516) and the explicit quotations (p. 517) at the basis of Blok's poetic world, but nonetheless evaluates them positively.

36. Tynyanov, an outsider to Symbolism, uses the word "eclectic" pejoratively.

37. Tynyanov (1967), p. 538.

38. Ibid.

oretical presuppositions can influence critical evaluation. Bely praises Khodasevich highly by emphasizing the "direct succession" that links his verse to that of the masters of Russian nineteenth-century poetry.[39] Tynyanov, noting essentially the same characteristics, rejects Khodasevich as a poetic voice that is not "genuine."[40]

Ivanov's conception of cultural tradition, forgotten or dismissed in Soviet Russia, nevertheless took root in Western Europe, most prominently in the work of the German literary critic Ernst Robert Curtius. In his twenty-five year exile, Ivanov came into contact with a number of leading European thinkers. However, his relationship to Curtius deserves special consideration. In this regard, one can speak with certainty of Ivanov's palpable and enduring influence on one of the twentieth-century's major scholars and cultural figures. It is particularly worth emphasizing this connection because Ivanov's importance has been consistently overlooked in the substantial secondary literature on Curtius.

Curtius first encountered Ivanov's writings in 1931, at a critical juncture in his own development. A distinguished professor of French literature at the University of Bonn, Curtius was at this time turning his attention and intellectual energy to the "spiritual crisis" in contemporary Germany. In a series of articles that later formed the basis of the book *Deutscher Geist in Gefahr* (*German Spirit in Danger*), he subjected the most recent political and intellectual developments to a blistering critique. In the course of his work on this subject, he read (with "*passionate* interest," as he noted in a letter of 8 December 1931 to Charles Du Bos)[41] the *Correspondence from Two Corners*. The impact of this work on Curtius's thinking proved to be decisive. A month later, in another letter to Du Bos, he exclaimed (in English, underlined): "The ideas of Ivanov have supplied me with the missing link which I needed for the chain of my thoughts."[42]

In *German Spirit in Danger*, Curtius treats topics as diverse as university policy, sociology and politics. Throughout, he brings an extensive tradition of poets and philosophers to bear on his argument. This methodological strategy underscores one of his central convictions: the relevance of the past for the present. Curtius repeatedly criticizes "the overevaluation of the present and the simultaneous underevaluation of the past and future...this confusion of the sense of time that we find today everywhere, in the general and individual con-

---

39. Bely (1923), p. 377.
40. Tynyanov (1967), p. 549.
41. Herbert and Jane M. Dieckmann, p. 314.
42. Ibid., p. 318.

sciousness."[43] According to Curtius, an apathy toward past achievement reflects an "indifference to culture," and, ultimately, "a decisive will to destroy culture."[44] He perceives this tendency in all aspects of society: in the politicians (of all parties) as well as the cultural establishment.

The so-called "nationalists," for example, seek to isolate Germany from its European context. Curtius rejects such a program because it is based on an untenable premise. All European countries, he argues, combine a common heritage (Roman antiquity and Christianity) with certain indigenous elements. Without denying the individuality of national literatures, Curtius emphasizes their indebtedness to a common ancestor.[45] On the other side of the political spectrum, Curtius assails Bolshevism, which he views as fundamentally inimical to culture.

In the book's final chapter, Curtius elaborates an idiosyncratic conception of humanism as an antidote to the ills of modern Germany. In contrast to the usual textbook definitions of this term, Curtius's subject is an "eternal humanism," i.e., a universal concept rather than a specific historical movement.[46] As a constantly evolving creative impulse common to numerous historical periods, it encompasses and unites extremely diverse phenomena. In Curtius's words, "It is the intoxicating discovery of a beloved archetype [Urbild].... In this way Hölderlin discovered the gods of Olympus. In this way all the reception of antiquity in the art of the Middle Ages and Renaissance took place."[47] Based on continuity and connection, Curtius's conception of humanism allows modernity to build productively on past accomplishments.

In order to give a concrete example of this ideal, Curtius turns to the *Correspondence from Two Corners*. This work, an epistolary dispute between Ivanov and Mikhail Osipovich Gershenzon, came into existence in 1920, during the Civil War, when its two authors were coincidentally assigned to the same room in a sanatorium outside Moscow. Their twelve letters concern the fate of culture in an era of revolution. Gershenzon assumes the role of "cultural anarchist," emphasizing the utter irrelevance—and, in any case, the unrecuperability—of cultural tradition for contemporary Russia. Ivanov takes the opposite position, arguing for the necessity of preserving the tradition. In essence, their debate was not new. Gershenzon followed a line of argument that can be found in Descartes and Rousseau; Ivanov, rely-

43. Curtius (1932), p. 41.
44. Ibid., pp. 19, 21.
45. Ibid., p. 22.
46. Ibid., p. 105.
47. Ibid., p. 107.

ing on explicit allusions, draws on such thinkers as Plato, Goethe and Tyutchev.

In the context of the cataclysmic events of the twentieth century, the issue of cultural continuity gained special urgency. The *Correspondence from Two Corners* served as the cornerstone of Ivanov's fame in emigration. Martin Buber, who published the work's first translation in his journal *Die Kreatur*, considered it "one of the most important spiritual documents of our time."[48] Charles Du Bos, who supervised the first French edition, summed up its importance by saying that "never has the fundamental contemporary opposition (which today truly marks the parting of the waters) between the hope of the 'thesaurus' and the obsession with the 'tabula rasa' been better expressed than in these pages."[49]

In the final chapter of *German Spirit in Danger*, Curtius gives a detailed summary of the *Correspondence*, quoting extensively from Ivanov and placing special emphasis on his definition of culture as memory. Ivanov had written:

> For me, however, culture in its true sense is not a surface extending only horizontally, nor is it a plain of ruins or a field strewn with bones. Culture, for me, is something truly sacred; it is the memory not only of the earthly and external features of our ancestors but also of the initiations that they achieved: a living, eternal memory, which does not die in those who partake of those initiations. These have been transmitted by the ancestors to their most distant descendants, and not one iota of this message, since the first letter was inscribed on the tablet of the human spirit, shall be effaced. In this sense, culture is not only monumental but initiative in character. Because memory, the highest ruler of all culture, allows its servants to partake of their forbears' experience. To those who rejuvenate themselves in these initiations, it transmits the strength of new beginnings. Memory is a dynamic principle; forgetting is exhaustion, interruption of motion, decay and return to a condition of relative indolence.[50]

According to this unabashedly mystical and generative notion of culture, no accomplishment or thought is ever lost. Ivanov conceives of tradition as a memory that retains "historical" impressions (texts, arti-

---

48. Letter to Ivanov of 21 August 1926 (Rome archive).
49. Letter to Ivanov of 11 July 1930 (Rome archive).
50. *SS*, vol. 3, pp. 395–96. My translation is adapted from Lisa Sergio's in Ivanov and Gershenzon, pp. 26–27.

facts, personal experiences) as well as the "initiations of ancestors" (mystical experience, metaphysical truth). Most importantly, such a memory does not impede evolution, for true culture is a continuing process that builds on the accomplishments of past generations. It is opposed to decadence, which Ivanov defines as "the feeling of the finest organic connection with the monumental tradition of a high culture that has passed, together with the emphatically proud awareness that we are the last in this series."[51]

It cannot be doubted that Ivanov's conception of memory was the "missing link" that allowed Curtius to complete his book *German Spirit in Danger*. Soon after the book appeared, Curtius wrote to Ivanov: "Your conversation with Gershenzon has become for me much more than the crystallization point of my thoughts; it has penetrated into the substance of my most profound certainties. Your dialogue came to me like the liberating word, the solution which I was waiting for without knowing it.... I am grateful to you for an 'initiation' in the true sense of the word. There are few people to whom one can write this. I am happy if my little book can help to spread your deep wisdom."[52]

Until 1940, when military censorship caused a lengthy hiatus, Ivanov and Curtius maintained a regular correspondence and exchanged articles and books. In addition, the two met frequently during Curtius's visits to Rome.[53] In 1934, Curtius contributed a brief essay on Ivanov to the Italian journal *Il Convegno*, which was devoting an entire issue to his work. Once again, Curtius focused on Ivanov's humanism.

> We are not concerned here with a "Christian humanism" in the sense of Erasmus or the Jesuits. We are also not concerned with a political link between classical concepts of order and trident theology. Ivanov's humanism is not the external conformity with an historical model, but anamnesis: that is, the reawakening of a primordial knowledge about the initiations and mysteries of the fathers. For this reason he can recognize in the seemingly most distant and most alien a renewal of antiquity: in Dostoevsky the Attic tragedy, in Gogol the aristophanic choir.[54]

51. *SS*, vol. 3, p. 396. English in Ivanov and Gershenzon, p. 27.
52. Letter of 26 February 1932. In Wachtel (1992), p. 76.
53. Cf. Curtius's letter to Herbert Steiner from 5 March 1948. "I was very moved by your mention of Ivanov's 82nd birthday. In the thirties I visited him repeatedly in Rome and I admire him deeply." (Deutsches Literaturarchiv, Marbach.)
54. For the original (German) text, see Wachtel (1992), pp. 88–90.

The references to the Dostoevsky book and the essay on Gogol and Aristophanes indicate that Curtius understood Ivanov's literary-critical work as an application of the "humanistic" principle he had discovered in the more philosophical *Correspondence*.[55] Curtius points with obvious approval to Ivanov's "ahistorical" methodology, which allows him to connect writers who are separated by space and time.

Further evidence of such approval can be found in a letter of 1935. At this time, Ivanov was at work on an essay on "Symbolism" for an Italian encyclopedia. Apparently in response to a request for relevant secondary literature, Curtius included a list of fourteen general works on French Symbolism. In the accompanying letter, however, he himself cast doubt on their value: "But I assume that you will only touch on the so-called 'Symbolism' of the eighties and nineties. Your real topic is after all eternal symbolism, for which Dante and Goethe are much more important than Mallarmé and his contemporaries."[56] The term "eternal symbolism" (which would eventually appear as the concluding phrase of Ivanov's encyclopedia article)[57] recalls the notion of "eternal humanism" that Curtius had developed in *German Spirit in Danger* to designate his own timeless spiritual ideal.[58]

With the publication in 1948 of the monumental *European Literature and the Latin Middle Ages*, Curtius became something of an international celebrity. By examining topoi (which he understood as repeating motifs) that can be found in various national literatures, Curtius sought to demonstrate the essential unity of the Western poetic tradition. In an introduction written for the work's English translation, Curtius emphasizes the way that *European Literature and the Latin Middle Ages* developed organically from *German Spirit in Danger*.[59] The theme of continuity, which appeared as an ideal in the polemical essays of the earlier work, becomes the central principle of a theory of literature.

---

55. Curtius had read Ivanov's works on Dostoevsky and Gogol in German. English translations now exist of both; for the former, see Ivanov (1966), for the latter, see Maguire, pp. 200–214.

56. Letter of 7 April 1935. In Wachtel (1992), p. 94.

57. *SS*, vol. 2, pp. 659, 667.

58. Curtius (1932), p. 105.

59. "In 1932 I published my polemical pamphlet *Deutscher Geist in Gefahr*. It attacked the barbarization of education and the nationalistic frenzy which were the forerunners of the Nazi regime. In it I pleaded for a new humanism, which should integrate the Middle Ages, from Augustine to Dante.... What I have said will have made it clear that my book is not the product of purely scholarly interests, that it grew out of a concern for the preservation of Western culture." In Curtius (1973), pp. vii–viii.

Curtius's conception of "topos" oscillates curiously between a strictly historical approach to literary influence and, when such influence cannot be proven empirically, a more mystical sense of tradition.[60] In his introduction, Curtius stresses his indebtedness to Jung, who, through recourse to a "collective unconscious," attempted to explain connections between cultural phenomena of disparate countries and cultures.[61] Yet the fact that Ivanov figures prominently in the book's crucial methodological chapter suggests that Jung was not the sole source of Curtius's ahistoricism. In a section entitled "Continuity," Curtius once again includes the citation from the *Correspondence from Two Corners* concerning culture as memory. A

---

60. Richards, p. 250, notes: "In Curtius's writings one is struck by the frequent attempts to bring irrational, intuitive elements in harmony with philological and literary-historical analysis."

61. Curtius (1973), p. ix: "In my book things will also be found which I could not have seen without C. G. Jung . . . " Already in *German Spirit in Danger* (pp. 41–42), Curtius had praised Jung ("our age's wisest expert on the soul") for recognizing the ideal of continuity as a necessary condition of spiritual health. The complicated question of the relationship of Jungian psychology to Russian Symbolism has attracted much scholarly attention and conjecture: Averintsev (1970), pp. 129–30, 136; Hansen-Löve, e.g., p. 375; and Aleksandr Etkind (1994). The central figure in this discussion is Emil Metner, who became a patient, friend, and disciple of Jung. Metner insists that Jung shared a number of basic Symbolist presuppositions (cf. Medtner, pp. 574–75). Ivanov, on the other hand, disagreed profoundly. While the fleeting references to Jung in Ivanov's published works seem positive (e.g., SS, vol. 3, pp. 272, 483), archival sources make clear his vehement rejection of Jung's principles. On 6 July 1929, Ivanov wrote to Metner: "I must admit to my complete ignorance of Jung and his psychological school, in which you have evidently found something extremely valuable. I would hope that you will initiate me into its mysteries." RGB, f. 167, k. 14, ed. khr. 10. Metner promptly sent Ivanov a Russian edition of Jung's *Psychological Types* (which Metner himself had just published in Berlin under the "Musaget" aegis). In a letter to Metner of 22 November 1929, Ivanov shared his impressions of the book. He disliked everything about it: "its rhapsodic structure and useless, essentially dilettantish digressions and excurses, the indefinite explanation of the basic theory, the absolute (in its nihilism) attempt to reduce everything, without exception, to psychology alone, more precisely to Jungian psychology, and—finally (this is already the height of an author's hubris)—its sermonizing." RGB, f. 167, k. 14, ed. khr. 10. In a letter of 22 August 1930 to Herbert Steiner (Deutches Literaturarchiv, Marbach), Ivanov decried Jung's "efforts to interpret religious experience from a purely psychological standpoint." It is not surprising that these polemics, so uncharacteristic of Ivanov's tone and approach, are hidden away in letters, rather than published in essays. To some extent, this is surely connected to what Averintsev (1986), p. 43, has called Ivanov's "cultural diplomacy." It should also be emphasized that, in general, Ivanov was far more critical of his contemporaries than of his predecessors. "Death canonizes, it turns people into heroes" (in Al'tman, p. 310).

few pages later, he writes: "Culture as initiatory memory... Ivanov recorded his thoughts in 1920 in the Moscow convalescent home 'for workers in science and literature.' Since then, cultural collapses have ensued whose effects cannot yet be measured. In the present situation of the mind, there is nothing more pressing than to restore 'memory.'"[62] This goal recalls the fundamental program of *German Spirit in Danger*, where the spiritual health of a nation was dependent on its ability to remember the past and build upon this recollection. Curtius's *European Literature and the Latin Middle Ages* represents an attempt, using largely philological methods, to revive this memory. His repeated allusions to the *Correspondence from Two Corners* indicate that Ivanov contributed to the fundamental idea behind this work.

According to Ivanov, each new artistic work affirms and creatively continues the tradition. The central unifying concept is memory, understood not merely as a *thesaurus* of past accomplishment, but also as an instrument of innovation: "the source of all individual creation, brilliant insights and prophetic initiative."[63] At the basis of Ivanov's theory lies a belief in the inexhaustibility of cultural achievement. This idea, implicit in the deliberately ambiguous title of his 1912 "Goethe on the Border of Two Centuries,"[64] becomes explicit in that essay's concluding line: "But there can be no doubt that in the twentieth century, people will reread Goethe's work and draw from it something different than people of the previous century."[65]

Ivanov's belief in the open-ended nature of an artistic work anticipates much recent critical thinking. In 1970, in an open letter to the editorial board of a leading Soviet journal, Mikhail Bakhtin supplied what appears to be a gloss on Ivanov:

> It seems paradoxical that . . . great works continue to live in the distant future. In the process of their posthumous life they are enriched with new meanings, new significance: it is as though these works outgrow what they were in the epoch of their creation. We can say that neither Shakespeare himself nor his contemporaries knew that "great Shakespeare" whom we know now. . . . Modernization and distortion, of course, have existed and will continue to exist. But that is not the reason why Shakespeare has grown. He has grown because of that which actually has been and continues to be found in his

---

62. Curtius (1973), p. 396.
63. *SS*, vol. 3, p. 92.
64. The border is that between the eighteenth and nineteenth centuries (which Goethe had crossed) as well as the nineteenth and twentieth centuries (which Ivanov and his contemporaries had recently crossed). Cf. Gronicka, vol. 2, p. 192.
65. *SS*, vol. 4, p. 157.

works, but which neither he himself nor his contemporaries could consciously perceive and evaluate in the context of the culture of their epoch.[66]

Indeed, in the Bakhtin of 1970, Ivanov seems to have completed his circuitous path from Russia to the West and back again. Bakhtin, an internal exile in terms of Soviet scholarship, articulates a methodology remarkably reminiscent of Ivanovian notions: "We usually strive to explain a writer and his work precisely through his own time and the most recent past. ... We are afraid to remove ourselves in time from the phenomenon under investigation. Yet the artwork extends its roots into the distant past. Great literary works are prepared for by centuries, and in the epoch of their creation it is merely a matter of picking the fruit that is ripe after a lengthy and complex process of maturation."[67] These thoughts lead Bakhtin to a hermeneutic ideal based on a curiously familiar notion of memory: "*creative understanding* does not renounce itself, its own place in time, its own culture; and it forgets nothing."[68]

Throughout his life, Bakhtin had admired Ivanov's works, yet this coincidence in views is particularly striking.[69] It seems that, even (or perhaps *especially*) in periods of radical discontinuity, there remain thinkers whose erudition and convictions allow them to discover resemblances and to posit further connections. In the intellectual history of the twentieth century, Ivanov, Curtius, and Bakhtin belong to a small number of scholars who were capable of discerning order amidst cultural chaos. Isolated in their specific historical circumstances, they were nonetheless united by a conception of memory as a creative and liberating force that extended far beyond the confines of their own era.[70]

---

66. Bakhtin (1986), p. 4.
67. Ibid., pp. 3–4.
68. Ibid., p. 7. In the same essay, Bakhtin discusses "great time," a loosely defined but crucial concept that has a number of points of contact with Ivanov. As glossed by my colleague Caryl Emerson, great time "is some temporal level where all unexpressed or potential meanings are eventually actualized, where every idea finds a context that can justify and nourish it. Great time is neither abstract, nor ahistorical, nor systematic; it is simply an open, and very long, sequence of concrete historical moments." Averintsev (1992), p. 308, has described Ivanov's approach to earlier literature in Bakhtinian terms, as a "translation from 'small time' to 'great time.'"
69. For a discussion of Bakhtin's attitude toward Ivanov, see Clark and Holquist, pp. 25–26.
70. Buber, in many respects a kindred spirit, commented on Ivanov's "Letter to Charles Du Bos": "The Letter belongs to the most important testaments of the time. You have recognized and articulated the most essential thing: memory." From Buber's letter to Ivanov of 4 May 1932 (Rome archive).

While it is always dangerous to make predictions, the recent surge of interest in such thinkers may well signal a shift in Western literary theory from consciously fragmented, antitraditional approaches (heirs of Formalism) toward holistic, syncretic, and mystical systems. In terms of cultural developments in Russia, there can be no doubt that the demise of the Soviet system has made possible a search for new models and, consequently, has contributed to the renaissance of Vyacheslav Ivanov as poet and thinker. For even in the early years of the tragic experiment called Communism, from the depths of the Russian Civil War, with his country facing total economic and political anarchy, Ivanov could write to Gershenzon that "the aim of the struggle is not to do away with the values of the cultural past; the great thing being fought for is the revitalization of everything from the past that has a permanent validity—an urgent and supreme task of revaluation, to be carried out as soon as possible.... In addition to self-preservation, every living thing seeks self-revelation, certain in its depths that this must lead to self-exhaustion, self-destruction, and death—and also, perhaps, to eternal remembrance."[71]

---

71. From the ninth letter of the *Correspondence from Two Corners*. Translation adapted from Ivanov and Gershenzon, pp. 46, 48.

WORKS CONSULTED

INDEX

Works Consulted

Alexandrov, Vladimir. *Andrei Bely: The Major Symbolist Fiction* (Cambridge, 1985).

Alferov, A. D. *Sochineniya V. A. Zhukovskogo v dvukh tomakh* (Moscow, 1902).

Allen, Thomas W., and Edward E. Sikes. *The Homeric Hymns* (London, 1904).

Al'tman, M. S. "Iz besed s poetom Vyacheslavom Ivanovichem Ivanovym" in *Trudy po russkoi i slavyanskoi filologii*, no. 209 (Tartu, 1968), pp. 304–25.

Aseev, Nikolai. "Moskovskie zapiski" in *Dal'nevostochnoe obozrenie* (24 June 1920). Reprinted with an introduction by Aleksandr Parnis in *Russkaya Mysl'*, no. 3933 (Paris, 12 June 1992), p. 13.

Auslender, Sergei. "Goluboi tsvetok" in *Apollon*, no. 3 (1909), pp. 41–42.

Averintsev, Sergei. "Analiticheskaya psikhologiya K. G. Yunga i zakonomernosti tvorcheskoi fantazii" in *Voprosy Literatury*, no. 3 (1970), pp. 113–43.

Averintsev, Sergei. "Struktura otnosheniya k poeticheskomu slovu v tvorchestve Vyacheslava Ivanova" in *Tezisy vsesoyuznoi (III) konferentsii "Tvorchestvo A. A. Bloka i russkaya kul'tura XX veka"* (Tartu, 1975), pp. 152–55.

Averintsev, Sergei. "The Poetry of Vyacheslav Ivanov," in Robert Louis Jackson and Lowry Nelson, Jr., eds. *Vyacheslav Ivanov: Poet, Critic and Philosopher* (New Haven, 1986), pp. 25–48.

Averintsev, Sergei. "Vyach. Ivanov i russkaya literaturnaya traditsiya," in V. A. Keldysh, ed. *Svyaz' vremen. Problemy preemstvennosti v russkoi literature kontsa XIX–nachala XX v.* (Moscow, 1992), pp. 298–311.

Azadovskii, K. M. "Put' Aleksandra Dobrolyubova" in *Blokovskii sbornik*, no. 3 (Tartu, 1979), pp. 121–46.

Azadovskii, K. M. "... 'U nas s vami est' chto-to rodstvennoe' (Belyi i Iogannes fon Gyunter)" in Balashov, V. P., ed. *Andrei Belyi: Problemy tvorchestva* (Moscow, 1989), pp. 470–81.

Azadovskii, K. M. "Vyacheslav Ivanov i F. F. Fidler" in Wilfried Potthoff, ed. *Vjačeslav Ivanov: Russischer Dichter—europäischer Kulturphilosoph* (Heidelberg, 1993), pp. 35–57.

Azadovskii, K. M., and D. E. Maksimov. "Bryusov i 'Vesy'" in *Literaturnoe nasledstvo*, vol. 85, (1976), pp. 257–324.

Bailey, James. "Blok and Heine: An Episode from the History of Russian dol'niki" in *Slavic and East European Journal*, vol. 13, no. 1 (1969), pp. 1–21.

Bakhtin, M. M. *Speech Genres and Other Late Essays* (Austin, 1986).

Balashov, V. P., ed. *Andrei Belyi: Problemy tvorchestva* (Moscow, 1989).

Balmont, K. D. *Stikhotvoreniya* (Leningrad, 1969).

Beketova, M. A. *Pis'ma Aleksandra Bloka k rodnym* (Leningrad, 1932).

Belyi, Andrei. *Arabeski* (Munich, 1971).

Belyi, Andrei. *Chetyre simfonii* (Munich, 1969).

Belyi, Andrei. *Mezhdu dvukh revolyutsii* (Leningrad, 1934).

Belyi, Andrei. *Na rubezhe dvukh stoletii* (Leningrad, 1930).

Belyi, Andrei. *Simvolizm* (Moscow, 1910).

Belyi, Andrei. "Tyazhelaya lira i russkaya lirika" in *Sovremennye zapiski*, no. 15 (1923), pp. 371–88.

Belyi, Andrei. *Vospominaniya o Shteinere* (Paris, 1982).

Berdyaev, Nikolai. *Samopoznanie* (Moscow, 1991).

Bezrodnyi, M. V. "Iz istorii russkogo neokantianstva (zhurnal 'Logos' i ego redaktory)" in *Litsa*, vol. 1 (Moscow, 1992), pp. 372–407.

Blinov, Valerii. "Vyacheslav Ivanov i vozniknovenie akmeizma," in Fausto Malcovati, ed. *Cultura e memoria: atti del terzo Simposio Internazionale didicato a Viačeslav Ivanov*, vol. 2, (Florence, 1988), pp. 13–25.

Blok, Aleksandr. "Geine v Rossii" in Aleksandr Blok, *Sobranie sochinenii*, vol. 6 (Moscow, 1962), pp. 116–28.

Blok, Aleksandr, and Andrei Bely. *Perepiska* (Munich, 1969).

Bloom, Harold. *Poetry and Repression* (New Haven, 1976).

Boym, Svetlana. *Death in Quotation Marks* (Cambridge, 1991).

Braginskaya, N. V. "Tragediya i ritual u Vyacheslava Ivanova" in E. S. Novik, ed. *Arkhaicheskii ritual v fol'klornykh i ranneliteraturnykh pamyatnikakh* (Moscow, 1988), pp. 294-329.

Braun, F. A. "Novalis" in F. D. Batyushkov, ed. *Istoriya zapadnoi literatury*, vol. 1 (Moscow, 1912), pp. 289-332.

Bristol, Evelyn. "From Romanticism to Symbolism in France and Russia," in Paul Debreczeny, ed. *American Contributions to the Ninth International Congress of Slavists* (Columbus, 1983), pp. 69-80.

Bryusov, Valerii. *Dnevniki 1891-1910* (Moscow, 1927).

Bryusov, Valerii. *Sobranie sochinenii v semi tomakh* (Moscow, 1975).

Burgi, Richard. *A History of the Russian Hexameter* (Hamden, 1954).

Carlson, Maria. "Ivanov-Belyj-Minclova: the Mystical Triangle," in Fausto Malcovati, ed. *Cultura e memoria: atti del terzo Simposio Internazionale didicato a Viačeslav Ivanov*, vol. 1 (Florence, 1988), pp. 63-79.

Cassedy, Steven. "Bely's Theory of Symbolism as a Formal Iconics of Meaning" and "Bely the Thinker," in Malmstad, John, ed. *Andrey Bely: Spirit of Symbolism* (Ithaca, 1987), pp. 285-335.

Cassedy, Steven. *Selected Essays of Andrey Bely* (Berkeley, 1985).

Chulkov, Georgy. *Pokryvalo Izidy* (Moscow, 1909).

Clark, Katerina, and Michael Holquist. *Mikhail Bakhtin* (Cambridge, 1984).

Curtius, Ernst Robert. *Deutscher Geist in Gefahr* (Stuttgart, 1932).

Curtius, Ernst Robert. *European Literature and the Latin Middle Ages* (Princeton, 1973).

Davidson, Pamela. *The Poetic Imagination of Vyacheslav Ivanov: A Russian Symbolist's Perception of Dante* (Cambridge, 1989).

Dieckmann, Herbert, and Jane M. Dieckmann. *Deutsch-Französische Gespräche 1920-1950: La Correspondance de Ernst Robert Curtius avec André Gide, Charles Du Bos et Valery Larbaud* (Frankfurt am Main, 1980).

Donchin, Georgette. *The Influence of French Symbolism on Russian Poetry* (The Hague, 1958).

Doubrovkine, Roman. "Nemetskaya versiya melopei 'Chelovek.' Popytka interpretatsii" in *Cahiers du Monde russe*, vol. XXXV [1–2] (1994), pp. 301–30.

Durylin, Sergei. "Russkie pisateli u Gete v Veimare" in *Literaturnoe nasledstvo*, vol. 4–6 (Moscow, 1932), pp. 83–504.

Eikhenbaum, Boris. "Theory of the Formal Method" in Ladislav Matejka and Krystyna Pomorska, eds. *Readings in Russian Poetics* (Ann Arbor, 1978), pp. 3–37.

Ellis. *Russkie simvolisty* (Moscow, 1910).

Engel-Braunschmidt, Annelore. *Deutsche Dichter in Rußland im 19. Jahrhundert* (Munich, 1973).

Eskhil. *Tragedii* (Moscow, 1989).

Etkind, Aleksandr. "Vyacheslav Ivanov i psikhoanaliz" in *Cahiers du Monde russe*, vol. XXXV [1–2] (1994), pp. 225–34.

Etkind, Efim. "Poeziya Novalisa: 'Mifologicheskii perevod' Vyacheslava Ivanova" in Fausto Malcovati, ed. *Cultura e memoria: atti del terzo Simposio Internazionale didicato a Viačeslav Ivanov*, vol. 2 (Florence, 1988), pp. 171–85.

Falk, Johannes. *Goethe aus näherm persönlichen Umgang dargestellt* (Leipzig, 1832).

Filosofov, Dmitrii. "Nemetskii romantizm i russkaya literatura" in *Rech'* (6 January 1914), p. 3.

Frank, Horst Joachim. *Handbuch der deutschen Strophenformen* (Munich, 1980).

Friedrich, Theodor, and Lothar I. Scheithauer. *Goethes Faust erläutert* (Leipzig, 1956).

Gasparov, M. L. "Bryusov i bukvalizm" in *Masterstvo perevoda* (Moscow, 1971), pp. 88–128.

Gasparov, M. L. *Ocherk istorii russkogo stikha* (Moscow, 1984).

Gasparov, M. L. "Semanticheskii oreol trekhstopnogo amfibrakhiia" in *Problemy sturkturnoi lingvistiki* (Moscow, 1982), pp. 174–92.

Gasparov, M. L. *Uchebnyi material po literaturovedeniyu: russkii stikh* (Tallin, 1987).

Gerasimov, Yu. K. "Neokonchennaya tragediya Vyacheslava Ivanova 'Niobeya'" in *Ezhegodnik rukopisnogo otdela pushkinskogo doma na 1980 god* (Leningrad, 1984), pp. 178–203.

Gerbel, N. V. *Nemetskie poety v biografiyakh i obraztsakh* (St. Petersburg, 1877).

Gertsyk, Evgeniya. *Vospominaniya* (Paris, 1973).

Ginzburg, Lydia. *On Psychological Prose* (Princeton, 1991).

Goethe, Johann Wolfgang. *Gedichte* (Munich, 1982).

Goethe, Johann Wolfgang. *Poetische Werke*, vol. 1 (Berlin, 1965).

Gronicka, André von. *The Russian Image of Goethe*, 2 vols. (Philadelphia, 1968, 1985).

Guenther, Johannes von. *Ein Leben im Ostwind: Zwischen Petersburg und München* (Munich, 1969).

Gumilev, Nikolai. *Sobranie sochinenii*, vol. 4 (Washington, 1976).

Hansen-Löve, Aage A. *Der russische Symbolismus: System und Entfaltung der poetischen Motive*, vol. 1 (Vienna, 1989).

Haussmann, J. F. "German Estimates of Novalis from 1800–1850," in *Modern Philology*, vol. IX, no. 3, (January, 1912), pp. 399–415.

Heiseler, Henry von. *Zwischen Deutschland und Rußland* (Heidelberg, 1969).

Hesiod. *The Homeric Hymns and Homerica* (Cambridge, 1974).

Hiebel, Friedrich. *Novalis* (Bern, 1972).

Hinck, Walter. "Goethes Ballade *Der untreue Knabe*. Zur Geschichte der siebenzeiligen Strophe in mittelalterlicher und neuerer deutscher Lyrik" in *Euphorion*, vol. 56 (1962), pp. 25–47.

Holthusen, Johannes. *Studien zur Ästhetik und Poetik des russischen Symbolismus* (Göttingen, 1957).

Holthusen, Johannes. *Viačeslav Ivanov als symbolistischer Dichter und als russischer Kulturphilosoph* (Munich, 1982).

Ivanov, Dimitri. "Recurrent Motifs in Ivanov's Work" in Robert Louis Jackson and Lowry Nelson, Jr., eds. *Vyacheslav Ivanov: Poet, Critic and Philosopher* (New Haven, 1986), pp. 367–89.

Ivanov, Vjačeslav. *Durchsichtigkeit* (Munich, 1967).

Ivanov, Vyacheslav. *Ellinskaya religiya stradayushchego boga* in *Novyi put'*, no. 1 (1904), pp. 110–34; no. 2 (1904), pp. 48–78; no. 3 (1904), pp. 38–61; no. 5 (1904), pp. 28–40; no. 8 (1904), pp. 17–26; no. 9, pp. 47–70. In *Voprosy zhizni*, no. 6 (1905), pp. 185–220; no. 7 (1905), pp. 122–48.

Ivanov, Vyacheslav. *Freedom and the Tragic Life: A Study in Dostoevsky* (New York, 1966).

Ivanov, Vyacheslav. "Rasskazy tainovidtsa" in *Vesy*, no. 8 (1904), pp. 47–50.

Ivanov, Vyacheslav. *Sobranie sochinenii*, 4 vols. (Brussels, 1971–1986). Referred to as *SS*.

Ivanov, Vyacheslav. *Stikhotvoreniya i poemy* (Leningrad, 1976).

Ivanov, V. I. and M. O. Gershenzon. *Correspondence Across a Room* (Marlboro, 1984).

Ivanova, Lidiya. *Vospominaniya; kniga ob ottse.* John Malmstad, ed. (Paris, 1990).

Iwanow, Wjatscheslaw. *Das alte Wahre* (Berlin, 1951).

Jakobson, Roman. *Language in Literature* (Cambridge, 1987).

Kayser, Wolfgang. *Geschichte des deutschen Verses* (Munich, 1981).

Keys, Roger. "Bely's Symphonies" in John Malmstad, ed. *Andrey Bely: Spirit of Symbolism* (Ithaca, 1987), pp. 19–59.

Khodasevich, Vladislav. *Nekropol'* (Paris, 1976).

Kluge, Rolf-Dieter. *Westeuropa und Rußland im Weltbild Aleksandr Bloks* (Munich, 1967).

Knigge, Armin. *Die Lyrik Vl. Solov'evs und ihre Nachwirkung bei A. Belyj und A. Blok* (Amsterdam, 1973).

Knipovich, E. F. "Blok i Geine" in E. F. Nikitina, ed. *O Bloke* (Moscow, 1929), pp. 167–81.

Knipovich, E. F. "Ob Aleksandre Bloke" in *Literaturnoe nasledstvo*, vol. 92, book 1 (Moscow, 1980), pp. 16–44.

Kogan, P. S. "Novalis. Geinrikh von Ofterdingen" in *Golos minuvshego*, no. 5 (1915), pp. 266–70.

Kogan, P. S. "Pis'mo o zapade" in *Russkaya mysl'*, no. 5 (1901), pp. 102–14.

Kotrelev, N. V. "K istorii 'Kormchikh zvezd'" in *Russkaya mysl'*, no. 3793 (Paris, 15 September 1989).

Kotrelev, N. V. "Vyach. Ivanov—Professor Bakinskogo universiteta" in *Trudy po russkoi i slavyanskoi filologii*, no. 209 (Tartu, 1968), pp. 326–39.

Kreid, Vadim. *O russkom stikhe* (Antiquary, 1988).

Kupreyanov, N. N. *Literaturno-khudozhestvennoe nasledie* (Moscow, 1973).

Kuznetsova, O. A. "Diskussiya o sostoyanii russkogo simvolizma v 'Obshchestve revnitelei khudozhestvennogo slova'" in *Russkaya literatura*, no. 1 (1990), pp. 200–207.

Kuznetsova, O. A. "Gete v poeticheskom samoopredelenii Vyach. Ivanova" (as yet an unpublished manuscript).

Kuznetsova, O. A. "Perepiska Vyach. Ivanova s S. A. Vengerovym" in Tsar'kova, T. S., ed. *Ezhegodnik rukopisnogo otdela pushkinskogo doma na 1990 god* (St. Petersburg, 1993), pp. 72–100.

Kuznetsova, O. A. *Russkie poety serebryanogo veka* (Leningrad, 1991).

Kyukhel'beker, V. K. *Puteshestvie, dnevnik, stat'i* (Leningrad, 1979).

Landa, E. "A. Blok i perevody iz Geine" in *Masterstvo perevoda* (Moscow, 1963), pp. 292–330.

Lavrov, A. V., and V. L. Toporov. "Blok perevodit prozu Geine" in *Literaturnoe nasledstvo* no. 92, book 4 (Moscow, 1987), pp. 658–65.

Liberman, Anatoly. "A Note on Translating Russian Poetry" in *International Journal of Slavic Linguistics and Poetics*, vol. 33 (1986), pp. 121–26.

Maguire, Robert. *Gogol from the Twentieth Century* (Princeton, 1974).

Mähl, Hans-Joachim. "Goethes Urteil über Novalis. Ein Beitrag zur Geschichte der Kritik an der deutschen Romantik" in *Jahrbuch des freien deutschen Hochstifts* (Tübingen, 1967), pp. 130–270.

Malmstad, John. "Mandelshtam's 'Silentium': A Poet's Response to Ivanov" in Robert Louis Jackson and Lowry Nelson, Jr., eds. *Vyacheslav Ivanov: Poet, Critic and Philosopher* (New Haven, 1986), pp. 236–52.

Mandel'shtam, Osip. *Sobranie sochinenii v dvukh tomakh*, vol. 2 (New York, 1966).

Markov, Vladimir. *Manifesty i programmy russkikh futuristov* (Munich, 1967).

Markov, Vladimir. "Some Remarks on Bal'mont's Epigraphs" in Julian W. Connolly and Sonia I. Ketchian, eds. *Studies in Russian Literature in Honor of Vsevelod Setchkarev* (Columbus, 1986), pp. 212–21.

Medtner, Emil. "Bildnis der Persönlichkeit im Rahmen des gegenseitigen Sich Kennenlernens" in *Die kulturelle Bedeutung der komplexen Psychologie* (Berlin, 1935), pp. 556–616.

Mirsky, D. S. *A History of Russian Literature* (New York, 1949).

Novalis. *Schriften*, vol. 5 (Stuttgart, 1988).

Novalis. *Werke* (Hamburg, 1977).

Novalis. *Werke in einem Band* (Munich, 1981).

Novalis. *Werke, Tagebücher und Briefe Friedrich von Hardenbergs*, 3 vols. (München, 1987).

Obatnin, G. V. and K. Yu. Postoutenko. "Vyacheslav Ivanov i formal'nyi metod" in *Russkaya literatura*, no. 1 (1992), pp. 180–87.

Obatnin, G. V. and S. Sobolev. "Sovest' narodnaya uzhe smushchena: Vyacheslav Ivanov o sobytiyakh semnadtsatogo goda" in *Nezavisimaya gazeta* (30 September 1992), p. 5.

Parnis, Aleksander. "Vyacheslav Ivanov i Khlebnikov" in *De Visu*, no. 0 [sic!] (1992), pp. 39–45.

Potthoff, Wilfried. "Zur Vermittlung Goethes durch Vjačeslav Ivanov" in Hans-Bernd Harder and Hans Rothe, eds. *Goethe und die Welt der Slawen* (Giessen, 1981), pp. 193–207.

Richards, Earl Jeffrey. "E. R. Curtius' Vermächtnis an die Literaturwissenschaft. Die Verbindung von Philologie, Literaturgeschichte und Literaturkritik" in Walter Berschin and Arnold Rothe, eds. *Ernst Robert Curtius: Werk, Wirkung, Zukunftsperspektiven* (Heidelberg, 1989), pp. 249–69.

Ronen, Omry. *An Approach to Mandel'stam* (Jerusalem, 1983).

Ronen, Omry. "Tri prizraka Mayakovskogo" in *Shestye tynyanovskie chteniya: Tezisy dokladov i materialy dlya obsuzhdeniya* (Riga, 1992), pp. 9–13.

Rozanov, Vasily. "Tut est' nekaya taina" in *Vesy*, no. 2 (1904), pp. 14–19.

Scherr, Barry P. *Russian Poetry: Meter, Rhythm, and Rhyme* (Berkeley, 1986).

Seidel, Margo. *Novalis' Geistliche Lieder* (Frankfurt am Main, 1983).

Serman, Ilya. "Vyacheslav Ivanov and Russian Poetry of the Eighteenth Century," in Robert Louis Jackson and Lowry Nelson, Jr., eds. *Vyacheslav Ivanov: Poet, Critic and Philosopher* (New Haven, 1986), pp. 190–208.

Shklovsky, Victor. "Art as Technique" in Lee T. Lemon and Marion J. Reis, eds. *Russian Formalist Criticism: Four Essays* (Lincoln, 1965), pp. 5–24.

Smith, G. S. "A Note on the Equimetrical Translation of Russian Poetry" in *International Journal of Slavic Linguistics and Poetics*, vol. 33 (1986), pp. 127–30.

Solov'ev, V. S. *Sochineniya*, 2 vols. (Moscow, 1988).

Solov'ev, V. S. *Stikhotvoreniya i shutochnye p'esy* (Leningrad, 1974).

Stacy, Robert Harold. *A Study of Vjacheslav Ivanov, Cor Ardens (Part I)* (Ph.D. dissertation, Syracuse University, 1965).

Stammler, Heinrich. "Bely's Conflict with Vjačeslav Ivanov over War and Revolution" in *Slavic and Eastern European Journal*, vol. 18, no. 3 (1974), pp. 259-70.

Stepun, Fedor. *Mystische Weltschau: Fünf Gestalten des russischen Symbolismus* (Munich, 1964).

Stepun, Fedor. "Vyacheslav Ivanov" in *Russkaya literatura*, no. 3 (1989), pp. 123-33.

Szilard, Lena. "Roman Andreya Belogo mezhdu masonstvom i rozenkreitserstvom" in *RossiyaRussia* (1991), pp. 75-84.

Taranovsky, Kiril. *Essays on Mandel'stam* (Cambridge, 1976).

Taranovsky, Kiril. "O vzaimootnoshenii stikhotvornogo ritma i tematiki" in *American Contributions to the Fifth International Congress of Slavists*. vol. 1: Linguistic Contributions (The Hague, 1963), pp. 287-322.

Terras, Victor. "The Aesthetic Categories of *Ascent* and *Descent* in the Poetry of Vjačeslav Ivanov" in Thomas Eekman and Dean S. Worth, eds. *Russian Poetics* (Columbus, 1983), pp. 393-408.

Terras, Victor. "Viacheslav Ivanov's *Kormchie zvezdy* in Relation to the Poet's Philosophy of Art" in Kenneth N. Brostrom, ed. *Russian Literature and American Critics* (Ann Arbor, 1984), pp. 211-18.

Terras, Victor. "Vyacheslav Ivanov's Esthetic Thought: Context and Antecedents," in Robert Louis Jackson and Lowry Nelson, Jr., eds. *Vyacheslav Ivanov: Poet, Critic and Philosopher* (New Haven, 1986), pp. 326-45.

Tomashevskii, Boris. "Literature and Biography" in Ladislav Matejka and Krystyna Pomorska, eds. *Readings in Russian Poetics: Formalist and Structuralist Views* (Ann Arbor, 1978), pp. 47-55.

Toporov, V. N. "Zametki o poezii Tyutcheva (Eshche raz o svyazyakh s nemetskim romantizmom i shellingianstvom)" in Yu. M. Lotman, ed. *Tyutchevskii sbornik* (Tallinn, 1990), pp. 32-107.

Trunz, Erich. *Goethes Werke*, 14 vols. (Hamburg, 1976).

Tschöpl, Carin. *Viačeslav Ivanov: Dichtung und Dichtungstheorie* (Munich, 1968).

Tynyanov, Y. N. *Arkhaisty i novatory* (Munich, 1967).

Tynyanov, Y. N. "Blok i Geine" in *Ob Aleksandre Bloke* (Petrograd, 1921), pp. 237–64.

Tynyanov, Y. N. "On Literary Evolution" in Ladislav Matejka and Krystyna Pomorska, eds. *Readings in Russian Poetics* (Ann Arbor, 1978), pp. 66–78.

Venclova, Tomas. "Viacheslav Ivanov and the Crisis of Russian Symbolism" in J. Douglas Clayton, ed. *Issues in Russian Literature before 1917* (Columbus, 1989), pp. 205–215.

Veselovskii, A. N. *Izbrannye stat'i* (Leningrad, 1939).

Voloshin, Maksimilian. *Liki tvorchestva* (Leningrad, 1988).

Voloshin, Maksimilian. *Stikhotvoreniya*, 2 vols. (Paris, 1982).

Wachtel, Michael. "Die Korrespondenz zwischen E. R. Curtius und V. I. Ivanov" in *Die Welt der Slaven*, new series, vol. 16, nos. 1–2 (1992), pp. 72–106, 399–400.

Wachtel, Michael. "Iz perepiski V. I. Ivanova s A. D. Skaldinym" in *Minuvshee*, vol. 10 (Paris, 1990), pp. 121–41.

Wachtel, Michael. "'Russkii Faust' Vyacheslava Ivanova" in *Minuvshee*, vol. 12 (Paris, 1991), 265–73.

Wachtel, Michael. "The Veil of Isis as a Paradigm of Russian Symbolist Mythopoesis" in Peter I. Barta, ed. *The European Foundations of Russian Modernism* (Lewiston, 1991), pp. 25–49.

West, James. "Kant, Kant, Kant: The Neo-Kantian Creative Consciousness in Bely's *Peterburg*" in Peter I. Barta, ed. *The European Foundations of Russian Modernism* (Lewiston, 1991), pp. 87–136.

West, James. "Ivanov's Theory of Knowledge: Kant and Neo-Kantianism," in Robert Louis Jackson and Lowry Nelson, Jr., eds. *Vyacheslav Ivanov: Poet, Critic and Philosopher* (New Haven, 1986), pp. 313–25.

West, James. *Russian Symbolism* (London, 1970).

West, James. "Ty esi . . . " in Fausto Malcovati, ed. *Cultura e memoria: atti del terzo Simposio Internazionale didicato a Viačeslav Ivanov*, vol. 1 (Florence, 1988), pp. 231–38.

Woloschin, Margarita. *Die grüne Schlange* (Frankfurt, 1982).

Yampolskii, I. G. "Ivan Konevskoi: Pis'ma k Vl. V. Gippiusu" in *Ezhegodnik rukopisnogo otdela pushkinskogo doma na 1977 god* (Leningrad, 1979), pp. 79–87.

Zhirmunskii, V. M. *Gete v russkoi literature* (Leningrad, 1937).

Zhirmunskii, V. M. *Nemetskii romantizm i sovremennaya mistika* (St. Petersburg, 1914).

Zhirmunskii, V. M. *Religioznoe otrechenie v istorii romantizma* (Moscow, 1919).

Zhirmunskii, V. M. "Roman o golubom tsvetke" in *Russkaya mysl'*, no. 3 (1915), pp. 94–101.

Zhovtis, A. L. "Problema formal'nogo analoga" in Barry P. Scherr and Dean S. Worth, eds. *Russian Verse Theory* (Columbus, 1989), pp. 509–14.

Zhukovskii, V. A. *Sobranie sochinenii* (Moscow, 1959).

Index

Titles of works are listed under the names of the authors.
The index is drawn only from the main text, not from the footnotes.

Akhmatova, Anna, 217
Ascent/descent paradigm: in Ivanov, 70, 79, 80, 87, 208
Aseev, Nikolai, 125
Auslender, Sergei, 120

Bakhtin, Mikhail, 225–26
Ballad, 60; Goethe's use of, 43–45, 60; in Russian tradition, 46, 193; Ivanov's use of, 58–60, 185. *See also* Goethe, Johann Wolfgang, "Bride of Corinth"
Baratynsky, E. A., 13
Batyushkov, F. D., 122
Beethoven, Ludwig van, 10, 16, 148
Bely, Andrei, 14, 15, 219; on Symbolism, 4–5, 210–11; Ivanov on, 14–15; on Novalis, 122; on Ivanov, 126, 214
Berdyaev, Nikolai, 7
Blok, Aleksandr, 14, 15, 184
Bloom, Harold, 3–4, 17
Bobrov, Sergei, 125
Braun, F. A., 122–23; Ivanov on, 124
Buber, Martin, 13, 221
Bryusov, Valery, 5, 8, 14, 218; and Ivanov, 12, 212–14; on Ivanov, 22, 50, 212; on Novalis, 118; on Symbolism, 145, 213; as translator, 183, 184; on Zhukovsky, 198

Carlyle, Thomas, 117, 118
Classical antiquity: prosody, Ivanov's use of, 50, 85, 148, 183, 206; myth, Ivanov's use of, 73, 79, 100–101, 102, 108, 174, 175; tragedy, Ivanov's use of, 99–100
Curtius, Ernst Robert, 13, 219–20; Ivanov's influence on, 219, 221–25

Dactylic hexameter, 199, 201
Dante Alighieri: for Ivanov, 38, 40, 41, 42, 71, 150, 169, 176
Demeter, 52–53
Derzhavin, Gavrila, 179, 180
Deschartes, Ol'ga, 101
Dionysus: Ivanov's view of, 100–101, 148, 174, 175
Dmitrievskaya, Dar'ya Mikhailovna (Ivanov's first wife), 7, 30, 34
Dobrolyubov, Aleksandr, 144
Dostoevsky, Fedor, 6, 15, 95
Du Bos, Charles, 219, 221

Elegiac distich: Goethe's use of, 10; Ivanov's use of, 10–11, 104, 158, 159–60, 175–76; Novalis's use of, 157
Etkind, Efim, 186, 187, 190

Falk, Johannes, 215
Fiedler, Friedrich, 12, 13
Filosofov, Dmitri, 123
Formalists, 217–18
Futurists, 217

George, Stefan, 16, 17
German culture: and Russian tradition, 6; and Ivanov, 6, 9, 12, 13, 15–17; and Russian Symbolism, 14, 15, 118
German Romanticism, 15, 113, 136, 155; and Ivanov, 17; and Russian Romanticism, 115–16; and Russian Symbolism, 119, 122–23, 127. *See also* German culture
German Romanticism and Contemporary Mysticism (Zhirmunsky), 123. *See also* Zhirmunsky, Viktor
Gershenzon, Mikhail, 220, 227
Gluck, Christoph Willibald, 149
Gnedich, Nikolai, 182–83, 199

244   Index

Goethe, Johann Wolfgang: in Russian tradition, 6, 22, 23, 30; Ivanov's reception of, 17, 18, 30, 41–42, 45, 65–67, 68, 83, 94, 96, 216; as life-model for Ivanov, 21–22, 30, 35, 36; translated by Ivanov, 97, 111; and Novalis, 145–46, 214–15, 216. Works: "Blessed Yearning" ("Selige Sehnsucht"): Ivanov's translation of, 97; in Ivanov's works, 97–98, 101–5, 107, 108; "Bride of Corinth" ("Die Braut von Korinth"), 44–45; for Rozanov, 46; in Ivanov's works, 43, 45–48, 50, 53–58, 60, 61, 136, 185; "A Complaint in Advance" ("Vorklage"): in Ivanov's works, 39–40; *Complete Works* (edition of 1815), 38; for Ivanov, 38–39, 40; "Demon" ("Dämon"): in Ivanov's letters, 31; *Elective Affinities (Die Wahlverwandtschaften)*: in Ivanov's letters, 32, 33–34; *Faust*, 68–69, 78–79, 80–81; for Ivanov, 21, 22–23, 28, 31, 33–34, 35, 62–63, 67–68, 69–71, 74, 76–77, 78–83, 86, 87, 90–96, 148; in Russian tradition, 23, 62, 63; for Solovyov, 63–64, 65; "Ganymede", 84–85; for Ivanov, 85; "Permanence in Change" ("Dauer in Wechsel"): Ivanov's translation of, 111; "Prometheus": Ivanov's translation of, 111; *Urfaust*, 23, 24, 26; "West-easterly Divan" ("West-östlicher Divan"), 103; *Wilhelm Meister*, 38; "The Wonderful Flower" ("Das Blümlein Wunderschön"), 31–32, 34, 35
Guenther, Johannes von, 12, 62
Gumilev, Nikolai, 128, 217

Heine, Heinrich, 6, 15; for Ivanov, 15
Hirschfeld, Otto, 11
History of Western Literature (Batyushkov), 122
Hoffmann, E. T. A., 13, 16
Holthusen, Johannes, 86, 100
Homer, 52–53, 54, 136

Ivanov, Dimitri (son of V. Ivanov and V. Shvarsalon), 9, 177
Ivanov, Vyacheslav, Collections of verse: *Cor Ardens*, 97, 98, 102–5, 107, 128, 129, 150, 159, 171, 178; *Pilot Stars (Kormchie zvezdy)*, 8, 10, 22, 28, 37–40, 42, 46, 63, 71, 78, 84, 133; *Tender Mystery (Nezhnaya taina)*, 58, 90, 92, 170–71; *Transparence (Prozrachnost')*, 84, 86, 89; *Vespertine Light (Svet vechernii)*, 178. Poems and cycles of poems: "The Alpine Horn" ("Al'piiskii rog"), 80, 81–82, 83; "Beauty" ("Krasota"), 48, 54, 55, 56, 57, 60, 100, 135–38 *passim*; "Beethoveniana", 51; "Boat of Love" ("Lad'ya lyubvi"), 142; "The Cologne Cathedral" ("Kel'nskii sobor"), 9; "The Dispute" ("Spor"), 105–8, 158; "The Dream" ("Son"), 92–94, 96, 100; "Epirrhema", 83; "Fräulein [H?]", 10–11; "Ganymede", 84, 85; "Gastgeschenke", 12; "Goethe" ("Gete"), 10, 29–30; "The Grave" ("Mogila"), 178–80; "Infancy" ("Mladenchestvo"), 177–78, 185; "Into the album of a student-aesthete" ("V al'bom studenta-esteta"), 90–92; "Into the City of Minnesang" ("V gorod Minnesang"), 9; "Isis", 159–60, 161, 162; "Love" ("Lyubov'"), 106–7; "Love and Death" ("Lyubov' i smert'"), 105, 136, 138–41 *passim*; 149, 158, 178, 185; "Man" ("Chelovek"), 14, 54–58; "The Missa Solemnis of Beethoven" ("Missa Solemnis, Betkhovena"), 10; "Moonlit Roses" ("Lunnye rozy"), 46–48, 60–61; "Morning Star" ("Utrennyaya zvezda"), 68–77, 78, 185; "On the Wings of Dawn" ("Na kryl'yakh zari"), 80; "On the Rhine" ("Na Reine"), 9; "Oreads"

("Oready"), 78–80; "The Poet's Mysteries" ("Mysterii poeta"), 82–83; "Psyche", 101–2; "The Rainbow" ("Raduga"), 88–90; "Rainbows" ("Radugi"), 86–88; "Rosa Centrifolia", 161; "Rosarium", 160, 161, 170–71, 175, 178; "Russian Faust", 10, 23–29, 43, 63; "Saturnia Regna", 175; "Snows" ("Snega"), 140; "Sub Rosa", 170–71; "Tidings" ("Vesti"), 170, 171–76, 180; "To a German Professor of History" ("Germanskomu professoru istorii"), 9; "The Tsar's Departure" ("Ukhod Tsarya"), 58–60, 61, 92. Prose works: "Anima", 94–95, 97, 102; "Autobiographical Letter" ("Avtobiograficheskoe pis'mo"), 9, 16; "Correspondence from Two Corners" ("Perepiska iz dvukh uglov"), 97, 219, 220, 221, 224, 225; "Goethe on the Border of Two Centuries" ("Gete na rubezhe dvukh stoletii"), 62, 102, 225; *The Hellenic Religion of the Suffering God* (*Ellinskaya religiya stradayushchego boga*), 100, 148; "Manner, Personality, and Style" ("Manera, litso i stil'"), 98; "On Novalis" ("O Novalise"), 169; "On the Russian Idea" ("O russkoi idee"), 97; "Phantoms" ("Prizraki"), 22–23; "The Poet and the Mob" ("Poet i chern'"), 130; "Stories of a Visionary" ("Rasskazy tainovidtsa"), 66; "The Symbolism of Aesthetic Principles" ("Simvolika esteticheskikh nachal"), 51–52; "Tale of Prince Svetomir" ("Povest' o tsareviche Svetomire"), 14; "The Testaments of Symbolism" ("Zavety simvolizma"), 67, 146–47; "Thoughts on Poetry" ("Mysli o poezii"), 111, 198; "Thoughts on Symbolism" ("Mysli o simvolizme"), 83; "Two Elements in Contemporary Symbolism" ("Dve stikhii v sovremennom simvolizme"), 120, 147. Translations: Goethe, "Blessed Yearning" ("Selige Sehnsucht"), 97; Goethe, "Permanence in Change" ("Dauer in Wechsel"), 111; Goethe, "Prometheus", 111; Novalis, "Christendom or Europe" ("Die Christenheit oder Europa"), 137; Novalis, "Es giebt so bange Zeiten" ("There are such fearful times"), 152–5; Novalis, "Hymns to the Night" ("Hymnen an die Nacht"), 136, 139–42, 151, 177, 185, 187, 188, 189–94, 195–98, 199–209; Novalis, "I do not know what I could seek" ("Ich weiß nicht, was ich suchen könnte"), 131–33; Novalis, "The meadow became green" ("Es färbte sich die Wiese grün"), 137–38; Novalis, "One man succeeded–he raised the veil of the goddess of Sais" ("Einem gelang es—er hob den Schleyer der Göttin zu Sais"), 158–59; Novalis, "Pilgrim's Song", *see* "Tears of Love, Flames of Love"; Novalis, "Sacred Songs" ("Geistliche Lieder"), 130, 131–36, 152–55, 174, 185; Novalis, "Tears of Love, Flames of Love" ("Liebeszähren, Liebesflammen"), 162, 165–70, 173, 174, 176, 185
Ivanova, Lidiya (daughter of V. Ivanov and L. Zinov'eva-Annibal), 8, 58

Jung, C. G., 224

Kablukov, S. P., 121–22
Kant, 16. *See also* Neo-Kantianism
Khodasevich, Vladislav, 218–19; on Symbolism, 143, 145
Kogan, P. S., 117, 118
Konevskoi, Ivan, 118
Kühn, Sophie von, 114–15, 139, 179, 180, 193
Kuzmin, Mikhail, 148, 188
Kuznetsova, Ol'ga, 37
Kyukhel'beker, Wilhelm, 116–17

Lermontov, Mikhail, 183, 190, 202
Lunacharsky, A. V., 9

Mandel'stam, Osip, 216–17

Metner, Emil, 118, 119
Mintslova, Anna, 14, 119, 120
Mirsky, D. S., 129
Muth, Karl, 13
Myth, for Ivanov: 94, 95, 98–103 passim, 108. See also Classical antiquity, Demeter, Dionysus, Mythopoesis
Mythopoesis, 6; for Ivanov, 54, 95, 98. See also Myth

Neo-Kantianism, 14–15
Nietzsche, 16, 126; for Ivanov, 12, 35, 148; for Bely, 210–11
Novalis: Ivanov's translations of, 13, 111–12, 120, 121, 122, 128, 136, 151, 156, 157, 161, 176–77; Ivanov's reception of, 17, 18, 120, 124, 126, 129, 176–77, 189, 216; early Western reception of, 113, 117; in Russian tradition, 115–17, 122, 123, 125; Symbolist reception of, 117–19, 121–22; Ivanov's proselytizing of, 120–21, 124, 125–26, 127; and Goethe, 145–46, 214–15, 216. Works: "The Alpine Rose" ("Alpenrose"): in Ivanov's works, 175–76; "The Apprentices at Sais" ("Die Lehrlinge zu Sais"), 125, 157; in Ivanov's works, 160; "Christendom or Europa" ("Die Christenheit oder Europa"), 113; Ivanov's translation of, 137; "Fragments" ("Fragmente"), 125; Heinrich von Ofterdingen, 188, 164–65; "Hymns to the Night" ("Hymnen an die Nacht"), 118, 120, 129, 139, 185–86, 188; Ivanov's translations of, 136, 139–42, 149, 151, 171, 185, 186–88, 190–209; "The meadow became green" ("Es färbte sich die Wiese grün"): Ivanov's translation of, 137–38; "One man succeeded–he raised the veil of the goddess of Sais" ("Einem gelang es–er hob den Schleyer der Göttin zu Sais"), 157; Ivanov's translation of, 158–59, 160; "Pilgrim's Song" (see "Tears of Love, Flames of Love"); "Sacred Songs" ("Geistliche Lieder"), 129; Ivanov's translations of, 120, 130–36, 152–55, 169, 174, 185; "Tears of Love, Flames of Love" ("Liebeszähren, Liebesflammen"), 162–65; Ivanov's translation of, 162, 165–70; in Ivanov's work, 173, 174, 176, 185

Petrarch, 105, 138–39, 176, 185
Platen, August Graf von, 16
Potemkin, Petr, 128
Pushkin, Aleksandr, 10, 23, 181, 190; in Ivanov's works, 13, 26, 27, 80, 81, 82, 185

Rickert, Heinrich, 14–15
Rilke, Rainer Maria, 13, 16
Romanticism, German. See German Romanticism
Romanticism, Russian. See Russian Romanticism
Rozanov, Vasily, 46
Russian Romanticism, 36, 144, 182; and Novalis, 114, 116–17; Ivanov on, 146
Russian Symbolism, 4, 5, 6–7, 14, 18, 143, 147, 210, 211, 212; Ivanov on, 8, 17, 18, 65–68, 83, 84, 95, 146–47, 148, 213–14; interest in German culture, 14–15; and "zhiznetvorchestvo", 37, 144–45; reception of Novalis, 117–19; and German Romanticism, 123–24, 127, 138; Bely on, 210, 211; and translation, 184, 198; Bryusov on, 213

Schiller, 6, 10, 16, 17, 126, 157, 198; for Ivanov, 35, 68, 158, 198
Schmidt, Erich, 23, 24
Schopenhauer, Arthur, 9, 16, 126
Shklovsky, Viktor, 217
Shvarsalon, Vera (daughter of L. Zinov'eva-Annibal, third wife of V. Ivanov), 8, 9, 170
Smile: as motif in V. Solovyov's works, 51; as motif in Ivanov's works, 51–52, 88, 138

Solovyov, Sergei, 119
Solovyov, Vladimir, 51, 65, 66; for Ivanov, 10, 38, 40–41, 42, 50–51, 64, 108; "Three Meetings" ("Tri Svidaniia"), 50, 53, 54, 136; reception of Goethe by, 63–64; and "zhiznetvorchestvo", 144–45
Stacy, Robert, 104
Steiner, Rudolf, 119
Stepun, Fedor, 7
Symbol: Ivanov on, 64–65, 67, 68, 83. *See also* Russian Symbolism
Symbolism. *See* Russian Symbolism

Tepl, Johannes von, 105
Terras, Victor, 53
Theurgy: V. Solovyov on, 64, 144–45; Ivanov on, 64–68, 145, 146, 147. *See also* "zhiznetvorchestvo"
Tieck, Ludwig, 17, 113–15, 116–17, 186
Translation, 182–84; Ivanov's approach to, 13, 184, 185, 186–87; Zhukovsky's approach to, 115–16, 183; Symbolists and, 184, 198

Tynyanov, Yury, 218–19
Tyutchev, Fedor, 6, 116; for Ivanov, 13, 79, 80, 221

Veselovsky, A. N., 161

Wagner, Richard, 16

Zhirmunsky, Viktor, 122–23, 124, 155
"Zhiznetvorchestvo", 37, 144; Ivanov on, 146, 147. *See also* Theurgy
Zhukovsky, 6, 46; as translator, 115–16, 183; metrical innovations of, 189, 193, 194–95, 198, 199, 203; "Teon and Eskhin", 194–95; for Ivanov, 195–98 *passim*, 203
Zinov'eva-Annibal, Lidiya Dimitrievna (second wife of Ivanov), 7, 8, 9, 31, 34, 148, 149, 151, 161, 162; death of, 8, 106, 126, 138, 147, 150, 176, 178, 180, 197; Ivanov's letters to, 31–34, 35; in *Cor Ardens*, 103, 104, 107

Disastrous Fires

by George S. Fichter

Franklin Watts
New York/London/Toronto/Sydney/1981
A First Book

*Cover photograph courtesy of
The New York City Fire Department*

Photographs courtesy of
The New York City Fire Department: pp. vi (photo by Fr. A. Corr), 66 (photo by Fr. Benson); The New York Public Library Picture Collection: pp. 15, 21, 26, 28, 52; The Bettmann Archive, Inc.: pp. 17, 22 (top and bottom); United Press International: pp. 33, 40, 49; NASA: p. 45; The U.S. Forest Service: p. 56.

Library of Congress Cataloging in Publication Data

Fichter, George S.
Disastrous fires.

(A First book)
Includes index.
Summary: Presents accounts of several fires which resulted in numerous deaths or considerable loss of property.
1. Fires—Juvenile literature.
[1. Fires] I. Title.

| TH9448.F5 | 363.3'72 | 81-2448 |
| ISBN 0-531-04325-8 | | AACR2 |

*Copyright © 1981 by George S. Fichter
All rights reserved
Printed in the United States of America*
5 4 3 2 1

Contents

1
1 Fire—the Awesome Demon

2
4 A World Without Fire

3
7 The Nature of Fire

4
10 Twin Disasters—A Worst and a Most Famous

5
19 The San Francisco Fire

6
24 The Great Fire of London

7
31 Fire at Sea—and on the Docks

8
37 Show-stopping Fires

9
44 Fire in the Sky

10
51 Fire, a Weapon of War

11
55 The Woods Afire

60 For More Information

63 Index

Disastrous Fires

1

Fire— the Awesome Demon

Piercing, wailing sirens!
Clanging bells!
Flashing lights!
People shouting!
The smell of smoke and a cherry-red glow in the sky.
Fire! Fire!
If you are near, you can hear the crackle of flames, or even an ominous roar.

The flames lick their way up the sides of a building and grope hungrily at the sky, searching for more fuel on which to feed.

This time the fire is in an apartment house only two blocks from where you live. As you get closer, you hear a dull explosion. Apparently the fire has reached a fuel tank in the basement.

People are screaming for help. Some are huddled in the corner of the roof farthest from the fire. Nobody knows at this point how many others might be trapped inside the burning building.

But now the giant fire trucks have arrived. Mounted on one is a tremendously long extension ladder. A fireman rides it upward through the smoke to the people on the roof. Soon the people are scrambling down the ladder to safety. One person is being carried by a fireman, and as soon as they get to the bottom, a rescue team begins administering first aid.

Fire fighters wearing gas masks have already entered the building and are searching it for other victims. They carry special tools so they can easily cut through wood or metal that may be in their path or trapping victims. They have inhalators and resuscitators. If they find anyone overcome by fumes, they may be able to start their breathing again. Those seriously injured will be rushed to the nearest hospital.

Still other fire fighters are dousing the blaze with big streams of water, their hoses spewing out thousands of gallons per minute. Very quickly the rampaging flames are tamed, but the fire fighters continue their work. From another truck they get a pipe that blows the smoke from the building. This helps them continue their search for victims. Each fire fighter also carries special equipment that helps in putting out blazes not reached by the hoses.

The apartment building is in ruins, but you are relieved that apparently no one was seriously injured. You are grateful, too, that the fire did not break out where you live. You decide to check the very next day with the fire department to find out how to prevent fires and also what to do if a fire occurs where you live. This is something you should have done long ago, but it took a fire nearby to make it seem important.

If you were to cross the United States, Britain, or any other country in a low-flying airplane at night, you would be astonished at the number of flickering lights from fires below. In the United States, for example, an average of thirty people die in fires every night. Nearly a hundred are seriously burned. Property damage over a year's time amounts to almost $4 billion.

Yes, fires are indeed demons of destruction, leaving only charred remains in their wake. Some fires have been so catastrophic they will never be forgotten.

But fire is also a friend.

2

A World Without Fire

Can you imagine a world without fire?

Maybe you've never even thought about it, but in a world without fire you would not survive—at least not for long.

Fire keeps us warm in winter and, indirectly, cool in summer.

Fire cooks our food.

Fire gives us light in darkness.

Fire is essential in making and operating nearly every product we use, from automobiles and airplanes to the book you are now reading.

Fire does all of these things for us even though you may never strike a match to light a fire yourself. Of all the phenomena in nature, fire works hardest for us and in the greatest variety of ways.

Can solar energy replace fire? Yes, at least for many things. But solar energy comes from fire, too—the constant inferno on the sun. It is still fire, though in an indirect form, that provides the heat and light.

It was the taming of fire perhaps more than anything else that set humans apart from the beasts. Exactly how and when this happened is not really known, but it did occur long, long ago, maybe a million years or more. Some daring human captured fire and put it to work. The fire might have been a smoldering one around a volcano or a blaze started by a bolt of lightning in a forest. Or it might have been a much smaller blaze, a tiny fire started perhaps by friction when two branches rubbed together or a spontaneous blaze in dry rubble.

We may never know precisely how it happened, but overcoming the fear of fire and putting it to work was probably the biggest and most important step ever taken by humans.

People soon learned that fire could be kept alive only by feeding it fuel. Left alone, it eventually died out. Somebody had to watch the fire constantly and add more fuel to keep it going. Also, the fire had to be protected from the wind and rain. When people moved, they took glowing coals with them so that a fire could be started wherever they went.

No one knows how many years or centuries went by before humans learned how to make fire themselves or even what techniques were first used. Perhaps it was learned first that two of the right kinds of stones struck together could make sparks and thus start a smoldering fire. Gentle blowing would then turn the little fire into a big one. Or maybe the first fires were started by rubbing two dry sticks together. A stick rotated very rapidly in a groove inside another piece of wood can create enough heat to cause the bits of wood dust to catch fire. Soon people learned how to wrap the stick with the string of a bow to make it rotate faster. This method of starting fires is still used today by some primitive peoples.

It was thousands of years—not until 1827, in fact—before matches were invented. The first matches, invented by John

Walker of England, were called "friction lights." They were quite primitive and inefficient compared to the matches we now use. A friction light consisted of a splinter of wood with a head made of two chemicals, chlorate of potash and sulfide of antimony, mixed with gum arabic to make the mass stick to the wood. When this mass was drawn firmly and quickly between two pieces of sandpaper, it ignited—and often the head popped off also! But it was a beginning. The first of these friction lights were made and sold as novelties rather than as useful tools.

Improvements came rapidly, one of the most significant being the use of phosphorus, which ignites very quickly and easily. This eliminated the need for sandpaper. Phosphorus matches could be lit by rubbing them against a wall, rock, trouser leg —anything providing a bit of friction. But a pocketful of phosphorus matches would ignite if one were accidentally rubbed against the other. Sometimes they would even ignite spontaneously at room temperature. They were dangerous.

Nowadays we use safety matches. Invented in Sweden in 1855, safety matches need to be struck against a special surface provided on the box or match cover. Hundreds of millions of these matches are struck daily. The special phosphorus compound used in them does not give off the poisonous fumes that the original matches did when they burned. Matches are indeed so common in our lives now that we would have difficulty imagining life without them.

In a sense, matches were another step in the taming of fire, for they have allowed people to carry fire in their pockets or keep it on their shelves, dormant but ready to be put to work whenever needed.

Fire becomes an awesome, devastating, and killing monster only when it is permitted to escape its shackles.

3

The Nature of Fire

We have come to understand the nature of fire only in recent years. For a long time, fire was believed to be a substance, like water. Finally, but not until the 1700s, scientists recognized that fire is really a process. The process is called *combustion*.

Three conditions are necessary for fire. They are heat, fuel, and oxygen. A fire can be stopped by eliminating any one of these three. Once started, of course, a fire generates its own heat and at the same time produces light. The fuel is consumed as the fire burns, though, and so more must be added constantly. In controlled fires, like the soothing and gentle fire in a fireplace, fuel is brought to them. Fires out of control seek their own fuel. Oxygen is supplied from the air, which consists of about 20 percent oxygen under normal conditions. In a confined area, a fire will quickly use up all of the available oxygen and burn itself out.

Technically, some fires do burn without oxygen. Hydrogen, for example, will burn in chlorine or in fluorine. When combined in special circumstances, other gases may also "burn"—that is, produce heat and light. But all ordinary fires, such as the ones we use for heating and cooking, need oxygen.

There is a simple experiment you can perform that not only proves the need for oxygen but also shows roughly how much oxygen is in the air. Do not do the experiment, however, unless an adult is present.

Put some water in a shallow dish, then set a candle in the center of the dish and light it. Now turn an empty glass jar upside down and put it on the dish, over the candle. Very shortly the candle will begin to sputter and then go out. It has used up all of the oxygen in the jar. You will also notice that the water level rises in the jar. If you mark the level at the beginning and then again after it rises, you will find that the water is replacing roughly 20 percent of the space in the jar. This will not be exact, of course, because some gases are also produced as the candle burns.

Not all things burn easily or at the same rate. Some materials do not burn at all. Each substance has a different "kindling" temperature, the point at which it begins to burn. Using just a match, for example, you can easily set a piece of paper on fire. Paper has a low kindling temperature. In fact, we use the word "kindling" to mean pieces of paper or small bits of wood used to start a fire. But except for a few kinds, you cannot start a piece of wood burning by touching a match to it. You might cause the wood to char, but most kinds will stop burning about as quickly as the match.

By using one or several pieces of paper and maybe two pieces of wood, you can generally get a fire going. The paper burns long enough to raise the temperature of the wood to its kindling point. Two pieces of wood, one against the other, are better than one because they help to keep the temperature high enough for the wood to catch fire. Then the blaze generates its own heat.

Phosphorus has a kindling temperature so low that it will begin burning on its own, sometimes even at room temperature. But try to set fire to a piece of steel! Asbestos, sand, and many other substances that already contain large amounts of oxygen will not burn.

As a fire burns, some parts of the substance do not catch fire as quickly as other parts. Some of these rise as smoke, which consists of carbon and other unburned particles. There are also minerals in substances. Those that do not burn are left behind as ashes.

4

Twin Disasters—A Worst and a Most Famous

From the beginning, the year 1871 was unusual. Snows were light that winter, and when spring thaws came, the streams scarcely filled to capacity. All through spring, in fact, the sky remained uncommonly bright and clear. By early summer, the forest floors had given up their moisture and were tinder dry. When the wind blew, the forest crackled. Woodsmen insisted it was the driest year they had ever known. And the drought was widespread. Almost no rain fell anywhere in North America.

Then on July 8, the rains came. People breathed more easily, as more than an inch (2.54 cm) of water fell on the parched forests of Wisconsin. They were sure that the drought was finally broken. But they were wrong. There was no more rain again until September, and then only a light drizzle. By October, the forests in northern Wisconsin and Michigan were once again as dry as kindling.

Always there were small fires burning in the wilderness. Some were set intentionally—and foolishly—where crews building a railroad to Peshtigo, Wisconsin, were cutting away trees and brush to make room for their track. Peshtigo was a boom town. It was so prosperous that some people said it would soon surpass Chicago in size. It thrived on the forests that were pushed in close about it. The timber and a great variety of wood products produced in Peshtigo went by ship from the harbor at Green Bay to Chicago and from there throughout the nation and the world. With the arrival of the railroad, Peshtigo products would move even faster. The forest was Peshtigo's friend, its livelihood.

But smoke hung in the air persistently that fall. The fires crept through the bogs, smoldering and then breaking out wildly here and there. In October, in fact, the glow of burning fires at night was constant. During the day, the sun could be seen only through a haze of smoke. It shone like a copper penny in the smoky sky. Ships traveling on the big lake had to navigate by compass even during daylight hours.

Telegraph lines connecting Peshtigo with the rest of the world burned. The roads corduroyed with logs also burned. Peshtigo became essentially an island.

Some of the people living in Peshtigo were genuinely worried, but most were not greatly concerned. They were confident that the autumn rains would come as they always had in the past. But in 1871, the rains did not come—not in time, at least.

Hot, smoky air—even a steady rain of ashes—had become so common in Peshtigo that few people gave it a second thought that autumn. On Sunday evening, October 8, conditions were worse than usual, however. There was even a rumbling roar from the fires burning in the nearby forest, and the sky was an ominous yellow. As the noise of the fire increased, so did the concern of the people in Peshtigo. It was about 9:30 that night when the storm of flames engulfed the town.

Some people were sure it was Judgment Day. They fled in

panic, trying desperately to escape the sweeping flames, toppling trees, and choking smoke. A rain had indeed come—but it was a rain of sparks, ashes, and smoke. And it had rushed in on tornadolike winds.

The wisest people headed for the Peshtigo River. Some went to the bridge, thinking that it might be safer on the other side. But midway across the bridge they met people coming from the other direction. Then the ends of the bridge caught fire, and the bridge collapsed. People either jumped or were dumped into the cold, rushing river. Others dived into the river from its banks, going in as deep as they could and then ducking their heads under the water to keep away from the roaring rush of flames overhead. Now and then they would come up for a breath of air, which was almost impossible to get, and then they would quickly go under again to escape the flames, heat, and smoke.

But the fire had descended on Peshtigo with such suddenness there was really no time to think. Only those who acted with instinctive quickness survived. The town of Peshtigo was totally destroyed within only a few minutes, and about a thousand people in the town became fuel for the raging fire. No one is sure exactly how many people died in Peshtigo and the surrounding region, but estimates put the total death toll at well over 1,200. As in the majority of fires, most people perished due to asphyxiation. The fire itself quickly consumed the oxygen, and the people were forced to breathe in scorching gaseous fumes. In addition to destroying the town, the fire demolished hundreds of farms in the region, plus the livestock and wildlife. More than 200 square miles (520 sq km) of forest became smoldering ashes in the swift and devastating holocaust.

Paradoxically, the waited-for rains did come the very next day—heavy, cool fall rains that drenched the embers and left only charred skeletons on the landscape. No other fire in North America has been as catastrophic.

—12

IN CHICAGO
THE SAME DAY

Oddly, the Peshtigo disaster got a minimum of attention, despite the heavy losses, because of another fire that started at the same time. It was a fire spawned by the same long drought and also fanned by brisk winds.

It was that same Sunday night in 1871, strange as it may seem, that Mrs. O'Leary's cow is said to have kicked over a kerosene lantern and set the city of Chicago ablaze. (Mrs. O'Leary denied that the cow had anything to do with starting the blaze, though the fire did apparently start in her barn.) Strong winds—like those in Peshtigo, several hundred miles to the north—fanned the Chicago fire into an uncontrollable monster.

Chicago firemen were already worn out from fighting fires that autumn. Most of the buildings in the fast-growing city were made of wood, and they were built one against the other. Even the sidewalks were wooden. A fire on the preceding Saturday night, in fact the worst to that point in Chicago history, had leveled a four-block area despite the efforts of the firemen. The city had a population of more than 330,000 but fewer than 200 firemen. About a third of them had been injured in the Saturday night fire, and the others were exhausted. Further, some of their fire-fighting equipment had also been damaged.

Some people had warned about what would happen if a fire ever really got out of control in Chicago, and there were indeed many fires—an average of more than two a day to which the overworked firemen responded. Big insurance companies refused to write fire protection policies, and they canceled those already written. They declared Chicago to be one giant heap of kindling.

Sunday was a day of churchgoing and rest for the people in Chicago. No one was anxious to be aroused about anything, even the fire alarm that sounded that evening. As mentioned, the fire had started in the O'Learys' barn, which was filled with hay to feed their cows, a calf, and a horse. Legend has it that a cow had grown tired of waiting to be milked and had expressed her annoyance by kicking. Maybe she intended to hit Mrs. O'Leary, but she is said to have struck a lantern instead, spilling the burning kerosene onto the floor of the barn. Mrs. O'Leary poured some milk she had in a pail onto the blaze, but with the kerosene from the lantern, the fire was well provided with starter fuel and had a full loft of hay to turn to. Within seconds the whole barn was ablaze.

The fire watch stationed in the tower of the courthouse saw the flames shoot up, but in his excitement, he gave a signal that sent the first fire engines a mile (1.6 km) out of their way. The fire trucks were drawn by horses, and so the loss of a mile made a big difference in their time of arrival. Several residents in the area had turned in alarms using the newly installed alarm signal boxes, but the boxes had not been tested. They failed to work. By the time the first fire engine arrived, several dozen houses were already burning.

By the time five engines were on the scene, the wind was at work, too—blowing with gale force. It picked up pieces of the burning wooden buildings and tossed them through the air like torches, starting fire after fire. Even so, the experienced firemen, cheered on by a growing crowd of spectators, seemed to be managing to keep the fire from spreading. Then came news that St. Paul's Church, several blocks away, had caught fire. Part of the fire-fighting crew had to be dispatched to get the church fire

The Chicago Chamber of Commerce (top) *and the Crosby Opera House burn to the ground as citizens flee.*

CHAMBER OF COMMERCE.

under control, but it was too late. The fire quickly consumed the church and an adjacent factory, then began racing through the close-packed tenement houses along the street. Soon the two separate fires joined to become a single giant one that jumped the Chicago River and began its uncontrollable march through South Chicago. The narrow streets and alleys acted as draft channels through which the fire was sucked so fast that it screamed, howled, and roared. Flaming pieces of wood were hurled hundreds of feet.

The firemen continued to fight valiantly, but the battle was hopeless. The men became more and more exhausted, and the fire grew stronger. All of Chicago now seemed doomed. The people began to panic. They ran in all directions, trampling over each other as they went. Messages asking for help were telegraphed to Milwaukee, Cincinnati, and other cities.

The fire raged on. Fortunately, because an engineer released the gas into the sewer system, the gas works did not explode, as many feared it would. Some gas did explode underground, however, though it caused little damage. About 2 A.M., the courthouse fell victim to the fire. The blaze continued on northward, jumping the main branch of the Chicago River.

Officials were confident that at least the building containing the city's waterworks was safe. After all, it was a stone structure with walls 2 feet (.6 m) thick. The roof was formed of big timbers, but they were covered with thick slate, impermeable to fire. The waterworks was badly needed now to continue supplying water to help quench the flames.

But somehow the hungry fire got into the building, probably through ventilators. It ate the great timbers of the roof and tumbled the heavy slate onto the machinery. Now there was no water. The firemen had no way to fight back, and all that could be done was to let the fire run its course. By the trainload,

Chicago lies in smoldering ruins, but already (right) the cornerstone of the first new building has been erected.

help came the next day from Cincinnati, Milwaukee, and other places, but there was really nothing that could be done. The fire burned on northward into the prairie.

It was about 11 P.M. on October 10 when it finally began to rain. At about 3 A.M. the next morning, the swift-moving fire came to a sizzling halt.

Some 300 people were dead. It is miraculous that there were not many more deaths. About 100,000 were homeless. The complete heart of the city was destroyed, including all of the important government buildings and their documents, the railroad depots, elegant hotels, factories, businesses—all were charred ruins and ashes.

Some people said Chicago would never be able to recover and rebuild. Others vowed to turn this catastrophe into a boon and to build a new Chicago that was bigger and better than before. The nation and the world rallied to the devastated city's aid, sending money, clothes, food, and other needs to the people. And even while some parts of the city were still smoldering, other areas began to rebuild. The best architects were called in to make certain the new city was beautiful—and also fireproof. Within a year Chicago was half rebuilt. Within ten years it was difficult even to find scars of the big fire. Half a million people called the new Chicago home.

5

The San Francisco Fire

San Francisco was still young and boisterous in 1906. The millionaires lived in an area called Nob Hill. One whole section of the city, the Barbary Coast, thrived on gambling and vice. Chinatown was packed sardine-solid with houses, shops, and people. And all around were shacks stuck in the valleys and gripping the sides and tops of the hills. To get from one place to another, even up and down the steep hills, there was a newly installed cable-car system.

San Francisco was wild and loud. Ever since the Gold Rush of 1849, it had been growing. Now it had a population of nearly half a million.

Occasionally the earth shook from minor earthquakes. But these quakes alarmed and frightened only the newcomers. Old-timers shrugged them off and told how many times they had felt "shakes" over the years. Nothing ever happened. There was no need to be afraid. Some may have tried to say the same thing when the shaking began early in the morning on April 18, 1906, but they had to talk fast.

The earthquake itself lasted only about a minute, but in that brief time, much of the city was crumbled. Chimneys fell down, walls caved in, and chasms opened, splitting buildings and dividing streets in half. And almost instantaneously, fires began to break out all over the city. Some were started from downed electric power lines, others from upset stoves or lamps. At the start it is believed there were no fewer than thirty fires. But soon there were more. They spread rapidly and began merging.

San Francisco's fire department boasted more than 600 men, and all were soon hard at work. From the beginning, however, they were fighting a losing battle, for the earthquake had robbed them of their most effective weapon—water. All of the water mains in the city had been broken.

The mayor declared martial law almost immediately, and federal troops moved in rapidly to maintain order and to keep people from looting. San Francisco authorities did not want panic. Dynamite was called for quickly, too, so that buildings could be blown up to stop the spread of the gargantuan fire. But at first the dynamite was poorly used. Buildings were blown up so close to the fire that the rubble could not be moved away. It only added fuel in a convenient size for the fire to consume.

Even though there was almost no wind to help it spread, the fire was kept on the move by the convection currents created by its own heat. Sweeping down Market Street, it destroyed the city's entire business district, including the imposing twenty-story *San Francisco Call* building. With no outside help available, peo-

From the surrounding hills, the people of San Francisco watch their city burn.

ple began to fight their own battles against the flames, trying to save their homes and belongings. Some succeeded; others failed.

On the second day of the fire, April 19, officials moved to the wide Van Ness Avenue and began dynamiting and burning buildings far in advance of the fire. They hoped to create a stop line over which the fire could not jump. Roughly a mile of buildings were demolished—and it worked! The fire's forward movement was halted, and by the next day, all of the fires were under control.

But 75 percent of the city was in rubble or in charred ruins. An estimated 500 people were dead, and some 300,000 were homeless.

Yet San Francisco soon plunged into the ruins to clean up and rebuild with the same pioneering spirit and energy that had made the city the exciting and enterprising place it had been before the disaster. Within three years there was a new, stronger, and bigger San Francisco.

Top: *dining with a view of the ruins of San Francisco after it was hit by both earthquake and fire.* Bottom: *rebuilding begins almost immediately. Here, new telegraph lines are being erected.*

6

The Great Fire of London

Over the years many big cities have been devastated by fires. Some have been set intentionally to burn the city rather than allow invaders to ravage. Other cities have been captured by invaders and then burned after they were looted of their treasures. In various ways, cities have been victims of wars, with fire the ultimate weapon.

But the big fire that swept London in September of 1666 had nothing to do with war. London, like most older cities, had grown without planning. Many of the streets were so narrow that the roofs of the houses on each side touched each other, their overhangs making a canopy over the street below. The buildings were also pushed one against the other. London was a crowded and foul-smelling accumulation of humanity.

The fire started in Pudding Lane, where the buildings literally pinched each other for space. Most were coated with tar for waterproofing and also for preserving the wood. A baker had neglected to put out the fire in his ovens when he finished his work for the night, and for a reason not known, the fire escaped its confines and began eating at the building. Fanned by a brisk wind, the blaze was soon moving from the bakery to the building next to it, from there to another, then another, and so on.

But the fire was along the Thames River, near the Old London Bridge. Water was plentiful in the river, and so the few authorities roused from their beds to inspect the blaze assumed that it could be put out quickly, as had other fires in the same part of the city in the past.

The fire blocked access to the pumps at the bridge, however, and also it was kept on the move by the wind. It spread onto the bridge itself and then into the warehouses along its banks. Men worked hard trying to douse the flames with water, but the fire had become too gigantic to be affected by the meager amounts of water tossed on it.

People living in the path of the fire began to vacate their homes. They tried to take their most treasured belongings with them. It seemed safest to get to the other side of the Thames River, but because the Old London Bridge and all of the shops built along it were now in flames or smoldering, the best way to cross was by boat. Boat owners did a brisk business that morning.

The famous diarist Samuel Pepys, then clerk of the King's Navy, was the first high official to visit the fire and to recognize that it had become a danger to the entire city. After surveying the situation, he concluded that it would be necessary to demolish buildings in the path of the fire to stop it, removing its fuel. This meant destroying valuable property, and the city's mayor refused to accept the plan. Pepys then went to King Charles II and got the necessary authorization. Soldiers were dispatched to

the fire scene immediately, and they began pulling down the houses in front of the flames, then moving the rubble far enough out of the way to prevent it from becoming tinder.

London's mayor still resisted the operation. He was concerned that he would be held financially responsible for replacing the torn-down buildings. He would not be blamed, though, if the buildings were eaten up by fire. King Charles responded by putting the Duke of York in command, and from that point on, the evacuation of the people and the destruction of buildings to stop the fire from spreading was under military control. The blaze had already eaten a hole in the city 2 miles (3.2 km) wide.

London boasted more than a hundred churches in those days. It was their spires that gave the city its distinctive skyline. Almost all of them were destroyed. Among them was St. Paul's Cathedral, a monstrous church with a steeple that stood 500 feet (152 m) high. Most of the church was stone, and there was a wide courtyard. Everyone believed that St. Paul's Cathedral was the safest of all places in London, and so it was here that many brought their valuable books and papers for safekeeping until after the fire.

It was this very mass of material carried to the church by people who had evacuated their homes that gave the fire its start plus ample fuel with which to grow quickly. By the time it was detected, the fire was racing up the wooden scaffolding on the sides of the church where repair work was under way. Soon it had climbed to the very top of the tower. Every piece of

People carrying their most treasured belongings flee the fire by boat.

The Great Fire of London, September 1666

paper and wood in and around the church rapidly became ablaze. The heat of the roaring fire became so intense that the rocks in the walls of the church began to explode. The heavy lead roof melted and was dumped onto the church's rock floors. Then the floors gave way and crashed into the basement.

On the fourth day, London was still burning despite the fact that the wind had subsided. However, the eastward spread of the fire was now slower. If the fire continued on its present course, all of London would be entirely leveled by the blaze. The Duke of York decided to use gunpowder to blow up row after row of houses to make a path so wide the fire could not possibly leap across it. Sailors hauled barrel after barrel of gunpowder from the navy's storehouses and put them under the houses well in advance of the fire. Then they trailed powder from house to house and laid another trail to become the fuse. A torch was touched to the gunpowder trail, and in one explosion after another, the houses fell into heaps. As fast as possible, the rubble was cleared away, and the fire stopped at that line.

London lay in blackened ruins. Only the parts inside the old walls of the city had escaped the flames. About 200,000 people were homeless. Yet most astonishing—truly incredible, in fact—the number of deaths was small. Some records show four, others six. Most of what we know comes from Samuel Pepys' diaries. Though the fire rampaged, the wind had been almost constantly from the east and close to the ground. This had allowed people to guess the direction of the fire and its speed. Though there was some panic and pandemonium, most people had miraculously managed to keep out of the way of the flames.

Immediately London began to rebuild. This time the streets were made wider, and most of the buildings were built of brick and stone rather than wood. A new water system was constructed to assure a flow of water everywhere in the city. New churches sprang up, soon giving the city its familiar skyline again. The rebuilding of St. Paul's Cathedral was started in 1675, but the new church was much larger and more elaborate than the first. It would not be completed for thirty-five years.

From the Great Fire of London came two long-lasting benefits. Fire insurance companies were organized to protect people from losses by fire. And it was these insurance companies that organized the first fire departments.

7

Fire at Sea— and on the Docks

Surrounded by a sea of water, a ship would seem to be one of the safest of all places from the ravages of fire. But in fact, at sea and along the waterfront, fires are common and some rank high on the list of major fire disasters.

Topping the sea disasters in American waters was the tragedy of the *General Slocum* in 1904. It cost more than a thousand lives, about half of them children. The *General Slocum* was an excursion boat, and the passengers were mostly women and children out for a Sunday afternoon of fun when the vessel burned, trapping most of the passengers aboard.

But the best-known fire disaster at sea involved the *Morro Castle* in 1934. A popular luxury vacation ship that traveled from New York to Havana, Cuba, the ship was equipped with all the luxuries available at the time plus the latest fire-detecting and fire-fighting equipment. On Sunday night, September 8, 1934, the *Morro Castle* was on its return voyage from Cuba to New York. Everything was routine. People vacationing aboard the ship had to be at work the next morning, and most of them were sleeping off their last night of frivolity. Nearly everyone had been saddened by the sudden death of the ship's master, Captain Robert R. Wilmott, who had died of a heart attack before the traditional captain's dinner the night before. Captain Wilmott had skippered the *Morro Castle* since its maiden voyage. Captain William F. Warms had taken command to see the ship safely into port.

It was nearly 3 A.M. when what was presumed to be a minor fire was reported in a writing room aboard the ship. If the fire door to the room had been kept tightly closed, the fire might have been kept confined, but the door was open and the fire quickly moved out. Sensing an emergency, the radio operator asked whether he should send an SOS, the emergency signal. He could not do so unless authorized by the skipper. At this time, Captain Warms was apparently not sure of himself, and so he kept the *Morro Castle* steaming ahead at full speed.

Meanwhile, the fire was spreading rapidly. Half an hour passed before the radio operator was given the go-ahead to send out the distress signal. And it was that half-hour that may have made the difference in the lives of many people aboard the ship.

The *Morro Castle* had a crew of 240. Almost none of the crew had been rehearsed in the use of the fire-fighting equipment aboard the vessel. When the fire alarm was sounded, most of the crew responded by trying to save themselves. They had little concern for the ship or its 318 passengers. In the panic for survival, it became "every man for himself."

Some people made it to safety by getting into lifeboats. Others jumped directly into the sea. But it was the last night

The Morro Castle

aboard the ship. Many passengers were under the influence of alcohol and so were not in the best condition to respond to an emergency. The ship was equipped with every known fire-protection device, and thus in the final tally of deaths—some 137 people—it was ruled that negligence was the primary cause. Three lifeboats, for example, were never lowered into the water. They could have saved many lives. And Captain Warms was notably slow in acknowledging the ship's plight and stopping its forward motion. It was the movement of the ship that caused the fire to sweep over it.

Confusion is perhaps the most apt word to describe the situation. No one seemed to know his or her responsibilities; no one seemed willing to assume authority or to accept the seriousness of the situation. It is a sad commentary that 92 of the first 98 people to escape in lifeboats were members of the untrained and undisciplined crew. To his credit, Captain Warms at least did not desert his ship. With thirteen other crew members, he stayed aboard even when the *Morro Castle* had been essentially reduced to no more than a charred hull.

Fires on ships at sea are not uncommon, but they occur most often when the ships are docked. In the ports, ships are crowded one against the other. In the dock areas, too, there are excesses of gasoline, oil, trash, and highly combustible cargoes, and on most ships there are at these times only skeleton crews taking only the minimum safety precautions. For all these reasons, most ports have well-staffed fire departments and fireboats to respond quickly to the inevitable fires that break out either aboard the ships or in the warehouses at the docks. Even so, accidents do occur.

One Saturday afternoon in June of 1900, for example, four big German freighters were docked on the Hudson River at Hoboken, New Jersey. They were taking on cargo and coal in prep-

—34

aration to depart again the first of the week. On the ships were a number of sightseers. Suddenly, a small fire erupted in some bales of cotton on the dock. Somebody saw it, and an alarm was turned in immediately. But within only a few seconds, the fire had spread to kegs of whiskey on the dock. The kegs exploded, and aided by a brisk wind, the flames spread rapidly.

It was later determined that a quarter of a mile (.4 km) of dock area was in flames in less than fifteen minutes. People in the ships were trapped, and soon the ships were also ablaze. The fire became huge so rapidly that fire fighters could not approach either from shore or from the water. Burning cargo thrown from the ships continued to burn in the oil-slick waters. Many people jumped from the ships to escape. Some drowned; others were picked up by tugboats or other small boats that arrived quickly in the area. The rest of the people stayed aboard the ships, hoping the fire would be put out in time to save their lives.

The huge *Kaiser,* both a freighter and passenger ship, was towed out into the river, where the fires on its decks were put out. None of the more than 400 people aboard the vessel lost their lives, and the ship itself was ready to resume its schedule by the following Tuesday. But the *Bremen, Saale,* and *Main* were severely damaged, with people trapped inside them.

It was early the next morning before the flames were finally brought under control. About 300 people had been killed, though an accurate count was difficult because many of the dead had been crew members or dock workers, caught below deck sleeping.

In April 1947, an even worse fire occurred at Texas City, Texas. The *Grandcamp,* a French ship, was docked when a fire was detected in a hold where fertilizer was being loaded. Firemen were called to put out the flame, but before they could do so, the ship exploded. All of the fire fighters were killed, as were several hundred people on or near the dock. Two small airplanes flying overhead were literally knocked out of the sky, and the four people inside were killed. The Monsanto Chemical Company plant near the dock was soon engulfed in flames, too, and was also rocked by explosions. No house within a mile (1.6 km) of the dock was left standing after the explosions.

Broken fuel lines and tanks released gas, gasoline, and other chemicals, most of them flammable and explosive and some giving off poisonous fumes. Both the water supply and the electricity of Texas City were knocked out, leaving the area at the complete mercy of the flames. No matter, because most of the fire-fighting equipment had also been destroyed by the blasts. And with the fire still raging out of control that evening, a second ship exploded, spawning a whole new batch of fires. Like the first, this ship was loaded with fertilizer, which is chemically akin to dynamite.

For two days the fires raged before finally subsiding. No one really knows how many people died in the Texas City disaster, but most authorities put the figure at well over 500. Because there were many migrant workers and also roving seamen on the ships, an accurate count was difficult. More than 3,500 seriously injured people were treated in nearby hospitals.

The dock fire at Texas City is not an isolated case, of course. There have been many such incidents in the past. But at Texas City, the human-life casualties were perhaps the highest for a dock fire in recorded history.

8

Show-stopping Fires

A huge fire that gutted The Theatre in Canton, China, in May 1845 killed 1,670 people trapped inside the building. In all history, this was the most disastrous fire in one building. But over the years there have been numerous killing fires in theaters and similar places where people have gathered in large numbers for fun.

Why?

At such gatherings, people are jammed together and often are completely disorganized. They panic easily, and no one can exert command or control to keep them from trampling each other. Too often, also, far less than adequate thought has been given to fire protection. In the past, at least, large structures erected for temporary or limited use have been flimsily built and only limited provisions have been made for extinguishing fires or evacuating people. Further, the people at these "fun" gatherings are there for a good time. Their attention is on entertainment, not safety. They are careless with their smoking, and few are aware of the danger until it is too late.

One of the most memorable of all fires in the United States occurred on July 6, 1944, under the "big top" tent of Ringling Bros., Barnum and Bailey circus. The tent, 425 feet (127.5 m) long, was set up in Hartford, Connecticut, and more than 6,000 people, most of them children, were crowded under it for a special afternoon performance. All of the smells and other excitement of a circus outing were there that afternoon.

The tent had seven openings. There was the big main entrance on the west plus three smaller ones on the north and three more on the south. But four of these entrances were blocked by chutes used to get performing animals into the arena and then out again. Normally there were buckets of water and fire extinguishers well distributed around the tent "just in case," but because this was a special rush performance, these usual safety details had been neglected. Four fire trucks, however, each with an 800-gallon (760-l) water capacity, were outside the tent.

The big tent, which was the most important and expensive piece of equipment the circus company owned, had been waterproofed with paraffin thinned with gasoline. This made it highly flammable. Neither the tent itself nor the tent area had been inspected by local fire marshals before the performance, as was usually done.

All went well through the first act and into the beginning of the second. The Flying Wallendas were on their way up the poles to start their breathtaking trapeze performance. It was about this time that a Hartford policeman noted a small flame near the tent's main entrance. When he first saw it, the flame was no bigger than what might have been started by a single cigarette.

But within seconds, the flame had climbed to the top of the tent. Nobody else noticed it right away, and the Wallendas

—38

were about to begin their act when the bandleader saw the flame. Instantly he ordered the band to play "Stars and Stripes Forever," which in circus language meant an emergency. Circus employees dreaded the sound, but they responded by quickly rushing to their assigned posts. When they saw the flames, they tried to douse them with water. But already the fire was out of control.

The Wallendas rapidly slid down their ropes to the ground. An animal trainer tried desperately to get his leopards out of the ring and back into their cages. The crowd was at first confused, thinking that perhaps all of this activity was somehow part of the show. For critical seconds, they watched the unsuccessful attempts to quench the flames rather than trying to exit the already blazing tent. Those who realized what was happening had confidence that the experienced circus people knew how to handle the situation and that the blaze would soon be under control.

Then suddenly a wind, the greatest ally of a fire, whipped the blaze. Ropes quickly burned in two, and the tent's huge support poles began to fall. Flaming hunks of canvas also rained downward. From this point on there was complete confusion in the crowd as they began a mad rush for an exit. Some were blocked with chutes reserved for the lions, leopards, and other animal performers. Many of the people turned to the main exit, but by now it was too late. In less than ten minutes the entire tent was ablaze, and those still trapped inside were doomed.

Though the Hartford fire department responded quickly, there was little that could be done. Fire hydrants were 900 feet (270 m) away. The water in the nearby tank trucks had already been used, and the fire in that short time had already taken its toll—163 people dead, almost half of them children, with 261 people seriously injured.

With the big top now in flames, panicked patrons of the circus flee for their lives.

Ironically, it was discovered in the investigation later that the fire had apparently been started by a deranged circus employee—a pyromaniac later sentenced to prison. Some of the other circus employees were also sentenced to prison for not having taken the required precautions in regard to fire-extinguishing equipment.

About two years earlier, in November 1942, another crowd of people gathered for pleasure had been caught in a similar senseless holocaust in the fashionable Coconut Grove nightclub in a Boston suburb. The gathering was supposed to have been a football victory celebration for Boston College's defeat of Holy Cross, but in a surprise game, Holy Cross had won by an embarrassing 43 points.

Most of the Boston College officials and boosters kept out of sight that night, but the crowd in the club was nevertheless overflowing. Those who were there had decided to "live it up" despite the defeat. Win or lose, they were geared for a good time. It is doubtful that anyone entering the club that night gave fire a second thought, and even if they did, they must have felt comfortable. A fire inspector's recent check of the establishment had given it a rating of "good" in terms of required safety features. Even the swollen capacity—about 1,000 people as opposed to the absolute maximum of 600—did not concern anybody. Coconut Grove was a place to have a good time, to shed the worries of the world. Nobody was allowed to dwell on such undesirable thoughts as fires.

The Coconut Grove was decorated with palm trees, bamboo, rattan, and blue skies. The blue skies were actually a drapery of blue satin on the walls and ceiling, and the effect was overpowering for those wanting to escape from the wintry world outside into a kind of paradise. After a drink in the Melody Room, the patrons were ready for hours of entertainment. There was no place in Boston better for getting away from everyday problems.

It was about 10 o'clock that night when a light bulb that spotlighted a graceful palm went out. A waiter was asked to replace it, and he did so without apparent difficulty. But only a few minutes later, the blue satin drapes above the palm began to show signs of fire. It was a small fire, though, and seemingly nothing to be alarmed about. Some waiters tried to put it out with seltzer bottles and wet towels.

But by now the palm tree below the drapes was in flames, and there was sufficient worry for a cry of "Fire!" It came too late. During the shoving, pushing, climbing, and rushing for exits, everything went dark. Either the fire had cut off the electricity or the envelope of smoke had become so thick the lights could not shine through. The entire building was soon in flames. It is miraculous that as many people escaped as did, some through the kitchen door, others by shutting themselves inside the giant walk-in refrigerators, still others by plunging through narrow windows. But many others were trapped so suddenly that they were later found still at their seats, overcome by the gases generated by the fire.

Those who did make it to the top of the stairs of the newly opened cocktail lounge found a locked door. Some 200 people were later discovered near the main door, close to escape but unable to get outside. Meanwhile, in other parts of the club business went on as usual for a while. The fire swept in with such suddenness that survivors later said it seemed that the air itself was in flames. There was total pandemonium—again in darkness except for the seething flames.

Later estimates calculate the time as only twelve minutes from the start of the blaze near the palm tree to the death of 492 people. Investigations also failed to reveal absolute proof of what had started the blaze. Perhaps it was a carelessly placed lit cigarette. It is more likely that the cause was defective wiring, especially since an unlicensed electrician had been employed to install the electrical wiring in the new room. Officially, the cause was listed as "undetermined."

The tragic fire at the Coconut Grove was unfortunately not the last of fires of this kind, although the incident did spawn the reworking of fire codes and inspection systems throughout the nation.

9

Fire in the Sky

The countdown proceeded on schedule. Aboard the *Apollo* spacecraft were astronauts Virgil I. Grissom, Edward H. White II, and Roger B. Chaffee. The date: January 27, 1967. This was a routine check of the equipment in preparation for a scheduled February lift-off of the spacecraft on a flight to the moon.

Ten minutes remained in the simulated countdown. The command and service modules were sitting atop the 218-foot (65.4-m) launch vehicle, and the astronauts were sealed in their spacecraft. With closed-circuit television, technicians were watching the craft.

One of the crew members reported fire aboard the spacecraft. During the next eighteen seconds, there were more urgent calls, then a flash on the television screen, after which all communications were lost. The outside of the *Apollo* heated rapidly, flames spurting out and then heavy smoke. Ground crewmen rushed quickly to reach the spacecraft, but it was all over in a matter of seconds. The heat was so intense that rescue crews were unable to open the spacecraft for five minutes after

Exterior of the Apollo *spacecraft that burned on January 27, 1967, killing the three astronauts trapped inside.*

the flames first appeared. By this time the astronauts were dead, asphyxiated almost immediately by the noxious fumes of the fire. But the fire itself had burned for less than half a minute.

What had caused the disaster?

Inside the spacecraft, the highly pressurized atmosphere was almost pure oxygen. Oxygen, which supports combustion, is even more likely under pressure to trigger combustion. The materials inside the cabin were highly flammable too, contributing to the rapid spread of the flames from the originally small fire. The fire itself was later attributed to faulty wiring.

Three men had died. A pall fell over the *Apollo* project. Redesigning of the equipment for greater safety got under way immediately.

Fires aboard aircraft on the ground and in the air are not uncommon, of course. They have occurred ever since humans invaded the world aboveground. Many have involved only one person or a few people. Others have been major disasters commanding international attention.

One fire that may never be forgotten occurred on May 6, 1937, at Lakehurst, New Jersey. The giant *Hindenburg,* a German dirigible, or airship, was scheduled for a landing at Lakehurst. Each trip the *Hindenburg* made was a newsworthy event.

The *Hindenburg* measured 803 feet (241 m) long. Inside its gigantic metal framework were sixteen huge gasbags, each filled with hydrogen—a total of 7,300,000 cubic feet (219,000 cu m) of highly flammable gas. Hydrogen, when mixed with oxygen and ignited, burns explosively, and so the bags were inspected regularly to detect possible leaks. The dirigible was built so that escaping hydrogen could be vented quickly through the top. Even the inspection catwalks were padded and the crew wore special boots to prevent them from accidentally igniting sparks as they moved about inside the ship. The danger was known, but every possible precaution had been taken to prevent disaster. The engines, for example, were powered by diesel fuel, much safer than gasoline. And smoking was prohibited aboard the vessel except in special fireproof rooms.

Helium, which is not flammable, might have been used rather than hydrogen. But the major producer of helium fuel was the United States, which had banned its sale to Germany. The Germans preferred the much lighter hydrogen anyway and so far had experienced no difficulties, thanks to the detailed safety measures taken. The United States, however, had. Three U.S. dirigibles had crashed, killing nearly a hundred people.

On that fateful day in May 1937, the *Hindenburg* was nearing the end of another successful trip across the Atlantic. About noon it had flown over Boston. By midafternoon it had cruised directly over Times Square, the Statue of Liberty, and Ebbet's Field in Brooklyn—all part of its "show" approach to the United States. It had arrived in Lakehurst, New Jersey, late in the afternoon, but landing had been delayed because of a thunderstorm. Hundreds of people waited on the ground for the ship's landing, and more than 200 were there to assist the big ship.

Shortly after 7 P.M., the *Hindenburg* made its descent at Lakehurst. The tremendous silvery ship was a glorious sight in the setting sun. The first landing ropes were dropped, and the ship was only about 75 feet (22.5 m) off the ground when it happened. Suddenly the ship burst into flames, the blaze starting in the tail section but rapidly engulfing the entire ship. Within only seconds the dirigible was a flaming mass on the ground.

Some of the passengers made miraculous escapes by jumping or by scrambling free of the burning wreckage. But forty-one people died, twenty-seven of them crew members, thirteen of them passengers, and one a member of the ground crew.

Among the dead was Captain Lehman, skipper of the ill-fated ship.

What had caused the fire?

A study commission ultimately put the blame on escaping hydrogen believed to have been ignited by static electricity. The Germans thought it was sabotage. We will probably never know for certain.

But the burning of the *Hindenburg* removed nearly all dirigibles from the skies for many decades. Only recently has talk about them begun again. Dirigibles are now, in fact, proposed as the workhorses of the air in the years to come. They are far slower than jets but are extremely economical to operate and can handle tremendous loads of cargo. Their fuel, of course, will not be the highly flammable hydrogen.

Like other kinds of aircraft, airplanes are not at all immune to fires. Most often the fires occur during landings or on impact in crashes, the plane's fuel igniting and quickly swamping the craft in flames. When airplanes skid on the runway, belly-land (land without wheels), or have other mishaps at airports, airport fire-fighting crews rush to the aircraft. Since water will only spread the burning fuels used by the airplanes rather than extinguish the flames, the airplanes are sprayed with a thick chemical foam. This cuts off the fire's supply of oxygen and puts out the fire almost as soon as it starts. Many crash landings have been prevented from becoming disasters by this quick action.

Some mishaps occur in midair, however. In 1963, for example, a jet airliner exploded in midair over Elkton, Maryland, killing the eighty-one people aboard. The following year, an in-flight fire caused an airplane to crash in Tennessee, and thirty-nine people aboard died. Thirty-eight people died in an in-flight explosion of an airplane over Ohio early in 1967, and later that year, thirty-four people lost their lives in the crash and burning

The Hindenburg *in flames, May 6, 1937*

of an airplane in Pennsylvania. The worst airplane calamity in history occurred in 1977 when a KLM 747 jet ran into a Pan American jumbo jet on a runway on Tenerife Island, the largest of the Canary Islands, located off the coast of Africa in the Atlantic Ocean. In that crash 582 people died. Over San Diego, in 1978, a small plane ran into a commercial jet, causing it to explode in flames and killing 144 people. And in May 1979, an airplane disaster in Chicago resulted in the deaths of 272 people in a fire that rescuers were unable to extinguish in time.

All this should not worry you unduly, though, if you are planning to fly. The air traffic record is really exceptionally good. It is far better, in fact, than the safety records for ground traffic. In terms of statistics, airplanes are still in the top category for safety. But airplanes are not immune from fire, no more so than are objects built to stay on the ground.

10

Fire, a Weapon of War

No sooner had fire been tamed than it was turned into a weapon.

Turned loose against an enemy, fire could destroy dwellings, whole villages, or cities. In the War of 1812, for example, Washington, D.C., was set afire and burned to the ground by the British.

Fire could burn crops in the field or grain in storage, causing starvation. It could create pandemonium or kill people. Attacked by fire, an enemy's encampments, fortresses, and cities could be left in smoldering ruins. One of the reasons ancient castles were surrounded by moats was to make a barrier of water to reduce the possibility of the enemy's using fire as a weapon of destruction.

Throughout history, in fact, fire has been the most destructive of all weapons of warfare.

Daring attackers carried lit torches into enemy camps or dwellings. They threw spears or shot arrows that were flaming. Carts or wagons filled with burning hay or brush were pushed into enemy fortresses or against their walls. Ships or boats were set afire and then floated into enemy fleets or docks.

—51

The Capitol is burned down by the British during the War of 1812.

The most sophisticated weapons of today still depend on fire as their ultimate means of destroying the enemy. Fire remains one of the most feared weapons of warfare.

Some people under siege have turned to fire to destroy their homes and possessions rather than permit them to fall into the hands of the enemy. In 1812, for example, the Russians purposely set fire to Moscow and destroyed some 30,000 houses—more than 90 percent of the city. This prevented the city from falling into Napoleon's hands.

One early Roman weapon was called a springald. It released a barrage of incendiary darts that kept the enemy busy trying to extinguish a multitude of fires. The springald was a primitive kind of flamethrower, and it took only one well-placed fire dart to start a devastating conflagration.

Gunpowder did not really reduce the reliance on fire in warfare, for gunpowder must be ignited to fire its missiles. In the early days, cannons were fired by lighting a fuse that in turn caused the gunpowder to explode and thus force the firing of the missile. Very early handguns were fired in the same manner. First they required two people to manage—one to hold the weapon and the other to set fire to the powder by touching it with a lighted brand. In the early days, guns fired rocks. Iron balls were a later invention, and when they could be fit tightly into the weapon's muzzle, they were expelled with greater velocity. It was not uncommon in the early days for the weapons to blow up, and so the experts continued to refine them. This really constituted a tighter harnessing of fire.

Our weapons today are much more sophisticated, of course, but fire is still their basic force, launching the missiles and generally causing the greatest damage at the target site. One of the most fearsome weapons of World War II and even today is the flamethrower. It consists of oil and gasoline under pressure. This mixture is ignited and then shot out as a stream of flame under pressure, like water from a fire hose. The flamethrower is an effective weapon against pillboxes, tanks, and similar enclosures. The flames can easily enter the smallest apertures in these structures and then consume all of the oxygen inside, asphyxiating the occupants. The flamethrower is not an expensive weapon, but it is one of the most effective ever devised.

Incendiary bombs are even more devastating. The refined bombs used in recent years contain napalm, a "jellied" gasoline. When the bomb strikes, the gasoline ignites. In its jellied condition, the gasoline clings to whatever it hits, and as it burns, it builds up the necessary heat to create a general fire. Incendiary bombs dropped in large numbers on Tokyo in 1945 resulted in the deaths of more than 80,000 people in less than six hours.

The most incendiary of all, of course, are the nuclear weapons—the atom bomb, employed to bring World War II to an end, and the hydrogen bomb. The fires resulting from the intense heat are secondary to the explosions and radiation but are no less devastating in terms of deaths and property damage.

11

The Woods Afire

Every year millions of acres of valuable forestland are destroyed by fire. Some of the fires—and this is especially true in the northwestern United States—are started by lightning. But overall, about nine out of ten forest fires are started by humans. Some are the result of carelessness in the burning of trash or brush. Others are caused by the discarding of cigarettes. But an astonishing number are caused by arsonists. These are fires deliberately set by humans; fire fighters call them incendiary fires.

Incendiary fires are the most difficult of all to control, especially if they are started when conditions are just right for their burning and spread—with sufficient fuel and the wind in the proper direction. Many are started in the lowlands, then easily sweep down canyons and up slopes. The devastating fires that break out in California hill and canyon country, a section where there are many valuable homes, are of this sort. Lightning-caused fires, in contrast, generally start on mountains, hills, or ridges—the very highest parts of a region. They have less fuel for getting under way and for keeping going, and though there

The woods afire

are exceptions, fire spreads more slowly going down rather than up a slope.

Why do people start fires? Some are set in revenge to destroy the property of a neighbor or an enemy. Others are set by people wanting to collect fire insurance money. Still others are started by individuals who get an emotional thrill from seeing a fire burn. These same people may set fire to houses. People who are totally possessed by the urge to set fires are called pyromaniacs.

Forest fires are far from being new. In 1825, a fire burned about 3 million acres (1.2 million hectares) of forestland in Maine and nearby New Brunswick (Can.); it killed at least 160 people. Another huge fire in Silverton, Oregon, in 1865 destroyed an estimated million acres of valuable timber. The fire at Peshtigo, Wisconsin, in 1871 (Chapter 4) ranks as the worst forest fire in United States history. Ten years later another million acres (405,000 hectares) of Michigan forestland were burned, killing 138 people. These are just a few of the big fires, of course, for there have been numerous smaller fires every year throughout history.

Nor are all of the big fires in the distant past. Fires burned 2 million acres (810,000 hectares) of forest in Kentucky and West Virginia in 1952, and they destroyed 5 million acres (2 million hectares) of forest in Alaska in 1957. Every drought year is marked by another outbreak of fires, but dry weather only means the fires are more difficult to extinguish. Every year there are more than 200,000 separate fires in the United States. Most are small, burning only 10 acres (4 hectares) or so, but a few become very large and consume thousands of acres before they are extinguished.

One of the still talked-about big forest fires was at Tillamook, Oregon, in 1933. The fire had an unusual start, for it was caused by the friction of a log dragged by a steel cable over extremely dry brush. Rain had not fallen for about two months, and it was a hot, windy, mid-August day when the fire started. The blaze was seen immediately, but all efforts to put it out or to stop its spread failed. It continued to burn for nearly two weeks, destroying more than 250,000 acres (101,250 hectares) of virgin timber—huge and highly valuable Douglas-firs that were turned into giant torches by the flames.

Fire is indeed a great enemy of our forests. Within a few hours, trees that have been growing for years become charred pillars. The piled-up litter beneath the trees also burns and no longer serves as a sponge to hold water. Gone are not only the fortunes in timber but also the beauty of the forest and all of its wildlife unable to escape the flames. And forest fires can travel at great speed. Aided by winds, a fire burning through the crowns of trees may move at a speed of 20 miles (32 km) per hour or faster. Some ground fires travel as fast as 4 miles (6.4 km) per hour, though usually more slowly. Fires in peat bogs can smolder undetected for weeks, months, or even years, until conditions are "just right" for them to become uncontrollable monsters.

From lookout towers on the highest ground in the area, foresters keep a twenty-four-hour watch for fires. They know that a fire is easiest to stop when it is small, and so even a whisp of smoke is sufficient to put the fire fighters into action. With modern fire-fighting equipment and well-trained professional fire fighters, most fires can be extinguished if they are detected early enough.

In major forest fires, crews of 20,000 or more may be working on the ground. A hundred or more airplanes and dozens of helicopters fight the flames from the sky or transport fire fighters and supplies rapidly to places where they are most needed. Among the airplanes are huge tankers that can carry thousands of gallons of water plus special chemicals that slow down the burning.

But professional forest fire fighters are only readily available to the big forests—the 28 percent owned by the government and the 14 percent owned by industry. All of the remaining forestland in the United States—58 percent of the total—is privately owned. It is on these lands that fires, large and small, are least watched for and where little help is available to control them once they do break out.

For More Information

In this book you learned about a few of the big fires that have occurred in history—those that have killed many people or destroyed great amounts of property. Other fires have been included because they were especially dramatic or tragic episodes.

But even a small fire can be a disaster to those personally involved. You may already know someone who has been a victim of fire. If not, you probably will in the future. Fire touches everyone's life at some time.

Below is a list of organizations that can supply more information about fires—how to avoid them, what to do if you are in a fire yourself, and how to help in case of fire. You, or perhaps your class, might want to get information from these sources to help keep fire from becoming a foe rather than a friend.

Action Against Burns, Inc.
P.O. Box 347
Burlington, Maryland 01803

American Mutual Insurance Company
Institute for Safer Living
Wakefield, Maryland 01380

Burger King Corporation
G.P.O. Box 1472
New York, New York 10001

Chicago Fire Department
Bureau of Fire Prevention
444 North Dearborn Street
Chicago, Illinois 60610

Consumer Product Safety Commission
1111 18 Street N. W.
Washington, D.C. 20207

Film Communicators
11136 Weddington Street
North Hollywood, California 91601

Hartford Insurance Group
Junior Fire Marshal Headquarters
Hartford Plaza
Hartford, Connecticut 06115

National Fire Protection Association
470 Atlantic Avenue
Boston, Massachusetts 02210

National Technical Information Service
U.S. Department of Commerce
Springfield, Virginia 22151

Project Burn Prevention
BURNS
Boston, Massachusetts 02114

Underwriter's Laboratories, Inc.
207 East Ohio Street
Chicago, Illinois 60611

United States Fire Administration
Public Education Office
P.O. Box 19518
Washington, D.C. 20036

Walt Disney Educational Materials Company
500 South Buena Vista
Burbank, California 91505

Index

Airplane fires, 48, 50
    worst, 50
Airship fire, 46
Air traffic record, 50
Apollo spacecraft fire, 44–46
Arsonists, 55
Asbestos, 9
Asphyxiation, 12, 46, 54
Atom bomb, 54

Bellylanding of airplanes, 48
Benefits of fire, 4–6
"Big top" fire, 38–39
Bog fires, 58
Bombs, 54
Building fires, 37–43
    most disastrous, 37
Burns, national average, 3

Cannons, use of fire, 53

Canton, China, theater fire, 37
Capitol's 1812 fire, 52
Chaffee, Roger B., 44
Chemical foam, use in extinguishing
    fires, 48, 59
Chicago Chamber of Commerce fire, 15
Chicago fire, 13–18
Circus fire, 38–39, 40
Coconut Grove fire, 41–43
Combustion, 7, 46
Conditions necessary for fire, 7
Controlled fires, 7
Convection currents, 20
Cooking, use of fire, 4
Cooling, use of fire, 4
Crosby Opera House fire, 15

Deaths by fire, national average, 2–3
Destructive use of fire, 51–54
Dirigible fire, 46, 48

–63

Dock fires, 34–36
Drought, danger of fire during, 10–12, 13–18

Earthquakes, as cause of San Francisco fire, 19–20
Equipment, fire-fighting, 2
Extension ladder, 2

Fire alarm boxes, 14
Fire as a weapon of war, 51–54
Fire at sea and in the docks, 31–36
Fire codes, reworking of, 43
Fire departments, 2
    first, 30
Fire fighters, 2, 58, 59
Fire inspection systems, reworking of, 43
Fire insurance companies, organization of, 30
Fire in the sky, 44–50
Fire line, use of to halt progress of fires, 25, 29
First use of fire, 5
Flamethrower, 53–54
Foam, use in extinguishing fires, 48, 59
Forest fires, 12, 55, 56
Forests, privately-owned, fires in, 59
"Friction lights," 6
Fuel, as necessary for fire, 7
Fumes, poisonous, 46
    from matches, 6

Gases, poisonous, generated by fires, 42

Gases that "burn," 8
Gas masks, 2
General Slocum fire, 31
Grandcamp fire, 35
Great Fire of London, 24–30
Grissom, Virgil I., 44
Gunpowder, use of fire, 53

Heat, as necessary for fire, 7
Helium, as fuel, 47
Hindenburg fire, 46–48, 49
Hoses, use of, 2
Hydrogen, as flammable fuel, 47, 48
Hydrogen bomb, 54
Hydrogen fires, 7

Importance of fire in growth of civilization, 5
Incendiary bombs, 54
Incendiary fires, 55
Information about fires, 60–62
Inhalators, 2

"Jellied" gasoline, 54

Kindling point, 8
Kindling temperature, 8
King Charles II, 25–26

Light from fires, 4
Lightning, as start of fires, 55
Lookout towers, 58

Matches, invention of, 5–6
Morro Castle fire, 31–34
Moscow fire, 53

—64

Most catastrophic fire in North America, 12
Mrs. O'Leary's cow, 13, 14

Napalm, 54
Nature of fires, 7–9
Nuclear weapons, 54

O'Leary's cow, 13, 14
Organizations to contact for more information about fires, 60–62
Oxygen, as necessary for fire, 7, 8, 46
    experiment to prove, 8

Panic during fires, 32, 37, 42
Peat bog fires, 58
Pepys, Samuel, 25, 29
Peshtigo, Wisconsin, fire, 10–12
Phosphorous
    kindling temperature of, 9
    use in matches, 6
Primitive peoples' use of fire, 5
"Process" of fire, 7
Property damage, national average, 3
Pudding Lane, London, 24
Pyromaniacs, 41, 57

Radiation, from hydrogen bomb, 54
Rebuilding after fire
    Chicago, 17
    London, 29–30
    San Francisco, 23
Resuscitators, 2

Ringling Bros. Barnum and Bailey Circus fire, 38–39

Safety matches, 6
St. Paul's Cathedral, London, 26–27, 30
Sand, as substance that does not burn, 9
Sandpaper, use with early matches, 6
San Francisco fire, 19–23
Ship fires, 31–36
Show-stopping fires, 37–43
Solar energy, 4
Spacecraft fire, 44–46
Speed of fire, 58
Springold, 53
Substances that do not burn, 9

Taming of fire, 5, 6
Tenerife Island, 50
Texas City, Texas fire, 35–36
Theater fires, 37
Tillimook, Oregon, forest fire, 57–58
Tokyo, use of incendiary bombs on, 54
Twin disasters—a worst and a most famous, 10–18

Walker, John, 5–6
Warmth, from fire, 4
War of 1812, 51
Washington, D.C., fire, 51
Weapon, fire as a, 51–54
White, Edward H., II, 44
Wind, as an ally of fires, 25, 39, 58
Woods afire, 55–59
World without fire, 4–6

—65

7